PRAISE FOR DENNIS McDOUGAL

For *Dylan*

"A gleefully acid-etched biography . . . McDougal presents his caustic indictment with energy and panache." —*Publishers Weekly*

"A sometimes-scholarly, sometimes-snarky life of the songwriting and singing legend. . . . Richly detailed." —*Kirkus Reviews*

For *Five Easy Decades: How Jack Nicholson Became the Biggest Movie Star in Modern Times*

"Dennis McDougal is a rare Hollywood reporter: honest, fearless, nobody's fool. This is unvarnished Jack for Jack-lovers and Jack-skeptics but, also, for anyone interested in the state of American culture and celebrity. I always read Mr. McDougal for pointers." —Patrick McGilligan, author of *Jack's Life* and *Alfred Hitchcock: A Life in Darkness and Light*

For *Privileged Son: Otis Chandler and the Rise and Fall of the L.A. Times Dynasty*

"A great freeway pileup—part biography, part dysfunctional family chronicle, and part institutional and urban history, with generous dollops of scandal and gossip." —Hendrick Hertzberg, *The New Yorker*

"McDougal has managed to scale the high walls that have long protected the Chandler clan and returned with wicked tales told by angry ex-wives and jealous siblings." —*The Washington Post*

For *The Last Mogul: Lew Wasserman, MCA, and the Hidden History of Hollywood*

"Real glamour needs a dark side. That is part of the fascination of Dennis McDougal's wonderful book." —*The Economist*

"Thoroughly reported and engrossing . . . the most noteworthy trait of MCA was how it hid its power." —*The New York Times Book Review*

"Over the years, I've read hundreds of books on Hollywood and the movie business, and this one is right at the top." —Michael Blowen, *The Boston Globe*

DYLAN

Also by Dennis McDougal

Angel of Darkness

Fatal Subtraction: How Hollywood Really Does Business (with Pierce O'Donnell)

In The Best of Families

Mother's Day

The Last Mogul: Lew Wasserman, MCA, and the Hidden History of Hollywood

The Yosemite Murders

Privileged Son: Otis Chandler and the Rise and Fall of the L.A. Times Dynasty

Blood Cold (with Mary Murphy)

Five Easy Decades: How Jack Nicholson Became the Biggest Movie Star in Modern Times

The Candlestickmaker

DYLAN

THE BIOGRAPHY

DENNIS McDOUGAL

WILEY

Turner Publishing Company/Wiley General Trade
424 Church Street • Suite 2240 • Nashville, Tennessee 37219
445 Park Avenue • 9th Floor • New York, New York 10022

www.turnerpublishing.com

BOB DYLAN: THE BIOGRAPHY

Cover design: Maxwell Roth
Cover photograph: Lisa Law
Book design: Lissa Auciello-Brogan

Library of Congress Cataloging-in-Publication Data
McDougal, Dennis.
 Bob Dylan : the biography / Dennis McDougal.
    pages cm
Includes bibliographical references and index.
ISBN 978-0-470-63623-7
1. Dylan, Bob, 1941- 2. Rock musicians--United States--Biography. I.
Title.
ML420.D98M18 2014
782.42164092--dc23
[B]
                           2014008603

Printed in the United States of America
14 15 16 17 18 19 0 9 8 7 6 5 4 3 2 1

To Lola Irvin, who headed out for the West Coast almost 70 years ago and never looked back. It's all right, Ma. I'm only writing.

CONTENTS

PREFACE

When the van rolled up to the Chateau Marmont Hotel on Sunset Strip to fetch Bob Dylan for his sold-out concert at the nearby Pantages Theater on the evening of May 14, 1992, the legendary singer-songwriter was already spaced out on tequila, and more.

"He was on smack," declared one of his handlers that night. "He was nodding off time and again."

By the time the driver had coaxed him into the van and ferried him to the Pantages, Dylan was slurring his words and had to be helped to an easy chair behind a curtained-off section at the loading dock out back of the theater, where he fell into a trance watching black-and-white TV reruns of *Gilligan's Island* until his stage call.

He made it by rote through his 90-minute set that night, leaning on his keyboard for support, seemingly oblivious to the chorus of boos as the audience reacted to the fact that his vocals were indecipherable and the arrangements loud but unrecognizable. When he'd finished, Dylan left the stage without having said a single word to the audience. He walked directly out of the rear of the theater where, rather than wait for his driver to take him back to the Chateau Marmont, he climbed into the van, threw it into reverse, and nearly backed over one of his roadies.

It's hard to imagine that anyone in the Pantages audience left that night satisfied with what had occurred. The fact that any fan showed up in the first place was a testament to Dylan's distant past, not his recent achievements. It had been 30 years since "Blowin' in the Wind" first thrust him into the public consciousness, 17 years since his album masterpiece *Blood on the Tracks*.

Since then a string of 18 mostly forgettable albums had produced few hit singles.

Dylan had continued to tour, playing smaller venues and sometimes selling them out. But the faithful[1] who paid to see him frequently came away disappointed, saddened, and even unnerved to watch the great musical hero of their youth so reduced. What was the deal, they wondered. Was it age? Boredom? Did he just not care anymore?

Those who'd grown up with him couldn't believe the dissipated wraith they'd once known as vibrant and wise beyond his years.

"I felt bad the last two times I saw him on TV," Hibbing High School classmate Dave Beckers said at the time. "Whatever life he's lived, it looks like he's had it hard."

The people closest to Dylan knew what was wrong. Singer Judy Collins, a friend for more than 30 years, almost blurted out the secret to a TV camera crew that was interviewing her for a news magazine segment about Dylan turning 50 in May 1991. "I'm worried about Bobby; we all are," she said while the camera was turned off. The look of anguish on her face telegraphed that she was concerned he might die.

The public at large got a hint of the problem during the broadcast of the Grammy Awards earlier that year. Having failed to recognize Dylan with a single award for his astonishing output in the 1960s and most of the 1970s, the National Academy of Recording Arts and Sciences was doing a make-good by giving him a lifetime achievement award. Dylan not only showed up to accept, he also chose to perform his brilliant 1963 antiwar anthem "Masters of War" against the backdrop of the recently launched Gulf War in the Mideast. It

---

[1] "Bobcats" followed Dylan from city to city the way "Deadheads" unofficially caravanned with the Grateful Dead.

was a moment tailor-made for career resurrection, but Dylan did not rise to the occasion. He looked puffy-faced, was twitchy, and sounded worse, rushing through a garbled rendition of the song without its passion or point.

A forgiving audience nonetheless gave him a standing ovation when he accepted his plaque from one of his biggest fans, Jack Nicholson. The indulgent crowd, which included his twice-widowed 76-year-old mother, Beatty Rutman, applauded until Dylan began to speak in a clear if jaded growl, "Well, my daddy, he didn't leave me much. You know he was a very simple man, but what he did tell me was this, he did say, son, he said, you know it's possible to become so defiled in this world that your own father and mother will abandon you and if that happens, God will always believe in your ability to mend your ways."

As Dylan walked off stage without thanking a single soul, Nicholson watched with a slack-jawed what-the-fuck expression that indicated he wasn't sure whether Dylan's words were a put-on or a dead serious hallucination.

A year later, as he careened down Sunset Boulevard in a rented van on his way back to his hotel room following the Pantages show, Bob Dylan, the so-called "voice of his generation," looked like he was over. Done. It was only a matter of time before he would literally be knocking on heaven's door.

■■ ■■ ■■

Flash forward 20 years. On the heels of back-to-back-to-back critically acclaimed, bestselling, Grammy-winning albums, Bob Dylan's music routinely enters both the U.S. and U.K. charts at or near No 1. He hosted his own weekly satellite radio show, authored the bestselling 2004 memoir *Chronicles*, and won an Oscar for his hit song "Things Have Changed," featured in director Curtis Hanson's *Wonder Boys* (2000). And he became a musical hero to a new generation, the so-called Millennials, all of them born after 1980.

As he approached his 72nd birthday, Dylan could not help but be alternately flattered and astonished by the huge age range represented by his audience.

The original 1960s counterculture hero, he'd anticipated the Tweet generation by half a century, reducing cultural norms, politics, and mythology to phrases, epigrams, and memes. Like highly quotable haiku that short-circuited human discourse among texting Millennials and aging baby boomers alike, Dylan's poetry kept pace with the ever-shortening attention spans promoted by Facebook, Google, and Twitter. In his bestselling 2010 novel *Freedom*, Jonathan Franzen fittingly described Dylan as "the beautifully pure kind of asshole who made a young musician want to be an asshole himself."

Ever the student of both human nature and the American character, Dylan summed up the secret of his roller-coaster career in a single sentence: "It's always good to know what went down before you, because if you know the past, you can control the future."

Dylan's string of twenty-first-century hit albums are among the most influential and vibrant in a career that is stronger than ever. To mark the 50th anniversary of the civil rights movement in 2010, President Barack Obama invited Dylan to the White House to perform "The Times They Are a-Changin'." Accompanied only by piano and standup bass, his words rolled from his despoiled throat like ragged dirge, not anthem. And yet his challenge to another generation was as fresh as it had been 45 years earlier: get out of the new road if you can't lend a hand . . .

Perhaps prophetically, Dylan once told *Chicago Daily News* reporter Joseph Haas in the autumn of 1965 that condemning the older generation had never been his message at all. "It happened maybe that those were the only words I could find to separate aliveness from deadness," he said. "It has nothing to do with age."

Dylan seemed so much older then. Nowadays the firebrand from yesteryear is nominated regularly for the Nobel Prize in Literature. In 1997, Bill Clinton named Dylan one of the esteemed recipients of the Kennedy Center Honors. In 2012, President Barack Obama honored him with the nation's highest peacetime accolade: the Medal of Freedom.

He is the subject of scores of essays, books, and treatises. Lately, he's been exhibiting another side of his creativity with SRO gallery showings of his paintings. His Van Gogh-esque *Brazil* acrylics and *Drawn Blank* series of post-Impressionist landscapes, nudes, and brooding portraits have brought him a whole new audience.

College poetry courses dissect his phrases while biographers, theologians, and philosophers try to match those words to the highs and lows of an eclectic life, looking for the wellspring that transformed an ambitious Jewish misfit from the remote outback of northern Minnesota into poet, painter, and, for some, prophet.

The undisputed laureate of our time, Robert Allen Zimmerman has described himself as a mere song-and-dance man, though his legions of fans would beg to differ. More than any of his contemporaries, his influence has been global. He has been quoted by half a dozen U.S. presidents and honored for poetry that resonates so intensely that his observations of the human condition arguably stand beside those of Mark Twain, Charles Dickens, perhaps even William Shakespeare.

But how is any of this even possible, given the road he'd chosen a generation earlier?

■ ■■ ■■

In the autumn of 2012, as Dylan launched *Tempest,* his 35th studio album, Will DeVogue announced that he had found his sister—the second illegitimate child of Bob Dylan to surface in as many months.

"Isabella Birdfeather," said DeVogue. "Izzy for short."

Several weeks earlier, DeVogue rattled Bob's world with his assertion that he was Dylan's eldest child. A 48-year-old mortgage banker from Portsmouth, Rhode Island, DeVogue devoted much of his adult life to tracking down his biological parents. Once he located his mother, a recovering heroin addict from the early Greenwich Village folk scene, it didn't take long to narrow the field of prospective sperm donors. Dylan topped the list.

"I started Googling, read everything I could, and compared my photos with his," said DeVogue. "Then I contacted his manager."

Dylan's longtime gatekeeper Jeff Rosen seemed genuinely interested. Far from blowing him off, Rosen pumped DeVogue for details. Where exactly did Bob and Will's mother meet? How long did they know each other? Rosen promised to get back once he spoke with Mr. Dylan. He followed up with an e-mail saying Bob had no recollection and ignored all of DeVogue's subsequent calls.

"I didn't want anything from him," said DeVogue. "I just wanted a simple blood test to see if he really is or isn't my father."

A year later, DeVogue heard from Isabella Birdfeather. The 31-year-old daughter of underground L.A. radio deejay Barbara Birdfeather, Izzy bore an even stronger physical resemblance to Bob than DeVogue: same hooked nose, same bad teeth, curly hair and piercing myopic blue eyes. Like DeVogue, Isabella had a heroin addict for a mom.

Before she died in 2009, Barbara Birdfeather told her daughter that she probably inspired Dylan's "If You See Her, Say Hello." Izzy subsequently researched enough of her mother's itinerant lifestyle to determine that she had in fact been in Tangier[2] during the early '70s when Bob wrote the song for *Blood on the Tracks*. Triangulating a map of Manhattan, she further found her mother to have been within conjugal proximity of Bob when he recorded his 1981 LP *Saved*.

"Nine months later," she said, "I was born."

It disappoints but does not surprise either Will or Isabella that Bob would not acknowledge them. Wary to the point of paranoia, Dylan controls even the most trivial facts about himself. Since his divorce from presumed second wife Carolyn Dennis in 1992, no one has been able to confirm whether he ever remarried, though he confessed to *USA Today*'s Edna Gundersen ten years ago, "I've been married a bunch of times." He did not elaborate.

His security is so complete that he can't even get backstage without a pass. When he was barred from his own concert once for failing to present the proper laminate, instead of firing the guards Dylan praised them. "I told them they did a great job," wryly adding: "There's no exception, except for one."

When not on stage, Bob Dylan vanishes behind a curtain of misrepresentation, half-truths, and romantic claptrap designed to preserve his legend while revealing nothing about who he really is. He once made a *Time* magazine reporter meet him at a diner "somewhere in the Midwest." A condition of the interview was that he would reveal no further geographical detail.

Even in his dotage, Dylan routinely misdirects or ignores the truth, as he did when his most famous guitar recently resurfaced after vanishing nearly half a century ago.

---

[2] *If you see her say hello she might be in Tangier*
   She left here last early spring is living there I hear

PBS's *History Detectives* purportedly located the fabled Sunburst Stratocaster that Dylan played at the 1965 Newport Folk Festival when he famously "went electric" and changed the course of pop music history. Program producers spent months verifying the instrument's provenance, tracing it from a private plane Dylan used to get between performances in the early '60s. His pilot Vic Quinto tried returning it to Bob, as did his daughter Dawn Peterson after Quinto's death in 1977, but neither Dylan nor his staff showed any interest.

About the same time that Will DeVogue and Isabella Birdfeather first called Dylan "dad," *History Detectives* aired its findings. They included matching the wood grain of the legendary guitar to high-resolution color photos shot during Dylan's first electrified public performance of "Like a Rolling Stone." Confronted with the proof, which included Dylan's authenticated guitar case and a sheaf of half-written songs[3] and notes written in Dylan's hand,[4] Bob's lawyer maintained the *real* Stratocaster was and always had been in Bob's possession and would not be put on display.

Because lesser guitars played by Eric Clapton and Jimi Hendrix during rock's Pleistocene era had auctioned for more than $1 million, Dawn Peterson and the *History Detectives* producers were left to conclude that Dylan's position had to be about how much money the instrument might command or the preservation of his own myth—or, more likely, both.

Early estimates from Christie's predicted the guitar would fetch up to $500,000 and the assorted song lyrics another $30,000. On

---

[3]   "Medicine Sunday" (originally titled "Midnight Train"), "I Wanna Be Your Lover," and "Jet Pilot."

[4]   American hedge-fund manager Adam Sender paid $422,500 for the original lyrics of "The Times They are a-Changin'." Handwritten lyrics of "Let Me Die in My Footsteps" went for $70,000. A prerelease copy of *Freewheelin'* containing "Talkin' John Birch Paranoid Blues" sold for more than $20,000. And so on . . .

December 6, 2013, the Stratocaster sold for $965,000, a world record for an axe at auction.[5] Of the lyrics only a handwritten and typed copy of "I Wanna Be Your Lover" sold, for an additional $20,000.

Hovering over the Bob legend, almost from its beginning, is a whiff of desperation—an unspoken fear that at any moment, the truth might out and the boy who first reported that the emperor had no clothes might himself stand naked for all to see. In the age of the Internet, Dylan has been caught cribbing more than once, borrowing lines from a little-known Japanese novelist and an equally obscure Confederate poet. Most recently, his "Asia Series" of original oil paintings were exposed as copies of photos taken by some of the most famous photographers of the twentieth century, including Henri Cartier-Bresson.

And yet, despite the fraying of his carefully crafted legend, Bob Dylan remains "a national treasure," in the words of Barack Obama.

"I think he's gone in with nothing and come up with great things," said his contemporary and close rival, Leonard Cohen. "That is to say that my impression about Dylan is that he's used all the approaches: the spontaneous, the polished, the unhewn, the deliberate. He masters all those forms."

With all his imperfections, Bob Dylan remains trenchant, relevant and touched with grace. By his own hand, he is still a riddle wrapped in a mystery inside an enigma, and the question remains: How did a feckless, foolish poseur, a middle-class *schnorrer* from the Minnesota outback, become the Bard of his generation?

How indeed.

---

[5]   The honor formerly went to Eric Clapton's Fender named "Blackie," which sold in 2004 for $959,500.

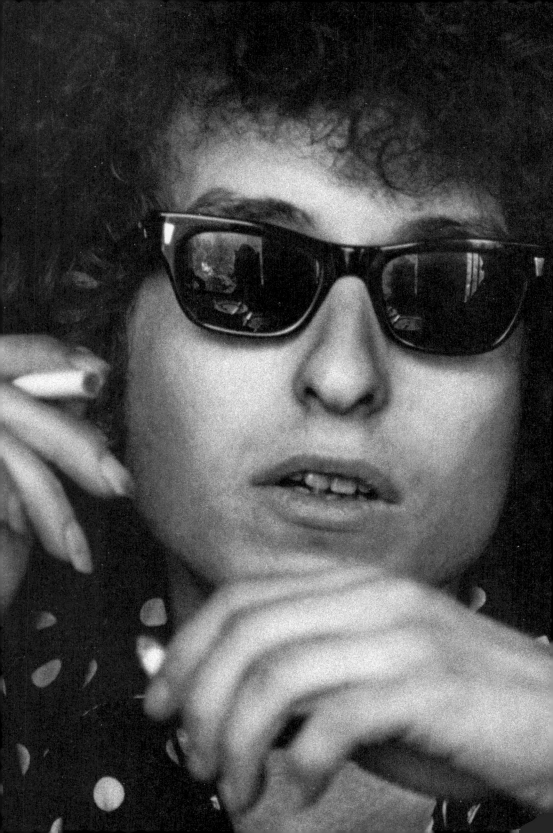

PART I

REBEL WITHOUT APPLAUSE

1941–1966

The poet is the unsatisfied child
who dares to ask the difficult
question which arises from
the schoolmaster's
answer . . .

—Robert Graves

1

HIBBING

Teetering at the brink of the deepest iron-ore pit mine on earth,[6] the North Country settlement where Robert Zimmerman evolved into Bob Dylan remains nearly as remote an American outpost today as it was when he left half a century ago.

Some 250 miles north of the twin cities of Minneapolis and St. Paul, Hibbing is small-town America writ large in primary colors: the summer sun cuts flat like a bloody disc against a vast azure horizon while emerald forests rise from rusting hillocks of crimson slag that still stretch for miles, decades after being exhumed. During the long, deep winters, street lights and smoking chimneys stand vigil against five-foot-high snow drifts that blow out of the Canadian Arctic. Wind howls off of Lake Superior and blows over the immigrant population[7] of northern Minnesota, thrashing them incessantly until the suffocating winter skies finally give way to a colossal spring, completing the cycle of seasons that transforms Bob Dylan's hometown once more into as vivid and improbable a setting as any ever imagined by Norman Rockwell or Thomas Kincade.

There is silence here, huge and tense. God and man coexist in uneasy symbiosis. Yet despite its many primordial elements, Hibbing was as much an invention of the twentieth century as the celebrated song-and-dance man who became its most illustrious

---

[6] In 1928, President Calvin Coolidge toured the mine and observed, "That's a pretty big hole."

[7] Twenty-seven different ethnic groups called northern Minnesota home during the 1950s.

emissary.[8] When the Vikings allegedly navigated into Middle America in 1362, they bypassed Dylan's rough and frigid North Country altogether, leaving their runes 100 miles to the west in Alexandria,[9] near the more hospitable eastern edge of the Great Plains. No American Indian tribe permanently settled the unwelcoming Mesabi[10] Iron Range. The eerie lights of the aurora borealis haunted the hills at twilight, and the Ojibwa regarded the land as sacred—a burial ground, but no place to put down roots and raise a family.

When the pioneers rolled through in the 1800s, most kept their wagons moving toward arable land. Hibbing's history didn't actually begin until the height of the Industrial Revolution, when a German entrepreneur named Franz Dietrich von Ahlen discovered iron ore and began buying up real estate. In typical immigrant fashion, he Americanized his name to Frank Hibbing and after his death, the company he founded and the city that he created out of whole cloth began inviting in anyone who wanted to work the mine, regardless of race, religion, creed, politics, or national origin.

Frank Hibbing's company town prospered through two world wars and didn't begin its long, slow decline until a far longer cold war. Hibbing taught its citizens tolerance and good will by binding them together in affluent isolation. Getting to know one's neighbors during a long Minnesota winter went way beyond going next door to borrow a cup of sugar. Slavs and Finns had to coexist with Irish and Italians; Roman Catholics mingled with German Lutherans, Methodists, and Russian Jews. Like Manhattan's Lower East Side,

---

[8]   Among Hibbing's other notable natives were Manson Family prosecutor Vincent Bugliosi, American Communist Party chief Gus Hall, and Yankee home run king Roger Maris.

[9]   "The birthplace of America," according to Dylan.

[10]   "Land of Giants" in Ojibwa.

Hibbing harbored pockets of secret, often petty prejudice but could never afford the metropolitan luxury of open bigotry.

Robert Zimmerman and his younger brother, David, came from third-generation Russian and Lithuanian stock. They were born[11] in a Catholic hospital in the Lake Superior port of Duluth two hours to the east of Hibbing. They might have grown up there in a more urban environment if their father hadn't suffered from polio following World War II. Bob was in kindergarten when he witnessed Abram Zimmerman brought low by disease. Once an award-winning athlete and a semi-pro baseball player, his father spent a week in the hospital followed by six months of excruciating rehab. Abe crawled up the stairs to the family's second-story apartment where he learned how to hobble around their living room again. During a 1984 interview, Dylan recalled: "My father was a very active man, but he was stricken very early by an attack of polio. The illness put an end to all his dreams I believe. He could hardly walk . . ."

Even when he was finally able to stand upright, one leg remained permanently crippled. To his children, Abe appeared taciturn, brooding, stern. He addressed his elder son as "Robert," never "Bobby" or "Bob."

Abe Zimmerman lost his senior manager's position at Duluth's Standard Oil refinery and had to rely on siblings to survive. Thus, in 1947 when Bob was six and David was just a year old, Abe moved his family 75 miles to the northwest to take a sales position with his older brothers Maurice and Paul Zimmerman who owned and operated Micka Electric, soon to become Hibbing's largest furniture and appliance store.

---

[11] Born May 24, 1941, Robert Allen Zimmerman's Jewish birth name was Shabtai Zisel ben Avraham. A passport issued to Robert Dylan in 1974, twelve years after he'd changed his name, gave his birth date as May 11, 1941. His brother, David Bernard Zimmerman, was born five years later.

Able, gregarious Beatrice "Beatty" Zimmerman effectively succeeded her husband as the senior partner in the marriage and once they'd resettled, the Zimmerman household tilted toward matriarchy.

"Beatty was sort of classic: what they used to call a hysterical personality," recalled author Toby Thompson, who met her in the late '60s. "Very theatrical, very over-the-top. A flying-off-the-handle kind of person, but very protective of Bob."

Beatty's mother, Florence Stone, invited the Zimmermans to stay in her front parlor until they could afford a place of their own. As effusive as her daughter, she gave up her home following the drinking death of Beatty's father[12] and moved in. Grandma Florence[13] lived down the hall from Bob and David's cowpoke-themed bedroom and became a second mother. A few days shy of his fifth birthday, Bob dedicated "Some Sunday Morning" to her and belted it out to a room full of adults. The boy was musical, said Florence.

For the next 15 years, his grandmother stayed home while Beatty took a job selling frocks and foundation garments downtown at Feldman's Department Store. Both women alternately scolded and coddled the boys, saturating them with music, Judaism, and the clipped, fabulist tradition of Yiddish storytelling. Beatty made up stories as easily as she mangled Mother Goose. In her version, "Hey-diddle-diddle" could precede "a house in the middle" or "a mouse with a riddle"[14] just as often as "the cat and the fiddle."

---

[12]   Hibbing was home to 68 saloons before Prohibition and nearly as many once booze was legal again. Ben Stone, Bob's grandfather, died of cirrhosis on May 17, 1945.

[13]   Like her son Abram, Dylan's other grandmother, Anna Zimmerman, was disabled. She had but one leg, smoked a pipe, and lived alone in her Duluth apartment overlooking Lake Superior. She "possessed a haunting accent—face always set in a half-despairing expression," according to Dylan's *Chronicles*.

[14]   As a teen Bob spun stories about a character he named "Herbie the Mouse."

A huge mahogany radio stood in the front room. Beneath its heavy lid, a hidden turntable provided further rhymes and riddles.

"I opened it up one day and there was a record on, a country record, this song called 'Drifting Too Far From Shore,'"[15] Bob recalled half a century later. "The sound of the record made me feel like I was somebody else and that, you know, I was maybe not even born to the right parents or something."

Abe bought a Gulbranson Spinet piano and set it up in the living room next to the radio while Bob was still in grade school, but it was Beatty and Grandma Florence who urged the boys to learn music. David was subdued and serious; Bob, impatient and restless. He quit in a huff after a single session with his teacher, Rose Zygmanski. He'd play the piano the way *he* wanted to or not at all. Zygmanski told his parents he had no talent while his brother David was the gifted member of the family.

It was no surprise that Bob eventually took up an instrument better suited to the strong-willed who prefer trial-and-error over sheet music and metronomes. He never did learn to read music, but began a lifetime of strumming guitar after Hank Williams showed him the way.

Through the filter of Dylan's own memory, growing up in Hibbing was both stirring and stifling: "If I had any advantage over anybody at all, it's the advantage that I was all alone and could think and do what I wanted to. . . . I don't know what I would have been if I was growing up in the Bronx or Ethiopia or South America or even California."

A curiously cosmopolitan settlement of immigrants enriched during the 1940s and early '50s by America's ever-expanding hunger

---

[15] Written and performed by Hank Williams. Dead of alcoholism in 1953, 29-year-old Williams was Nashville's first superstar and author of dozens of country standards.

for steel, Hibbing was an isolated outpost of blue-collar affluence in the midwestern outback. Residents outwardly espoused the *Father Knows Best* values of the 1950s, placing an enormous premium on patriotism and education. A child's upward mobility demanded twenty years of schooling. Perhaps Frank Hibbing's most enduring legacy was the high school that bore his name.

Now protected as a state historic landmark, Hibbing's three-story high school remains the grandest palace of higher learning in the northern half of the state. Built in 1923 for $4 million, Hibbing High seems a campus better suited to the Ivy League than a remote corner of rural Minnesota. From a million-dollar pipe organ and crystal chandeliers in an ornate rococo auditorium to its Olympic-sized indoor pool to priceless murals depicting the pioneer sweep of American history, Hibbing High would cost closer to $100 million if it were built today and if, indeed, craftsmen and materials could still be found to complete the task.

Add a first-rate faculty and its students never wanted for a more sophisticated exposure to the wider world beyond the Mesabi Range. Two of Bob's instructors, social studies teacher Charles Miller and English instructor B. J. Rolfzen, grounded Bob early in literature, liberal arts, and history.

"We used to sing the Mickey Mouse (Club) song to loosen up a little bit," said Miller.

Still revered by former students, both men turned teaching into a daily classroom adventure.

"Mr. Miller didn't teach so much as talk and tell stories," recalled John Bucklen, Bob's best friend growing up. "He made a deep impression on Bob, especially when he talked about the rough early days of the labor unions."[16]

---

16   When Abe worked for Standard Oil, he started in the stock room but rose to head the company union.

Miller's stirring accounts of the Industrial Revolution were perfect counterpoint to "Bonnie" Rolfzen's stentorian brand of English lit. Like Miller, Rolfzen taught in front of his desk, not behind it, performing passages from the classics rather than ordering up rote memorization. He and his wife lived next door to the Zimmermans and, like his most famous student, Rolfzen also had early paternal issues that translated into lifelong distrust of authority.

In his 2005 memoir about growing up dirt poor and Catholic in rural Minnesota, Rolfzen bitterly recalled the self-pitying alcoholic who sired himself and his ten siblings. He had lost both arms in a drunken accident at the very nadir of the Great Depression, consigning his entire family to abject poverty. When Rolfzen spoke to Bob's class about slogging through miles of snow with holes in his shoes to get to school, or sleeping in a deep-freeze hovel with nothing to eat, it was no exaggeration. But Rolfzen finished college and went on to teach, serving Bobby Zimmerman as both a sober role model and a passionate mentor who believed in the saving grace of poetry.

Encouraged by such brilliant, nonconforming teachers during the bland years between World War II and Vietnam, Bobby Zimmerman savored their stories. But even before Rolfzen had assigned *Uncle Tom's Cabin* or *Ben Hur*, Sir Walter Scott or John Steinbeck, before Charles Miller ever roused with breathless accounts of the Civil War or head-busting battles between Wobblies and company goons, Bob's extended family had already steeped both Zimmerman brothers in the Old Testament. The aging laity of Hibbing's Agudath Achim synagogue elected Abe president in the early '50s, and with little fanfare, an Orthodox rabbi was imported from Brooklyn to educate Bob.

"Suddenly a rabbi showed up under strange circumstances for only a year," Dylan recalled. "He and his wife got off the bus in the middle of winter. He showed up just in time for me to learn this stuff."

The couple lived above the L&B Café where the bearded patriarch taught the Torah after school and in the evenings. He officiated during Bob's 1954 bar mitzvah and then disappeared just as mysteriously as he'd arrived, leaving the Reform Jews of Agudath Achim once more without a rabbi.

Bob's proficiency in the Bible did not translate to his schooling. He carried a low B average all the way through high school. He flunked physics and scored 106 on his Stanford Binet—a perfectly respectable I.Q., but no indication of genius.

Puffy-cheeked, nearsighted, chunky, and dependent on glasses, grade-school Bob dressed like a nerd before there was such a term. Beatty and Grandma Florence sent him off to junior high with his hair slicked into place and his long-sleeved shirts buttoned all the way to the neck. He had asthma for a time and took his share of heat for being different. When classmates inevitably razzed him, he lashed back lamely with "Don't call me Zimbo!" By the time he entered high school, he'd changed strategy. Honing sarcasm to a lethal weapon, he leveled his acid tongue against the "bongs," i.e., anyone not a member of his small but exclusive clique of fellow misfits.

While there is no record of Bob engaging in fistfights, no one dared take him on in a war of words. He was the undisputed master of *glissendorf,* a cruel adolescent mind game in which school-yard pals conspire to confuse an innocent third party with nonsense and misdirection for no other purpose than to humiliate. Bob occasionally reduced his victims—pubescent girls, more often than not—to tears.

"Bob used to tell girls that the iron in the water gave him certain talents, that it made him creative, and they'd believe him," said John Bucklen. "If you were Bob, you'd say just about anything."

"He had a wicked way with words," testified LeRoy Hoikkala who, along with Bob and Monte Edwardson, completed the close-knit trio of high school rebels who would later identify themselves as the Golden Chords. Once they all decided rock 'n' roll was a far more effective way to get babes than *glissendorf,* Bob traded in sarcasm for a guitar.

■ ■ ■

In December 1955, 14-year-old Robert Zimmerman saw *Rebel Without a Cause* at the Lybba Theater,[17] and it was a revelation.

"James Dean changed all of our lives," recalled Bucklen.[18]

Jim Stark, the aloof outsider James Dean portrayed in *Rebel,* had a stern but ineffectual father (Jim Backus) and a hysterical if well-meaning mother (Ann Doran), neither of whom understood a thing about their brooding son. Bob went back to see it three more times, soaking up Dean's angst, savoring the details of his real-life reck-lessness and early death.[19] He studied his method acting in the

---

[17]   Now the Sunrise Deli, the First Avenue cinema where Bob spent many a mat-inee first opened in 1947. Like the rest of the Iron Range's theaters, the Lybba was founded by his great-grandfather Benjamin Edelstein, who named the theater for Beatty's grandmother. In 2009, Bob's son Jesse named his health-care nonprofit for her: the Lybba Foundation.

[18]   Hoikkala maintained that *Blackboard Jungle* had a similar effect when it pre-miered a year later, further justifying Bob's contempt for adults. The other big teen hit in 1956 was *The Girl Can't Help It,* which introduced Bob to Gene "Be Bop A Lula" Vincent as well as his high school role model, Little Richard.

[19]   James Dean wrecked the Porsche 550 Spyder, which he'd nicknamed "Little Bastard," and died on Friday, Sept. 30, 1955, in Cholame, California. He was 24.

postmortem releases, *Giant* and *East of Eden.* Masking his sarcasm so he could sneer at adults without them being the wiser, Bob taught himself to mimic the actor's sly, low intonations when inflicting *glissendorf* on unsuspecting bongs.

Bob convinced himself he even looked like James Dean, insisting that friends compare his profile with the actor's fanzine photos. They both had blue eyes. They stood roughly the same height (5'8"). Over time, Bobby Zimmerman the Nebbish perfected Dean's slouch, morphing into Bob Zimmerman the Rebel, down to his shades, sideburns, and red leather jacket.[20] He set up a shrine in the basement and tacked Dean portraits to the wall.

The night he sneaked out to see *Giant,* his folks waited up for him. Beatty was in high dudgeon. She wouldn't let him go upstairs until he told her why he was out roaming the streets at all hours. When he mumbled, Abe ordered him not to sass his mother. Bob simmered, did an about face, and retreated to the basement, his father at his heels. According to Dylan biographer Robert Shelton, Abe hollered: "Robert, you come back here! We've given you a good home. We buy you the best of everything. What more do you want? I never had it so soft when I was your age . . ."

His father tore James Dean from the wall, ripped the picture in two, and tossed the shreds at Bob's feet. Crushed but chastened, Bob's escalating war with his old man stalemated if only for an evening. His father struck him uncharacteristically speechless: they *did* give him everything—clothes, car, and spending money that he blew on Lucky Strikes, Wurlitzer tunes, and cherry pie á la mode down at the L&B Café.

---

[20] He browbeat his parents into buying it for him.

When his classmates scrounged for summer jobs, Bob got packed off to Camp Herzl[21] in northwestern Wisconsin where he canoed with cousins, perfected his Ping Pong, wrote poetry,[22] hit on chicks, and sang around the piano on the front porch of the social hall. It was there Bob bonded with fellow campers Howard Rutman and Larry Kegan, who both hailed from the Twin Cities and knew a thing or two about the thriving rhythm and blues subculture emerging on St. Paul's eastside.

The trio developed a doo-wop act, named themselves the Jokers, and performed at parties. Once, they appeared on a televised Minneapolis talent show. Their parents beamed at their white bread a cappella, but when the Jokers were alone, they tended toward double-entendre race records like the Toppers' "Baby Let Me Bang Your Box."[23]

The Jokers wore matching red and gray cardigans embroidered with their names, and even got their parents to spring for an eight-song demo at Terlinde Music. But two-thirds of the Jokers lived in St. Paul and before the third one was old enough to drive, Larry Kegan broke his neck.

---

[21] Named for Theodor Herzl, leader of the first organized Zionist meeting in 1897, the "independent, trans-denominational, Zionist overnight camp" was founded in 1946 to "create lasting Jewish friendships, and develop commitment and love for Judaism and Israel."

[22] Fifty years later, one of his earliest songs, "Little Buddy," surfaced at a Christie's auction. It turned out to be a revision of a Hank Snow composition that 16-year-old Bobby Zimmerman called his own and tried to publish in the Camp Herzl newsletter. The handwritten pages fetched $78,000.

[23] *I been playin' piano large and small*
But you got the best piano of all . . .
I got a shuffle, a backbeat, a boogie-woogie too
But when I play my jelly roll you don't know what to do
Baby le me bang your box . . .

While vacationing with family in Florida, Bob's earliest rock 'n' roll running buddy dove off a seawall into three feet of water. He woke up paralyzed from the waist down. Once Bob got his driver's license, he visited Kegan often, but any hope the Jokers might rise again died in the summer of '57.

Abe let his son tool around Hibbing in the family Buick, but Bob kvetched until his parents bought him a pink-and-white '51 Ford convertible. He immediately primered the car a more manly grey, but one mode of transportation would never do. Bob cajoled Abe into helping him buy a used Harley, too.

At Abe's insistence, Bob did earn his keep after a fashion. He helped out after school at Micka, where his father boasted to the other Howard Street merchants that his boy was growing up as sturdy as a football player. Abe might fantasize his son as a future Green Bay Packer star like defensive end Bobby Dillon,[24] but Bobby Zimmerman held no great interest in athletics.

"I didn't play too much baseball because my eyes were kind of bad and the ball would hit me when I wasn't looking," Bob recalled. "Football I never played at all, not even touch football. I really didn't like to hurt myself."

He did like boxing, however, which was part of the P.E. curriculum during the '50s. "You didn't need to be part of a team," he said. "And I liked that."

He shot baskets and played hockey some. Learning to skate was virtually required in northern Minnesota.

Mostly, he stuck to spectator sports and found someplace to hide when physical labor looked like it might be in the offing. When Abe

---

[24]   Despite being blind in one eye, Bobby Dan Dillon became a North Country hero during the 1950s and still holds the Packers' record for career interceptions: 52.

called on the boy to help deliver Frigidaires, Bob would vanish to the backroom and pound on an old piano.

As Micka's bookkeeper it fell to Abe to order repossessions and part of Bob's job involved hauling away half-paid-for TV sets or appliances—an odious task he performed reluctantly or not at all.

"He saw Abe as a kind of new-world Shylock extracting a pound of flesh from the backsides of impoverished laborers, sapping their pride," observed Dylan biographer Bob Spitz.

Bob lived inside his own head and the older he got the more he thought about climbing aboard a Greyhound[25] or an outbound freight. Until that day came, he stayed current with the latest flicks and further explored American pop culture through dispatches from *Life* magazine, the *Hibbing Daily Tribune,* and the emerging novelty of television,[26] but mostly he listened to the radio. Late at night, Bob bonded with the blues.

Hibbing might have been ground zero for beer barrel polka and hayseed country & western during the Eisenhower Administration, but the deep southern AM broadcasts that bounced up and down the Mississippi River Valley after dark descended on Bob's transistorized ears like messages from outer space. From early Elvis to clear channel R&B, he and his posse tuned in after everyone else headed to bed. Following those brooding autumn evenings and long, isolating winter nights, he and Hoikkala, Edwardson, and Bucklen one-upped each other at school the next day about their latest discoveries: Memphis Minnie, Howlin' Wolf, Etta James, Fats Domino, Muddy

---

[25] Founded in Hibbing in 1914, Greyhound went national 13 years later and become the premier mode of cheap transportation in the U.S. In 1989 the Greyhound Bus Museum opened in Hibbing, half a mile from the brink of its iron mine. The museum features a dozen antique buses, including Greyhound's original seven-seat Hibbing Hupmobile.

[26] As Micka's junior partner, Abe was among the first in town to buy a TV set for his family in 1952.

Waters—all erupting out of 50,000-watt powerhouses in Chicago, Memphis, Little Rock, or St. Louis. Bob sent away regularly to "Stan's Rockin' Record Shop Review" on KWKH Shreveport for impossible-to-find 45s by Blind Lemon Jefferson, Big Bill Broonzy, and Chuck Berry.[27] Once he'd unearthed the racial roots of rock and roll, Bob's James Dean facade slowly coiffed higher, fluffing at the top of his head into a Little Richard[28] pompadour.

Bob's postmidnight radio club was not exclusively male. The rock 'n' roll goddess who would remain an inspiration throughout his early career turned out to be an echo—literally—of the best Hibbing had to offer. While Dylan fans still differ over the identity of "The Girl from the North Country," Marvel Echo Star Helstrom[29] inevitably gets the most votes.

The hard-scrabble daughter of Scandinavian immigrants who actually lived in a windowless tar paper shack (no exaggeration) on the other side of the tracks (true) at the outskirts of town (can't make this stuff up) due south of the Maple Hill Cemetery on Dillon Road (yes!)—Bob's first steady girlfriend was a poverty-stricken platinum-haired knockout[30] whose tough-girl looks (think Olivia Newton-John, final frames of *Grease*) made her a pariah among Hibbing's country club set . . . but welcome among Bob's eccentric entourage. He recalled her as "my Becky Thatcher"[31] in *Chronicles* and compared Echo's tough chick beauty to Brigitte Bardot.[32]

---

[27] Six records for $3.49.

[28] Bob's favorite Little Richard tunes were "Jenny Jenny" and "True Fine Mama."

[29] A Portland, Oregon, rock trio took her name when they began recording in the early 2000s.

[30] She washed her hair daily with Joy dishwashing liquid.

[31] . . . but not his first girlfriend. That honor went to Gloria Story, "the first girl that ever took a like to me," according to Bob.

[32] Apparently lost to history, Bob's first musical composition was a sophomoric paean to the French actress.

They became a couple through junior and senior years. Echo introduced him to such cultural disparities as the sauna (a clapboard outbuilding adjacent to her ramshackle home) and her parents' oddball record collection, including hard Bakelite 78s of Jimmie Rodgers[33] and the Carter Family.

Matt Helstrom dug wells and welded for a living, but played guitar after work. He owned several, including a solid-body Hawaiian. While Echo's father could be as stern as Abe Zimmerman (especially when it came to Bob keeping his daughter out after curfew), he at least had a deep appreciation for the grassroots music that inspired Bob to buy his own solid-body electric.

Dylan later maintained he found his first turquoise Silvertone in a Sears Roebuck catalogue for $20 down, but friends from those early days remembered him paying $22 for that first guitar at a First Avenue music store. Regardless of which was true, Bob only confessed his purchase to Abe after the fact. When he stepped up to a $60 Ozark Supro, he was equally reticent to tell his old man, especially after discovering the guitar didn't work so well without the additional expense of an amplifier.

Though he remained dependent on Abe's grudging generosity for nearly every rebellious symbol in his rebellious young life, Bob's mumbled gratitude for everything from his motorcycle to his high-decibel guitars scarcely masked a deeper resentment. Once, while out riding with Echo strapped tight around his waist, his Harley stalled and the fuel gauge registered empty. Bob stayed with the bike and sent Echo for gas when, of all people, Abe Zimmerman rolled

---

[33]   Like James Dean, the Depression-era yodeling brakeman from Meridian, Mississippi, died young. Proclaimed "the Father of Country Music," Rodgers was 35 when tuberculosis claimed him in 1933. Sixty years later, Dylan eulogized him as "one of the guiding lights of the twentieth century, whose way with song has always been an inspiration to those of us who have followed the path."

by in his Buick Roadmaster. Abe drove Echo to a service station, helped her pump a gallon, drove her back to Bob, and waited until the Harley fired up. Once Abe drove away, Bob turned to his hapless girlfriend and snarled: "What'd you do that for? Why'd you let him give you a ride?"

Echo learned to put up with the petulance. He smuggled her up to his room once, only to hear Grandma Florence puttering down the hall. Panicking at having a *shiksa* in the house, he ordered Echo out his window. Instead of protesting, she climbed to a ledge above the garage, eased herself over the edge, shinnied to the ground and made her way home on her own.

Giggly, petite, and thriving on male attention, Echo tolerated Bob's mercurial moods. She fit right in with the oh-so-serious rock 'n' rollers who cycled in and out of the Golden Chords: LeRoy Hoikkala on drums, Bob on piano, Monte Edwardson on lead guitar and vocals. Inevitably, Echo cheered them all on during after-school practice in Hoikkala's garage or Edwardson's den.

John Bucklen, who mimicked Elvis's sideman Scotty Moore on rhythm guitar, dropped by on occasion, but played with rival bands despite his bond with Bob. Like Abe Zimmerman, Bucklen's father was disabled. Norman Bucklen lost a leg in a mining accident, never fully recovered, and died in December 1957 after years of poor health. His 16-year-old son discovered the body and for months thereafter, John didn't hang with Bob or Echo or the rest of the Chords. Suddenly thrust into the role of the man in his mother's house, he began to distance himself from his peers.

Death was an infrequent visitor in Bob's privileged life, so when it happened, the unsettling effect lingered. On Memorial Day 1957, an 18-year-old classmate named Leonard Venditto who lived next door to John Bucklen fractured his skull in a motorcycle accident just outside of town. LeRoy Hoikkala acted as honorary pallbearer.

After the funeral, Hoikkala sat with Bob in his convertible for a long time discussing the meaning of Lenny's death.

About the same time, Bob had his own brush with mortality. Both Hoikkala and Bucklen remember Hibbing's Harley delinquents out cruising one afternoon just as a freight train rolled through. Bob led the impatient revving as they waited for the caboose to clear. He shot forward, but hadn't counted on an unseen second train rolling by on a parallel set of tracks in the opposite direction. Only Bob's split-second decision to ditch the Harley saved him from sliding beneath a boxcar.

"He wasn't a very good driver," Bucklen recalled.

In the days before more practical, soft contact lenses or laser eye surgery, vanity could be hazardous for a nearsighted rebel. Whenever he bent a fender, he phoned Abe to bail him out, always mumbling a preemptive irony, "I broke the fan belt."

Abe settled Bob's first big accident out of court, reportedly for $4,000. Another near miss on his Harley came way closer to tragedy. Again it was Abe to the rescue. Bob didn't see a three-year-old dart into the street from between two parked cars until it was too late. All he remembered was the boy holding an orange as Bob struck him down with his motorcycle. When the child's Hibbing physician ordered him transferred to a hospital in Duluth, Abe arranged for an ambulance. The youngster recovered, but a shaken Bob agreed to sell his Harley.

"I can still see that orange rolling across the street," he later told Echo.

■ ■ ■

Little Bobby Zimmerman vanished between Bob's junior and senior year. Bob the Rebel took his place—a rock 'n' roll James Dean who melded the shoulder-rolling stage presence of Elvis Presley with the TV detective cool of *Peter Gunn*. The leader of the Golden Chords convinced himself that he oozed unruffled composure.

"I had a couple of bands in high school, maybe three or four of 'em," Bob told *Rolling Stone* a quarter century later. "Lead singers would always come in and take my bands because they would have connections, like maybe their fathers would know somebody, so they could get a job in the neighboring town at the pavilion for a Sunday picnic or something. And I'd lose my band. I'd see it all the time."

The Chords had a deafening, memorable, if short-lived run at Moose Lodge potlucks, Friday night dances, and school talent shows in the spring and summer of 1958.

"We were just the loudest band around, it was mostly that," Bob recalled. "What we were doing, there wasn't anybody else around doing . . ."

Bob led the Chords in their ear-splitting debut at the annual Hibbing High Jacket Jamboree that winter. The Chords shook, rattled, and rolled the million-dollar chandeliers of the school auditorium and while it was Bob standing center stage, an alter ego named Elston Gunn already waited in the wings. He whacked at the eight-foot-long Steinway like a tone-deaf Jerry Lee Lewis, kicking the pedals so hard that one busted off.

"Little Richard's trademark at the time was putting one leg up on the piano and Bob did it just that way," recalled classmate Jean Shore.

Principal Kenneth Pederson ordered the curtains pulled and the house P.A. system cut, but Bob brayed on through the amps he and the Chords set up on stage.

"I gotta girl, way over town," he shrieked in imitation of Ray Charles.

Even Echo couldn't handle Bob's raspy voice as it twisted the melody high then low so that he never repeated himself, never sang the lyrics the same way twice. Down in the audience, she cringed at the sneers and laughter, covering her own ears until her girlfriend Dee Dee Seward gripped her elbow: "Listen!"

"I gotta woman, she's good to me, and her name is Echo!"

So what if Pederson pulled the plug. Screw *him!* Echo went to the prom that year with Bob. She was radiant in blue chiffon while he twitched in a new suit and tie. After the postprom party at the Moose Lodge, they fell asleep in his convertible. Bob got her home without Matt Helstrom being the wiser, but whenever they heard "Wake Up Little Susie" thereafter, they heard more than just the Everly Brothers. Bob and Echo were definitely an item. Somewhere in the backseat of time, they lost their virginity to each other. They went steady; might even marry someday.

But selling his Harley hadn't lessened Bob's wanderlust. Echo frequently accompanied him in his convertible to neighboring Chisholm or the bigger burg of Virginia at the eastern edge of the Mesabi Range. It was there that he met and cozied up to James Reese, the only black deejay north of the Twin Cities. Going by Jim Dandy on local station WHLB, Reese played an hour of jazz each evening along with the kind of blues Bob couldn't even find on the postmidnight AM dial: Son House, Charley Patton, Willie Dixon . . .

Reese and his wife welcomed the white kid from Hibbing—even had him and the Chords up to the house where he let them paw through his personal record collection.

On weekends, Bob would tool in the opposite direction—west, toward Judy Garland's hometown of Grand Rapids, Minnesota, or maybe north toward International Falls and the Canadian border. His early road trips up and down Highway 169 quickly evolved into longer journeys, taking him far beyond the Range, all the way to

Duluth or its twin city of Superior, Wisconsin. Bob would sometimes spend the night there at a cousin's house or hang with his
Camp Herzl buddy Louis Kemp.[34]

There was frequent drinking—mostly beer and wine but maybe a
little Scotch if it could be successfully pirated from the old man's
liquor cabinet. Bob and the boys broke into summer cottages to
relieve winter boredom, performing no real vandalism but leaving
some signature behind. An ashtray filled with Lucky Strike butts.
Stite malt liquor empties. Once Bob and John Bucklen broke into
Bucklen's older sister's place and hung her husband's guitar from
the rafters. Hoikkala recalled another frigid night their car wouldn't
start after they'd decided to occupy a remote mountain cabin. To
keep warm, they burned whatever was at hand while minimizing
damage to the furniture. According to Hoikkala, Bob volunteered to
sacrifice his guitar. Hoikkala took the offer to be manufactured
melodrama but also an example of Bob's peculiar brand of moralism: he was first to party but also first to repent.

Over the next year, Bob circled farther and farther away from
Hibbing, testing the stamina and mileage of his convertible, seeing
how far south he could travel on a single tank of gas. By the middle
of his senior year, he'd made the trip to Minneapolis several times,
cruising through the black neighborhoods and the sprawling campus
of the University of Minnesota along the eastern bank of the
Mississippi. He paid special attention to the school's bohemian

---

[34] Perhaps Bob's most venerable companion for more than a century, Louis was
heir to A. Kemp Fisheries, which supplied Lake Superior white fish to generation after generation of midwesterners, dating back to the beginning of the
Great Depression. Credited with developing the imitation crab product *surimi*
after he took over in 1967, Kemp renamed the family business for himself
then sold it to an international food conglomerate 25 years later. As an Orthodox Jew, Kemp's wealth may have accounted in part for his long and loyal
kinship with an American folk rock hero who could give him nothing that he
couldn't buy himself, except enduring friendship.

quarter: six square blocks of cafés, bars, and bookstores called Dinkytown.

"He really loved Negro people like Jim Dandy," Echo told Bob biographer Robert Shelton. "Bob always used to come back from Minneapolis impressed by the way the colored people danced and made music."

Abe and Beatty wanted Bob to go to college of course but would have preferred something a little more substantial than music—perhaps engineering or prelaw. Abe even arranged for him to rent a room during the summer at the Sigma Alpha Mu house, a Jewish fraternity near campus. His folks suggested he might want to consider pledging.

Echo's parents couldn't afford college, and Bob was first to recognize they were coming to an end. When she accused him of seeing other girls in Minneapolis, he retreated to mumbles. Echo made the inevitable easier by demanding to know whether he wanted to break up. The mumbling persisted. They drifted apart.

So did the Golden Chords. To Bob's everlasting envy, Monte Edwardson moved on with Hoikkala to form another and far more successful band called the Rockets. They eventually landed a recording deal with Aladdin Records way out west in Hollywood.

Meanwhile, Bob remained a solo act. Angst and frustration defined his final year at Hibbing High. Bereft of his band, he hooked up briefly with others in a final attempt to make his mark before giving in to college. He and a couple of Duluth cousins partnered with a Finnish guitarist, billing themselves as "Three Hebes and a Swede." In another brief incarnation, Bob sang for a group that called itself the Satin Tones.

But without Echo or the Chords to ground him, he floundered until the evening of January 31, 1959. That night, he made a rock 'n' roll pilgrimage to the Duluth National Guard Armory overlooking

Lake Superior near State Highway 61. On a barebones stage that made the Hibbing High auditorium look like Versailles he witnessed one of pop's earliest road shows, joining several hundred shrieking teens packed together in midwinter homage to the soundtrack of their generation: Dion and the Belmonts, Ritchie Valens, the Big Bopper, and Buddy Holly.

Bobby Zimmerman completed his transformation into Elston Gunn that night. All that followed could be traced back to the joyous torment of a teenager in love with a girl named Donna, draped in Chantilly lace, enduring in generational memory that would not fade away.

When accepting the 1998 Grammy for his comeback album *Time Out of Mind,* 57-year-old Bob Dylan recalled, "When I was 16 or 17 years old, I went to see Buddy Holly play at the Duluth National Guard Armory, and I was three feet away from him, and he looked at me and . . ."

Hefting his Album of the Year trophy, Bob cleared his throat and continued, "I know he was with us all the time we were making the record in some kind of way."

Three days after that Duluth concert, in a frozen cornfield east of Mason City, Iowa, Buddy Holly died in a small plane crash along with Valens and J. P. Richardson, a.k.a. the Big Bopper. Bobby Zimmerman's pantheon of early death now included three new exemplars along with James Dean and Lenny Venditto. Twelve years later, "American Pie" composer Don McLean consigned to myth that first in a long line of rock-and-roll fatalities, dubbing February 3, 1959, "the day the music died."

Dead or alive, Buddy Holly restored Bob's faith in his own destiny. In Rolfzen's English class, he wrote a sort of I.O.U. to classmate Arnold Koski who held on to it for 50 years: "Arnie, I'm going to make it big," he said. "I know it for sure and when I do, you bring this piece of paper and for two months, you can stay with me, no matter where I am."

For the rest of his senior year, Bob rehearsed his stage persona so that wild man Elston Gunn could debut that summer when Bobby Shane and the Poor Boys needed a piano player for a gig in Fargo. Shane was the stage name for Bobby Velline, who was two years younger than Bobby Zimmerman, but far more sophisticated in the business of rock and roll. Velline agreed to let loud and raucous Elston Gunn join his group on piano. At Gunn's suggestion, Velline renamed his Poor Boys "the Shadows." But despite Gunn's wild energy on stage, Velline let him go after just two shows. Turned out he could only play in the key of C. Mostly the Zimmerman kid faked it, standing next to Velline and clapping out rhythm as he'd seen Gene Vincent do in the movies.

"We decided we weren't really making enough money to cut in another member," recalled Velline, who shortened his name a few months later to Bobby Vee.

With $500 he'd saved during summer gigs, Velline cut a demo with Soma Records in Minneapolis and a "Peggy Sue" knockoff he called "Suzie Baby" caught on locally on the radio. Nationally distributed Liberty Records signed Bobby Vee on the strength of "Suzie Baby" and before the year was over, a new teen idol was born.

Meanwhile, a beaten Bobby Zimmerman rode the Greyhound back to Hibbing alone. It was raining when he arrived. Bucklen remembered an odd episode after Bob's return. The phone rang one night and Bob threatened to "beat the crap" out of his old pal.

"And I thought: well that's really interesting," said Bucklen. "Why would he say something like that?"

He agreed to meet Bob on a corner near his house and waited until he saw him staggering from street light to street light, swinging his arms and swearing like a lunatic.

"He walks up to me just like it was in a movie," Bucklen recalled.

Bob swung and missed, falling to the sidewalk. Bucklen could smell the booze as he lifted him to his feet. "Are you okay?" he asked.

Bob continued snarling as Bucklen led him to his mother's nearby apartment. Bob doubled over as they mounted the stairs.

"Blam! He lost it all over the steps," Bucklen recalled.

He turned Bob around and marched him back to the Zimmermans' place three blocks away. Meanwhile a neighbor heard the commotion and called Mrs. Bucklen.

"So my mother had to clean the steps up and she was *not* happy . . . and I never did know what made Bob so pissed off."

The answer seemed as simple as one too many pilsners and a thousand frustrations. Despite his yearbook aspiration to "join Little Richard" as printed beneath his airbrushed senior portrait, Bobby Zimmerman just hadn't risen to the level of professionalism demanded by as rank an amateur as Bobby Vee. Rock immortality eluded him. His ephemeral career ended after a handful of gigs.

And yet, by autumn, Bobby Dylan was busy being born though Elston Gunn was all but dead.

2
MINNEAPOLIS

Abe and Beatty allegedly rewarded Bob for the Elston Gunn episode with a brief trip to Pennsylvania's Devereux Foundation,[35] which promised then and now to help "persons with emotional, developmental, and educational disabilities." By the beginning of his first semester at the University of Minnesota, Bob was living at the Sigma Alpha Mu house on University Avenue where classmate John Pankake remembered him as "well-groomed and neat in the standard campus costume of slacks, sweater, white oxford sneakers, poplin raincoat, and dark glasses."

He entered college introverted and standoffish, and sought counseling from Dr. James Janecek, a recent med school graduate who became one of the Vietnam era's earliest military psychiatrists. While Janecek wouldn't breach patient confidentiality, he did tell his children years later that their Pied Piper came from a troubled family.

"When I said I liked his music but the lyrics were a little weird, my dad said, 'What do you expect? Fucked-up family. What else is new?'" recalled Sarah Janecek.

By his own recollection, Bob summed up his first semester as flunking biology because he wouldn't watch a rabbit die and getting

---

[35] Believed to be the model for the reformatory reviled in "The Walls of Red Wing," the counseling center near Valley Forge boasts of having successfully shaped square pegs to fit society's holes for more than a century.

kicked out of English for using four-letter words. He scored a D+ in music appreciation.

"Bob didn't think much of the college crowd," Abe Zimmerman rationalized later. "He considered most of them phonies."

Nevertheless, his parents paid his room and board while he grudgingly attended classes. As boring as life may have been, things seemed to work out fine from Abe's perspective until Christmas 1959. When Bob returned to Hibbing for the holidays, he discovered Echo married and pregnant. Finding his first love carrying another man's child killed off the last of Bobby Zimmerman. He returned to campus early, spending Christmas alone and miserable. In short order, fast-fading Elston Gunn vanished. By the beginning of 1960, chunky Bobby Zee had turned his myopic vision toward the insular coffeehouse culture of Dinkytown.

He'd moved on with the ladies too, falling for—among others—a honey-haired young Minneapolis actress named Bonnie Jean Beecher.[36] He also hooked up for a time with Camp Herzl alumna Judy Rubin, also a freshman. Some biographers suggest they represented the yin and yang in Bob's evolving taste for women: the unattainable *shiksa* versus the Beatty Zimmerman clone. Beecher and Rubin both lived across campus from the all-Jewish "SAMMY" house, which remained Bob Zimmerman's official campus address at the beginning of the winter semester.

But with the turn of the New Year, Zimmy morphed into Dylan[37]— a name he later claimed to have pulled from the ether rather than as

---

[36] Believed by Dylanologist Paul Williams to be the true "Girl from the North Country," Beecher was the "actress girl who kneed me in the guts" by breaking it off with Dylan. She later changed her name to Country Pie and finally Jahanara when she married comedian Hugh "Wavy Gravy" Romney in 1965 at a Greenwich Village wedding that was attended by Bob and officiated by blind balladeer Rev. Gary Davis.

[37] In Welsh folklore twins born at the beginning of the world were named Llewellyn ("light") and Dylan ("darkness").

homage to the late Welsh poet Dylan Thomas.[38] However he came by his alter ego, Bob had already determined his future lay in music. Once he quit college,[39] his father stopped paying his rent and Bob became a *schnorrer* drifting from couch to couch, pretending to depend on the kindness of strangers despite the occasional money order that wafted in from Hibbing.

"He was very much 'the Homeless One,'" recalled Davis Matheny, who was five years older than Bob and himself a would-be troubadour. "He had a boyish, vulnerable quality, but I thought he was playing a part: 'People don't care for me,' or whatever."

Bob took his cues from transient balladeers, mediocre Beat wannabes, stand-up comics, and upstart radicals who demanded racial equality and nuclear disarmament at the same time that they cut class or drew unemployment.

"I ended up shoplifting for him," recalled Beecher. "Stealing food from my sorority house."

Though he could always count on an allowance from Hibbing, he bummed meals, partied deep into the wee hours, and frequently got loaded on cheap burgundy or Grain Belt lager. He honed his fashion sense at Goodwill and gave up Lucky Strikes for whatever brand he could mooch.

Dinkytown's first bona fide coffeehouse, the Ten O'Clock Scholar,[40] opened that same year on the east side of Fourteenth Avenue half a block north of the busy Fourth Street intersection. The instant folkie Mecca paid a few bucks to anyone willing to entertain

---

[38] Thomas began drinking himself to death at the White Horse Tavern in Greenwich Village and finished the job while a permanent resident of Room 103 in the Chelsea Hotel, four days after his 39th birthday.

[39] Officially, he remained enrolled in the arts college for three semesters, though he quit attending classes after the first.

[40] In January 1966, Linda Mingo, a call-in on Bob Fass's Radio Unnameable, reported that the Scholar had burned down just before Christmas 1965.

for four hours on a Saturday night. There were other Dinkytown dives where budding balladeers could pass the hat,[41] but the Scholar best fit the stereotype of the true Beat establishment then mushrooming in Bohemian neighborhoods across the nation. Thimbledeep philosophical debates punctuated overly intense chess games with jazz and folk for a soundtrack. Bob, who fit the Mother Goose definition of a dubious academic,[42] had found his new home.

Late into the night, the Scholar thrummed with discord and blank verse, absorbing campus rebellion and the first stirrings of a national folk revival that had kicked off the previous year with the Kingston Trio's surprise No. 1 single "Tom Dooley." An onslaught of golden oldies followed, ranging from one-hit wonders like the clean-cut Highwaymen's "Michael Row the Boat Ashore" to country western star Johnny Horton's "The Battle of New Orleans" to down-and-dirty vintage blues like Lloyd Price's "Stagger Lee." Beside No. 1 *Billboard* status, they all shared roots in folk balladry.

Tuning in to the zeitgeist, Bob's allegiance easily shifted from Little Richard to Woody Guthrie. He abandoned garage-band rock for hoedowns, hootenannies, and an unwholesome hobo image, carting a steel-string Martin from café to café in his black-on-white plaid guitar case. During the transition, he borrowed and modified Bobby Velline's stage name, briefly incarnating as country western crooner Bobby Dee.

But his Hank Snow–Hank Williams cowboy phase died both on and off stage, and soon he began to pattern himself after older,

---

[41] Bob became a regular at Purple Onion Pizza and St. Paul's Bastille coffeehouse after establishing himself at the Scholar.

[42] *A diller, a dollar, a ten o'clock scholar!*
      What makes you come so soon?
      You used to come at ten o'clock,
      But now you come at noon.

shabbier, and more cosmopolitan Dinkytown dissidents. He dramatically emerged from storefront alcoves and snow-covered alleys in long gray scarf and ankle-length black wool coat, striking a pose that shifted from shy to overconfident and back again. To his mother's everlasting horror, the wispy curls at the sides of his head blossomed to a JewFro so that at a distance he resembled a sparkler on the Fourth of July.

Ellen Simer, whose father ran the Minnesota Folklore Society, maintained that he brushed his teeth so seldom they turned green. "And the idea of kissing somebody with his green teeth was like, 'How would you want to do that?'" she recalled.

Still, his bashful intensity trumped hygiene and Bob continued to intrigue his pals as well as invite the mothering instincts of the ladies.

"I first met Bob when a bunch of us guys got together on the loading dock at the [University of Minnesota] Chemistry Building to drink and sing," remembered "Spider" John Koerner. He recalled Dylan joining in but remaining aloof, sopping up tunes as if he were attending a seminar instead of a beer bust.

A former Marine and former engineering student who dropped out to take up the blues, Koerner became the first of several older Dinkytown denizens who took Bob under his wing. For a short time during that winter, they roomed together in a Seventh Street apartment until their money ran out and they stiffed the landlady. Even then, Koerner sensed that this edgy, awkward kid had talent far beyond petty larceny and hustling coeds. "Bob had the knack, you know—simple, but all-encompassing."

Koerner's wife, Jeane, wasn't so sure. Her most enduring memory of Bob was the night she drove him back from a West Bank bacchanal where he'd tanked up on free booze. He barfed in her backseat and never apologized or offered to clean up the mess.

"He told a lot of lies, was not very nice, especially to women, and knew about two chords on the guitar," she recalled. When Bob stopped in to visit Spider, Jeane—who was pregnant at the time—remained invisible. Bob focused on what John might be able to teach him, ignoring all else.

"He had a kind of undeserved sense of entitlement," Jeane recalled. "Maybe you have to have that to become a big star."

The voice Bob brought with him from Hibbing was soft and reedy and full of elocution; when he first sang of lost love on the four-inch-high dais at the front of the Ten O'Clock Scholar, the lyrics came out crisp and clean, more James Bond than James Dean. It didn't take long for him to recognize he'd turn more heads with a sandpaper slur and nasal whine than a carefully enunciated tenor. The first time Dave Metheny saw him clawing his guitar strings, several young honeys were hanging on his every mumble.

"I don't remember what he sang," Metheny recalled. "Just one of those things from the *Treasury of Folk Songs* that had flowers and maidens and dying fawns gazing into brooks."

Dave Whittaker, another seasoned Dinkytown dropout, lent Bob his borrowed copy of the long out-of-print *Bound for Glory,* Woody Guthrie's bestselling 1943 autobiography. Soon thereafter Bob became a Woody avatar.

Law student Lynn Castner, acquainted with Bob through his sister Flo, let him listen to his extensive Woody record collection, completing the transition from Zimmerman to Gunn to Guthrie. Bob incorporated the Okie laureate into his act, absorbing the talking blues style while abandoning whatever clarity B. J. Rolfzen once evoked in the classroom. After Bob began using a mouth harp, the ghost of James Dean returned with a vengeance and he punctuated like e. e. cummings. His ramblin', gamblin' participles forever lost their climactic "g"s.

Whittaker, who'd just returned from Israel, lived in an apartment eight blocks from the Scholar with his girlfriend Gretel Hoffman. They happily put Bob up in a backroom, sharing their food, wine, records, books, and passion for politics. Until then, the only thing Bob had ever protested was working weekends at Micka Electric.

"Bob Dylan was never political," recalled Dave Morton, who claimed his jug band to be the first act ever staged at the Ten O'Clock Scholar. "He was kind of straight when he first showed up. But Dave Whittaker was political. He was *real* political. Dave was the one who introduced Bob to politics."

Morton recalled Whittaker's instructing Bob on the world beyond Minnesota, where blacks were beaten, Jews reviled, and powerbrokers' faces remained always well hidden. By his 22nd birthday, Whittaker had already traveled to Europe and London, as well as Tel Aviv. He'd hung with Jack Kerouac[43] and Allen Ginsberg at Lawrence Ferlinghetti's City Lights bookstore in San Francisco and sat in on some of Dave Van Ronk's earliest performances at the Café Wha? in Greenwich Village. Besides introducing apolitical Bob Zimmerman to polemics, protest, and the prose of Woody Guthrie, Whittaker also turned him on to pot, while Gretel turned him on to Odetta.

In the early '50s, Odetta Holmes dropped her last name at the same time she swapped a maid's uniform for show business. By 1960 she'd moved up from minor roles in off-Broadway musicals like *Finian's Rainbow* to a guest spot on fellow folk star Harry Belafonte's 1959 network TV special.[44] With the lungs of Ma Rainey and the stage

---

[43] Published in 1957, Kerouac's *On the Road* joined *Bound for Glory* in becoming Bob's lifelong blueprint for finding solace in the open road. Kerouac's *Mexico City Blues* was "the first poetry that spoke to me in my own language," Dylan later told Allen Ginsberg.

[44] Directed by Norman Jewison, "Tonight with Belafonte" won an Emmy as well as a whole new audience for the Harlem-born actor-turned-Calypso king.

presence of Hattie McDaniel, the regal performer had a signature contralto that evoked comparisons to Mahalia Jackson. Once she belted out "Water Boy" over CBS, her career flourished, and she quietly advanced the cause of civil rights into mainstream America.

When the "Voice of the Civil Rights Movement" passed through the Twin Cities on the college concert circuit, Bonnie Beecher made a point of getting Bob in front of her. Odetta stopped at the Scholar and Bob was able to rasp a song or two. Odetta's benign encouragement gave him the resolve to take his own act on the road.

"She played that upstroke-downstroke kind of rhythm where you don't need the drum," Dylan recalled. "It's kind of like a Tex-Mex rhythm and I thought, well, I could use that rhythm for all kinds of things."

By 1960, Odetta had signed with Chicago club owner Albert Grossman to manage her career. Grossman's 100-seat Gate of Horn[45] was a magnet for stand-ups like Lenny Bruce and Lord Buckley as well as minstrels like Shel Silverstein, Bob Gibson, and Hamilton Camp. The corpulent promoter pledged every promising act who came through Chicago a record deal and bookings in exchange for 10 percent of their earnings and a share of their music publishing. Odetta was among Grossman's first coups.

Whether Bob made a mental note of Grossman's name on the outside chance he'd someday play the Gate of Horn, Odetta's example definitely helped him decide to get out of town.

From Boston to San Francisco, young America was on the move in 1960 and Bob meant to join the migration. John Kennedy's New Frontier agenda would soon blend with Kerouac's mandate to take

---

[45]   Located in the basement of the Rice Hotel, Grossman's club opened in 1956 and played host to folk balladeers as well as jazz acts and comics passing through Chicago's Near North Side. In Greek myth, the Gate of Horn was the portal of true dreams while the Gate of Ivory evoked the false.

in *all* of America, from inner city slums and intoxicating brothels to high-rise urban majesty and heartland waves of golden grain. Assimilating restless rock 'n' roll energy with "can-do" ethics, Bob calculated that stardom must be just down the road a piece. Abe and Beatty's bourgeois hopes for their elder son might have prevailed in another time or place, but in Dinkytown during the final year of the Eisenhower Administration, Bob determined he'd hitch from town to town until he found his destiny . . . once he'd fine-tuned his folkie identity and worked out enough chord progressions, that is.

When Dave Whittaker married Gretel, Bob moved out, only half-joking when he told Gretel to call him after the divorce. Drifting from place to place, he prevailed on girls and guys alike to take him in.

He stayed for a time with Dave Ray, another of John Koerner's young acolytes and one of his few Dinkytown peers younger than Bob himself. Ray still hadn't graduated from high school when he began developing an act with Koerner and harmonica player Tony "Little Son" Glover. They replicated street corner stomp and field holler blues and Bob studied the trio closely, borrowing shamelessly. If Ray howled about "Ol' Black Betty" from the Scholar stage on a Friday night, Bob wouldn't think twice about doing precisely the same on Saturday.

Mostly Bob drifted from place to place that winter and spring until he settled on a $30-a-month one-room walk-up above Gray's Drugs[46] that he romanticized in *Chronicles* as "an empty storage room with a sink and a window looking into the alley. No closet or anything. Toilet down the hall. I put a mattress on the floor, bought a used dresser, plugged in a hot plate on top of that—used the outside window ledge as a refrigerator when it got cold."

---

[46]   Reincarnated in 2001 as Loring's Pasta Bar.

Leaning out his window at the southwest corner of Fourteenth and Fourth he could see Bridgeman's Restaurant and the Victorian facade of McCosh's Books[47] half a block to the south, the newly shuttered Varsity movie theater half a block to the north. He had a clear view of the Varsity's abandoned art deco past and Bridgeman's cafeteria present, but just off to the east on Fourteenth Street glowed the Scholar, representing the folkie future.

Bob wasn't alone in his new passion for old music. The folk revival swelled from coast to coast. High school and college students alike rummaged through their parents' scratched-up 78s in search of the next "Tom Dooley." Bob spent as much time listening to Lynn Castner's copies of Cisco Houston, Josh White, and the Weavers as he did suffering trial-and-error boos on the Scholar stage. Mostly, he absorbed the old ballads and moved on, but there was one album he simply had to have.

One of the true gems among those early records was a rare copy of oddball archivist Harry Smith's 1952 six-LP *Anthology of American Folk Music*.[48] Budding Dinkytown folklorist John Pankake owned the rare out-of-print compendium of 84 songs, and Bob could not get enough. When the recordings went missing from Pankake's apartment, his first suspicion turned to the scruffy kid from Hibbing. He confronted Bob, who heatedly denied taking it, but a week later the *Anthology* mysteriously reappeared in Pankake's collection.

Like many earlier albums, tracks on the *Anthology* originally recorded between 1927 and 1932 were "jury texts" with lyrics that

---

[47]   Bob prowled the store for old records and sheet music, but not books. "He never read anything," Kevin McCosh told biographer Tony Scaduto.

[48]   Recognized with two Grammys, Smith's eclectic Folkways collection was reissued by the Smithsonian Institution six years after his death in 1991 and lauded as *the* wellspring of the '60s folk revival, influencing every roots-inspired artist from Joan Baez to Bruce Springsteen. Like Dylan Thomas, Smith died an alcoholic and a permanent tenant of the Chelsea Hotel.

varied from performance to performance, even though the tunes remained constant. Bob not only covered many of those ballads, incorporating them into his act and occasionally claiming authorship, he used the music as the basis for many of his subsequent compositions. It is no accident, for example, that the melody for "Hard Times in New York Town" bears a strong resemblance to the Bently Boys' 1929 recording of "Down on Penny's Farm," featured on Vol. I of the *Anthology*. At least 30 other early Dylan songs can also be traced to *Anthology* tunes.[49]

While purists call such appropriation thievery, Bob saw his borrowing differently. Even as a Golden Chord, he had boasted that Bobby Freeman's 1958 hit single "Do You Wanna Dance?" was actually his composition. When a blithe young Scholar groupie batted her lashes and asked where he'd learned "Man of Constant Sorrow" or "The Water Is Wide," who could resist simply claiming authorship? Until he finally got his footing as a lyricist, plagiarism was Bob's sincerest form of flattery—and, according to many a peer, it remained thus long after his popularity soared.

■ ■ ■

Listening to lifted records launched Bob's folkie education, but rambling and gambling in the Guthrie tradition also required some hard traveling.[50] He'd been as far west as Fargo and thoroughly explored the Lake Superior shoreline north and south of Duluth, but Bob

---

[49] He borrowed lyrics, such as from Jim Jackson's "Old Dog Blue," to write "Oxford Town." Influences continue to appear in his work up to the present day.

[50] There is anecdotal evidence that he'd been as far away as Arizona and California, among other destinations when he was growing up, but that was in the backseat of Abe's Buick during family vacations and didn't count.

didn't begin zealous wayfaring until after he'd celebrated his 19th birthday. From Scholar regulars he began to hear about an emerging folk scene in Denver where Kerouac's *On the Road* vagabonds stopped off on their amphetamine odyssey across America. Specifically, a bar on Colfax Avenue called the Satire sounded like it might be the Ten O'Clock Scholar of the Rockies.

But when Bob arrived during the summer of 1960, the Satire's audience[51] didn't warm to nasal laments and three-chord progressions the way folks did in Dinkytown. He didn't last a week before the manager, Walt Conley, invited him to leave. Conley did let Bob crash at his place for a few weeks, and when he heard about the Gilded Garter, a new club looking for free talent in a dying gold rush town 40 miles west of Denver, he told Bob. Clad in chambray work shirt, tortured Levis, Huck Finn cap, and black leather boots, Bob set out for Central City.

Once dubbed the "Richest Square Mile on Earth," the one-horse town had been reduced to a frontier facade that made Hibbing look like Shangri-La. Down to 250 residents with more leaving each day, Central City was suitable only for tourists. Bob's disappointment didn't end there. The Gilded Garter turned out to be a faux saloon on the main drag where bored dance-hall waitresses wore bustiers for tips, leaving little or nothing for faux Okie entertainers when they passed the hat. Bob failed even more quickly than he had in Denver but never forgot the hungry women there who seldom waltzed for free.

After returning to Denver, Bob checked into a fleabag and knocked around the bars and coffeehouses for a while, but his tendency toward larceny finally caught up with him. Late one night,

---

[51]   According to biographer Bob Spitz, he briefly shared billing with the Smothers Brothers, neither of whom could stomach Bob's performances.

Conley showed up outside his hotel room door with banjo player Dave Hamil, another one of Conley's crash pad guests. It seemed that several of Hamil's LPs had gone missing around the same time as Dylan. Bob denied taking them, but a search beneath his mattress did indeed turn up the records. Bob tossed them out his window and Hamil called the cops. Moved by Bob's tearful plea that he'd only borrowed them to learn some songs, the police asked Hamil if he really wanted to press charges. Once he'd retrieved his collection and Conley talked him out of it, Hamil said "no." Within the week Bob hightailed it back to Dinkytown.

"He ran out of money or something, ended up washing dishes in North Dakota, so the story goes," recalled Dinkytown resident Marilyn Matheny. "But when he came back no one believed him, that he had really gone on this trip or done these things. They just thought he was making stuff up. So they kind of dumped on him a lot. I felt kind of bad for him. It was just really not a good time for him."

That fall, he sulked and began jotting things down on napkins, bits of paper, and the backs of envelopes. Sometimes he scribbled spontaneously in a sweeping, hurried hand; other times he pondered his words so that they came out crimped and bore erasures and the smudges of editing. When his meter finally matched his metaphor, he'd corner people to give his prose a listen. When Dave Metheny heard one of Bob's compositions, it ended their friendship.

"It included a highly disparaging line about someone who went off sniffing drainpipes and reciting the alphabet," Metheny remembered. "I suspected it was about a friend named Max Von Rabenau. I hated the reference, and asked him coldly if that was who he was referring to, and he said it was, snickering, and I tore into him for disparaging a friend of mine. We never exchanged friendly words again."

Most reacted favorably to Bob's doggerel, perhaps because they seldom knew the targets of his sarcasm. His jottings became a permanent part of his arsenal, pouring from his notebook like burning coals to fuel future verse, maybe even a memoir like *Bound for Glory*. His Woody obsession had grown exponentially since his Central City escapade and whenever he got shitfaced—which turned out to be quite often—Dinkytown pals and rivals alike baited him the way Bob had once *glissendorf*ed the bongs of Hibbing High. "Woody's outside, Bob!" they'd yell. "Woody's here! Woody wants to see you!" Blitzed enough, Bob would actually stumble out to the street, looking for his hero.

Dave Morton remembered teasing him once that Woody had called from New York. Bob nearly tripped racing for the phone. "Hello! Hello!" he hollered into a receiver, but all he got was dial tone.

Sober, Bob might wish it so, but knew it couldn't be, for Guthrie was dying in New York, slowly, by degrees. As winter closed in, he decided that Woody's torch awaited him there. Fifty years later, Bob recalled the day he left Dinkytown.

"I didn't bring the past with me when I came to New York," he said. "Nothing back there would play any part in where I was going."

A fond and dramatic sentiment today, perhaps, but throughout Bob Dylan's several lives the past was seldom far behind. His parents subsidized his expedition on the pretext that he had a year to prove himself or return to the University of Minnesota.

3

GREENWICH

When Dylan first blew in from Minnesota four days after the inauguration of President John F. Kennedy, the towering five-story arch at the entrance to Washington Square wore a frosty white topknot while New York shivered through its coldest winter in 60 years. Snow drifted 10 feet high along the edges of Manhattan's canyon boulevards as Bob wandered into the Café Wha?. Manager Manny Roth looked doubtfully at this latest in a continuing migration of folkies hitting New York that season, but waifish Bob always inspired mercy as a first impression. Greenwich Villagers like Roth volunteered to steer him toward a warm place to stay that night, and many more thereafter.

"Going to New York was like going to the moon," Bob recalled. "You might as well have been talking about China. It was some place [to] which not too many people had ever gone, and anybody who did go never came back."

Unlike his disappointing summer in Denver or his exasperating early Dinkytown experience, Bob felt instantly at home in frozen Greenwich. He played for the requisite nickels and dimes during Sundays in the Square and paid his dues in the basket houses[52] along MacDougal, Houston, and Bleecker Streets while constantly aspiring to headline at more established showcases like the Gaslight and Gerde's Folk City.

---

[52] Second-tier bars and coffeehouses that avoided New York's onerous cabaret laws and licensing fees by passing the basket for donations instead of paying performers.

But according to Greenwich godfather Dave Van Ronk, Bob assailed New York City for just one reason, and it involved neither fortune nor fame.

"In retrospect, even he says now that he came to New York to 'make it.' That's bullshit," Van Ronk recalled in his autobiography, *The Mayor of MacDougal Street*. "When he came to New York there was no folk music, no career possible. . . .What he said at the time is the story I believe. He came because he had to meet Woody Guthrie."

An unlikely hero, the dying, diminutive Okie troubadour embodied all Bob hoped to be. As with James Dean, Bob would go so far as to declare that he and Guthrie were dead-on doppelgängers. Even in his diminished state, Woody would cock his head and let a burning cigarette tremble from his lower lip, as much for dramatic effect as for the addictive pleasure of the nicotine. Bob aped the pose every chance he got during those first months, channeling Guthrie each time he got in front of an audience. Fellow folkie John Cohen said Dylan even convulsed his head á la Woody.

Named for the 28th president of the United States, Woodrow Wilson Guthrie came of age at the dawn of the Great Depression, melding an "ah shucks" stage presence he borrowed from Will Rogers with a radical progressivism, equal parts John Steinbeck and Karl Marx. Born into an upper-middle-class Oklahoma family in 1912, Guthrie quit high school and married at 19. After his parents' own fortunes plummeted following the 1929 stock market crash, he rejected their comfortable capitalism for a bumptious brand of socialism. Over the next 30 years, Guthrie spent more time manufacturing his hobo image than he did actually traveling on boxcars or finding his way back home to deserted wives and babies.

He took odd jobs, busked for quarters, and bummed rides and meals and living-room couches from old friends and new alike.

Drinking and philandering while studying the American landscape as he'd never done in school, Guthrie devoured books and newspapers like a doctoral student, belying his ignorant Dust Bowl pose by writing songs, essays, and a regular humor column for the Communist Party's *Daily Worker* in which he lampooned American racism, class discrimination, and economic hypocrisy. As early as 1941, the year Robert Zimmerman was born, J. Edgar Hoover himself began a file on Guthrie that grew to 120 pages over the next 20 years.

"From a confidential source," Hoover wrote in 1941, "information has been furnished this Bureau that one Woodrow W. Guthrie, who is employed by the Department of the Interior,[53] is allegedly a member of the Communist Party."[54]

Despite the FBI's relentless red baiting, Guthrie kept succeeding, first as a popular L.A. radio act, then as a member of the early folk quartet the Almanac Singers,[55] and finally—and most indelibly—as a songwriter. His most immortal lyric was an everyman response to Irving Berlin's *God Bless America*. Sick of listening to Kate Smith belt out the saccharine anthem over the radio during the winter of 1940, Guthrie wrote his earliest version of *This Land Is Your Land*[56]

---

[53] The federal Bonneville Power Administration hired Guthrie in 1940 to narrate a documentary that was never completed. Guthrie wrote "Roll On, Columbia" based on the experience and 50 years later Washington State claimed it as its official folksong.

[54] Guthrie never joined the Communist Party.

[55] Pete Seeger and Lee Hays went on to form the Weavers in the early '50s while Millard Lampell, the fourth member of the Almanacs, overcame the blacklist to become a successful Hollywood screenwriter.

[56] Originally entitled *God Blessed America*, the melody came from "Little Darling, Pal of Mine," which was based on an even older gospel hymn and first popularized by the Carter Family. The long-ignored final verse of Guthrie's subversive original reads:

> *One bright sunny morning in the shadow of a steeple*
> *By the relief office I saw my people*
> *As they stood there hungry, I stood there wondering if*
> *God blessed America for me.*

while holed up in New York's Hanover House. Berlin composed more than 1,500 sentimental tunes in his 60-year career, but Guthrie matched his legacy with more than 3,000 harder-edged songs in half as many years. He would have written more had he not been diagnosed in 1952 with Huntington's Chorea.

Along the way, Guthrie married and divorced three times and fathered eight children, few of whom he knew well while they were growing up. Woody's most famous son was only 13 when Bob Dylan knocked at the front door of the Guthries' Howard Beach home in the winter of '61.

"I could tell by his (boots) he wasn't coming by to sell something," recalled Arlo Guthrie.

While Bob maniacally praised their cantankerous old man as "genius, genius, genius, genius," Arlo and his sisters stood shivering at their front door. They told the jumpy stranger that their nomad dad no longer lived on the premises. In deep decline from the genetic disease that killed his mother and grandfather and would eventually claim Guthrie himself, as well as two of his daughters, Woody needed constant care and spent most of his days bedridden at a state hospital. Bob remained insistent.

Arlo remembered Bob as polite if prepossessed: an odd combination of self-deprecating humor and nervous tic. Even when he sat, his legs jiggled like those of an over-caffeinated Parkinson's patient. Despite their skepticism, Woody's children found his intensity beguiling.

Bob recalled the episode as a failed attempt to talk his way into the Guthries' basement so he could dig through Woody's unpublished songs.[57] He even offered up an impromptu performance of a

---

[57] In 1998, British folkie Billy Bragg and the American band Wilco recorded many of Woody's "lost" songs on the first of two Elektra albums named for the street near Coney Island where Arlo and his sisters grew up: *Mermaid Avenue*, Vol. I & II.

couple of Woody's talking blues right there on the front porch, just like another Jewish kid who'd taken up the folksinger's mantle ten years earlier. Robert Zimmerman, it seemed, was not the first Woody worshipper to show up at the Guthries' front door nor would he be the last.

Ramblin' Jack Elliott, née Elliot Charles Adnopoz,[58] was the original Woody clone. A Brooklyn surgeon's son who tracked Guthrie down while the Okie bard was still relatively healthy, Ramblin' Jack apprenticed himself to Woody when Bob was in junior high. Before the folk revival exploded in the late '50s but a few years after Guthrie entered the hospital, Jack took his act on the road as a solo, gaining the popularity in Europe that eluded him at home. He honed a leftie singin' cowpoke persona in England that required a Stetson as part of the image, not unlike the Huck Finn headgear Bob incorporated into his own stage uniform.

"The very first person I met when I came back from Europe was Bob Dylan," recalled Elliott. "I met him while we were visiting Woody in the hospital. I didn't know who the kid was, but there he was with his little black corduroy cap and round oval face. He had this peach fuzz. He looked kinda country and kinda cute."

In lieu of the Jimmie Rodgers yodel Ramblin' Jack used to fill in gaps on his own Woody mimicry, Bob substituted the harmonica.[59] Otherwise both performers' songbags consisted mostly of Guthrie talking blues: comic, fabulist recitations set against a simple three-chord progression. Their Woody homages were so similar that Jack

---

58 Before settling on Ramblin' Jack, he was Xerxes, followed by Buck Elliott, and then just plain Jack.

59 Fifty years later, the Hohner signature series of seven machine-autographed Dylan harmonicas sold on www.bobdylan.com for $700 or $120 for a single mouth harp. Individually signed harmonicas went for $5,000 while the entire collection of seven, signed, played by Bob, and presented in a handsome carved ebony box, sold for $25,000. "The harmonica is the world's bestselling musical instrument," said Dylan. "You're welcome."

took to introducing Bob as "the son of Jack Elliott," and thus, Woody Guthrie's "grandson."

By the time Bob tracked Woody down, his carefully crafted image—wisecracking hillbilly with a penchant for homespun polemic—had splintered beneath the weight of his mortality. Palsied and cramped by constant pain, his disease so diminished the Dust Bowl balladeer that he couldn't hold a guitar, yet his sizeable pride remained intact.

Fellow folkie Len Chandler, who accompanied Bob on those early visits, recalled the cautionary instructions Marjorie Guthrie gave them both about her husband: "If he starts to smoke, do *not* attempt to help him light his cigarette because it's a big matter of pride for him to do it himself. So you just sit there and wait for him."

Guthrie struck match after match, letting each burn down to the tips of his quavering fingers. His hands shook so violently that he couldn't get a single match to the end of the cigarette and for ten excruciating minutes, Chandler and Dylan just sat there helpless at the side of his bed. After two boxes of matches, Guthrie got it lit, drew in a cloud of nicotine, and leaned back triumphant on his cot.

"And then we just sang him Woody Guthrie songs," said Chandler, "and he'd kind of moan a little bit, you know?"

Guthrie hardly spoke and could rarely be understood when he did, and yet he remained as hypercritical as Dylan remembered Abe Zimmerman once having been. He showed deep pleasure whenever Bob played a Woody composition but grew agitated when the kid's strumming strayed to other songs. Bob never lost patience, never overrode the master's wishes, never called Guthrie on his towering ego. Guthrie was "my last idol," according to Bob, but he was not so naive that he didn't realize that his Dust Bowl role model more closely resembled Tom Paine than he did Tom Joad. "Woody was a man who dwelled on simpleness because he was getting attention for it," said Bob.

More through osmosis than from any advice Guthrie might have given, Dylan mimicked the romanticized life of the man he read about in *Bound for Glory,* easily shape-shifting from bright mid-western Jewish kid to wandering Village troubadour. Off stage, Bob sat at the bar, studying his peers, inhaling every lick, chord, and audience-satisfying performance he could claim as his own. Like an admiring lamprey, he tapped into the lives of others. Like Van Ronk, whose raspy singing voice Dylan himself later likened to the sound of "rusty shrapnel," Bob's own mildly pleasant Dinkytown tenor devolved into "a voice you could scour a skillet with,"[60] as *The New Yorker*'s John Updike would write a few years later.

Bob could take the heat though. He suffered boos and paid dues and clowned and cooed and won the audiences over in the clubs along MacDougal Street. He'd met Woody in the flesh, after all, and mimicking the bard became a kind of armor whenever the heckling got too bad. All Bob Dylan needed now was a roadmap to take him down the line, where lady luck and a record deal might ease his fevered mind.

■ ■ ■

He spent just four months in New York before returning to Minnesota, but all Dylan mythology sprang from those first weeks in Greenwich when Bob came to accept his limits as a performer while calculating how best to break into the big time. The Jesse Fuller[61]

---

[60] "Dylan asks us not to listen to what he sings but to listen to how he hears," wrote Dylanologist Stephen Webb. "He is a great singer because he is a great hearer, not because he has an abundance of natural vocal talent."

[61] Composer of *San Francisco Bay Blues,* Fuller was a one-man band who hit his stride performing on kazoo, harmonica, cymbal, and 12-string guitar while scratching a washboard and banging on a drum with a foot pedal.

harmonica holder he wore around his neck became his trademark. Occasionally he waddled and winked for the audience imitating Charlie Chaplain's Little Tramp. At other times, he'd wail on the mouth harp while down on bended knee á la Al Jolson. Almost always, he lubricated his performances with Sartori wine.

Musicianship had never been Bob's strong suit. He wasn't much on the guitar and though he still played blues piano, his plinking was similar to "the way Dustin Hoffman plays the piano in *Tootsie:* not great," according to Marshall Brickman, another early Greenwich folkie.[62] Dylan himself admitted that witnessing New Lost City Rambler Mike Seeger coax divine harmonics out of every instrument he picked up, from dulcimer to mandolin, forced Bob to rethink his own path to stardom. If he practiced until his fingers bled, he'd never match Seeger's sounds.

Thus, when headline performer Fred Neil offered him $1 and a cheeseburger to back him on harmonica at the Café Wha?, Bob didn't bargain. The place stayed open from noon to 6 A.M., giving Bob the sort of work-study program he never had back in Dinkytown. It was his introduction to vaudeville. Twenty conga drummers followed Fred Neil, and then an Appalachian balladeer, a standup comic, a lounge crooner, and an impersonator. Then the entire variety show started up all over again.

Any sort of public exposure furthered Bob's trial-and-error search for an enduring stage persona. From that modest beginning, he moved up fast. Charlie Rothschild, the booker at Gerdes Folk City, reckoned Bob was ready for a professional solo gig by April 1961, when he offered Dylan shared billing with blues legend John Lee

---

[62]   After an early collaboration with The Mamas and The Papas' John Phillips, Brickman abandoned music and found his true métier with Woody Allen, co-writing the Oscar-winning screenplay for *Annie Hall*.

Hooker. "We made a deal in the kitchen and signed a contract for ninety bucks," Rothschild recalled.

And yet, for all his upward mobility and newly honed stagecraft, there was little that set Bob apart from the steady stream of folkies flooding the Village . . . until he began performing his own songs.

"The thing about Dylan, interestingly enough, was that I had known his songs long before I had known Dylan," recalled fellow folkie Richie Havens. "And they were not songs that were recorded at the time. He had not yet recorded. They were songs that other people learned, and I learned them from other people."

What Havens, Ramblin' Jack, Len Chandler, and even Dylan himself did not yet fully perceive was that Village singer-songwriters were about to detonate across the American landscape.

For the first half of the twentieth century, Tin Pan Alley dominated American song. The collection of drafty high-rise offices along Broadway that housed the pop music business had flourished since the Gilded Age. As a rule, the songwriters who composed the soundtrack of America rarely performed their own music. Urban sophisticates like George and Ira Gershwin, Cole Porter, Harold Arlen, and even the great Irving Berlin produced the poetry mouthed by Broadway casts or crooned nationally over homogenized network radio, but they never sang a note themselves and left the song plugging and music publishing to others. Singers who entertained the great unwashed with their own vernacular compositions, hayseeds like Hank Williams, A. C. Carter, and Woody Guthrie, tended to perform their own songs in down-market hubs like Nashville or Memphis.

But *real* singers—the Bing Crosbys, Frank Sinatras, Andrews Sisters, and Doris Days who fronted Big Bands and routinely topped the *Billboard* charts—sang what was written *for* them. As late as 1961, the Grand Ol' Opry and Tin Pan Alley polarized American popular music. Beyond rhythm and blues or rock 'n' roll, there was little crossover until a Village juggernaut fronted by Dylan changed all the rules.

Parroting Woody's style, most of Bob's early compositions were surreal talking blues lampooning everything from surviving New York's mean streets ("Talkin' New York") to the sinking of a Hudson River barge during an oversold family boat trip ("Talkin' Bear Mountain Picnic Massacre Blues") to cornpone Judaism ("Talkin' Hava Negeilah Blues"[63]). But satirical lyrics gave way soon enough to protest. Borrowing the tune from Guthrie's very own "1913 Massacre," Bob composed "Song to Woody," his earliest bona fide ballad, which paid tribute to his idol while simultaneously lamenting a United States that "looks like it's dyin' and it's hardly been born."

During his first months in New York, Bob spent as much time expanding his Village network as he did inventing lyrics.

"He had so much nervous energy, he couldn't sit still," recalled Dave Van Ronk. "And he was very, very evasive."

Van Ronk and his wife Terri Thal were among his earliest devotees along with Eve and Mac McKenzie and a Brooklyn couple, Mel and Lillian Bailey, who rescued Woody from the hospital on weekends and had him up to their apartment for klatches with friends like Pete Seeger and Ramblin' Jack. Like the Whittakers back in Dinkytown, all served as surrogate parents for prodigal Bob, letting him crash on their couches, snack on their groceries, and parse through their libraries.

In his fanciful *Chronicles*,[64] Dylan conjured a further eminence grise he dubbed Ray Gooch, and his live-in girlfriend, Chloe Kiel, neither of whom a small army of present-day Dylanologists who explore every available morsel of Dylan's life have ever been able

---

[63]   "Here's a foreign song I learned in Utah: Ha-va-ne-gei-lah o-de-ley-e-e-oo."

[64]   "I'll take some of the stuff that people think is true and I'll build a story around that," he explained to *Time* magazine at the time of *Chronicles*' publication.

to locate. In beguiling detail, Bob spelled out the opium-smoking lifestyle of this Bohemian couple who lived somewhere near Vestry Street in Tribeca amid a dazzling array of texts: Thucydides, Machiavelli, Clausewitz, Tacitus, Pericles, William Faulkner, Byron, Shelley, Longfellow, Poe, Freud, Milton, Pushkin, Tolstoy, Dostoyevsky, Jules Verne . . . everything from Ovid to the autobiography of Davy Crockett.

To hear Bob tell it some 40 years later, the Gooch trove represented a veritable canon of Western literature. *Chronicles* would have readers believe that Bob devoured most of Gooch's library before moving on to the microfilm archives at the New York Public Library to catch up on daily newspaper coverage during the Civil War. Weed, wine, and late-night gigs did not preclude his prodigious education, according to Bob. While his scholarship would indeed grow formidable with the years, it remains dubious that he did it all in Ray Gooch's backroom.

Like much of the hard-to-prove reminiscences that comprise *Chronicles*, Ray and Chloe are either one of young Bob's best-kept secrets or they are pure fiction. None who knew him well or slightly in those days can recall a thing about the Gooches, despite Bob's own remarkably detailed snapshot description of the couple's well-appointed opium den:

> Above the fireplace, a framed portrait of a wigged colonial was staring back at me—near the sofa, a wooden cabinet supported by fluted columns, near that, an oval table with rounded drawers, a chair like a wheelbarrow, small desk of violet wood veneer with flip-down drawers . . .

Add to that suspiciously precise catalog Bob's contention that the Gooch apartment was on the top floor of a Federal-style building located on the same block as the Bull's Head Tavern, "where John

Wilkes Booth used to drink," and his story falls apart. The Bull's Head Tavern is located near Gramercy Park on the east side of Manhattan, opposite Vestry Street.

Still, there is little doubt that a series of mentors did tutor Bob following his Dinkytown lapse. He never quit learning, even if it wasn't of the collegiate variety Abe and Beatty would have preferred. Van Ronk needled him over his narrow folkie focus and urged him to read Arthur Rimbaud's *Season in Hell,* François Villon's medieval testaments to bawd and booze, and Bertolt Brecht's experimental stage plays. Soon enough, Bob understood the surreal context of *Mack the Knife* to be more than just another Bobby Darin hit.

Bob also prevailed on girlfriends to educate him. The first he met in the Village claimed to be a professional thief while the second was an actress who let him sleep in her East Fourth Street apartment during the spring of '61 until she left for California. In both dalliances, according to biographer Bob Spitz, Dylan "perfected an ambivalence that protected him from intimacy."

After his return from Minnesota,[65] his first genuine muse shattered that ambivalence, however, and kicked his Village apprenticeship into high gear.

"I met Bob Dylan on a hot day at the end of July 1961 at a marathon folk concert at Riverside Church in upper Manhattan," wrote Suze Rotolo in her 2008 memoir *A Freewheelin' Time.* Thus began a rocky storybook romance.

The "red diaper baby" of openly Communist parents, Suze was just 17, but New York wise in ways that a 20-year-old hustler from Hibbing could never be. What was more, the grey-eyed blonde

---

[65]   He let on to none of his Village acquaintances that his return to Hibbing was occasioned by his 64-year-old grandmother Florence's fatal heart attack. Those who hadn't bought Bob's confabulations about being a rail-riding orphan still had no idea that he was actually a well-heeled Jewish kid from a middle-class Minnesota family.

might be full-blooded Italian, but her golden, arguably Semitic good looks rivaled those of any Camp Herzl nymphet. Her mother and recently deceased father had schooled Suze and older sister Carla as artists and activists, bucking the tide of John Birch and Joe McCarthy at a time when the execution of Julius and Ethel Rosenberg remained fresh in national memory. Indeed, the FBI had already begun compiling a file on Suze before she ever met Dylan. Couple her precocious politics with a girlish grin and come-hither intellect, and Bob fell hard.

Suze was more circumspect, especially after seeing Bob with a snootfull. "He has to be drinking to open up," she said. Suze responded to his awkward courting but took a hard line whenever he oscillated between passion and brooding indifference. She had no patience for his boozing or his "I'm-just-a-poor-country-boy" act.

During the first half of 1961, Bob preceded his finest stage performances by bingeing. He climaxed one Café Wha? appearance by puking on the front steps. He rarely played Folk City during Monday night hoots unless fully tanked. Upping the ante, he quit wearing glasses after Dinkytown. He wasn't just kidding when he called himself Blind Boy Grunt.

"We drove past this woman once in Brooklyn with *gigantic* breasts," recalled Len Chandler. "And I said, 'Dylan! Look! Look at those!' And he squints and says, 'What?' So the woman goes into a bar and I tell Dylan we gotta stop, go inside. 'You gotta see this,' I tell him. And she's there with these *enormous* breasts, so big she had 'em lying on top of the bar. And I tell Bob, 'Now, *see* what you're missing?'"

It was only at Suze's insistence that he abandoned vanity long enough to consult an optometrist. "Suze was the only one who wouldn't take any shit from him," said Chandler.

She mothered with steely resolve that even *glissendorf* couldn't touch. Gradually, he let his guard down. Around Suze, boozy empathy softened into sober compassion, finding its way into his earliest confessional ballads. Like Van Ronk, Suze was a student of Rimbaud and Villon and the Beats, as well as Lord Byron, Edna St. Vincent Millay, and Robert Graves, whose treatise on female influence on male poetics, *The White Goddess,*[66] would prove to be a potent early Dylan influence. She schooled him in the absurdist theater of Ionesco and Beckett as well as Brecht. They haunted the used bookstores along Canal Street and shopped for secondhand treasures at thrift stores. Together they discovered the emergence of transcendent stand-ups like Lenny Bruce, Bill Cosby, and Woody Allen.

A serious artist, Suze also introduced Bob to painting. Woody worship had already addicted him to doodling: charcoal caricatures and line-drawings abound in the pages of *Bound for Glory,* and Bob's earliest Thurber-esque sketches closely approximate those of his musical mentor.

On Sundays if Dylan wasn't visiting Woody or taking in a gospel show at Madison Square Garden, Suze got him on the subway uptown to Central Park and guided him through the Metropolitan Museum of Art, planting seeds that wouldn't germinate until long after she'd abandoned both Dylan and New York to study art in Italy. Similarly, at the Museum of Modern Art on West 53rd Street, she made him familiar with the work of former Village residents Jackson Pollock, Mark Rothko, and Willem de Kooning.

At first, Suze saw him as a sad Village joke, scruffing about like a Woody wannabe. But after a few encounters, she sensed a shrewd, funny manipulator, marveling at how quickly he assimilated people, absorbed their essence, and then moved on to the next customer.

---

[66] According to Graves, genuine poets were outlaws and vagabonds in the picaresque tradition of François Villon, Dante, Petrarch, and Lord Byron, not sterile Court-bound versifiers who pandered to the ruling class.

The Rotolos lived on Sheridan Square in the penthouse above the former Café Society[67] theater. A couple floors below, another Village Bohemian named Miki Isaacson "ran a kibbutz for strays," according to *New York Times* pop music critic Robert Shelton. Like Ramblin' Jack and a host of others, Dylan often slept on one of Isaacson's blow-up mattresses, stopping by the Rotolos' apartment to flirt with Suze in the morning.

Bob used friends and acquaintances to climb from basket houses to headlining hoots to the recording studio that summer, all with lightning speed. The bumbling Dinkytown amateur of just one year earlier evolved onstage and offstage, intuitively reaching for the door before opportunity had a chance to knock.

He made a deal with a Broadway tout named Roy Silver to manage him in exchange for a 20 percent commission. In *Chronicles*, Dylan dismissed his first manager as a "hustler"—one of the few in the Village in those days who still wore a suit. While Silver increased Bob's bookings both in frequency and quality, the pace wasn't fast enough to match Dylan's ambition.

When he heard that Harry Belafonte needed harmonica backup for the Leadbelly classic "Midnight Special" in the fall of '61, Dylan volunteered. Later, in his own venerable recording career, Bob came to tolerate little or no studio rehearsal before virtually every take,[68] but he sucked it up for the Calypso king and toed the line. Bob didn't last long under Belafonte's prickly perfectionism, but did get his foot in the door at RCA—his objective in taking the gig in the first

---

[67] One of two New York dinner theaters founded in the late 1930s, the integrated nightclub launched the singing careers of Billie Holliday, Lena Horne, and a host of other black performers in previously white-only venues south of Harlem. Producer John Hammond Jr. was one of its biggest benefactors.

[68] "I don't like hanging around studios," he said during a 1975 interview. "I'm not a technical wizard. I'm not interested in that aspect of *the* current recording, which the Beatles started with that Sgt. Pepper thing."

place. He'd been prepping for his Bobby Vee moment since the first time Elston Gunn kicked a piano. Landing a record deal was the next big item on Bob's career agenda.

It wasn't as if he hadn't rehearsed for this moment. Bob had been recording himself since high school when he and John Bucklen first fooled around with a tape recorder. Among his first "bootleg" recordings that surfaced in the late '60s were 27 traditional tunes he'd taped back in Dinkytown. By the time he got to Minneapolis, Bob sang whenever he saw an open mike.

He made the rounds and had already been turned down at Elektra, Vanguard, and Folkways when the call came in to back a rising folk chanteuse on her first Columbia Records album. He knew how to comport himself inside a recording booth. This time, he was ready.

■ ■ ■

"He had a sublime indifference to what people thought," recalled legendary Columbia Record producer John Hammond. "I found him an irreverent son-of-a-bitch who was going to change the face of the music business. He had a marvelously cynical view of what was happening in America."

During the recording session with singer Carolyn Hester, Dylan made his initial impression on Hammond, the first of three men who would propel his star far beyond Greenwich Village.

The independently wealthy great-great grandson of Cornelius Vanderbilt, Hammond[69] translated trust-fund autonomy into frequent defiance of record company executives. Despite opposition from the front office, he launched the careers of many of the

---

[69]   As early as 1941, the same year that the FBI first took notice of Woody Guthrie, J. Edgar Hoover cited Hammond as "one of the wealthiest Communist Party 'members-at-large'" with a trust fund that yielded $9,000 a year. Adjusted for inflation, that comes to about $140,000 in 2013.

most-enduring musicians of his time. Years before the Jim Crow South clashed with the rest of the nation over civil rights, Hammond introduced Count Basie, Bessie Smith, Lionel Hampton, Big Joe Turner, and Billie Holliday to mainstream white America. Several months before he met Bob Dylan, he signed the 18-year-old daughter of a Detroit preacher. Ten years after discovering Aretha Franklin, he would do the same for Asbury Park's Bruce Springsteen.

The second ally to boot Dylan up the ladder that season was *Times* pop music critic Robert Shelton, whose rave review of Dylan's stage performance at Gerdes Folk City further piqued Hammond's interest:

> Although only 20 years old, Bob Dylan is one of the most distinctive stylists to play in a Manhattan cabaret in months. Resembling a cross between a choir boy and a beatnik, Mr. Dylan has a cherubic look and a mop of tousled hair he partly covers up with a Huck Finn black corduroy cap. His clothes may need a bit of tailoring, but when he works his guitar, harmonica, or piano and composes new songs faster than he can remember them, there is no doubt that he is bursting at the seams with talent . . .

Credited with discovering 18-year-old Joan Baez at the inaugural Newport Folk Festival in 1959, Shelton was the most influential of a new kind of critic whose interests ranged far beyond Broadway. Shelton used his bully pulpit to promote new talent, writing seriously about cabaret, folk, and jazz. His reviews were read with equal seriousness. If Shelton anointed a rising star, that was what they became. That his friend Roy Silver urged Shelton to see his client perform also helped.

"I remember feeling, 'Gee, whiz, Shelton, you gave him a jet-propelled push there,'" recalled a jealous Jack Elliott. In a single newspaper article, Woody's "grandson" leapfrogged past Woody's "son."

Former Weaver Fred Hellerman, who shared a summer cottage on Fire Island with Shelton, hollered at his roommate: How could he get so rhapsodic about a kid trying to imitate Woody?

"I didn't get it," said Hellerman. "He couldn't sing and yet Bob [Shelton] is laying it on like he's the second coming of Christ."

From Bob's point of view, the article's most important readers were Abe and Beatty. Having given Bob a year to make it or return to Minnesota, Shelton's review was a reprieve.

"We figured that anybody who can get his picture and two columns in the *New York Times* is doing pretty good," Abe told the *Duluth News-Tribune*. "Anyway, it was a start."

Whether calculated or serendipitous, the *Times* article appeared shortly after Bob backed Hester on harmonica. Following the session, Hammond sidled up and asked, "Bobby, would you be willing to do an audition tape up here?"

As an incentive, Hammond gave Bob a couple of albums he'd recently produced, including a prerelease acetate of *King of the Delta Blues*. Ever the maverick, Hammond used his considerable influence to buck Columbia's conventional wisdom in releasing 16 scratchy tracks recorded 25 years earlier by the long-dead Mississippi bluesman Robert Johnson. *King of the Delta Blues* sold precious few copies during that Perry Como era but made an indelible impression on Bob.[70]

Johnson's romantic background also appealed to Dylan. A blues prodigy extraordinaire who drank like a fish, fooled around with

---

[70]   As it did on every significant blues guitarist of the second half of the twentieth century, from Jimi Hendrix and Eric Clapton to Keith Richards and Stevie Ray Vaughn.

other men's wives, and allegedly made a deal with the devil to guarantee his legend, Johnson died young and mysteriously, possibly poisoned by a jealous lover. Gone at 27, just three years older than James Dean and five years older than Buddy Holly, Johnson left behind an even smaller though equally hallowed body of work that might have been forgotten if not for Hammond.

"When Johnson started singing, he seemed like a guy who could have sprung from the head of Zeus in full armor," Dylan recalled. "I immediately differentiated between him and anyone else I had ever heard. The songs weren't customary blues songs. They were perfected pieces . . ."

Their bond in esoteric blues now sealed, Hammond got Dylan to sign a five-year Columbia contract.

"Dylan was a rebel and I wanted to record protest," said Hammond, who had already signed protestors like Pete Seeger and Malvina Reynolds. "This was when we were getting involved in Vietnam, and so I started at the right time."

By the end of November, Bob had recorded his eponymous first album. Except for "Song to Woody" and "Talkin' New York," all 13 tracks were one-take covers of traditional folk tunes that he taped over two days.

"Mr. Hammond asked me if I wanted to sing any of them over again and I said no," said Dylan. "I can't see myself singing the same song twice in a row."

Shelton, now Bob's biggest and most important fan, wrote the album liner notes under a pseudonym.[71] Cost of the entire project: $403.

Bob's third influential megafan to materialize that autumn was Odetta's manager. The pudgy Chicago promoter Albert Grossman migrated to New York about the same time as Dylan, taking up

---

[71] Stacey Williams.

semipermanent residence each night near the stages of both the Gaslight and Gerde's Folk City. He made no bones about his objective: he planned to cash in on the folk revival.

"He knew nothing about the business, but he had a sharp eye for what sells," recalled Fred Hellerman.

His arranger and business partner Milt Okun maintained that Grossman didn't have a musical bone in his body, but the *Billboard* 100 became his Bible. "He realized the folk thing was happening with groups made up of boys who all dressed alike: the Kingstons, Limelighters, Chad Mitchell Trio, Brothers Four," recalled Okun.

From his experience booking jazz acts back at the Gate of Horn, Grossman also knew that the most commercially successful jazz vocal group of the era was Lambert, Hendricks & Ross: two hip guys and a chick. What Grossman had in mind was a similar folk trio clad in beatnik attire. He offered the gig first to Bob Gibson and Hamilton Camp, but they had no interest in adding a girl to their act. Known around the Village as "the floating Buddha," Grossman studied performances the way a rancher studies cattle. At one point, he invited Van Ronk to anchor his ersatz trio, but after a tryout, Van Ronk declined. Too homogenous and artificial, he said.

Ultimately, Grossman settled on a more malleable set of Village newbies: a Cornell psychology graduate named Peter Yarrow, standup Baltimore comic Noel Stookey, and flaxen-haired Village vixen Mary Travers, who bore an uncanny resemblance to Echo Helstrom. Grossman changed Stookey's first name to Paul and debuted Peter, Paul and Mary[72] at the Bitter End that autumn. He invited Fred Hellerman.

---

[72]   The irony that three Jews might catapult to fame on the strength of Catholic saints' names was underscored by Capitol Records chief Joe Smith, who dubbed Peter, Paul and Mary "two rabbinical students and a hooker."

"They were fucking awful," said Hellerman. "Mary sang flat. They couldn't harmonize. I told Albert he was making a big mistake, but he told me he was sticking with them."

Grossman signed them to Warner Brothers and left the heavy lifting to his partner.

"It took them three hours a day for three weeks to learn one song," said Milt Okun, a high school music teacher who started his recording career as Belafonte's arranger. "Once they learned it, they did it the same way every time. Forty years later, they still sound exactly the same."

Grossman might have been preoccupied launching Peter, Paul and Mary, but when Shelton gushed over Dylan in the *Times,* he recognized a potential gold mine. He began circling like a benevolent grizzly. Without putting up his own money, Grossman helped arrange Bob's first big solo concert and stuck someone else with the bill.

Since he first landed in New York, Dylan's favorite Village haunt was Israel Young's Folklore Center[73] at 110 MacDougal Street a few doors down from the Gaslight. Founded in 1957, the Center was an emporium catering to the influx of folkies and tourists then flooding Greenwich. Young sold everything from capos to Jew's harps, but he barely made the rent most months.

To subsidize his shoestring business, he promoted festivals and produced concerts. At Grossman's urging, he produced Dylan's first appearance at Carnegie Hall on November 4, 1961. He could not afford the Hall itself, but the Carnegie Chapter Hall upstairs on the fifth floor rented for $75 an evening. Tickets and programs cost another $35. Young paid Dylan $20 to perform. Despite the manufactured Village buzz surrounding Dylan's upcoming first record

---

[73] Dylan penned a couplet for Young that he still used half a century later to advertise his Folklore Centrum in Stockholm, Sweden: "What did the fly say to the flea? The Folklore Center is the place to be."

album and the much-vaunted Shelton review, only 52 people showed up.[74]

"About 40 minutes late, Bob Dylan walks up on stage and talked about what a little country boy he was and how he got lost on the subway," said folk chanteuse Jean Ritchie. "Poor thing," she added.

Izzy Young lost money. Grossman lost nothing. He made a note of this hiccup in Bob's rising trajectory so that, in future, he could remind Dylan that his concert debut would have turned out far differently if Grossman had been in charge.

Despite bombing at Carnegie Hall, Bob returned to Dinkytown in triumph during December 1961. A new coffeehouse had opened on the far side of campus and when he played there, even his most cynical critics paid attention. This was *not* the punk-assed kid who set out to find Woody just one year earlier.

"I saw Bobby in a back room, looking a little older, a little more like what he wanted the world to think of him as," recalled Dave Metheny. "He had a huge 12-string guitar in his lap, dwarfing him, and was just in the middle of telling some pretty girls some line like 'Now, when ah play the 12-string, ah play this nex' song different.' He seemed to be striving to indicate he'd grown up in Tupelo, Mississippi, or somewhere."

Bob told old friends how he was "building a character that will sell," and only the most jaded among them doubted his intent.

After his return to New York, his first order of business was to rent a place at 161 Fourth Street above Bruno's Spaghetti Shop. It wasn't much larger than the hovel he'd once rented above Gray's Drugs. Both just happened to have a Fourth Street address. He asked Suze to move in with him, but she held out until after her 18th

---

[74]   The following week, Joan Baez sold out the 1,700-seat Town Hall 14 blocks south on 43rd Street.

birthday. When she finally agreed, she confided to friends that she had some reservations.

"I think he may need too much from a woman," she said. "Someone to take care of him and all of that. I don't know if I can do it."

FOURTH STREET

The chill winter day Bob received the first pressing of his premiere Columbia album, Len Chandler ferried him across the Brooklyn Bridge on the back of his Vespa to share his triumph with Woody.

"The hospital was fairly grim, you know. Gray, institutional," Chandler recalled. "Woody had a little cot, like a one-person lay bed, but he didn't have a record player so he just tucked the album under his pillow."

Guthrie had grown worse, more agitated, less tolerant. The rest of the afternoon, the two prodigies played guitar for the master, mostly shying away from their original compositions. True to form, Guthrie keened loudest over his own songs. On the twilight return to Manhattan, Dylan fell to brooding silence. Had Guthrie approved of "Song to Woody"? It was hard to tell. He and Chandler both avoided looking down through the metal slats on the bridge's lower level as they watched the East River flow beneath them.

"That ride is very scary on a motor scooter," recalled Chandler. "Wind blowing a little bit. And you're looking down and you think your tires are going to catch in those things and pull you down. Feels like you're fixin' to die."

Bob held on tight. He salted such moments away for future storytelling, like the night a few weeks later when three young black men approached them as they wandered, wasted on weed, observing and absorbing the neighborhood around Harlem's Apollo Theater.[75]

"Dylan became very alarmed, very antsy and worried," Chandler recalled. "I said, 'Take it easy.' But he thought we were gonna get mugged, so he threw his wallet down and continued walking. One of the kids came running up. Dylan cringed. The kid says, 'Hey, man, you dropped your wallet,' and handed it to him."

Bob saw no percentage in being brave, whether crossing the Brooklyn Bridge or loitering in Harlem after dark. He wanted to embrace all of New York, preferably stoned, but with minimal risk. He noted all the adrenaline moments though, "building a character that will sell" by weaving thrilling personal experience in with white lies and whoppers. He was so adept at disinformation that it often went undetected for years. By the time he finally did confess, his burgeoning celebrity trumped outrage. Even those he'd duped forgave him on grounds that poets sometimes play fast and loose. Suze had no idea who she was living with until one day she happened to see his draft card. Pissed at first, she got back at him with a new nickname: "RAZ," for Robert Allen Zimmerman. The seeds of distrust were sown, though.

"Trouble between us slowly grew out of his facility for not telling the truth," she said.

"You know, he mentions me a lot in *Chronicles,*" said Len Chandler, "but every quote that he attributes to me, I never said. I mean, I feel very flattered that he talks about me so nicely, I really do. He said I'm one of his favorite singer-songwriters. I mean, that's really nice to have it floating around in the world that Dylan said that. But most of what he writes is just made-up bullshit."

---

[75] "I used to go there on Monday night a lot," Dylan told an interviewer 15 years later, adding, "I've never had any trouble walking around in (black) neighborhoods."

When John Hammond asked Bob to have his parents cosign his Columbia contract, Dylan said he was an orphan. His only living relative was a degenerate uncle who dealt cards for a living in Vegas.[76] After Columbia assigned publicist Billy James to promote Bob's first album, Dylan spoke to him about fearlessly bouncing all over the West since age seven. Such "facts" found their way into press releases and by the time he landed his first radio interview on Oscar Brand's WNYC "Folksong Festival," the yarn had spun into a remarkable backstory of a sensitive, homeless urchin who rambled from Gallup, New Mexico, to Aptos, Texas—all the way to Sioux Falls and back again. With each retelling, his tale rose taller.

On WBAI's "Folksingers Choice," hostess Cynthia Gooding questioned him between each of a dozen songs he performed live, and Dylan's fantasies intensified. Instead of going to school, he'd spent six years on South Dakota's Art B. Thomas carnival circuit running Ferris wheels, manning midway booths, reading palms, and befriending freaks. He went into great detail about the plastic side-show lady whose skin slickened to polyurethane after she'd been burned over most of her body. Gooding humored him, but at the end of the interview couldn't resist asking: "When you're rich and famous are you gonna wear the hat too?"

"Oh, I'm never gonna become rich and famous," said Bob.

■■ ■■ ■■

Even with local airplay and Shelton's hype, sales of *Bob Dylan* languished. When he saw his album collecting dust on the counter at the In-and-Out coffee shop, Bob moped around his new Fourth

---

[76] He did indeed have such an uncle, but he was neither degenerate nor his only living relative.

Street apartment for days. Sales stalled at 4,200 copies and Columbia Records considered dumping him. He became known as "Hammond's Folly."

But Albert Grossman begged to differ, and a more formidable Village ally would have been hard to find. Before he left for the West Coast where he would organize The Mamas and The Papas, folkie John Phillips asked Grossman to manage him.

"I'll tell you something," said Grossman. "I think I'm gonna take Dylan instead of you."

"You must be kidding," said Phillips, then leader of a slick trio called the Journeymen. Unlike Dylan, he said, the Journeymen could carry a tune. Grossman matched Phillips's contempt with his own.

"Dylan will sell more records off his first album than you'll sell in your whole lifetime," he said.

Famously inarticulate and as corpulent as his surname implied, Bob's future manager was persistent, slightly menacing, and as avaricious as Elvis Presley's obnoxious Col. Tom Parker. Dylan characterized him as a latter-day Sidney Greenstreet, "all immaculately dressed every time you see him, you could smell him coming." Like Abe Zimmerman, Grossman tended first to the bottom line.

"Albert didn't just *help* Dylan succeed," said Milt Okun. "Bob Dylan would not have happened without Grossman."

For most of Bob's inaugural year in New York, before and after he met Roy Silver, Dave Van Ronk's wife Terri Thal handled his out-of-town bookings. Under the impression that she was Dylan's manager, Thal was up in Boston during the winter of '62 getting him gigs while Bob was back in the Village quizzing Hammond about Grossman. Both men had served together on the board of the Newport Folk Festival, so Hammond seemed to Dylan to be the right person to ask.

Hammond remained unenthusiastic. Ignorant of Dylan's dealings with Roy Silver or Terri Thal, he told Bob that Grossman was "not the grooviest guy around, but if you want to sign with him go ahead."

There was another obvious candidate. Harold Leventhal had already managed the successful careers of Pete Seeger and Joan Baez. A former Communist who got his start plugging songs for Irving Berlin, Leventhal hooked up with fellow lefties Seeger and Guthrie in the late 1940s. Shrewdly sensing opposition to the black-listing paranoia that was gripping postwar America, Leventhal pro-moted the Weavers to enormous success and was credited with launching the '50s folk revival.

"Everybody loved Harold. Everybody hated Grossman," recalled Fred Hellerman. "Harold was never motivated by money. His atti-tude was, 'Hey, that guy's got talent and deserves a hearing.' Gross-man's attitude was 'Oh boy! I can make a million bucks!'"

Steering Bob to an old-line Tin Pan Alley publisher that winter, Silver promised that Lou Levy, husband of one of the Andrews Sis-ters and a successful song plugger since the '30s, would get "Song to Woody" plus Dylan's growing trove of talking blues into the com-mercial mainstream. Dylan signed for a $500 advance and Levy copyrighted Bob's work with his Leeds Music, shipping demos off to potential performers; then he sat back and waited to collect half the profits. Levy's share amounted to a one-cent royalty on every song recorded[77] (the writer got the other penny) plus half of every-thing generated by radio airplay, concerts, or other commercial use.

By springtime, Dylan was cranking out songs daily—some good, most not, and a few pretty spectacular, but Roy Silver remained his manager. Bob knew that had to change, but took months to act.

---

[77] In 1962, a million-selling single or LP would generate $20,000, split between publisher and songwriter. The two-cent royalty has increased over the years and today, it is nearly a dime.

Ultimately the naive kid in the Huck Finn cap who cared little about fame or fortune would opt for the fat man who could make him a millionaire.

∷ ∷ ∷

There's little doubt what song catapulted Bob Dylan from local hero to spokesman for his generation. Village legend has it that at a table in the Commons[78] in April 1962, Bob wrote a traditional "riddle" song[79] that asks an absurd question in the lyric followed by a poignant answer in the refrain.

"He gave me his guitar and asked me to play various chords while he worked on the words," recalled fellow folkie David Blue.[80] The tune came from Odetta's "No More Auction Block," [81] but the poetry, as awkward and tentative as it may have been, was pure Dylan. Rough-hewn lines like "How many times must a man look up before he can see the sky?"[82] gave an otherwise slick protest song the rustic flavor of the Woody/Ramblin' Jack tradition.

"When he'd finished it we went over to Folk City and Bob played it for Gil Turner who thought it was fantastic," said Blue. "Then Gil

---

[78]   Just off MacDougal Street, the basement café was later renamed the Fat Black Pussycat.

[79]   "I Gave My Love a Cherry" or "Where Have All the Flowers Gone?" for example.

[80]   Born in Rhode Island Stuart David Cohen just four months before Robert Zimmerman was born in Minnesota, Blue had a Jewish father and Irish Catholic mother. Like Dylan, he grew up conflicted, alienated, and overweight, with "the constant feeling that I had to get away"—common ground that would bind his friendship with Bob for the next 20 years.

[81]   Alternatively entitled "Many Thousands Gone."

[82]   Author, Judaic scholar, and Dylanologist Seth Rogovoy maintained the song is a "midrash" or Biblical interpretation of passages in the Old Testament books of Ezekiel and Isaiah.

got up on stage and played it for the audience while Bob stood in the shadows at the bar."

The following month, Turner put Bob on the cover of the sixth issue of his newly minted *Broadside* magazine, publishing the lyrics to "Blowin' in the Wind" for the first time.[83] Dylan stopped in at Len Chandler's East Broadway apartment a few days later to celebrate.

"We adjourned to the fire escape because my wife didn't like us smoking dope in the house," said Chandler. "Across the way lived Sally Golden and her sister. They both played guitars and were singing, straight out of *Broadside:* 'How many roads must a man walk down?' Dylan's jaw dropped. They were singing *his* song!"

Following Hammond's pep talk about writing more protest songs, Dylan hit his songwriting stride around Christmas. He moved quickly past talking blues to topical ballads (the martyred Emmett Till, [84] a condemned Texas murderer named Donald White, etc.) and first-person testimonials about life in Cold War America ("Walkin' Down the Line," "Let Me Die in My Footsteps," etc.). But each of those efforts merely put him in the middle of a pack of talented singer-songwriters then flooding the Village: Tom Paxton, Phil Ochs, Fred Neil, Peter La Farge, Tim Hardin, and his close pals Len Chandler, Paul Clayton, and David Blue. What set Bob apart by the spring of 1962 was a very personal way of seeing the world around him.

"He early on realized that he was like a bee putting his stinger in, getting all the sap, then moving on to the next place where there was

---

[83] Then-entitled "Talking John Birch" was featured in Issue No. 1—the first time any Dylan song was published.

[84] While he admitted stealing the tune from Len Chandler, "The Ballad of Emmett Till" became one of Dylan's first well-known civil rights anthems—the saga of a 14-year-old Chicago boy murdered for whistling at a white woman during a summer visit to Mississippi.

more sap," said Ochs biographer Marc Eliot. "And he left behind a
bunch of saps."

"The guy saw things," testified Suze Rotolo. "He was definitely
way, way ahead. His radar was flying. He had an incredible ability
to see and sponge—there was a genius in that. The ability to create
out of everything that's flying around. To synthesize it. To put it in
words and music. It was not an intellectual approach that he had to
research something—he did it on his own."

Suze joined Bob and Paul Clayton on a road trip in May '63 to
explore Virginia's Blue Ridge Mountains where Clayton went to
college, and Bob used the opportunity to parachute into Appalachian
poverty á la James Agee.[85] Like anthropologists on Spring Break,
they drove from windowless shack to windowless shack, Bob channeling Woody at every stop.

"That boy's got it!" rasped a toothless old Virginia man sitting on
his filthy mattress, the only furniture in a hovel that made Bob and
Suze's Fourth Street apartment look like a suite at the Waldorf. "The
boy's got music in him."

When the old man picked up a guitar and sang from his own repertoire, Bob filed the songs away for future reference. Dylan himself
later described his poetic logorrhea as a compulsive gift, bestowed
by some power beyond his ken: he didn't invent songs so much as
snatch them out of the air. He never acknowledged to what degree
wine, weed, amphetamine, and the wholesale appropriation of others' efforts might have helped, but there seemed little question that
the alchemy worked. Bobby Zimmerman's transformation to Bob

---

[85] The year Bob was born, Agee published *Let Us Now Praise Famous Men*, a
literary study of the grinding poverty of southern sharecroppers. Scorned by
critics and remaindered at the time (it sold just 600 copies), it had been rediscovered and was well on its way to becoming an American classic by the time
Dylan visited Virginia.

Dylan was complete. Pete Seeger himself introduced him at a spring-time hoot as *the* new voice of the Village. However the words came to him, Bob matched them with the right folk tune. "Blowin' in the Wind" marked his graduation to first-among-equals in Greenwich's mushrooming singer-songwriter community.

But there was a postgraduate course yet to tackle. Two months after his "Wind" triumph, Suze left to study art in Italy. Thus began Bob's seven-month apprenticeship in confessional love songs.

■ ■ ■

"She had a mind of her own," recalled Len Chandler. "They would break up and get back together and break up and get back together . . ."

Over Bob's protests, Suze accompanied her mother to the University of Perugia to study art that summer. Like Suze's older sister Carla, Mary Rotolo made no secret of her growing contempt for Dylan. She saw her daughter's Italian sojourn as an opportunity to bust up the romance.

Chandler joined Dylan in seeing Suze off, but Bob kept a stoic bearing. As the ocean liner left, he betrayed none of the farewell angst he'd soon spew in his songs. Maintaining his stiff upper lip, Bob planned a July appearance at the Gaslight where he'd publicly perform others' material—Woody, Robert Johnson, Jessie Fuller, *American Anthology* ballads—for what would turn out to be the last time in quite a long while.

That same month, Roy Silver used the growing cachet of "Blowin' in the Wind" to convince Witmark, the publishing arm of Warner Brothers music, to buy Bob's songs for $1,000. What Silver neglected to reveal was that six months earlier Bob had sold those rights to Lou Levy. When Witmark's Artie Mogull learned the truth, he blew up. He waved another $1,000 in front of Levy on the outside chance he'd void the Leeds Music contract. Persuaded by the lousy sales of Bob's first album, Levy cut his losses. Forty years later, Mogull still marveled at his shortsightedness: "Believe it or not, the guy at Leeds gave them back their contract."

But Lou Levy wasn't alone in selling Dylan short. Grossman paid Silver[86] $10,000 to tear up his contract with Bob that summer. Hammond cautioned Bob to sign for no more than two years, but Dylan signed with Grossman for seven. In so doing, he turned over a quarter of his Witmark publishing revenue to Grossman in addition to a whopping 20 percent management fee of every dollar Bob generated.

Grossman had been on a roll since March when Warner Brothers launched Peter, Paul and Mary's inaugural album. Their hit single "Lemon Tree" [87] climbed to No. 35 on the *Billboard* Hot 100. The follow-up single, "If I Had a Hammer (The Hammer Song)," was released that autumn. A second LP reviving Woody's "This Land is Your Land" and a slate of mostly traditional folksongs was already in the works.

But with Dylan in his back pocket, Grossman had more than enough material for a third PP&M album. All he needed to do was switch his newest client from Columbia to Warner Brothers and he'd have his very own hit machine. His first order of business was to break Bob's Columbia contract. Halfway through producing

---

[86]   Silver went on to manage comedians Bill Cosby, Joan Rivers, and Richard Pryor as well as Cass Elliot, Jackson Browne, and Dr. John, migrating to L.A. in the 70s where he began a second career as a restaurateur. His eponymous Chinese eatery on Sunset Boulevard, which became an after-hours hangout for musicians, was notorious for a menu of cocaine and chow mein.

[87]   A Broadway librettist who borrowed the tune from a Brazilian folksong, Will Holt later sold TV commercial rights to S.C. Johnson for a Lemon Pledge advertising campaign.

Dylan's second album, John Hammond began receiving legal threats. He asked Columbia's legal counsel what to do after learning Bob had been underage when he signed with the label.

"Has he been in the studio lately?" asked attorney Clive Davis.

"Sure," said Hammond. "Lots of times."

"Well, you can tear up that letter from Dylan's lawyer," said Davis. "If he's been in the studio for us on his own free will since he's been 21, then that supersedes anything else."

Grossman was furious. He wasn't as ruthless a song shark as those who'd blatantly stolen from Dylan heroes like Little Richard or Buddy Holly, but he did have a feudal lord's passionate belief in indentured servitude.

"I'm sure that if Grossman had *told* Bobby what he was signing, they wouldn't have had a problem later on," said Milt Okun. "But he didn't. He did the same thing to Gordon Lightfoot and all the other acts he signed, which was not right. I eventually dissolved my partnership with him."

At the time, Bob was oblivious to Grossman's maneuvering. He poured himself into his music while awaiting Suze's return, wringing out his poignant "Tomorrow Is a Long Time" just weeks after she departed. He recorded it for the first time during an August visit to Minnesota, where he also broke the news to Abe and Beatty that he'd legally changed his name. His father wept.

After returning to New York, Bob found a letter from Suze saying she wouldn't be back until January. Bob's poignant lyrics turned to spite. His most famous love song of those early years was arguably no love song at all. Like the self-pitying bile that spills from "Boots of Spanish Leather,"[88] which was written about that same time, "Don't Think Twice, It's All Right" is less an enduring testament to

---

[88] "I think it's a child's song, crying out for his mother," said pop historian Marc Eliot.

amore than it is a callous kiss-off from a jilted lover. His rebuff of the fickle lass to whom he'd given his heart while "she wanted my soul," became every bit the adolescent anthem of the early '60s as "Blowin' in the Wind": one tapped into baby boom outrage over racial iniquity and Cold War brinksmanship while the other spoke to every teenaged boy trying to maintain his dignity after his heart has been drop-kicked to the side of the road.

In what had become routine, Bob took the tune for "Don't Think Twice" from Paul Clayton who himself borrowed it from an earlier folksong.[89] While Dylan later acknowledged Clayton's "Who's Gonna Buy Your Ribbons (When I'm Gone)" as the source for "Don't Think Twice," their respective publishers sued each other over the alleged plagiarism. Clayton eventually got a $500 settlement, but they remained friends.

Similarly, Jean Ritchie's Geordie Music accused Bob of stealing the melody for "Masters of War" from "Nottamun Town," a traditional tune Ritchie had copyrighted. Dylan successfully claimed his lyrics constituted a new composition and there was no settlement.

His other masterwork that season was another protest song, but so different from "Blowin' in the Wind" or anything that wafted out the windows of the Brill Building that it defied classification.

The man who would become Dylan's best friend, roadie, and chief confidante for the next seven years rolled in from L.A. that summer—a "silent and creepy buddy bodyguard," according to Suze. Victor Maymudes, who informally entered the Beat brotherhood as a regular at L.A.'s first coffeehouse,[90] hooked up with Jack Elliott during an expedition to explore the Village scene. Jack

---

[89]   The more closely entitled "Who's Gonna Buy Your Chickens When I'm Gone?"

[90]   Herb Cohen's Unicorn next door to the Whiskey on the Sunset Strip was home base for Lenny Bruce as well as West Coast way station for Odetta, Judy Henske, and other Eisenhower-era troubadours. Maymudes became a fixture from the day it opened in 1955.

introduced Maymudes to Bob at the Gaslight Café just as Dylan began to noodle with his latest song.

"When we came in, Bob Dylan was in the backroom[91] where the performers hang out," Maymudes recalled. "He had been typing on an old typewriter . . . he was a two-finger typist. He was writing a new song. This one would be a hard rain that was going to fall."

Not a folksong or a love song or talking blues, "A Hard Rain's A-Gonna Fall" was a timeless, apocalyptic message that resonated with all that Dylan had assimilated since he first landed in New York: Brecht, Kerouac, Baudelaire, Ginsberg, an Italian poet from the 13th century[92] . . . every kitchen-sink influence from the Bible to the *New York Times*.

Using the medieval Child ballad "Lord Randall"[93] as a template, Dylan finished "Hard Rain" in the basement of the Village Gate a few days later and first performed it publicly three weeks before the Cuban missile crisis. His timing turned out to be so prescient that for years afterward, critics and biographers alike believed his apocalyptic vision must have been inspired by the Kennedy-Khrushchev faceoff.

---

[91] The room and the Remington typewriter both belonged to Hugh "Wavy Gravy" Romney, "the illegitimate son of Harpo Marx and Mother Theresa," according to New Left satirist Paul Krassner. After Maymudes became his manager and he'd wed Bonnie "Jaharana" Beecher in 1965, Romney established celluloid immortality by warning the half-million concertgoers at Woodstock against taking the brown acid.

[92] He lifted lines directly from *The Divine Comedy* in which Dante "stumbled on the side of a misty mountain" in the opening Canto and later wandered into "the depths of the dark forest" (Canto II) and saw a "black branch with blood dripping." (Canto XIII).

[93] A sixteenth-century Anglo lament of a young man poisoned by his lover, the song begins: "O where have you been, Lord Randall, my son? Oh where have you been, my handsome young man?"

Fellow folkie Richie Havens first heard it played by Gene Michaels,[94] yet another would-be singer-songwriter, and assumed he had written it.

"I was singing Dylan's 'A Hard Rain's Gonna Fall' for two years before he heard me sing it, and a year or so before he recorded it," said Havens. "It was the hardest song for me to learn. It took me three days to learn it because the imagery was so disjointed. It was difficult as all hell, but I learned it. I sing it very slowly, which made the song three times as long as it was, and it was already seven minutes. It was a very moving, heavy song."

When Dylan first heard Havens perform his version at Folk City, he approached the stage afterward, stoned and weepy.

"Man, you're my favorite singer," he said. "You really sang that song so beautiful."

Later, down in the basement, Dave Van Ronk buttonholed Havens.

"Do you know who that was?'

"No," said Havens.

"That's the guy who wrote that song."

■ ■ ■

Milt Okun[95] took Dylan's Witmark demo of "Blowin' in the Wind" to the Chad Mitchell Trio, who became the first to record it that autumn on an album of protest songs entitled *In Action*. The trio's

---

94   Teamed with a young singer from Florida named Tina DeVogue, Michaels was an early Village dropout. He and DeVogue married, fell into drugs, and disappeared, but their brief relationship with Dylan would carry significant resonance half a century later.

95   Okun initially took "Blowin' in the Wind" to his mentor Harry Belafonte, whose assistant Bob Ballard nixed it. When Belafonte chastised Okun a year later for not giving him first crack, Okun told him that he had. "It was the first time I ever saw Harry turn white," said Okun.

label refused to release it as a single because the lyrics contained the word "death." Kapp Records believed deejays would shun anything that reminded listeners of their own mortality. By year's end, Warner Brothers Records would demolish that taboo when Grossman ordered up "Blowin' in the Wind" as Peter, Paul and Mary's first single from their third LP.

Dylan recorded "Blowin' in the Wind" too for John Hammond's follow-up to his poorly received *Bob Dylan*, but releasing it as a single was out of the question. When it came to Top 40 radio, Bob's Woody whine was worse than "death."

"'Blowin' in the Wind' is not a natural vehicle for Dylan the performer," Dylanologist Paul Williams understated a generation later. "It's not very elastic."

But elastic enough for *avant garde* BBC-TV producer Philip Saville, it seemed. At year's end, while Bob continued to pine for Suze, Saville invited him to England to tape *Madhouse on Castle Street*,[96] a one-man tour de force about a recluse who descends into lunacy in a London rooming house.

Saville had seen Bob perform at the Gaslight during a visit to the Village and guessed he'd be perfect for the role, but when Dylan arrived and read the script, it was clear his folkie stage presence did not mean he could act. He displayed all the emotive presence of a two-by-four. Instead, Saville opted for young Shakespearean David Warner to play the madman while Bob strummed four songs for the soundtrack from the shadows, including "Blowin' in the Wind."

Madhouse flopped, but Bob did get a taste of pop-star luxury at the Mayfair and ran into none other than Robert Graves near the hotel. As Bob started in on how *The White Goddess* had inspired

---

[96] Because of the then-common practice of tape wiping as a way for networks to save money, no full recording is known to exist.

him, the great man snubbed the young pup. Back in the States, Dylan switched from admiration to calling Graves an "old bastard."

Bob earned 500 British pounds for his TV gig and used it to extend his European visit so he could surprise Suze with a visit to Italy. After the first of the year, however, she'd already boarded a ship[97] headed back to the U.S. When Bob arrived in Perugia, she was gone and he had to settle for a tour of Rome[98] as his consolation prize.

His low-profile success as budding Village phenom built exponentially during his absence. Once he and Suze reunited, the time had come to put the finishing touches on his second album and he wanted her on the cover with him.

"We went down to Dylan's place on Fourth Street, just off Sixth Avenue, right in the heart of the Village," recalled photographer Don Hunstein. "It was winter, dirty snow on the ground . . . I can't tell you why I did it, but I said, 'Just walk up and down the street,' There wasn't much thought to it. It was late afternoon. You can tell that the sun was low behind them. It must have been pretty uncomfortable, out there in the slush."

"It was freezing out," Suze said. "He wore a very thin jacket, because image was all. Our apartment was always cold, so I had a sweater on, plus I borrowed one of his big, bulky sweaters. On top of that I put on a coat."

Bushy-haired Bob wore a chambray shirt beneath his suede jacket while Suze bundled up "like an Italian sausage," as she remembered it.

And yet a more iconic portrait of Romeo and Juliet circa 1963 simply does not exist. The cover of *Freewheelin' Bob Dylan*

---

[97]   Appropriately named the *Christoforo Colombo*.

[98]   Inspiration for "When I Paint My Masterpiece," a minor hit for the Band ten years later. In an outpouring of nostalgia, he also wrote "Girl from the North Country" while in Italy.

remains such a powerful image of what it meant to be young, defiant, and in love during the early '60s that Apple Computers licensed it nearly 50 years later for a campaign aimed at selling iPads to baby boomers.

That winter Warner Bothers released Peter, Paul and Mary's second album, *Moving*. And while it wasn't the instant *Billboard* smash their first album had been, Peter Yarrow's children's classic "Puff the Magic Dragon" built *Moving*'s audience and kept the LP on the charts for more than a year. "Blowin' in the Wind," the painstakingly well-rehearsed breakout single from their third album *In the Wind*, hit on Top 40 radio that spring, and sold over 300,000 copies in two weeks. By contrast, *Freewheelin'* had been out over a month and wasn't doing much better than *Bob Dylan*.

But as *Moving*'s momentum built, sales of *Freewheelin'* kept pace and "Blowin' in the Wind" became an anthem. Over the next few years, more than 50 other artists recorded versions of the song, running the gambit from Duke Ellington to Spike Jones.

Before the year was over, Peter, Paul and Mary's *In the Wind* spawned nearly a half-dozen more hits, including "Don't Think Twice," and *Freewheelin'* exploded across America in its wake. Bob Dylan, "a character that will sell," catapulted into the national conversation, and while the parents of those who bought his records might criticize what they did not understand, their sons and their daughters grasped every idea, absorbed every word, and savored every detail of the growing Dylan legend.

5
ON THE ROAD

Bob's network extended well beyond the Village at the beginning of 1963. Like the restless teen who once circled his '51 Ford in an ever-widening gyre beyond the Mesabi Range, Dylan wandered farther and farther from his Fourth Street base. He had hardly relaxed after one compulsive road trip before planning the next.

"Bob soaked up everything and glommed onto whatever taught him something new," said Suze.

Saratoga. New Haven. Long Island. Wherever there was a festival or a folk event, he absorbed it and then moved on. He visited Boston often, poaching ideas and melodies at Club 47 or the Golden Vanity[99]—the Cambridge equivalents of the Gaslight or Gerde's Folk City. Suze accompanied him, but usually only on shorter jaunts. While he was off peregrinating, she cocooned in the Village. When they were together, his attention could be stifling.

"They had a photographer friend who lived in Schenectady," recalled Len Chandler. "Joe Alper did a lot of candid shots whenever they went up to visit and they got very close to him and his family, but when Bob found out Suze posed topless once—tasteful, artsy stuff—he went nuts. He was finished with Alper. That was

---

[99] While in Boston, Bob heard a University of Massachusetts undergrad play a minor key variant of the old English folk tune "Nottamun Town" and used it for "Masters of War." The undergrad gave up a career in animal husbandry to follow Bobby Zimmerman's example. He changed his name from Henry Fredericks to Taj Mahal and took up the highway blues.

typical. No argument. No explanation. If Dylan was done with you, he was done."

Bob's double standard dated back to Hibbing, where it was okay for him to philander with Echo's best friend while he went into passive-aggressive rage over any male who flirted with *his* girl. When amateur photographer Arnie Maki once asked Echo to pose without her blouse, Dylan ordered her never to see the sonofabitch again.

He hated to be reminded of his hypocrisy and ostracized anyone who did—a character trait Albert Grossman would play like a fiddle. Bob's new career architect believed Greta Garbo had the right idea: say little, reveal less, then disappear. Grossman advised clients: don't speak during performances, always preserve an air of mystery, and don't be a comedian. [100]

"(Bob) started to grow very aloof after Grossman got him," said Kevin Krown, an early Greenwich friend who watched Dylan's Charlie Chaplin phase do a slow fade.

"Bob was a lot more calculating about his career than most people imagine," said guitarist Barry Kornfeld. "He had this image that he created. He ceased to be [a] funny, Woody, cheerful cherub peeking over a harmonica holder with a little cap. I think it was a conscious decision that he needed more mystique. You can't be funny and have mystique, you know."

Grossman encouraged Bob's natural bent for hyperbole, both on stage and off. Never explain, never elaborate, keep a flippant upper hand, and then just vanish. Never play it for laughs and, when in doubt, brood.

---

[100] In one of his final clown routines, Dylan wandered the fringes of the 1963 Newport Folk Festival sucking on a cigar while snapping a bullwhip at anything that moved. Bob and whip later appeared on the cover of a French bootleg album.

"They were kindred spirits," Suze recalled. "Albert never denied who he was, but he had that way of observing and not being forthcoming. Bob never gave a straight answer. He couldn't at that time. He was creating his own legend and his own fiction of himself."

When he first took over, Grossman booked Bob with better-known acts as a guest performer on the college circuit, but at warp speed Bob became a big enough noise all on his own. Whenever Peter, Paul and Mary or Pete Seeger sang a Dylan original, they acknowledged and praised him from the stage. His brand blossomed.

■ ■ ■

Following Bob's success from afar, Abe and Beatty began pestering Grossman's office to let them come see their boy work his magic in New York. Dylan ducked his folks as long as he could, but reluctantly invited them to his Town Hall concert during the rollout of *Freewheelin'* and they drove all the way out from Minnesota. Still passing as gentile, Bob did not acknowledge the middle-aged Jewish couple sitting in the audience. Instead, he aped the drawl and mannerisms of his adopted father figure.

"Well I'm just one of those ramblin' boys," he enunciated in his best Woody. "Ramblin around and makin' noise."

But the noise was all Dylan that night. He wrote each of the 15 songs he performed, concluding his one-man *tour de force* by reciting a long poem that declared his independence as much from Woody as from his real forebears. In "Last Thoughts on Woody Guthrie," Bob mocked Abe and Beatty's lifestyle, from country club[101] to conspicuous consumption. None of that shop-at-Macy's,

---

[101]   According to B. J. Rolfzen, Jews weren't allowed to play at Hibbing's Mesaba Country Club in the '50s and early '60s—a particular blow to Abe, who loved hobbling around golf courses.

televised *Life* magazine half-truths for Bob. It was his final message in an evening crammed with messages.

"That stuff ain't real!" he hollered from the stage.

The printed concert program contained a similar sermon. Written in quasi-autobiographical blank verse that foreshadowed *Chronicles* by half a century, "My Life in a Stolen Moment" mixed fact with fiction so deftly that only those who knew the truth could tell the difference. Abe and Beatty's boy praised Hibbing as "a good ol' town" but condemned the University of Minnesota as a failed educational experiment. Once Bob lit out for the territories, his fibs conflated from little white myths to absolute bullshit. Mark Twain had nothing on Bob Dylan.

Like Huck Finn, Bob ran away from home "when I was 10, 12, 13, 15, 15 1/2, 17, an' 18." He'd hitchhiked and/or ridden the rails from Gallup to Galveston to California, Kansas, Florida, Iowa, Washington, and beyond. Along the way, he'd been busted for both armed robbery and murder and "for lookin' like I do."

Following the concert, Bob did not invite his folks back to his apartment. He did agree to meet them for dinner near their Midtown hotel. Suze remembered Beatty as bubbly while Abe remained mute. If either had reservations about their Bobby sleeping with a shiksa, they didn't show it; neither did they seem bothered by his many distortions about his past. There was tension though.

"In hindsight, I'm sure they wished I hadn't been there so they could have visited with their son alone," said Suze.

■■ ■■ ■■

Ramblin' Bob made up for lost time over the next several months, traveling for real this time from Chicago to Boston to New York, all the way west to California and back again—not by thumb or boxcar, but by airliner. He flew Suze to Puerto Rico for a weeklong Columbia Records sales retreat where they fit in like a pair of cockneys at Buckingham Palace. Neither minded lapping up a little bourgeois luxury at the Americana Hotel. They checked in as Mr. & Mrs. Dylan.

Bob debuted on network TV during the spring of '63 as part of an ABC folk anthology, but further enhanced his principled young rebel's legend by refusing to appear on the most popular variety program in the country. After CBS censors told him he couldn't sing "Talkin' John Birch Paranoid Blues,"[102] he walked off *The Ed Sullivan Show.* Columbia executives also removed the cut from *Freewheelin'* because it was potentially libelous. When Clive Davis tried to sympathize, regaling Bob with recollections of his own rebellious college days, Dylan shouted "Bullshit!" and stomped from his office.

Both the song and the dispute might have gone unnoticed if Grossman, Robert Shelton, and other Dylan acolytes had not informed the wire services of Bob's complaint to the FCC, accusing CBS of exercising "a form of censorship and economic tyranny."

Here was a pop star with principles. Respected *Village Voice* music critic Nat Hentoff joined the growing Dylan fan club with a write-up in *Playboy* and Bob wowed Chicago talk-show host Studs Terkel with his impassioned Holden Caulfield[103] pose. A huge Guthrie fan himself, Terkel accepted as gospel Bob's claim that his uncle took him to see Woody in California when he was just 10 years old. Bob also claimed he was deep into writing his own *Bound for Glory*-type memoir. Like Hentoff, Terkel was charmed.

---

[102] Since dumping its resident humorist John Henry Faulk in 1956, the network whose news division got credited for breaking the back of McCarthyism remained sensitive to charges of blacklisting in primetime.

[103] Talent agency MCA tried unsuccessfully to cast Dylan in a film version of *The Catcher in the Rye.*

In this new, charismatic incarnation and just in time for his 22nd birthday, Bob traveled to the Monterey Folk Festival where he formally encountered Joan Baez. Their paths had crossed before, both in Greenwich and Harvard Square, but Bob was still hungry back then and folk was already Joan's world.

As evidenced by three *Billboard*-topping LPs since her 1959 debut at the Newport Folk Festival, Baez had already established a character that would sell. She owned a Jaguar XKE and a home in pricey Carmel Valley, belying her waifish stage persona. Joan's long dark mane and pitch-perfect soprano helped her supplant the formidable Kingston Trio as *the* commercial standard for folk purity in 1963. She didn't just sing "Barbara Allen": she *was* Barbara Allen. And yet, while Baez oozed exotic grace on stage, her insecurities off stage often turned petty.

"Joan could be very difficult, very arrogant, rude, hysterical," recalled Joyce Kalina, cofounder of Boston's Club 47, where Baez first cemented her reputation. Len Chandler was more blunt: "Joan could be a very nasty bit of business."

She pulled the plug on rival performers' amplifiers, stole their songs before they took the stage, and sang like a siren above their voices from the back of the room, drowning out their performances.

"She had stage fright half the time," explained Kalina. "She used to go out in the alley and throw up, she was so scared."

Her disdain extended to Dylan. More than a generation later, Judy Collins recalled her own first Village encounter with Bob. With Baez at her side, the two budding folk queens spied a rumpled, drunken Bob sitting at the bar in Café Wha? Curious at his growing reputation, neither was impressed by his appearance.

"He looks like a toad," remarked Baez.

After "Blowin' in the Wind," Joan altered her opinion. She set out to turn the toad into a prince. The folk revival's Virgin Princess knew platinum poetry when she heard it.

Baez felt no compunction about using peers to boost her to the next level before pulling the ladder up behind her. Al Grossman's client Bob Gibson, one of the nation's best-known folkies in 1959, introduced barefoot Joan to the world at the first Newport Folk Festival, but Baez wouldn't return the favor four years later after Gibson's star began to slip.[104]

After Monterey, she didn't mind introducing Dylan though. By then, he was a star on the rise and she knew it. During her summer concert tour,[105] Baez brought him out as a mystery guest who'd recently knocked them dead at the 1963 Newport Folk Festival.

Dylan further enhanced his revolutionary image by formally attaching himself to the civil rights movement. During his first-ever visit to the Mississippi Delta, he joined folkie/actor Theodore Bikel and Pete Seeger in a voter registration drive in Greenwood, Mississippi.[106] Dylan performed his "Ballad of Emmett Till" on Silas Magee's farm before moving on to Ole Miss, an hour's drive to the

---

[104] An alcoholic since his teens and Grossman's Chicago roommate for two years before they both moved to New York, Gibson had become a speed freak and heroin addict by the early '60s. "Gibson was doing straight folk music with a kind of Ray Charles, Elvis, Everly Brothers attitude," recalled the Byrds' Roger McGuinn. "To me, that was the first attempt at mixing rock 'n' roll and folk music." After Grossman turned his back on him, Gibson did jail time in Chicago, Cleveland, and Canada, dropping out of music all together until the mid-70s, when he joined Alcoholics Anonymous. He remained sober until his death in 1996.

[105] As early as November 1962, Time named Bob as a Baez disciple. In a cover story about her growing influence, Bob's nasality registered "just the right clothespin-on-the-nose honesty to appeal to those who most deeply care," the magazine reported.

[106] Ten miles south of Money, Mississippi, where Emmett Till was murdered eight years earlier.

east. It was there he sang an in-your-face "Oxford Town" to an alternately jeering, cheering crowd of undergrads. TV producer Arthur
Barron captured both performances for a televised documentary that
aired in New York a few days before the historic March on
Washington.

Dylan joined Baez on stage that August day in an iconic prelude
to Martin Luther King Jr.'s "I Have a Dream" speech. The King and
Queen of Folk sang "Only a Pawn in Their Game" and "When The
Ship Comes In" to the largest throng ever to converge on the National
Mall. Peter, Paul and Mary were there, too, as were members of the
Movement's old guard like Mahalia Jackson and Marian Anderson.

"But what I remember, see, was Bob and I ducking behind the
Lincoln Memorial to smoke us a joint," said Len Chandler. "You
won't read that in any history book."

Chandler and Bob drifted apart after that. He saw Dylan and Baez
riding through Manhattan in a limousine several months later. Bob
called out to him when the limo stopped at a light. But as Chandler
ran across the street to greet him, Joan reached over and rolled up
the window. Bob's face slowly slid behind the smoked glass, the
light changed, and Chandler didn't see his oldest Village friend
again for another 30 years.

■■ ■■ ■■

During a break in Joan's concert tour late that summer, she and
Dylan stopped over in Woodstock, where they explored the arts colony during the day and each other at night in a room upstairs over
Tinker Street's Café Espresso. In the liner notes to *Joan Baez in
Concert Part 2*, Dylan waxed saccharine over their postadolescent
dalliance: *For the breeze I heard in a young girl's breath/Proved
true as sex an' womanhood/ An' deep as the lowest depths a death/*

An' as strong as the weakest winds that blow/ An' as long as fate an'
fatherhood . . .

When fellow folkie Eric von Schmidt comments on how wired
Dylan always seemed, both on stage and off, Joan arched her brows
and offered her own coy observation: "Eric," she said, "he doesn't
jiggle like that when he's asleep."

Suze's friend Sue Zuckerman, who took the credit (or blame)
for first introducing her to Bob, saw Dylan's pent-up energy as
"fascinating." In much the same way Budd Schulberg's Sammy
Glick enticed the opposite sex in the pages of *What Makes Sammy
Run?* Dylan infected women with a "crazy desire to know what it
felt like to have all that driving ambition and frenzy and violence
inside of me."

While Bob and Baez were trysting, Albert Grossman was looking
to purchase his own Woodstock retreat in neighboring Bearsville.
Still very much the Sleepy Hollow envisioned a century earlier by
Washington Irving, Woodstock compared to Manhattan the way a
rain forest contrasts to a moonscape. Rip Van Winkle still dozed
deep in its meadows while Ichabod Crane raced the Devil past tav-
erns and cemeteries on moonless nights.

Outfitted with antiques, swimming pool, and a commercial-sized
automated car wash for his new Silver Dawn Rolls Royce, Grossman's estate became a sanctuary for clients as well as himself and
his fiancée. A sign at the property line read, "If you haven't tele-
phoned, you are trespassing."

Dylan quickly acclimated to the relaxed Catskills atmosphere. He
bought himself a Triumph motorcycle to blow off steam on the rural
roads and Grossman refurbished a room over the barn for him. In the
years ahead when the going got tough, Bob got off to Woodstock. It
never occurred to him that he might be paying for it all.

Suze's suspicions roused after Newport, though she had no tangible proof.

"Bob was charismatic," she said. "He was a beacon, a lighthouse. He was also a black hole."

From the moment Mary Rotolo first laid eyes on him, she knew Dylan was all wrong for her daughter. "She felt I was better off without the lyin', cheatin', manipulatin' bastard," recalled Suze. In a notebook entry from that time, she summed Bob up as "an extraordinary writer, but I don't think of him as an honorable person. He doesn't necessarily do the right thing. But where is it written that this must be so in order to do great work in the world?"

One of Bob's trio of buddy-bodyguards[107] confirmed Suze's suspicions late that summer. Geno Foreman dropped by the Fourth Street apartment and blurted: "Hey Bobby, hey, man, heard about you and Joanie in California being, y'know, together, man."

Bob hustled Foreman to another room, but the damage was done. Suze moved into her sister Carla's apartment on Avenue B several blocks west of Fourth Street and discovered a few weeks later she was pregnant. According to Carla, she tried to gas herself. Suze considered a return to Puerto Rico for an abortion, but chose instead to visit a discreet Pennsylvania doctor—one who didn't mind bucking the law in those pre–*Roe v. Wade* days.

Meanwhile, Bob continued to juggle Joan and Suze and any number of other women as best he could while he laid down studio tracks for his upcoming album, *The Times They Are a-Changin'*.

On October 26, Abe and Beatty revisited New York, this time for Bob's triumphant return to Carnegie Hall. Almost two years had

---

[107] Victor Maymudes and Albert Maher rounded out the salaried "thought guard" entourage Albert Grossman hired to protect his investment. Maher and Maymudes flanked Bob while Foreman, who died in 1966 of ulcerative colitis aggravated by drug and alcohol abuse, kept fans at bay with a hand-carved shillelagh.

passed since their son first sang upstairs in the Chapter Hall, but this time he was booked into the *real* Carnegie Hall, which was packed and not just with a handful of groupies. Bob Dylan's time had arrived. Included among protest anthems like "Blowin' in the Wind" and "With God On Our Side"[108] were mesmerizing apolitical originals—timeless ruminations like "Percy's Song" and "Lay Down Your Weary Tune,"[109] which he'd composed in California, in Joan's cottage by the sea.

At the concert's climax, Abe and Beatty stood and cheered. No longer huddled like anonymous poultry at a crow convention, the Zimmermans swelled with pride. "That's my Bobby!" Beatty whispered to any who would listen.

After their return to Minnesota, Abe confided in the same Hibbing High principal who once pulled the plug on the Golden Chords: "It's great the way he can pull people in with his lyrics because he certainly can't sing very well."

Dylan cleared more than $8,000 from a single night's performance, but less than a week later, his juggernaut began to stall. *Newsweek* published a "gotcha" profile exposing Dylan as Bobby Zimmerman. Abe and Beatty had both been interviewed for the article, as well as his brother, David, and Bob raged at them afterward for months. Adding insult to injury, none other than Robert Shelton reported that a Rutgers University professor claimed that Dylan had

---

[108] He laid his words directly over the melody of Dominic Behan's "The Patriot Game."

[109] Author Stephen Webb called the song "a lullaby to the end of time, God's good night kiss to us in the form of a song . . . one of the greatest theological songs since King David composed his psalms." He performed the haunting quasi-gospel song just once, and never again, leaving it to the Byrds to carry the folk rock madrigal to a far larger audience.

plagiarized "Blowin' in the Wind."[110] True believers remained loyal to their new messiah.

"We admired Dylan's ability to smuggle the subversive into mass-circulated trappings," wrote New Left historian Todd Gitlin. "Whether he liked it or not, Dylan *sang for us;* we didn't have to know he had hung out in Minneapolis's dropout nonstudent radical scene in order to intuit that he had been doing some hard traveling through a familiar landscape. We followed his career as if he were singing our song; we got into the habit of asking where he was taking us next."

But Dylan would not be drafted as the baby boomers' tour guide. Offstage, he shunned the spotlight. If he didn't have Victor Maymudes or Geno Foreman to run interference for him, he hid behind newspapers or wore a disguise. If he did get cornered, he removed his prescription Ray-Bans long enough to signal with his ice-cold baby blues that the conversation was over.

"When asked if you care about the world's problems, look deeply into the eyes of he that asks you," Dylan preached. "He will not ask you again."

One effervescent teen recalled years later as a middle-aged adult the day that he spied his hero crouching in a booth at Healy's Café on East 18th Street. As he approached with his question about the meaning of life, Bob tried first to stare him down. When that failed, he fell back on existential *glissendorf.* Pointing through the plate-glass window, he told the kid, "Y'see that lamp post over there? How do you know it's over there?"

The kid dropped his jaw and Dylan went in for the kill.

---

[110] A Sigma Alpha Mu fraternity brother said Dylan plagiarized the song during his brief stay at the Sammy house while a New Jersey high school student made a similar claim. Neither contention held up.

"Man, you don't know *nuthin'*. You don't know *shit* about nut-hin'. How am I supposed to tell you if you don't know nuthin'? Whaddaya coming to me for?"

Dylan paid his bill and left his adoring fan by the cash register, dumbstruck and close to tears.

■ ■ ■

On December 13, 1963, Bob appeared in the Grand Ballroom at New York's Americana Hotel, where the National Emergency Civil Liberties Committee[111] had asked him to sing for its 10th Annual Bill of Rights Dinner. Maymudes and the rest of his ragtag entourage weren't allowed inside, so Dylan banished stage fright with wine.

The crowd of 1,400 of Manhattan's well-heeled, middle-aged liberal elite came to see the Left's newest Pied Piper, but all Bob saw from the stage were "bald-headed, pot-bellied people sitting out there in suits." They gave him a standing ovation when master of ceremonies John Henry Faulk presented him with the organization's annual Tom Paine Award.[112] Surprised, Bob tried to leave, but was persuaded to the podium. Surveying the crowd, he slurred, "I only wish that all you people who are sitting out here today weren't here and I could see all kind of faces with hair on their head."

Glissendorf might work one-on-one when dressing down a fan, but not to cow a crowd. Ovation faded to boos. Boozed-up, Bob would neither temper his scorn nor leave the dais. It was almost as

---

[111] Listed by the House Un-American Activities Committee as a subversive orga-nization, the Committee was a leading Cold War opponent of Jim Crow rac-ism and Joe McCarthy, challenging First Amendment breaches in court while honoring dissidents like Dylan. NECLC director Clark Foreman fathered Geno Foreman, one of Bob's bodyguards.

[112] British pacifist and philosopher Bertrand Russell won the previous year.

if he'd been given the chance to spew all over Abe and Beatty and their entire generation. He would not shut up.

Three weeks earlier, JFK had been assassinated and the nation with God on its side still mourned, so Dylan's rant caught the NECLC crowd utterly off guard. He identified more with Lee Harvey Oswald than he did bleeding-heart liberals. "I'm so sick a hearin' we all share the blame," he snarled.

At a visceral level, the JFK assassination[113] chilled Bob's lust for the spotlight. If a lone gunman could hit a moving target in Dallas, how about a minstrel on stage armed only with a guitar?

He shied away from performing for a while and concentrated on a novel. His latest hero was Hemingway, whose spare style worked in prose but not poetics. In an open letter he published in Gil Turner's *Broadside*, Dylan confessed:

> my novel is goin' noplace.
> absolutely noplace.
> like it don't even tell a story.
> its about a million scenes long,
> and it takes place on about a billion scraps of paper . . .
> certainly I can't make nothin' of it

Late in January, following the release of *The Times They Are a-Changin',* he and Maymudes joined Paul Clayton and tabloid journalist Pete Karman on a road trip. Aboard Bob's new blue Ford station wagon, they lit out for concert dates in San Francisco and L.A., adopting a see-America-first approach heavily influenced by

---

[113] He wrote a free verse eulogy after the killing that later became a blueprint for "Chimes of Freedom":

. . . the colors of Friday were dull as cathedral bells were gently burnin', strikin' for the gentle, strikin' for the kind, strikin' for the crippled ones an' strikin' for the blind.

cannabis and Kerouac. One of Suze's closest friends, Karman, joined the troupe at her request to keep an eye on her wayward boyfriend.

"Victor was little more than a gofer hired by Grossman to road manage," he recalled. "Apart from his lickspittle attention to Dylan, I can't remember a thing about him except that he was dark, skinny, and had a Levantine beak. Paul, on the other hand, was a tragic character. He was a gay pill popper living in the reactionary south. He was madly in love with Dylan, who treated him badly for it."

Meaning to turn his "Life in a Stolen Moment" fantasy into fact, Dylan demanded they stop off to visit striking coal miners in Kentucky, dissident students at Tougaloo College in Jackson, Mississippi, boozing revelers in New Orleans's Vieux Carré during Mardi Gras, and the ghosts of Dealey Plaza in Dallas. Envisioning another "passing-of-the-torch" moment similar to his bedside visits with Woody, Bob first directed his companions to Chicago poet laureate Carl Sandburg's rural farm in North Carolina. After muttering to his wife that he'd never heard of Dylan, the cranky octogenarian gave him a few minutes and then told him he had to feed his goats.

Undaunted, the quartet drove on, smoking dope, buzzing on Benzedrine, and consuming mass quantities of Beaujolais, climaxing their odyssey with a San Francisco concert and Dylan's live performance of "The Lonesome Death of Hattie Carroll" on *The Steve Allen Show* in Los Angeles. But somewhere near Denver, Dylan later claimed, he first heard another quartet over the car radio, and it changed his life. At the time, eight of the top ten singles in the U.S. belonged to John, Paul, George, and Ringo.

"They were doing things nobody was doing," Bob recalled. "Their chords were outrageous, just outrageous; and their harmonies made it all valid. . . .

"Everybody else thought they were for the teenyboppers, that they were gonna pass right away. But it was obvious to me that they had staying power. I knew they were pointing to the direction music had to go."

Back in Bob's dope-smoking haunts like the Gaslight and the Kettle of Fish, the Beatles had already detonated. Located in the basement at 116 MacDougal a block south of Café Wha?, Gaslight regulars grudgingly gave the Beatles their due just as folk, rock, and pop reached a crescendo.

Former Chad Mitchell guitarist Jim McGuinn, who'd followed Albert Grossman to New York after making his debut at Grossman's Gate of Horn, wowed his peers night after night in the Gaslight's backroom with his rendition of "I Wanna Hold Your Hand." Hour after drunken hour, McGuinn did acoustic encores of the chorus, provoking shout outs of "one . . . more . . . time!" from the likes of Tom Paxton, Len Chandler, Phil Ochs, Dave Van Ronk, and Dylan.

Yet, while he might belittle the Beatles' puerile lyrics, McGuinn could not deny their sound. After he quit the Village for L.A. later that year, he switched his first and middle names, melded Dylan's poetry with Beatlemania, and formed the Byrds, pop's first folk-rock quartet. What Peter, Paul and Mary did to popularize Dylan among folkies, Roger McGuinn and his Byrds[114] would next do for devotees of rock 'n' roll.

Compared to PP&M and the Byrds, Dylan's third LP seemed a throwback to an earlier time. The close-up black-and-white portrait that Mary Travers's husband, Barry Feinstein, shot for the cover of *The Times They Are a-Changin'* looked like Dust Bowl Bob from his skinny neck to his squinty sneer. Like Woody, he'd become a

---

[114] Nominated for Best New Artist during the 1966 Grammy Awards along with Herman's Hermits, Sonny & Cher, Glenn Yarbrough, Marilyn Maye, Horst Jankowski, and Tom Jones, the Byrds were as close to cool as the NARAS judges would allow. With 47 categories and more on the way, Dylan wasn't nominated once, nor would he be for another 15 years.

heavy drinker with a brilliant aptitude for performance art, vernacular storytelling, and a lifelong conviction that the next woman would be a keeper. Instead of singing about being a travelin' man, he'd finally become one.[115] Never mind that the only things that made Bob's traveling hard were hangovers and a constant, gnawing ambition.

In the liner notes for *The Times They Are a-Changin'*, Bob briefed his growing fan base on his extended education since quitting the University of Minnesota. His required reading list: Villon, Brecht, Yevgeny Yevtushenko, William Blake, Lenny Bruce, Allen Ginsberg, Brendan Behan. Mimicking rhyme schemes from the 23rd Psalm to Pete Seeger's "The Bells of Rhymney," he entitled his blank verse "11 Outlined Epitaphs" and invoked almost every musical influence he'd incorporated into his act from Edith Piaf to Miles Davis to Marlene Dietrich. Listen to the jailhouse songs of Ray Bremser, the cabaret stylings of Charles Aznavour, he advised; go see François Truffaut's *Shoot the Piano Player*; check out Modigliani's paintings of long-faced *jeune filles* . . . "Epitaphs" also declared Bob's independence from the media. "I shall not cooperate with reporters' whims," he insisted, deprecating journalists as "hung-up writers, frustrated novelists."

"They don't hurt me none by putting fancy labels on me," he said. "They got all these preconceived ideas about me, so I just play up to them."

Of course, he was not above exploiting journalism whenever it benefited his career.

---

[115] In an abbreviated odyssey similar to his *On the Road* adventure with Karman, Clayton, and Maymudes, Dylan and Barry Feinstein co-piloted Grossman's Silver Dawn from Denver to New York, beginning with a pilgrimage to Central City where Dylan played piano for a stripper. They stopped off for a holy-roller revival in Iowa and raced a freight train across Nebraska, reveling in the natives' disapproving stares.

He reserved his grandest hypocrisy for "beautiful Sue with the lines of a swan . . .long hair spread out the color of the sun . . . the true fortuneteller of my soul," even as gossip about Baez buzzed from coast to coast. Had he consulted the true fortuneteller of his soul before the release of *The Times They Are a-Changin'*, he might have learned Suze was breaking it off for good.

In a self-pitying screed he included on his next album, Dylan blamed Suze's mother and sister Carla[116] for the breakup. "Ballad in Plain D" stood in stark adolescent contrast to "Mr. Tambourine Man," another song Dylan wrote on the occasion of their disintegration. In the liner notes for *Biograph* (1985) and again in *Chronicles*, Dylan credited Bruce Langhorne with inspiring "Mr. Tambourine Man" because he carried an oversized Turkish tambourine among his trove of instruments.

"I was house musician at Gerdes Folk City back then and, frankly, I didn't think he could sing," Langhorne recalled, "but Bobby had the gift of words. He was kind of quick and I started paying attention to what he was saying."

A ragged clown of a man who'd lost two fingers of one hand in a brawl, Langhorne was Dylan's first sideman to plug in, taking Bob electric on his *Freewheelin'* cover of Blind Lemon Jefferson's "Corrina, Corrina."[117]

"I'm just a musician," Langhorne said. "I never had that drive that Bobby did. I never even knew I was 'Mr. Tambourine Man' until I read about it."

---

[116] In keeping with inbred Village cronyism, Carla Rotolo acted as secretary to venerable folklorist Alan Lomax.

[117] Langhorne also backed him on "Mixed-Up Confusion," an outtake from the *Freewheelin'* sessions that wasn't released until 1985 on the three-LP *Biograph* set. A mock lament reminiscent of Eddie Cochran's "Summertime Blues," it is frequently cited by Dylanologists as Bob's first formal foray into electrified rock.

According to Suze, Dylan wrote "Mr. Tambourine Man" after wandering the Village streets all night. His poignant bacchanal sprang as much from their climactic breakup as it did from his acquaintance with Langhorne. Compared to the awkward "Ballad in Plain D," the sheer musicality of "Tambourine Man" showed Bob's range from the ridiculous to the sublime. With the Byrds' version, "Mr. Tambourine Man" became the first folk rock classic—a sound Dylan likened to "danceable Bach."

■ ■ ■

In addition to shadowing Bob on behalf of Albert Grossman, Victor Maymudes also kept him in pharmaceuticals. Before he set out on his second European trip, Bob dropped acid with Victor and Boston record producer Paul Rothchild[118] in April 1964. Rothchild recalled a tray of foil-wrapped sugar cubes Maymudes discovered in Albert Grossman's refrigerator one evening. They shared their treasure with Bob.

"It was a magical night of camaraderie and conversation, with Dylan strumming his guitar, but from that moment on his music changed," said Rothchild.

While Dylan later denied the drug's influence, his concert appearance at London's Royal Festival Hall the following month marked a subtle shift away from Bob the folksinger. The Woody influence still came across, but his repertoire had lost its political edge. Dylan first met the Beatles and the Rolling Stones on that trip. Whether through their influence or his new psychedelic sensibility, his music began to evolve.

---

[118] Rothchild migrated to L.A., produced the first five albums by The Doors, and presided over much of the '70s rock 'n' roll renaissance from his hilltop home in the Hollywood hills. He died in 1995.

Following their English sojourn, he and Maymudes traveled on to Paris where they connected with a German fashion model who echoed Echo's Scandinavian good looks. She went by the stage name Nico[119] and accompanied Dylan and Maymudes to a Greek village where Maymudes's ancestors once lived.[120] Bob finished writing several songs he planned to record on his next album while there and, again, the poetry differed from all that had come before— not yet rock and roll, but a far cry from his best-known previous efforts, which Bob described as "finger-pointin' songs." *Another Side of Bob Dylan,* recorded in a single evening, was a grab bag of funny, bitter, poignant, irreverent, and restless farewells to the pro- test phase of his relentless reinvention. Topics he once borrowed from TV news or the *New York Times* gave way to couplets laced with angst and whimsy that had little to do with civil rights or nuclear war. He left politics to Village rivals like Paxton and Ochs who jumped on the Woody bandwagon just as Bob abandoned it.

Phil Ochs in particular patterned himself after Dylan, almost to a degree of hero worship, but was never able to shake his own protest image. David Blue, an intimate of both songwriters, told Ochs his career stalled because he was a singing journalist who thought too hard about commercial success. While Dylan might be equally cal- culating, he trusted his gut. "That's the difference between you and Dylan," said Blue. "You operate from your head. Charts, plans, ideas, crusades. Dylan operates from his cock."

---

[119] Nico, née Christa Päffgen, appeared in Fellini's *La Dolce Vita* at the age of 21, and had begun a career as a model, actress, and singer. She later fronted Lou Reed's Velvet Underground with a signature moan á la Marlene Dietrich.

[120] One of Dylan's "things I'll always miss," which he related a quarter century later to *Interview* magazine, was sunset at Trebuki bay on the Aegean island of Skyros.

Dylan had "a calypso mind," according to Eric von Schmidt, and brought it to bear whenever he entered the recording studio, as he did on the wine-and-speed-fueled evening of June 9, 1964.

Bob met producer Tom Wilson at Columbia's Seventh Avenue recording studio to lay down tracks for *Another Side of Bob Dylan* and invited Nat Hentoff to observe the spectacle for *The New Yorker*. With no rehearsal and an endless supply of Beaujolais, the tentative Hibbing amateur John Hammond first led into the same studio two and a half years earlier took command to such a degree that Wilson just sat back, shut up, and did his best to capture the moment. He likened Dylan to "a white Ray Charles with a message."

"He's got a wider range of talents than he shows," said Wilson. "He kind of hoards them. You go back to his three albums. Each time, there's a big leap from one to the next—in material, in performance, in everything."

Bob zipped through 11 tracks plus four additional outtakes, all in less than six hours. Ramblin' Jack and Maymudes, their girlfriends, and even a couple of tots crowded the control booth. The late-night recording session resembled a boozy family outing, with grousing and effusive praise from the sidelines. During breaks, Dylan huddled with Hentoff, lying with utter sincerity about his fake biography. While the cat was out of the bag and halfway around the world about his Hibbing upbringing, Bob still floated lie after self-serving lie. He reinforced his carny/hobo/runaway image with a straight face,[121] Hentoff offered no challenge, and everything zipped right past *The New Yorker*'s vaunted fact-checkers.

Following the recording session they adjourned to a nearby Middle Eastern restaurant and drank even more Beaujolais. Dylan confided to

---

[121]   Bob purposely trained the humor out of his persona by sitting deadpan through comedy performances at Village clubs and stifling the urge to laugh at the likes of Bill Cosby, Tiny Tim, or Hugh Romney.

Hentoff, "You know Joanie—Joanie Baez—worries about me. She worries about whether people will get control over me and exploit me. But I'm cool. I'm in control, because I don't care about money, and all that. And I'm cool in myself, because I've gone through enough changes so that I know what's real to me and what isn't."

Dylan scoffed at the fleeting nature of fame,[122] assuring Hentoff that the spotlight would soon fade: "This so-called mass fame comes from people who get caught up in a thing for a while and buy the records. Then they stop. And when they stop I won't be famous anymore."

Nonetheless, when he returned to Hibbing for brother David's high school graduation[123] later that month, he dressed entirely in black and slouched in the back row so he wouldn't be recognized. His *New Yorker* profile was about to ratchet his notoriety to a whole new level. His asking price per concert now ran from $2,000 to $3,000 and cumulative sales of his first three albums topped 400,000, making Dylan respectable as a recording artist even if he was not yet a household name.

That summer, his fame seldom allowed for introspection, even though he hid out much of the time at Grossman's Bearsville retreat. He powered his 500cc Triumph Tiger through the Catskill countryside, swam in Grossman's pool, and dabbled in home movies. He added Johnny Cash and Allen Ginsberg to the expanding list of early heroes he finally got to meet in the flesh.

Ginsberg's verse "was the first poetry that spoke to me in my own American language," said Bob. Already famous for *Howl*, Ginsberg

---

[122] He liked keeping tabs on his celebrity though, working up some wine courage before polling customers as they entered Folk City or the Gaslight: "Do you know who I am?" He kept track in a notebook and whenever the "yeas" outnumbered the "nays," he'd grin before weaving up on stage and announce to his pals, "Yup. I'm famous."

[123] He attended St. Olaf College near Minneapolis on a music scholarship.

was one of only two people Bob described at that time as "saintly."[124]
Ginsberg waxed paternal, adopting Dylan as a sort of on-again, off-again little brother, though he made no secret of a lust for Bob that rivaled that of Paul Clayton, the other gay poet in Dylan's life. Both would have gladly played Verlaine to Dylan's Rimbaud, if only Bob weren't so doggedly hetero.

Like Johnny Cash, Dylan remained addicted to chicks, liquor, and other mind-altering substances. When he finally met Cash at the Newport Folk Festival in July, Bob circled him once, bending slightly forward with a grin before reaching out his hand. Dylan confessed his deep admiration for Johnny's earliest Sun Records releases while Cash bubbled over about all things Dylan. Cash fell in love with *Freewheelin'* shortly after its release. Finding common ground in women, weed, and wine,[125] they bounced on Cash's motel bed like a pair of zoned-out teens.

"I thought he was the best hillbilly singer I'd ever heard, I really did," said Cash. "I thought, he's gotta be from Mississippi, the best writer that ever came outa Mississippi."

Cash performed "Don't Think Twice"[126] on the Newport stage[127] that summer along with "Folsom Prison Blues" and his career-making

---

[124] The other, equally holy in her own way, was Mrs. Sara Lownds, the future Mrs. Dylan.

[125] One year later, Cash was busted near Reno for public drunkenness and again five months after that in El Paso for trying to smuggle Dexedrine and Equinal across the Mexican border. He paid a $2,000 fine. When the U.S. Forest Service charged him $125,000 in 1967 for starting a fire in California's Los Padres National Forest, Cash sobered up, found Jesus, moved to Tennessee, and convinced the California courts to reduce his penalty to $82,000.

[126] Continuing the long tradition of folk theft, Cash borrowed the tune of "Don't Think Twice" for "Understand Your Man," a diatribe he recorded in Nov. 1963, excoriating his first wife, Vivian Cash.

[127] Finally recognizing that "Hammond's Folly" was anything but, Columbia forbade the nonprofit Newport Folk Foundation from releasing any of Bob's stage performances that year or any thereafter.

1956 hit, "I Walk the Line." Cash shared a doobie with Bob backstage where they found even more in common. Their budding relationship led to an exchange of letters that continued for a decade.

"I'd write on airplanes, and I'd use air-sick bags as envelopes," Cash recalled.

Bob also renewed his acquaintance with Mavis Staples at Newport. He and Joan Baez seemed to be *the* item of the season, but offstage Bob sowed his seeds wherever and whenever he could. Among others, his roving eye fell on the youngest member of Chicago's Staples Singers.

"He just *loved* him some Mavis," recalled Len Chandler.

Forty years hence, Mavis recalled Dylan as a curly-haired "cutey." She bore a striking resemblance to an ample if sloe-eyed Supreme, from her dimpled smile to her helmet hair. Acknowledging what would become an on-again, off-again affair for the next seven years, she said Dylan literally asked her father Roebuck "Pops" Staples for her hand while they stood together in a buffet line.

"Dylan didn't ask. He *told* Pops: 'Pops I want to marry Mavis,'" she recalled. "He said, 'Don't tell me. Tell Mavis!'"

Still a cultural taboo,[128] Dylan's taste for black women only increased after he read *One Hundred Dollar Misunderstanding*, a 1961 underground novel about a white college student who falls for a black hooker. Without Suze to anchor him, Bob became an equal opportunity philanderer. He met up with Bonnie Beecher again following Newport, inviting her to accompany him to Hawaii while he played a concert there. Back in New York, Joan remained none the wiser. As soon as he was back in town, they picked up their trysts in the sweltering basement apartment next door to the Hotel Earle. Ten

---

[128]   Until 1967, when Barack Obama was six years old, miscegenation remained a crime in most outhern states.

years later, Baez immortalized the dive as "that crummy hotel over Washington Square" in "Diamonds and Rust."

Baez was already rubbing him the wrong way. She publicly mocked the Beatles during concerts, sneering the "yeah, yeah, yeah" chorus of their second U.S. hit "She Loves You" between renditions of Dylan songs and her own dead serious murder ballads. Now well past the finger-pointin' phase of his songwriting, Bob was never as dismissive of the Fab Four. He recognized apotheosis when he saw it.

Dylan and Maymudes personally welcomed the lads from Liverpool on their second visit to the colonies that August. Rock journalist Al Aronowitz, another in Dylan's growing entourage, later maintained (dubiously) that the Beatles were cannabis virgins[129] until Victor turned them on. All things considered, Bob still preferred wine.

"Alcohol was always Bob's number one drug of choice," recalled Aronowitz.

As shrieking females twice filled the 16,000-seat Forest Hills Stadium later that week to see the Beatles, Bobby Zimmerman could not help but observe with some envy the wet-panty effect that he'd once hoped Elston Gunn might have on the bobbysoxers of Hibbing High.

On Halloween, Bob climaxed his concert year at Lincoln Center's Philharmonic Hall[130] playing to a far more subdued crowd. Joan was the one now making cameo appearances as his "mystery guest." They sang "You've Lost That Lovin' Feeling" backstage as a warm-up. She spiked his drinks with Valium "to help him relax."

---

129 Dylan misunderstood "I Wanna Hold Your Hand," according to George Harrison's wife, believing the Beatles were saying "I get high" instead of "I can't hide." Bob accommodated with a joint, chased by several bottles of wine. The boys from Liverpool got and remained high for the rest of their visit.

130 It was renamed Avery Fisher Hall in 1973 after the founder of Fisher Audio donated $10.5 million to the New York Philharmonic.

"She really introduced him when she brought him out in her concerts," recalled Fred Hellerman. "She was something; he was nobody. But after he was doing his *own* concerts, he wasn't as gracious. He'd stumble over her lyrics, upstage her, and then stopped bringing Joan out at all."

Just as Baez once did during her rivals' performances, Dylan now sang above her, stepped on harmonies and shifted the melody, mixing up lyrics at her expense. He played the gaffes for laughs, behaving as if it were Baez's fault.

They did a duet of the finger-pointin' "With God On Our Side" that Halloween night—the last time Bob would perform the protest anthem for the rest of the year. Prophetically, the one traditional song they did was "Silver Dagger":

> *All men are false, says my mother,*
> *They'll tell you wicked, lovin' lies.*
> *The very next evening, they'll court another,*
> *Leave you alone to pine and sigh.*

The remaining two numbers were kiss-off ballads written for Suze Rotolo—"It Ain't Me Babe"[131] and "Mama, You've Been on My Mind."[132] It doubtless never occurred to Joan that both might just as easily have been written for her.

---

[131]   Bob credited a John Jacob Niles song—one of the first he'd ever learned—as the source for the tune.

[132]   Bob wrote the song in the backseat of Baez's car during a ride from the airport to Carmel.

6
CHELSEA HOTEL

With the release of his fifth LP just a month away, Dylan got loaded on the evening of February 17, 1965, before appearing on ABC-TV's *The Les Crane Show*. Bob's target audience listened mainly to radio, but Albert Grossman gave his blessing for a rare televised appearance. After all, Les Crane represented a new, cutting-edge kind of talk-show personality, not an aging emcee like Jack Paar or Ed Sullivan.

A liberal San Francisco radio presence who made the transition to late-night TV, the 31-year-old Crane peppered rat-a-tat-tat banter with approved youth lingo: all things were "groovy," "swingin'," or "hip," not unlike his guest list. He nixed stiff vaudevillians and Catskill comics, leaving them to rival Johnny Carson whose far more successful *The Tonight Show* on NBC delivered low-key, white-bread entertainment.

Crane was taking TV in a swingin' new direction. He dared to get political, bringing on Martin Luther King Jr., Bobby Kennedy, Muhammad Ali, and even Allen Ginsberg, who extolled the forbidden virtues of marijuana. Crane's co-host, black comedian Nipsey Russell, added yet another layer of self-conscious cool to the show. He booked performers who were equally edgy for the time—musical guests like Judy Collins,[133] Jesse Fuller, "Papa" John Phillips, and the edgiest "get" of all, Bob Dylan.

---

[133] She sang "Hard Rain" during her appearance on the show.

For all his ersatz cool, Crane harbored anxious cynicism. He might dabble in drugs off the air, but stayed straight as a Standards-and-Practices official in front of the cameras. Thus, his dialogue with Dylan served as illustrative disconnect between manic and mellow, and Crane became a tense, clueless model for "Ballad of a Thin Man,"[134] according to Mr. Tambourine Man.

"Crane didn't know what to do with a little hippie," recalled Bruce Langhorne. "Bobby was quick, definitely on top of it."

The Crane-Dylan dialogue remains a remarkable snapshot of the gulf between those traveling America's homogenized highway and those headed for the nearest off-ramp. With Langhorne backing him, Dylan sang "It's All Over Now, Baby Blue" from the new album before settling onto the obligatory talk-show furniture next to actor Tommy Sands[135] and French-Italian cabaret vocalist Caterina Valente.

Bob dismissed Crane's inquiries about the commercial success of "Blowin' in the Wind," plugging instead "Subterranean Homesick Blues," the first single off *Bringing It All Back Home*. He waved at Odetta sitting in the audience before answering Crane about who or what inspired him. Hank Williams and Cole Porter, but only after Woody, of course. Dylan squinted, his eyes casing the soundstage before he lapsed into stoned, snickering babble about bright lights, the yellow carpet, the claustrophobic studio space.

---

[134] In 1986, Dylan maintained the song was a response to "something that hap-pened over in England in '63 or '64" when a reporter named Max Jones dogged him with vapid questions. "Yeah, there were a lot of Mister Joneses at that time," he told author Bill Flanagan. "There obviously must have been a tremendous amount of them for me to write *that* particular song. It wasn't just one person. It was like, 'Oh, man, here's the thousandth Mister Jones.'"

[135] Reflecting 40 years later on his own short-lived career, Sands (who was mar-ried at the time to Nancy Sinatra) recalled that evening as a wake-up call that came too late for him and other Elvis clones. Bob "was the vanguard of it all . . . his whole trip was just right for the time."

"Apparently it looks bigger on the television than it does here in the studio," Crane conceded. "But it's a pretty big studio. We have one of the largest studio audiences of any (on) television."

Then Crane turned his questioning to Bob's nouveaux riches. Dylan ticked off a shopping list. He planned to buy boots, bananas, fruit, pears . . .

"Bought some very fancy ashtrays the other day," he deadpanned.

Bob also wanted a Maserati. Invoking the ghost of James Dean, Crane warned, "I don't want *you* riding around in any hot sports cars."

Chastened, Dylan promised to buy a three-wheeled Messerschmitt instead. He continued to mock Crane's inanities with monosyllables or one-liners—respectfully at first, but with increasing *glissendorf,* until out of desperation Crane asked Bob to dig his groovy new wardrobe.

> **Crane:** . . . I put on these duds for *you* tonight.
> **Dylan:** You did?
> **Crane:** In a tribute to you. And you're gonna sit there and put me on, right?
> **Dylan:** No, I'm not putting you on. Everybody always thinks that.
> **Crane:** Everybody always thinks you're putting them . . .
> **Dylan:** Yeah, yeah, it's weird, weird. That's a nice tie, though.
>
> *Crane removed his tie and handed it to Dylan.*
> **Crane:** Swing! Love!

Collapsing into laughter at the memory, Bruce Langhorne recalled, "Bobby didn't miss a beat! He takes the tie, points at Crane's feet, and says, 'I like your shoes!'"

Les Crane didn't give his boots away. It wouldn't have helped anyway. His talk show didn't survive the season. He faded fast, first from television and finally from showbiz altogether.[136]

But Dylan stole the show. His valedictory performance that night raised his profile again, this time with a national network audience. Switching instantly from clown to Cassandra, an electrified Dylan ended the program with the menacing message of "It's Alright, Ma" snarled into living rooms across America. Moments earlier, he'd been jiving Crane about portraying his own mother in a western horror movie written by Allen Ginsberg.[137] With the dire fulminations of "It's Alright, Ma," Dylan delivered very different tidings.

All Dylan's wealth that Les Crane insisted on discussing had no meaning for Bob. Money didn't talk; it swore. Advertisers that sponsored Crane's show were a con. Crane himself was nothing more than something in which he invested.

But that was alright, sang Bob. The thousands of baby boomers who got their first dose of Dylan that night understood. They had nothing to live up to.

■■ ■■ ■■

With the jarring, semi-electric *Bringing It All Back Home*, Bob left Woody in the Dust Bowl. From its symbol-laden cover to the hypnotic hymnal inside, the album supplied catch phrases for a generation and became a subliminal blueprint for all the tumult that

---

[136] Crane made one final showbiz splash with the 1971 hit "Desiderata" for which he won a Grammy for best spoken word recording. He finished out his career as a software and computer game executive. Crane died in 2008.

[137] With utter sincerity, Tommy Sands mistakenly encouraged Bob by observing: "I think as big and as successful as Bob Dylan is as a singer and writer of folksongs I think that he has a tremendous future as an actor."

followed. Whatever had sparked Dylan's expansive poetry after he'd wandered into the Café Wha? four years earlier now reached critical mass.

He recorded *Bringing It All Back Home* in 16 hours, over three January days. The album turned out to be the first of a mid-60s trilogy that would shift much of pop music from the mundane to the surreal. Were he never to make another record, Dylan could have retired to Carl Sandburg's Carolina goat farm and lived off his laurels and royalties for the rest of his life.

But his nerves were lit at the beginning of 1965, and two more masterworks—*Highway 61 Revisited* and *Blonde on Blonde*—followed in quick succession, dazzling elders and acolytes alike. With *Bringing It All Back Home,* the simple melodrama of black hats versus white that premised previous Dylan broadsides dissolved into the kind of layered nightmare vision Brecht and Kurt Weil staged with *The Threepenny Opera.*

Bob's new verbal landscape catapulted him overnight from musical realism to symbolic expression, beginning with "Subterranean Homesick Blues."[138] Introducing machine-gun rap to America a half dozen years before Tupac or Snoop Dogg were born, Dylan's first bona fide hit single peaked at 39 on the *Billboard* Top 40. The album it fronted rose to No. 6, higher than any previous Dylan effort. The thought dreams he put on vinyl sprang from pot and personal experience, but they resonated with a growing audience eager to find hidden meaning behind every word.

"It didn't matter that Dylan's lyrics, for example, were celebrations of strictly private experience," observed Todd Gitlin. "By

---

[138] At Allen Ginsberg's suggestion, Dylan flashed placards synchronizing rhymes from the song during the opening sequence of *Dont Look Back*, thus getting himself credited with creating the world's first music video 15 years before MTV hit the airwaves.

playing the music together, we transformed it into a celebration of our own collective intimacy, love, hilarity."

Thus, "Maggie's Farm" could be Bob's declaration of independence from his folkie past, when he'd played minstrel during the summer of '62 on Silas Magee's Mississippi farm; or it could be an anthem aimed at Secretary of Defense Robert McNamara and the escalating "police action" in Vietnam; or it could be a simple amplified rocker built on the spare thematic architecture of "Down on Penny's Farm," hijacked from Volume Two of the *Anthology of American Folk Music*. It could be all or none of the above, depending on who heard it. Dylan's rollicking rhymes meant many things to many listeners, the sure sign of a wordsmith who has hit his stride.

"You can't compromise very much at all and be an artist," observed Bob Neuwirth, a kindred spirit who crossed Dylan's path early as one of Jack Elliott's backup crew and remained Bob's alter ego (some said "evil twin"[139]) off and on over the next 20 years. "Bob has earned my respect that way. I don't think he's a great poet, but he knows how to have so much fun with words. He loves words! He loves the little permutations and the twistings and the playing. He instinctively falls into alliteration and onomatopoeia."

Even his love songs became cryptic. *Bringing It All Back Home* contained no paeans to North Country girls or restless farewells from the dark side of the road. Like Bob himself, his women were now artists who didn't look back. He might credit Hank Williams and Cole Porter on late-night TV, but his real muse was much harder to pin down. Once again, Dylan had moved on from confessional balladry to something far more ambiguous. "Love Minus Zero/No

---

139   "He and Neuwirth held court, mainly at the Kettle of Fish, the bar above the Gaslight, and pronounced sentence and declared truth to whoever approached them," recalled Suze. "It was depressing to see people bow and scrape to the reigning king and his jester."

Limit" resonated less with Tin Pan Alley than it did apocalyptic visions straight out of the Book of Daniel, where statues crumble into one another and faith is "true, like ice, like fire."

In the spring of '65, Dylan commanded $5,000 a concert, appearing regularly with Joan Baez on the college circuit. She still wore an Egyptian ring[140] he'd given her the previous summer, but she'd lost much of her Folk Queen sparkle. Amphetamine and alcohol tortured Bob's attention span, slowly strangling their relationship.

"I think Bobby comes closer to being psychotic than neurotic," said Baez. "I just say that because of the couple times that he got drunk and turned against friends—just turned on them—and I couldn't believe it."

When he headed to London in April for a series of concerts in the U.K., Joan tagged along, but he relegated her to a corner of his hotel suite. He never invited her to the stage.

"Seemingly Baez had found someone more ambitious and calculating, more cold-hearted than she was," recalled former Journeyman Dick Weisman. "She was transformed from a guest artist to a mere member of Dylan's entourage."

Ten years would pass before Baez appeared on stage again with Dylan. As filmmaker Donn Pennebaker famously chronicled in *Dont Look Back,* the King of Folk had morphed into the King of Pop and appeared not to care less. Comfortable as a solo act, he regressed to predatory *glissendorf* with the sycophantic support of Maymudes, Neuwirth, and the rest of his mocking posse.

Hysterical British nymphets greeted him at Heathrow, likely taking their cues from *A Hard Day's Night.* Bob took his from Elvis. He took full advantage of femme fans, attempting to bed the best of the

---

[140] The jacket and cuff links he wore on the cover of *Bringing It All Back Home* were gifts from Joan and got a bittersweet mention in her own confessional ballad about their breakup, "Diamonds and Rust."

flock, including a pregnant young canary name Marianne Faithfull. Just 17 and days away from marrying British artist John Dunbar, Dylan propositioned her: a song written exclusively for Faithfull in exchange for her virtue.

"I didn't go to bed with him, and he got cross," she recalled. "There went whatever he was writing. He tore it up in front of me."

As a predictor of future philandering, the Faithfull incident brimmed with Bob hubris. From the moment he set foot on British soil, Fleet Street hailed him as America's answer to the Beatles. Released the previous fall, *A Hard Day's Night* had been filmed in black and white, but its quasi-documentary style was carefully scripted, down to the staged teen frenzy. Not so with *Dont Look Back*. Like the rock star he'd wanted to be since Elston Gunn first kicked a piano, Bob learned what it was really like to see London from behind smoked limo windows while fans chased him from stage door to the Savoy. The reality of hiding out in hotel rooms under assumed names got old fast. Freewheelin' Bob took to signing autographs "The Phantom" if he signed them at all. Instead of reacting to the furor with compassion or modesty, the adulation only fueled the shitty side of Bob's dual nature.

Albert Grossman helped produce *Dont Look Back* and gave Pennebaker full range to capture forever the backstage pettiness of a bored, buzzed, pampered wunderkind. Dylan did not disappoint. He delighted in skewering friends and fellow musicians as well as fans and unsuspecting journalists. He showed as little mercy to Baez or Bob's adoring 18-year-old Scottish folk clone Donovan Leitch as he did some clueless deejay demanding to know how it felt to be an idol. Dylan sneered and sniped at critics and hangers-on with equal savagery.

Among others, Dylan seduced Donovan's 16-year-old girlfriend, Dana Gillespie. Leitch evened the score in his 2007 memoir, *The*

Hurdy-Gurdy Man, recalling Bob as "quite small and slight of frame, a very pretty young man with bad teeth and curiously solid hands. . . . Definitely the thinking girl's crumpet."

At one point, just before taking the stage, a petulant Bob turned to Neuwirth in *Dont Look Back* and pouted, "I don't feel like singing." Were it not for Neuwirth or Maymudes carefully coaxing him back into the spotlight, he'd have simply turned his back on 20,000 paying customers and bolted out the backdoor.

But he stiffed no ticket holder on that trip. As can be heard in the bootleg recordings that emerged several years later, Dylan masterfully mixed acoustic guitar with amplified backup, reflecting the same in-studio juggling act he'd perfected on *Bringing It All Back Home*. By the time he returned to New York early in June, just after his 24th birthday, he'd earned a rock star's right to wear prescription Ray-Bans after dark. He was a genuine idol, his days of happy Greenwich anonymity gone forever.

:: :: ::

"What I think happened to Dylan is this," said Paul Williams, perhaps the world's preeminent Dylanologist.[141] "He came to New York an ambitious kid, made the scene, wrote some songs, made some records, became famous, kept on going and did a whole lot of great work and got so famous so fast with so many expectations from all sides that finally it blew up in his face, and through some kind of saving grace there was a woman then to save him, protect him, allow him to go on with his life."

---

[141]   In addition to founding *Crawdaddy* magazine and writing several other books of rock 'n' roll criticism, Williams authored five successive volumes painstakingly tracing Dylan's career as a performance artist, concert by concert, from Hibbing High through the early years of the twenty-first century.

Sara Lowndes was a model, one-time Playboy Club hostess, and well-heeled trophy wife before she met Dylan. Married to Hans Lowndes, a fashion photographer twice her age, she bore him a daughter, Maria, in October 1961, ten months after Dylan arrived in New York. Shortly thereafter, she quit her modeling career and took a job with Time-Life films.

Like Bob, Shirley Noznisky changed her name when she came to New York. Hans insisted on Sara[142] when she made the rounds of Manhattan's modeling agencies. Born in Delaware in 1939 to a junk dealer father and a mother who sold dry goods, she too descended from Eastern European Jews. On the basis of her good looks and Lowndes's reputation as a commercial photographer, Sara landed on the client list of the prestigious Ford Agency, and the Lowndes family assumed an upper-middle-class lifestyle on the fashionable East Side. They lived in a 60th Street town house, four blocks from Albert Grossman's office. Before she left Hans, Sara tooled around Midtown in an MG, slumming on occasion in the Village. After the split, she and Maria moved into an apartment on MacDougal Street.

Albert Grossman's girlfriend Sally Anne Buehler befriended Sara while waiting tables at the Village club where she and Albert met. Both women shared a Jewish American princess's sense of privilege long before Sally introduced Sara to Bob.

"I remember the first time Bobby was ever on television, I watched the program with Sara," Sally recalled. "I probably shouldn't say this, but she thought we were going to watch Bobby Darin!"

Soon thereafter, Albert proposed and Sally moved into his new apartment in Gramercy Park, assuming regal control as if she'd never groveled for tips or wiped a counter clean. Grossman cast her

---

[142] Also Bob's grandmother Florence Stone's middle name and the wife of Abraham in the Old Testament.

as the dark-haired siren in the red dress lounging in the background of the *Bringing It All Back Home* album cover. She was 13 years his junior, but every bit as shrewd as her fiancé.

"Upward mobility and waiting tables in the Village were synonymous in those days," she said.

"Grossman had a very fancy wedding up in Woodstock, but I didn't get the feeling theirs was a real love affair," recalled Milt Okun. He saw chunky Al merely buying himself some svelte brunette arm candy.

The match between Bob and Sara, on the other hand, tingled with forbidden passion. Sara was married when they first met. Whether Bob helped her out of a jam remains as ambiguous today as the fate of her magazine husband. Once Bob moved in, Hans vanished. Only the trajectory of the affair during those first few months remains clear.

They were both on the guest list at the Grossmans' lavish Bearsville wedding on November 14, 1964, but Joan Baez was not. While Albert and Sally honeymooned in Europe, Bob and Sara holed up in their Gramercy Park apartment.

Shortly after the Grossmans returned, Bob gave up the Fourth Street apartment he shared with Suze and moved into Room 211 at the Chelsea Hotel. There he remained off and on over the next year, passing the ghosts of Dylan Thomas and Brendan Behan in the hallway. The balcony in Bob's room overlooked the lobby entrance, allowing him to step out for a smoke and a quick survey of the flotsam and jetsam cruising the lower West Side, some of whom inevitably found their way into Dylan's poetry.

"He lived there very quietly," recalled Stanley Bard, whose family owned and operated the famous fleabag on West 23rd Street for three generations. "Dylan became one of our most famous guests."

Bob and Sara's chemistry accelerated during the first half of '65. In her role as assistant to Time-Life photo editor Robert Drew, Sara recommended documentarian Donn Pennebaker's cinéma vérité style to Dylan and Grossman. Sara shared Dylan's fascination with film, demonstrating by example how a model makes the camera lens work for, not against, you. It was okay to wear Coke-bottle bottoms perched on the bridge of one's nose in private, for example, but never let a paparazzo capture a nearsighted moment.

Bob arranged for Sara and her three-year-old daughter to move in with him. Later that spring, they conceived their first child at the Chelsea. He claimed to have spent several sleepless nights banging out "Sad Eyed Lady of the Lowlands" on his Remington. With cadences straight out of the *Song of Solomon*, his elegiac tribute to the woman "with eyes like smoke" would eventually take up an entire side of *Blonde on Blonde*. Ten years hence, he'd romanticize "Sara" again on *Desire*:

> *I'd taken the cure and just gotten through*
> *Stayin' up for days in the Chelsea Hotel*
> *Writin' 'Sad-Eyed Lady of the Lowlands' for you . . .*

"Bullshit," wrote pop critic Lester Bangs in a scathing review of *Desire*. "I have it on pretty good authority that Dylan wrote 'Sad-Eyed Lady,' as well as about half the rest of *Blonde on Blonde*, wired out of his skull . . ."

Suze knew Sara briefly when she was living as a single mom on MacDougal Street. She felt sorry for her. "I just knew she was a Scorpio and she was in for it. I'm a Scorpio and he's a Gemini, and they don't mix."

Joan on the other hand didn't met Sara until the day she quit Bob's British concert tour, but any sympathy she felt for the future Mrs. Dylan didn't register until later. Shortly before the tour ended, Bob spurned Baez for the final time. Sara flew to England to join Bob and the Grossmans for a short vacation in Portugal. Bob didn't bother to tell Baez, who still believed they had one last chance as a couple.

"I mean, I wanted to tell him that I loved him, that I cared for him, that it didn't matter what was going on and everything, and I was glad Sara was there because she seemed to care for him you know, somebody to take care of him," Joan later confessed to Anthony Scaduto. "And I bought him a shirt and went to the door and I'd never met her but I guess that's who came to the door. And she took it and I never heard anything after that. That was the closest I got to seeing him. And then I left England."

▪▪ ▪▪ ▪▪

On June 15, Dylan and a five-piece band entered Columbia's Studio A in Midtown Manhattan, did 15 takes of an ex-lover's raging revenge fantasy, and changed the course of pop music.

"I never thought of it as a song until one day I was at the piano and on the paper it was singing, 'How does it feel?' in slow motion," Dylan explaining the following year. "It was like swimming in lava. You see your victim swimming in lava. Hanging by their arms from a birch tree. Skipping, kicking the tree, hitting a nail with your foot. Seeing someone in the pain they were bound to meet up with."

After their return from Portugal, he and Sara rented a Catskills cabin from Peter Yarrow's mother. There, Bob spewed somewhere between 6 and 20 pages of angry verbiage he later called "vomit," struggling to locate a song. He banged out a tune in G sharp on an old upright piano and by the time he and his new lady love drove back to New York City, he'd pieced together "Like a Rolling Stone."

No less a musical authority than Phil Spector[143] correctly noted the chord progression belonged to Richie Valens's "La Bamba," but the acid lyrics were pure Dylan.

It's impossible to overstate the impact of that long (6 minutes, 13 seconds), dense (406 words), and ambiguous (chrome horse . . . mystery tramp . . . Napoleon-in-rags . . .) anthem. "Like a Rolling Stone" [144] generated whole books dissecting its meaning. Dylanologists tried in vain to pinpoint its target (Joan? Suze? Echo? Dylan himself?).

And yet the angry screed that *Rolling Stone* magazine declared the No. 1 rocker of all time never even made it to the top of the *Billboard* 100. That honor went to one-hit wonder Barry McGuire and his "Eve of Destruction," which pandered to the protesting tastes of American youth in the summer of '65. At 299 words growled over 3 minutes and 37 seconds, "Eve of Destruction"[145] was explicit, obvious, and on-the-nose—the polar opposite of the No. 2 *Billboard* hit, but far better suited to the soundtrack of the summer of the Watts riots,[146] when troop strength doubled in Vietnam, and more boys came home in body bags than at any time since World War II.

Pop music still featured just as much drivel as drive. While the Beatles and Bob gained traction, the bestselling single for the year

---

[143] Before he became a felon, the Wall-of-Sound genius once approached Dylan about doing an opera together.

[144] Most assumed the title came from Hank Williams' "Lost Highway":

I'm a rolling stone, alone and lost

For a life of sin I've paid the cost . . .

[145] Songwriter P. F. Sloan (born Phillip Schlein) singled out Bob as his only peer who took him seriously. "Dylan recognized that I was a budding talent." He also predicted the music business would eat him alive and after some success (he also wrote "Secret Agent Man" and "From a Distance"), Sloan did fade from view.

[146] Some L.A. radio stations banned the song following the riots.

was "Wooly Bully" from Sam the Sham and the Pharaohs. Charting at 41, "Like a Rolling Stone" didn't even break *Billboard*'s top 40.

The folk revival from which Dylan sprang all but died that summer. Peter, Paul and Mary's popularity waned while the Kingston Trio was ancient history. The stage was set at Newport for Bob's nagging, perennial question: How does it *feel?*

"If you want to find out anything that's happening now, you have to listen to the music," said Dylan. "I don't mean the words, although 'Eve of Destruction' will tell you something about it. The words are not really gonna tell it, not really. You gotta listen to the Staples Singers, Smokey and the Miracles, Martha and the Vandellas. That's scary to a lot of people. It's sex that's involved.[147] It's not hidden. It's real. You can overdo it. It's not only sex; it's a whole beautiful feeling."

What Dylan *felt* was compulsion to abandon the past and embrace the future—a dicey proposition in a culture where the present dominates and change is almost always met with scorn. With "Like a Rolling Stone" about to explode across the AM radio dial, Bob's 20-minute electrified set at Newport late in July so shocked its audience that the performance instantly took on mythical status. As with the Beatles at Shea Stadium or the Rolling Stones at Altamont, thousands upon thousands would later swear they'd been there, just as millions would claim four years hence to have trekked to Bethel, New York, for the Woodstock Music & Arts Festival.

---

[147] Bob delivered no better illustration of the nonsensical seminal underpinnings of his poetry than "Sitting on a Barbed Wire Fence," an outtake from the *Highway 61* recording sessions that wasn't released until 26 years later on *The Bootleg Series Vol. 1–3*:

> Well this woman I've got, she's filling me with her drive
> Yes this woman I've got she's thrilling me with her hive
> She's calling me Stan or else she's calling me Mr. Clive

While critics would dwell for decades on Dylan electrified performance, his real break with the past was best illustrated by the
skirmish that preceded it. Fred Hellerman and "Spider" John Koerner
were among those who actually did witness Bob's heresy, but more
than a generation later both men recalled the fistfight between Alan
Lomax and Albert Grossman better than they did Dylan "going
electric."

"Here are these two stiff middle-aged white guys, pounding the
crap out of each other, rolling around in the dirt," recalled Koerner,
chuckling at the memory.

"Lomax was an anti-Semite," declared Hellerman. "He'd always
hated Grossman."

As one of Newport's founders, Grossman held elder statesman
status even after he quit the board of directors, took up cannabis,
grew a ponytail, and began dressing like "a freaked-out Benjamin
Franklin," according to Festival creator George Wein. Alan Lomax,
on the other hand, remained a revered folk figure, having captured
much of America's musical past on tape in his capacity as archivist-
in-chief for the Library of Congress.

Like John Hammond, Lomax was an unrepentant socialist who
descended from privilege. His father ran the folklore department at
the University of Texas, inspiring Lomax to take up the tape recorder
after graduating from Harvard in 1931. For the next 30 years, Lomax
crisscrossed the nation, capturing all manner of blues, sea shanty,
field holler, gospel choir, and murder ballad, plucked from a banjo
on the back porch or moaned low and mean from inside prison
walls. Like 12-string Leadbelly, the lutist John Jacob Niles, Jean
Ritchie and her dulcimer, and even fingerpicking Woody Guthrie,
Lomax remained loyal to an acoustic past he'd nurtured and sustained for a generation. In *Chronicles,* Dylan himself credited

Lomax with preserving much of the music on which Bob based his own compositions.

But Albert Grossman represented the electronic future. Thus, when he put the amplified Paul Butterfield Blues Band on stage just ahead of Dylan,[148] Lomax finally freaked. He ordered a lowering of the decibel level but Grossman objected. Watching from behind a chain-link fence several yards away, Koerner couldn't hear the shouting match, but he saw the slugfest escalate.

"I thought they were gonna kill each other," he said.

To Koerner, Dylan's cacophony later in the program was anticlimactic. The disaffected purists who hissed and booed at the ear-splitting opening blast of "Maggie's Farm" showed the same fury as the progressive crowd who groused at Bob's drunken blather before the National Emergency Civil Liberties Committee two years earlier. The effect on Dylan was the same.

"As soon as he came on, it was obvious he was stoned," recalled Irish folkie Liam Clancy.

Like Elston Gunn channeling Little Richard at the Hibbing High Jacket Jamboree, Dylan heard only the decibels that erupted from the stage. Pete Seeger[149] worried that his father's hearing aid would blow while New Lost City Rambler John Cohen's infant daughter had a different reaction: constipated from birth, Dylan moved her bowels.

Whether or not a sober Bob would have heeded the jeering crowd remains forever in doubt. When he unloaded "Like a Rolling Stone," he'd already been branded a traitor to the chaste folk tradition. Electric guitar embroidered parts of *Another Side of Bob Dylan* and occupied a whole side of *Bringing It All Back Home* but not like this. The

---

[148] Bob recruited three Butterfield sidemen including guitarist Mike Bloomfield for his backup that day.

[149] Though he was concerned about the screech of feedback, the oft-told tale that Seeger took an axe to the sound system cables is apocryphal.

in-your-face "Once upon a time . . ." overture of what would become Bob's signature song stunned the audience and led to a yearlong war among critics and fans alike at every concert stop, from Stockholm to Sydney. Even Robert Shelton panned Bob's performance.

"He was accused of selling out," wrote rock historian Gene Santoro, "and yet, he personified the folk revival's longing for a popular hero who would forge a new sound and, incidentally, a new sense of community."

Most important of all from Grossman's point of view, the Newport controversy forged new profit margins. The festival that summer earned $80,000 for the nonprofit Newport Folk Foundation. One year later, after Grossman pulled Dylan, Butterfield, and the rest of his clients from the lineup, the festival lost $15,000[150] even as Dylan ascended the *Billboard* charts with his musical recommendation that everybody get stoned.

Following his electrified onslaught at Newport, Dylan did return to the stage for an acoustic encore as a farewell gesture to his Lomax past. Armed only with harmonica and a Gibson lent to him by Johnny Cash, he mollified the crowd with a set that included "It's All Over Now, Baby Blue." And then he walked offstage and into the future.

Four days later he returned to Studio A to lay down the rest of his electrified emancipation declaration.

⋮⋮ ⋮⋮ ⋮⋮

Highway 61 Revisited took nearly twice as long to produce as *Bringing It All Back Home,* in part because Dylan started after dark and worked through the night, devoting much of his studio time to

---

[150] Apparently over their trauma by then, Festival goers did not boo Chuck Berry, Howlin' Wolf, or any of the other amplified acts at Newport '66.

"chucklefucking"—an *expression d'art* that session guitar maestro Mike Bloomfield defined as "people stepping on each other's dicks until it came out right."

Frequently aided by weed and amphetamine, words sped to him from out of nowhere. Whether under the influence or soberly setting one phrase in front of another, Dylan had returned to the top of his serendipitous game with *Highway 61 Revisited*. Celebrated British poet Philip Larkin publicly puzzled over the lyrics years later, wondering whether Dylan was being mysterious or just half-baked. Increasingly, Bob's songs defied interpretation, confounding those who tried. In their final form, such nonsensical working titles as "Phantom Engineer Cloudy," "Lunatic Princess No. 3," and "Black Dalli Rue" became, respectively, "It Takes a Lot to Laugh, It Take a Train to Cry," "From a Buick 6," and "Positively Fourth Street."[151] His self-explanatory song "Juarez" might reflect a psychedelic trip through the streets of a border town, but by the time the public heard it, the oddly affecting ballad had become "Just Like Tom Thumb's Blues."[152]

In an extended saga like "Desolation Row," he incorporated as much Fellini, Bergman, and Godard as he did Woody Guthrie. Session keyboardist Al Kooper later claimed the surreal imagery in Dylan's epic dirge came from watching the daily circus traipse up and down 8th Avenue—New York City's theater of the absurd as witnessed from his second-floor balcony at the Chelsea Hotel. According to Dylan's own suspect testimony, Shakespeare, T. S. Eliot,[153] Ma Rainey, Bette Davis—all those characters real and

---

[151] Some critics later proclaimed "Tombstone Blues" the first punk rocker.

[152] Bob Neuwirth maintained he came up with the opening line.

[153] While Bob merely has him fighting Ezra Pound in the captain's tower, Eliot's "The Wasteland" was believed by some critics to have been the model for "Desolation Row."

imagined that he'd absorbed during his post-Dinkytown education, spilled out on paper in a single cab ride from Soho to Studio A.

Whether intended or not, for many of his eager young followers "Desolation Row" became Dylan's bitter reply to President Lyndon Johnson's[154] disingenuous State of the Union address: everything was *not* great in the Great Society. When LBJ parroted the rallying cry of the civil rights movement, "We shall overcome" spilled hollow from his tongue.

"There's an old saying," said Bob. "If you want to defeat your enemy, sing his song."

Forty years after the fact, Dylan told *Los Angeles Times* pop music critic Bob Hilburn he had no idea where "Desolation Row" came from. All he was trying to do at the time was match words to meter.

"It's like a ghost is writing a song like that," he said.

For the first time since recording his eponymous debut album, Dylan again switched producers, dumping laid-back Tom Wilson in favor of a more worshipful Columbia staffer and John Hammond protégé named Bob Johnston. Johnston would later declare in all seriousness that Dylan was nothing less than "the only prophet we've had since Jesus."

Clearly, Dylan knew his Bible. All that rote memorization that led to his off-key bar mitzvah finally paid off in the flip opening stanza of "Highway 61" which summarized the 22nd Chapter of Genesis in just 60 words. More and more, he salted his sound with timeless literary reference and biblical allusion, even as he turned his back completely on politics. He'd been shifting gears for nearly a year, but fans still idolized the protest singer, not a Benzedrine-inspired dream meister pushing personal boundaries.

---

[154] Despite his claim that he did not want Barry Goldwater moving next door and marrying his daughter, Dylan declared his preference for the Arizona Republican because he reminded him of Tom Mix.

"I tell you, I'm never going to have anything to do with any political organization again in my life," Dylan affirmed in the months leading up to *Highway 61 Revisited*. He refused all who attempted to get him to commit to causes—most notably, Vietnam.

When his Village cronies joined in solidarity late that summer to play a benefit "Sing-in for Peace" at Carnegie Hall, Dylan's absence glared. Virtually everyone who'd had a hand in turning Bobby Zimmerman into Bob Dylan lent their name to the program, including John Hammond, Robert Shelton, Alan Lomax, and a host of talent, from Pete Seeger to Joan Baez. But neither Dylan nor any of Grossman's other clients participated. Fellow folkies like Phil Ochs and Tom Paxton might denounce Dylan's new sound as "folk rot,"[155] but Bob henceforth refused to stage any sing-ins unless the audience paid up front. He answered former colleagues' criticism with "Positively Fourth Street,"[156] his follow-up to "Like a Rolling Stone": they had some nerve, calling themselves friends.

"I guess they felt he was the spokesman for these things and he betrayed them," observed Suze. "But the music goes on. You can't stay in one spot."

On August 28, Dylan and his new backup band kicked off the *Highway 61* tour on the same Forest Hills stage where the Beatles played just one year earlier to sold-out, screaming fans. Suze sat in the audience, as stunned at her ex's showmanship as she was at his renewed musicality. As with *Bringing It All Back Home* and his Newport performance, he played half the set acoustic, the other half ear-splitting rock.

Mike Bloomfield and drummer Sam Lay dropped from Bob's ensemble at the end of the Studio A all-nighters, but were ably replaced

---

[155] Paul Simon called Dylan's poetry "punk and old hat," adding "I think it's just rehashed Ginsberg."

[156] Bob's favorite version of the song was recorded by Johnny Rivers.

on stage during the 33-city autumn tour by a pair of Canadian bar band veterans who'd been scratching out a living backing rotund American rocker Ronnie Hawkins. Levon Helm took over drums while Robbie Robertson played lead guitar. A week later at the Hollywood Bowl, the remaining members of Hawkins's Hawks—Richard Manuel, Rick Danko, and Garth Hudson—replaced the departing bassist Harvey Brooks and Al Kooper, who'd had enough of braying arena crowds Kooper contemptuously labeled "lemmings."

When journalists Nora Ephron and Susan Edmiston asked a few weeks later how he felt about being booed at Forest Hills, Dylan surprised them with an enthusiastic grin.

"I thought it was great, I really did," he said. "If I said anything else I'd be a liar."

"And at the Newport Folk Festival?" they asked.

"That was different," Bob replied, recalling the old guard's attempts to muzzle him. "They didn't like what I was going to play and they twisted the sound on me before I began."

The ring of the cash register drowned out the rude lemmings who still came, still paid full admission, and still bought his records. Dylan and Grossman invested $30,000 in a custom sound system they trucked from venue to venue. At the time, only Bob and his manager seemed to appreciate the irony of his chart-topping album and hit singles juxtaposed against the jeering that greeted him at every stop.

Clad in a flashy red-and-blue "Op Art" long-sleeve shirt, Navy blazer, and pointed high-heeled boots, Dylan met with Ephron and Edmiston in Grossman's Midtown office between concerts and got serious for a change. Despite the neon duds, he resembled "an underfed angel with a nose from the land of the Chosen People." His *Highway 61* album cover pose—slouching on the steps outside Grossman's Gramercy Park apartment wearing a satin blue long sleeve over a Triumph Motorcycle T-shirt[157]—gave way to a gentler, more pensive Bob.

"The thing that struck me was how delicate, even fragile, he looked," Edmiston recalled.

Despite an Elston Gunn pompadour coiffed into "fine spun soft froth," all trace of the little boy lost of his *Freewheelin'* period had vanished. Edmiston and Ephron came prepared to parry words with a *fashionista* put-on artist, but left impressed with his cool logic and frank language. That did not mean he'd dispensed entirely with *glissendorf*. Like many a Dylan fan, Ephron assumed the chastised marquee character of "Queen Jane Approximately" must be Joan Baez, but with his tongue planted firmly in cheek, Dylan corrected her: "Queen Jane is a man."

Nearly six months after his final split with Baez, reporters still inquired about their romance, as did *Chicago Daily News* reporter Joseph Haas. A few weeks after Dylan's interview with Ephron and Edmiston, he asked if they were still together.

"Oh, man, no," insisted Bob. "That was a long time ago."

"On her latest album, about half of her songs are Dylan songs," Haas persisted.

"Heaven help her," said Bob.

■ ■ ■

Outside of the studio and away from the media, prophet Bob poured profit into what would become a lifelong vanishing act.

"I need the money to employ people," he told Robert Shelton. "It all works hand in hand. If I had no money, I could walk invisible.

---

[157] Bob Neuwirth also achieved some measure of immortality, if only from the waist down, as the guy in the orange striped shirt holding a Nikon who stands behind Dylan.

But it costs me money now to be able to walk invisible. That's the only reason I need the money. I don't need the money to buy clothes or nothing . . ."

By year's end, U.S. sales of *Highway 61 Revisited* approached 350,000 copies. His Columbia deal guaranteed a 5 percent royalty, but the company had only been paying 4 percent on each album because of a contract snafu.[158] In addition to what he regarded as a relatively paltry percentage, Bob felt shortchanged by the recording industry's notoriously shady accounting practices and complained often to Grossman that other artists paid more to record his songs than Bob earned recording them himself. For the first six months of 1965, Dylan's royalties exceeded those of Richard Rodgers, Lorenz Hart, Oscar Hammerstein, George Gershwin, and Cole Porter combined.

"Even the record company figures won't be right," he said. "Nobody's going to be straight with you because nobody wants the information out."

To keep tabs on cash flow, he and Grossman created Dwarf Music to replace his expiring Witmark Publishing deal. Grossman neglected to tell Dylan that Dwarf was a 50-50 deal. Half the proceeds of the 237 songs he'd written for Witmark would go to Grossman forever.

His Ashes and Sand personal services corporation looked after concert cash, while Dylan watched his nickels and dimes as carefully as he did back in the days when he mooched cherry pie off of Echo and made Suze pay for her own meals. One of his few luxuries—and part of his new vanishing act—was limos.

"When I came back from England last time, I didn't buy a chauffeur, but I sure rented one," he said. "I make no bones about it."

---

[158] Columbia left out a standard escalator clause that would automatically bump his percentage from 4 to 5 percent after the first album. While the company agreed to pay the difference, doing so in a single tax year would have meant that the IRS would get most of the money.

For his extended *Highway 61* tour, Grossman leased him a two-engine 13-seat Lockheed Lodestar in which Bob and his entourage crisscrossed the U.S. quickly and quietly, far from the eyes of fans.

Meanwhile back in New York, Bob bought a Midtown town house about ten blocks north of his manager's Gramercy apartment while escrow closed on two parcels in Byrdcliffe, the hilltop Woodstock arts colony near Grossman's Bearsville spread. Dylan created Davasee Corporation as the repository for an 11-room manse on Camelot Road called Hi Lo Ha and the wooded acreage surrounding it. His personal privacy and that of his new family became *the* priority. During the same November week he spoke with the *Daily News*'s Joseph Haas, he married a very pregnant Sara Lowndes in a secret ceremony[159] in Mineola. Two months later, she bore him his first son, Jesse, but he mentioned none of this during interviews.[160]

Haas: "Do you ever hope to settle down to a normal life, get married, have kids?"

Dylan: "I don't hope to be like anybody. Getting married, having a bunch of kids, I have no hopes for it. If it happens, it happens. Whatever my hopes, it never turns out. I don't think anybody's a prophet."

Haas: "You sound quite pessimistic about everything."

Dylan: "No, not pessimistic. I don't think things can turn out, that's all, and I've accepted it. It doesn't matter to me. It's not pessimism, just a sort of sadness, sort of like having no hopes."

---

[159] They wed before a Justice of the Peace on Nov. 22, 1965, with Grossman and an attorney as witnesses. The day before, Dylan played a concert in Syracuse. The day after, he was on the road again.

[160] Had Edmiston not noticed a comely brunette in a striped sailor's blouse at a concert rehearsal in White Plains a few days after their interview, the marriage might have remained secret. She learned Sara was Dylan's wife and passed on the intelligence to Ephron, who broke the story on the front page of the *Post*.

Given Dylan's penchant for wholesale fabrication, the media could be faulted for failing to challenge such mordant declarations, but it was a pre-Watergate, pre-Internet era when even the president lied regularly, boldly, and with impunity. Dylan could utter most anything and be believed. At a famous December 3 press conference in San Francisco, he was asked "How many protest singers are there?" and after pondering a moment, he answered "I think there's about 136."[161] Most reporters chuckled, but some carefully jotted the number down.

Bob certainly lied about drugs. At the beginning of 1966, speed, grass, and hallucinogens fueled a creative mania unmatched in his neophyte career, adding to a music catalog so broad and deep it rivaled the outputs of Cole Porter, Irving Berlin, and Stephen Foster. On stage, his elongated phrasing and nasality might resemble W. C. Fields, but his words resonated with his lemming fans. Roaring past his long-sought Bobby Vee moment, Dylan now rivaled the Beatles. He took potshots at Paul McCartney for producing Tin Pan Alley treacle, even as John Lennon[162] tried rectifying the sins of "Yesterday" and "Michelle" by imitating Bob's poetics on *Help!* and *Rubber Soul*.

"For one moment, from roughly the time *Highway 61 Revisited* was released in the fall of 1965 to the end of his tour in the U.K. in May 1966, he truly did tower over everything around him—everything, not just other musicians, but other artists, other politicians, other philosophers, other evangelists," recalled rock historian Greil Marcus. "He knew it, and you could hear the fact and the knowledge in his sound, and you can hear it now."

---

[161] When pressed for more, he quipped "It's either 136 or 142."

[162] He and Dylan wrote a song together around that time, recording it at Lennon's London flat, but ultimately losing what would have been the sort of rarity that collectors would have killed for.

If *Bringing It All Back Home* marked his break with politics and his folkie past, and *Highway 61 Revisited* began his drug-enhanced pursuit of pure poetry, then *Blonde on Blonde* became his double-LP testament to speed, death, and testosterone.

"The whole album is about sexuality and its power, or, if you will, the war between men and women," concluded Dylan chronicler Paul Williams.

The sessions that produced *Blonde on Blonde* at the beginning of 1966 started in New York and ended a month later at Columbia's Nashville outpost. His trial-and-error chucklefucking behind him, Dylan now knew *exactly* what he wanted and didn't care who he inconvenienced to get it. Sidemen like bluegrass guitarist Peter Rowan recalled Dylan's "hit-and-run studio tactics" with session musicians sitting around smoking, drinking, playing cards or Ping Pong, and collecting union wages all night long, waiting for Bob to get the words and music just right.

"Dylan would sit there at the piano for hours with the Bible, and then he'd come and say 'OK, I'm ready,'" recalled keyboardist Bill Aikins.

Ever the enabler, producer Bob Johnston indulged his star, tolerating the expensive downtime. "He can't help what he's doing," explained Johnston. "I mean, he's got the Holy Spirit about him. You can look at him and tell that."

Not all agreed. "Everybody seemed bored," recalled Rowan. "Even *he* seemed bored."

But inside his skull, Dylan chased "that thin, that wild mercury sound" he tried describing to journalist Ron Rosenbaum a decade later: "It's metallic and bright gold with whatever that conjures up. That's my particular sound. I haven't been able to succeed in getting it all the time."

When he did succeed, he could, in spooky evocations like "Visions of Johanna,"[163] evince the eerie reading of Edgar Allan Poe after midnight, or summon up the world-weary funk of a French Quarter jazz funeral in "Rainy Day Women No. 12 + 35." As Bob banged on the piano, Johnston grumbled, "That sounds like the damn Salvation Army Band," to which Dylan replied, "Can you get one?"

He consumed so many candy bars and drank so many Cokes that Johnston began to suspect he might be a junkie, but Dylan's focus was far too keen for an addict. Some of his detractors later speculated he wrote "I Want You" about heroin, though Dylan perished that thought. From hanging out with Ginsberg and William Burroughs, he concluded that dabbling in heroin now and again did not automatically lead to addiction.

"A lot of people *think* I shoot heroin," he told Shelton, "but that's baby talk . . ."

He told Nat Hentoff that opium, hashish, and pot "aren't drugs; they just bend your mind a little," yet in other interviews he preached abstinence: "People just don't need drugs. Keep things out of your body."

There seemed little doubt he needed Dexedrine. During the recording of "Sad-Eyed Lady of the Lowlands," he began noodling with his harmonica at 6 P.M. and didn't release his weary musicians until daybreak. When he wasn't wide awake, singing, or playing an instrument, he sat on a stool off to the side of the studio, leafing through fanzines, humming or mumbling to himself.

"He would just do things like read off the names, like 'Melina Mercouri' or 'Anthony Quinn,'" recalled Rowan. "Then he'd say, 'Right?' And all his crew would all go 'Right.'"

---

[163] Originally entitled "Freeze Out."

Dylan ought to have collapsed from exhaustion by the spring of '66, but a protean drive kept moving him forward.

"It takes a lot of medicine to keep up this pace," he confided to Shelton two months after the *Blonde on Blonde* sessions. During a midnight flight between Lincoln, Nebraska, and Denver at the outset of a punishing international concert tour that spring, he rattled on for hours to *The New York Times*'s pop critic. While everyone else caught up on their sleep, Dylan remained wired to the gills, vamping, buzzing, leaping from topic to topic as Shelton let his recorder run.

"It's very hard, man. A concert tour like this has almost killed me. It's been like this since October," said Dylan.

Caught up in Renaissance Man hubris, Dylan's candor might have been gripping reading for *Times* subscribers, but Shelton abandoned whatever remained of his journalistic objectivity. He did not report what happened on that late-night plane ride until years later in *No Direction Home*, his long-gestating biography of Bob.[164] Even then he didn't reveal that Dylan confessed to a $25-a-day heroin habit until "I kicked it."[165] Instead, Shelton rhapsodized in the pages of the *Times* that before *Blonde on Blonde*, Dylan "used to sound like a lung cancer victim singing Woody Guthrie. Now he sounds like a Rolling Stone singing Immanuel Kant."

Shelton recognized Dylan as a prodigy from the first, but in the years since they'd met, he'd evolved into Bob's adoring Boswell, and would remain so for the rest of his life. He kept confidences, including the Jabberwocky contents of Dylan's much-anticipated first book, galley proofs of which Bob brought along with him to

---

[164] Promoted for a winter release in 1966, *No Direction Home* was written and rewritten again and again and wasn't published until 1986.

[165] That revelation didn't come to light until the week before Bob's 70th birthday when the BBC released transcripts of Shelton's unedited interview in which Dylan also claimed to have supported himself as a male prostitute during his first weeks in New York.

edit during the '66 concert tour. The novel he'd told Studs Terkel he was writing back in the spring of '63 wound up a thin volume of run-on sentences and quippy blank verse by the time he'd completed his first draft. When Shelton asked if he thought the book would legitimize his literary reputation, Dylan dodged the question.

"Hey, I would love to say that I am a poet," he said. "I would really like to think of myself as a poet, but I just can't because of all the slobs who are called poets."

His publisher anticipated a classic like *Catcher in the Rye* or *On the Road*—a bestselling instruction manual for the under 30 set along the lines of John Lennon's *In His Own Write*. But the volume Dylan first called *Side One,* then *Off the Record,* then *Walk Down Crooked Highway* and finally, *Tarantula,* turned out to be as baffling and pretentious as James Joyce's punctuation-free swan song *Finnegans Wake.*[166]

"It's just a lot of writings," said Bob. "I can't really say what it's about. It's not a narrative or anything like that."

Classic Dylan understatement. Bob had zero discipline for sustained storytelling, exposing a serious limitation to his art. As dense as any Dylan ballad, but with none of the restraint dictated by the form and format of a song, *Tarantula*[167] read like a tale told by an idiot savant on PCP. The "master of the revitalized cliché," according to Paul Williams, Bob could pluck a phrase from here and weld

---

[166] "Bob Dylan may someday be remembered with James Joyce (and who else? Yeats? Faulkner?) as one of the great celebrants and promoters of the English language in the twentieth century," concluded Paul Williams, but it must be remembered that Williams also called Dylan "the master of the revitalized cliché."

[167] California stage and TV actor Darrell Larson performed a musical adaptation of *Tarantula* in August 1974. He also staged a rock opera based on Bruce Springsteen's music. Neither effort lasted beyond a few performances.

it to another there to create an electric metaphor, but he could not tell an extended narrative to save his life.

"It didn't have a story, that was its trouble," Dylan acknowledged to *Chicago Tribune* reporter Hubert Saal after his publisher Macmillan declared the book hopeless.

After Random House resurrected it, *Tarantula* did not improve. The most recurrent "character" was simply called "aretha," as in the Detroit soul singer John Hammond discovered a few months before he signed Dylan. But a reader would be hard pressed to describe "aretha" or anyone else mentioned in *Tarantula*. Perhaps the most revealing line in all of its 149 pages was: "okay, so I shoot dope once in a while. big deal. what's it got to do with you?"

When the book was finally published in 1971,[168] rock critic Robert Christgau praised Bob but ripped *Tarantula* in his *New York Times* review.

"Dylan wrote like a word-drunk undergraduate who had berserked himself into genius," he concluded.

■■ ■■ ■■

Richard Fariña, on the other hand, wrote like a literary soothsayer who might challenge the likes of Philip Roth or Saul Bellow. While Dylan prepped for his return to the U.K. in the spring of '66, Fariña's first novel rolled off the presses. Before it hit the bookstores, *Been Down So Long It Looks Like Up To Me* had already garnered the kind of advance critical praise a first novelist lusts after.

Four years Bob's senior, Fariña rated high among the second-tier singer-songwriters who emerged from the Village, only to burn out

---

[168] In a 1966 interview, WBAI's Bob Fass observed, "You know, Truman Capote took six years to write his book," to which Dylan replied, "Oh, I wouldn't have to take six years."

early and fade from pop memory. He'd been writing and performing before Dylan got to New York—even provoked a commercial ripple with minor hits like "Birmingham Sunday" and "Pack up Your Sorrows." But long before his short-lived marriage to Carolyn Hester, Fariña had told friends his *true* calling was writing fiction. With his picaresque first novel, Fariña lived up to that promise.

His and Bob's paths had crisscrossed often since the summer of '61, when Fariña took Dylan under his wing in much the same way John Koerner mentored Bob back in Dinkytown. It was Fariña who urged his wife Carolyn Hester to use Dylan's harmonica as backup on her third LP, paving the way for Bob's introduction to John Hammond. As two Village vagabonds, they found much in common beyond music and the obligatory Woody worship: scoring weed, rambling after midnight, scribbling snatches of overheard dialogue in spiral notebooks, eyeing jail bait . . .

By the spring of '62, Hester and Fariña had separated over his wandering eye. When he met Joan Baez's kid sister in Paris, Fariña was 25 and Mimi Baez was barely 17, but old enough to provoke Fariña's final divorce decree. When he married Mimi the following year, Fariña's old college chum Thomas Pynchon stood up as best man. Already published and a fan of Fariña's writing, Pynchon encouraged his prose.

Like Dylan with *Tarantula*, Fariña labored on *Been Down So Long* for years. He was still at it when next he crossed Bob's path. He and Mimi lived in a cabin in Carmel during the spring of '63 while Dylan was holed up nearby in his sister-in-law's cottage, plinking out songs on Joan's grand piano.[169] In a magazine article Fariña wrote for *Mademoiselle* the following year, he marveled at

---

[169] Like Carla Rotolo, Mimi came to the defense of her sister when Bob's verbal sadism got to be too cruel, once bringing Dylan to tears after a particularly vicious put-down of Joan.

how quickly the kid from Minnesota had seduced a generation. Fariña compared Bob to James Dean[170] and the romantic bards of old who traded "bouts of hard writing with hard living."

"(Dylan) often runs the two together, courting all the available kinds and degrees of disaster, sleeping little, partying late, and taking full-time advantage of the musician's scene . . ." wrote Fariña. He recommended that his readers, "catch him now . . . next week he might be mangled on a motorcycle."[171]

On April 30, 1966, as Dylan headed for the U.K. after successful concerts in Australia, Fariña and Mimi had a blowout over his failure to remember her 21st birthday. Fariña climbed on the back of a friend's motorcycle and sped off in high dudgeon. Later pegged by Carmel police as wobbling out of control at 90 M.P.H., the motorcycle skidded through a barbed-wire fence at an S-curve and tossed Fariña head first into an open field. The driver survived. Fariña died instantly.

Dylan forged on through Europe that spring and did not attend the funeral, but Fariña's Leonard Venditto moment wasn't lost to him. *Been Down So Long* became a cult classic. Pynchon wrote the introduction in later editions. Though Mimi gathered together his remaining short stories and essays for a companion volume, all future Fariña stories were silenced.

---

[170] Bob reciprocated by calling Fariña "the king of the bullshitters with nothing to say."

[171] Dylan repaid Fariña's cautionary praise by calling him a "silent moving picture actor."

Death was much on Dylan's mind that season. The previous autumn, Peter La Farge[172] had killed himself in Liam Clancy's[173] apartment on Sullivan Street and Geno Foreman died after moving to London. Bob admitted to Shelton, "I have a death thing. I have a suicidal thing, I know."

"I thought the whole drug-and-booze thing was obscene, and not just because I recovered," said fellow folkie Ed McCurdy,[174] a friend to both Dylan and La Farge. "I thought it was obscene when I was doing it. It certainly didn't help the music. It gave people the feeling that they were creating something, so the next time they tried two bottles instead of one. This happened to Dylan. This happened to everyone . . ."

And still, Dylan pushed himself—promethean Bob, carrying fire to lemmings only to suffer their scorn.

"Judas!" howled a British fan during a concert that May at the Manchester Free Trade Hall, the same month that Columbia released *Blonde on Blonde*.

"I don't believe you!" Dylan yelled back. "You're a *liar!*" Turning to his band, he signaled for *Like a Rolling Stone* and defiantly hollered: *"Play fucking loud!"*

No sooner had Dylan returned from his grueling European run than Grossman signed him to a 64-city tour across North America.

---

[172] Whether by an overdose of Thorazine supplied by Johnny Cash or by slashing his wrists as Clancy told Dylan biographer Howard Sounes, the 34-year-old former boxer and rodeo cowboy died just as his career hit its stride. Cash had recently turned his best-known song, "The Ballad of Ira Hayes," into a country hit and La Farge had just signed with MGM after recording five albums for the much smaller, though influential, Folkways label.

[173] Bob subsequently claimed he shared girlfriends with La Farge and Clancy.

[174] Actor, singer, composer ("Last Night I Had the Strangest Dream"), McCurdy abandoned a successful TV and recording career in the late '60s, retiring to Canada where he recovered from booze and pills and began a second career as a character actor on Canadian TV.

Whether messianic or simply money-wise, Albert knew to strike while the iron was hot. Asked if he ever planned to give up touring and devote himself to writing, Dylan answered, "When I really get wasted, I'm gonna have to do something, you know. Like I might never write again. I might start painting soon."

Woodstock was his asylum and Sara his nurse during his infrequent downtime, but even hearth and home could not defuse the inevitable. In the three days prior to July 29, 1966, he didn't sleep a wink. He had no business getting out of bed let alone operating a motorcycle. That he didn't expire the way Richard Fariña and Lenny Venditto did seemed nothing short of a miracle—a commodity, as it turned out, that Dylan seemed to have in ample supply.

PART II

GOIN' UP THE COUNTRY

1966–1978

*I guess he felt he'd used up 'nuff
of the 'electric supply*

*I guess he knew that the
Angel of Death was nigh*

*I guess he sighed his
next mortal sigh . . .*

*—Allen Ginsberg,
"Blue Gossip"*

7
WOODSTOCK

Sara Dylan, the only known witness, never broke her silence. All other accounts vary; only she and her husband know the details of the accident. But according to Bob chronicler Howard Sounes, who went to great lengths to solve the mystery 30 years later, the spill heard 'round the world was equal parts authentic bone-cracking misery and opportunistic guile.

"I think we finally know what really happened," Sounes concluded.

Sounes's version: Following a morning visit to the Grossmans' Bearsville compound on Friday, July 29, the Dylans set out for Byrdcliffe some time before noon. Sally phoned Albert in Manhattan as Bob drove off on his motorcycle, Sara trailing close behind in the car. Moments later, while Sally was still chatting with her husband, the car zipped back into the driveway. A rattled Sara was at the wheel. Bob lay moaning in the backseat. The motorcycle was nowhere to be seen.

As Sara helped Bob to the front porch, Sally set the phone down and stepped outside to help. Sara warned her off.

"Keep away from him!"

Bob had taken a tumble, she hyperventilated. Sally saw no evidence of abrasions, cuts, or bruises, but hurried back indoors anyway to tell her husband. Before she could hang up and call an ambulance, Sara had loaded Bob back into the car and sped away.

No police report was ever filed, nor did Bob check into an emergency room. But the following day word went forth across the AM dial that the voice of a generation might lie dying in upstate New York, maimed with a broken neck, his future in serious doubt.

Artie Mogull, who'd quit Witmark to head Dwarf Music for Dylan and Grossman, heard the bulletin Saturday morning.[175] He stopped mowing his lawn, took a deep breath, and whined, "Why does everything happen to me?"

Still smacking their corporate lips over *Blonde on Blonde*, the first-ever double LP destined to go platinum, Columbia Records execs echoed Mogull. Concert promoters from sea to shining sea had already booked Bob for an extended fall tour, but there would be no tour, no press, no public appearances. As Bob biographer Anthony Scaduto reported, the media devolved at warp speed into rank speculation:

> Dylan was dead; his brain had been crushed and he was no more than a vegetable; he was an incurable drug addict, hospitalized for treatment; he was in a psychiatric ward somewhere, totally insane; he was so badly scarred his public would never see him again.

Whether the speeding bike skidded out of control (one story), the wheels locked (another story), or it toppled over and pinned him to the ground (a third version), his injuries were indeed severe enough to merit an extended stay at Dr. Ed Thaler's Middletown clinic.

"I had a bed up there in the attic with a window lookin' out," Dylan recalled. "Sara stayed there with me. I just remember how

---

[175] *The Saturday Evening Post* published a six-page cover story the same day anointing Dylan the "Rebel king of rock and roll."

bad I wanted to see my kids. I started thinkin' about the short life of trouble. How short life is."

He wore a neck brace after he left Thaler's. David Zimmerman later confirmed that his brother was laid up for weeks with a cracked neck vertebra. The injury scared him enough to ring up his old Camp Herzl buddy Larry Kegan. He'd last seen him lying helpless on a gurney in a Twin Cities hospital. When Kegan answered, Bob began, "Larry, I thought a lot about you because I was almost paralyzed."

A counselor with a graduate degree in speech therapy, wheelchair-bound Kegan had thought a lot about Dylan too, as it turned out.

"Bob, where ya been for the last ten years?" he said. "That's not the way you treat a friend. Let's get together."

Kegan was still very much the Joker. Paralysis hadn't lessened his sarcasm, sex drive, or love of music. They picked up their friendship where it had left off and Kegan applied some of his professional balm to Dylan's anxiety.

By the time he wrote *Chronicles*, Dylan had dismissed his fear. He called the accident little more than an excuse to escape the limelight.

"Truth is I wanted to get out of the rat race," he said.

But Bob also denied being "a walking Dow chemical plant." He was no speed freak. He blamed his rail-thin amphetamine physique in the months leading to the accident on poor dental hygiene.

"I just couldn't chew and the less I ate, the worse my teeth got," he said.

Root canal work during his recuperation gave him an opposite result.

"I began to have a bit of a weight problem."

According to his mother, he was getting fat.

"Bob goes to bed every night by nine, gets up in the morning at six, and reads until ten while his mind is fresh," Beatty Zimmerman told the *Village Voice*'s Toby Thompson. "After that the day varies, but *never* before."

Still, there's nothing like cheating death to refocus a man's priorities. In a single dramatic instant, Dylan had morphed again—this time from the frizzy nicotine-stained hipster depicted by photographer Daniel Kramer on the slightly out-of-focus cover of *Blonde on Blonde,* to a quiet, studious family man captured on camera by Woodstock photojournalist Elliot Landy. In conservative haircut, rimless spectacles, and casual suburban sportswear, Dylan resembled a junior CPA on a Catskills vacation.

One persistent rumor blamed Grossman for his vanishing act. Ever the bogeyman, Albert supposedly used drugs to keep his client under house arrest until his magic returned. Indeed, Grossman's psychedelic reputation had grown in direct proportion to his client roster and his waistline. Guest tepees began to dot his Bearsville estate. Invitees could expect a steady supply of booze, cannabis, mescaline, and mysticism.

"People would get really high and go sit in the tepee, where something spiritual was supposed to happen," recalled frequent Bearsville visitor Bebe Buell. "It usually turned into people going off and fucking."

Dylan did not participate. With Sara for a nurse, he sobered up—but with disastrous poetic results.

"Right through the time of *Blonde on Blonde,* I was writing songs unconsciously," he recalled. "Then one day I was half-stepping and the lights went out. And since that point, I more or less had amnesia. Now, you can take that statement as literally or metaphorically as you need to, but that's what happened to me . . ."

Calculated or serendipitous, the accident gave Grossman ample opportunity to torture Columbia Records. During extended contract renegotiations, MGM offered to boost his album royalties to 12 percent against a $1 million advance. Match it, said Grossman.

Columbia business affairs chief Dick Asher scrambled with counteroffers, but Grossman went into his Buddha routine. During meetings he stared at the ceiling, chewed his little finger, cleaned his glasses, played with his ponytail; he'd light a cigarette, hold it between ring finger and pinky, and draw the smoke through his fist. The stalemate lasted the better part of a year.

Ultimately, Grossman upped Bob's royalty to 20 percent an album with a $200,000 advance payable over three years. He also hiked the royalty on each of his previous LPs from 4 to 9 percent. In exchange, Dylan promised to deliver four albums within the next five years.

When Asher finally did drive up the Hudson River Valley to Grossman's place with the new contract, Dylan pulled up at the Bearsville compound in his blue Ford station wagon.[176] His neck brace was long gone; he showed no scars or any trace of an accident. Asher began to think he'd been conned.

■ ■ ■

"Dylan shut out the world of show business and all the Manhattan craziness and turned into such an ordinary guy that he was actually a little boring to be around," said Happy Traum, a Village veteran who moved to Woodstock around the same time as Bob.

Dylan took up painting, grew a scruffy beard, and read everything he could get his hands on. A month after the accident, Allen Ginsberg showed up at his front door with a truckload of books. A crudely

---

[176] Demonstrating a decade of brand loyalty, he bought a bay blue Mustang convertible shortly after they first rolled off the assembly line, but "a guy who worked for me rolled it down a hill in Woodstock and smashed into a truck," Bob recalled. The salvage value was $25.

carved sign nailed to a tree beside his four-acre retreat warned, "Private property. No Trespassing."

"Roadmaps to our homestead must have been posted in all 50 states for gangs of dropouts and druggies," Bob recalled. He bought a menacing St. Bernard named Buster and a large shepherd mix[177] named Hamlet. To further discourage the overly inquisitive, he purchased a handgun and a rifle he called "the great equalizer."

"You'd be surprised the number of strangers we get up here looking to bother him," a cab driver told the *Chicago Tribune*'s Hubert Saal, one of the first to drive out for an interview. "We figure it's his business. Why, one time I walked into the coffee shop downtown and some girls—tourists—were asking the owner where Bob Dylan lived. And Dylan was sitting at the counter having a cup of coffee. Nobody told nobody nothing."

Despite Bob's new contract, Columbia would get no LP for another year. Neither did he revise *Tarantula* to meet Macmillan's deadline. In addition to stiffing his publisher and his record label, Bob also used his convalescence to snub off ABC-TV. Fanzines breathlessly reported "Bob Dylan, Columbia's top folk recording artist, makes his big time TV debut[178] in October on *Stage 67 . . .*" but following the accident, the network postponed its much-hyped telecast.

American Broadcasting paid Dylan $100,000 to shoot his 1966 European tour and deliver a concert film similar to D. A. Pennebaker's *Dont Look Back*. The verité classic wasn't due for release until the following spring, but its buzz was already solid. When ABC asked Pennebaker to cobble together the 1966 tour footage for *Stage 67,* the director delivered a 45-minute documentary

---

[177] When Dylan discovered the dog had no pedigree, he gave it to Rick Danko.

[178] *Stage 67* planned to broadcast his first bona fide documentary, but his actual TV debut was years earlier.

entitled *Something Is Happening*. As with *Dont Look Back*, Bob did not come off looking very good.[179]

Dylan decided to go Pennebaker one better and set up an editing operation in the basement of his Woodstock home. When the network objected to his meddling, he bought the footage back. Bob would revolutionize documentaries the way William Burroughs's *Naked Lunch* revolutionized the novel.[180] Pennebaker wouldn't help him, but Dylan was able to draft his assistant to his cause.

Like a pair of chucklefucking *auteurs*, Bob and Pennebaker protégé Howard Alk tinkered with the black-and-white footage through the fall and winter of 1966. A former Grossman competitor, Alk forged a lasting friendship with Bob based on an elusive hope that one day, they would produce *the* great rock 'n' roll movie together. Alk was ten years older with far more extensive showbiz experience, but he was not the senior partner in the relationship.

In Chicago, Alk had operated a folk/jazz club that rivaled Grossman's Gate of Horn. He edited his first documentary in 1959,[181] when Bob was still in high school, and he cofounded an ensemble of Loop actors who evolved into Second City.

But once bitten by the film bug, he followed Grossman's example, sold off his interests, and moved to the First City where he ingratiated himself to Pennebaker. Alk apprenticed as editor for *Dont Look Back* and shot footage for the ABC project during Dylan's '66 concert tour. When the network postponed its broadcast indefinitely, he wouldn't walk away, but Alk wasn't Bob's only ally. Bob

---

[179] "I wanna go home to baseball games and TV," a drunken Dylan moans in one climactic scene, after which he throws up in the backseat of a limo.

[180] While the book made little sense, Norman Mailer immortalized Burroughs's heroin-laced masterwork as "a collage of extraordinary fragments."

[181] *Cry of Jazz* examined racism, jazz, and artist exploitation. In 2010, the Library of Congress added it to its National Film Registry.

Neuwirth had a similar "Hey, *anybody* can do *that!*" attitude about filmmaking and moved to Woodstock to join the cause.

A year earlier, when both Bobs were high much of the time, they got their first taste of self-indulgent cinema from Andy Warhol, who invited them up to his Factory on East 47th Street. The "director" of such epics as *Empire* (24 hours of a stationary camera trained on the Empire State Building), *Haircut* (a soundless, seamless shot of a man getting a trim), and *Blow Job* (close-up of a contorted face enjoying off-camera fellatio) was a living, breathing example that *anyone* could make a movie. Warhol fawned over Dylan and begged him to do a screen test[182]—flattery that inevitably provoked contempt.

"If you want to understand me, look at my surface," Warhol said. Taking him at his word, Bob saw an albino freak and understood that he had an ego the size of his own. Dylan did take note of Warhol's Kleig lights, editing equipment, and army of toadies though.

Neuwirth looked beneath the surface of Factory life and found Warhol "superstar" Edie Sedgwick.[183] Though he later denied it, Dylan reportedly had the first one-night stand with Warhol's best-known groupie.[184]

---

[182] He did agree to sit for a portrait in exchange for Warhol's so-called "Double Elvis" silkscreen. Bob swapped it for Albert Grossman's couch and later apologized when he tried to get Warhol to give him another painting. Following Albert's death, Sally auctioned "Double Elvis" for $750,000.

[183] Cousin to actress Kyra Sedgwick, Warhol's debutante slum goddess allegedly inspired Bob to write "Leopard Skin Pillbox Hat" and "Just Like a Woman." Warhol told friends Dylan was "the guy Edie's gonna marry." She signed briefly with Albert Grossman until he found no talent to manage. A hideously dissipated Sedgwick overdosed on barbiturates and alcohol in 1971—dead at 28, and the subject of Jean Stein and George Plimpton's bestselling oral history of the '60s, *Edie*.

[184] Actress Sally Kirkland, another Factory Girl, first met Bob through Warhol, but didn't get around to sleeping with him until she joined the Rolling Thunder caravan ten years later. She claimed to have introduced him to yoga.

"I don't recall any type of relationship," he declared. "If I did have one, I think I'd remember."

After Dylan threw her over, she became Neuwirth's "sex slave." They camped out at the Chelsea until Warhol's *Chelsea Girls* (1966) blew the hotel's bohemian cover. "The notoriety it had gotten from that movie pretty much destroyed it," observed Dylan, which was yet another reason to loathe Andy. After Dylan left, Neuwirth was right behind him.

Robbie Robertson also abandoned the Chelsea Hotel and headed north to Camelot Road in the winter of '66. He joined Neuwirth, Alk, and Dylan in matching sequences for a project they were now calling *Eat the Document.*

"I know Robbie kinda got into it too," said Pennebaker, "but he didn't know anything about film either, so there was a lot of bullshit flying around."

They shuffled and arranged clips again and again, like random poetry created with refrigerator magnets. The result was as successful a film as *Tarantula* was a novel. *Eat the Document* never did get an airing and disappeared without a trace only to resurface in later decades as an artifact of passing interest to die-hard Dylan freaks, and no one else.

And yet, at least for Robertson, moviemaking had the unintended bonus of luring him to Woodstock where he felt finally at peace after years on the road. In the spring of 1967, he sent for the rest of the Hawks. For $125 a month, they leased a pink hippodrome off of Stoll Road near the foot of Overlook Mountain just a few miles east of Bearsville and Dylan's hilltop sanctuary.

Garth Hudson concocted a makeshift sound studio in the basement where the Hawks could make music whenever the spirit struck. They hired Grossman to manage them, but showed as little interest in reentering the concert tour grind as Dylan. Renaming themselves the Crackers,[185] they holed up for the summer and several seasons thereafter, inventing music in the fat fuchsia barn they nicknamed "Big Pink." Bob visited often.

■ ■ ■

Before plunging into cannabis, psychedelics, and speedballs, Paul Clayton earned the abiding respect of Village regulars in the years before Dylan came to New York City. Born in Herman Melville's hometown of New Bedford, Massachusetts, and steeped in the folk tradition, he was an Alan Lomax–inspired musicologist who arrived in Greenwich in 1958 after a stint at the University of Virginia. While the Golden Chords were still practicing Little Richard in LeRoy Hoikkala's garage, Clayton signed with Folkways Records and solidified his reputation on the New England college concert circuit as well as in the clubs along MacDougal Street.

After arriving in '61, Bobby Zimmerman gravitated toward the older, gayer, and more drug-dependent folkie. For a time, he and Clayton developed the kind of symbiosis Dylan had with Ramblin' Jack, Dave Van Ronk, and Woody himself—all essential mentors during Dylan's early career. Ten years Bob's senior, Clayton recognized in Dylan a talent for synthesizing lyrics that Clayton coveted but never could master. Simultaneously, Clayton's obscure repertory of Cape Cod sea shanties and old Irish murder ballads appealed to Bob, as did his itinerant lifestyle.

"I *liked* the folk scene," Dylan declared in later years. "It was a whole community, a whole world that was all hooked up to different towns in the United States. You could go from here to California and always have a place to stay, and always play somewhere, and meet

---

[185]   They also considered calling themselves the Honkies.

people. Nowadays, you go to see a folksinger—what's the folk-singer doin'? He's singin' all his own songs. That ain't no folksinger. Folksingers sing those old folk songs, ballads."

Armed with guitar, self-deprecating humor, a golden voice, and a seemingly limitless supply of Dexamyl,[186] Paul Clayton was just such a troubadour. He started as Bob's tutor, then his equal, and finally his sometime bodyguard, mignon, and chauffeur. A year after John Hammond signed Dylan to Columbia, Clayton still sang Bob's praises while basking in his glow.

"There are about 20 people he feels safe with, and only about five or six of those whom he can spend much time with," said Clayton, confident he was among the favored few.

But Bob spent less and less time with him as he realigned alliances. Clayton still hoped his own career might blossom on Bleecker Street, but by the end of '64, he'd lost his grip on Dylan's coattails. Some believed "It's All Over Now, Baby Blue" might have been Bob's adios to his blue-eyed guru. After "Like a Rolling Stone," Dylan dropped Clayton altogether. Still, he acknowledged him as one who opened the door to the "old weird America" that he and the Band rediscovered in the basement of Big Pink.

"Folk music is the only music where it isn't simple," said Dylan. "It's never been simple. It's weird, man, full of legend, myth, Bible and ghosts. I've never written anything hard to understand, not in my head anyway, and nothing as far out as some of the old songs. They were out of sight."

By the time Dylan had recuperated to the point where he could return to making music in the spring of '67, Paul Clayton was out of sight and mind. Dylan and the Crackers rehearsed many an old-time Clayton tune in the basement of Big Pink, but they also wrote and

---

[186] Dexedrine to speed up; Miltown to slow down.

recorded at least 34 new songs,[187] including an apropos mystical dirge titled "I'm Not There." Dubbed by British Dylanologist John Bauldie as "Dylan's saddest song," "I'm Not There" embodied Clayton's morose soul-searching, and subsequently became the title and theme of director Todd Haynes's 2007 Dylan biopic that attempted to examine six of Bob's earliest lives.

On March 30, 1967, Paul Clayton stripped bare the copper wires at one end of an extension cord, plugged the other into a bathroom wall socket, and dressed himself for a funeral. He lay down in a tub of water clutching the naked wires to his torso. Days earlier, the 36-year-old traveling minstrel had insisted space aliens had tried hypnotizing him, using multiples of the number 12 to lure him to his death. Stephen Wilson, who chronicled Clayton's descent into madness, recalled a manic drug habit that heightened hallucination to living nightmare. By the time he died, Clayton was destitute, solitary,[188] and strung out—"as wild as a reindeer," according to Wilson.

"Paul Clayton was a beautiful young man, very intelligent, very educated, very smart," eulogized Izzy Young, whose Folklore Center had been Clayton's as well as Dylan's favorite Village refuge. "I felt bad when he killed himself."

If Dylan felt the same way, he did not acknowledge it. Instead, he poured himself into his music. He wrote "I Shall Be Released," "You Ain't Goin' Nowhere," "Tears of Rage," and "This Wheel's on

---

[187] These were nonsense songs that seemed straight out of Lewis Carroll. Along with his more serious meditative ballads, over half Dylan's compositions during his Big Pink period anticipated the future by liberally salting the word "gonna" among his lyrics.

[188] He began withdrawing from the world after a Feb. 26, 1966, marijuana bust in Charlottesville, near his alma mater. After he fled Virginia, a local newspaper headlined "FBI is ready to join hunt for folksinger." While the report was false, it fed both his paranoia and his schizophrenia, and Clayton lived his final year convinced he was an FBI fugitive.

Fire" that summer, though for another year or two nobody would know just how prolific he'd been. Dylan showed up daily at noon. He worked closely with the Band using what Robbie Robertson called "the clubhouse technique."

"Just like the Bowery Boys. Every day we'd all meet at the clubhouse. And we'd get together, and we'd talk about dreams, make a little music, cook a little food, throw a football around, play checkers. That's what life *was*. We did that every day."

Meanwhile, his fans were tuning in elsewhere. Columbia released a *Greatest Hits* album to fill the vacuum, but the 1967 *Billboard* 100 contained not a single Dylan song. As Vietnam persisted, dividing the Greatest and boomer generations into warring camps, the soundtrack for that uncivil war—sparked in part by Dylan's previous LPs—devolved into escapist pap. The Monkees, Supremes, Strawberry Alarm Clock, and Elston Gunn's former front man Bobby Vee[189] dominated the American charts. Peter, Paul and Mary even sidestepped Dylan for "I Dig Rock and Roll Music,"[190] Paul Stookey's snide jab at the pop abyss into which Bob appeared to have fallen just before his motorcycle accident:

> The message may not move me,
> Or mean a great deal to me,
> But hey, it feels so groovy to say!

But as Dylan himself declared in a Big Pink composition, he was *not there*.

---

[189] "Come Back When You Grow Up" by Bobby Vee and the Strangers charted at No. 15 that year.

[190] No. 91 on the 1967 *Billboard* 100.

"The dilemma that has chased Bobby through the years is, as amazingly prolific and communicative as he is through this material, he can't talk," Stookey reflected 40 years later. "One-on-one, he borders on autism."

While absent from public view, his musical skills caught up with his lyrics. He invented new ballads while perfecting "the mathematics of a song."

"He said Lonnie Johnson taught him how to do this triple beat," explained John Cohen, cofounder of Mike Seeger's New Lost City Ramblers.

Alonzo "Lonnie" Johnson influenced Dylan's earliest licks and chord progressions the way Paul Clayton inspired his poetics. Though Bob closely studied the New Orleans jazz maestro's system of "thematic triplets" during the summer of '61,[191] he rarely had the time or sanctuary to master what he'd learned until Big Pink. Melding Johnson's blues "geometry" with Clayton's folk repertoire, Dylan and the former Hawks[192]—Robbie Robertson, Richard Manuel, Rick Danko, and Garth Hudson—forged elements of Harry Smith's *Anthology of American Folk Music* into a new sound.

At first listen, the synthesis of old and new seemed a hodgepodge of brilliant musical gems salted amid garage band debris. But on a second and third trip around the turntable, the musical manifesto became clear. The mesh of hoary, hair-raising folklore combined with dreamscapes and amplified nightmare brought to critical mass a wholly original American libretto at the dawn of the Age of Aquarius.

---

[191]   Johnson came to New York to join blues queen Victoria Spivey in recording her Prestige Bluesville album *Idle Hours*. Six months later, Dylan played harmonica and sang backup for Spivey and Big Joe Williams on the LP *Three Kings and The Queen* released on her own label, Spivey Records. "When he walked into a room, there was an eeriness about him," said Bob.

[192]   Levon Helm did not join them.

■ ■ ■

"Abe was very excited about Bob's career," recalled Beatty's brother Max Edelstein, who lived a few blocks from the Zimmermans.

He watched his brother-in-law's metamorphosis from father of a college dropout to parent of a prophet. As early as Harry Belafonte's '62 *Midnight Special* album, which featured Dylan on harmonica, Abe boasted to the neighbors about his Robert. His son's protest phase generally left Abe cold, according to Edelstein, but once he'd moved on to confessional love songs, Abe bragged openly and regularly. Following the motorcycle accident, Bob's transformation into a "countrypolitan" with healthy interests in child-rearing[193] and renewed curiosity about his Jewish heritage absolutely delighted the Zimmermans.

"He came back here while his dad was still living," recalled Bob's high school history teacher Charles Miller. Abe phoned Miller and B. J. Rolfzen when Bob came home, bubbling over with the news. Could they drop by? "We spent an hour shooting the breeze with him, me and Bonnie Rolfzen," said Miller.

While hardly buddies, Bob and his father made amends after his move to Woodstock, but their differences still outweighed the similarities. Abe smoked cigars while Bob preferred Marlboros.[194] Abe moved up from his Buick to a Cadillac Coupe DeVille Bob bought for him; Bob still favored old Fords that he drove until the wheels fell off. Abe golfed; Bob shot hoops. Ironically, his father became a political firebrand at the same moment Bob shunned politics.

---

[193] Sara gave birth to Anna Leigh, her second child by Bob, on July 11, 1967.

[194] He briefly gave up smoking all together, saying that it improved his voice as well as his health. Eventually he returned to both cannabis and tobacco.

The Six-Day War reawakened Abe's dormant Zionism. Following Israel's surprise rout of Egypt, Syria, and Jordan in June of '67, he hit the streets of Hibbing, passing the *pushka* charity box around in support of the Jews in Palestine. He bought Israel development bonds and shared his renewed zeal with his sons. But Bob had forsworn war, whether in Southeast Asia or the Middle East, and their father-son dialogue remained as discordant as it had years earlier, when Bob preferred word-strangled Woody Guthrie over conversations with his own old man.

Beatty never stopped extolling Bob's virtues, even during those doubtful Dinkytown days. She subscribed to *Billboard,* clipped and saved every review, and mailed her signature fudge bars to critical journalists along with a mother's plea to show a little more kindness. Unlike her husband, Beatty accepted Bob's name change, his shaggy appearance, his shape-shifting music, his public denial that the Zimmermans ever existed. It was all showbiz. She had faith and, after visiting him on Camelot Road for the first time, she saw that faith rewarded. Known in her youth as Duluth's premiere Jewish matchmaker, Beatty breathed easier after meeting her Ashkenazi daughter-in-law. Ironically, it was Bob's brother, David, "the good son," who married a *shiksa.*[195]

Like Beatty's grandfather, Bob had become a latter-day Solomon. B'chezer (B. H.) Edelstein, the family patriarch, combined scripture with showbiz, investing in Mesabi Range movie theaters while providing wise counsel to his extended family. He died at 91 the same year Bob left for New York but his spirit seemed to live on in Dylan.

When Beatty spied a huge Bible in his living room resting atop a *shtender*—a traditional wooden stand like the one B. H. once

---

[195] Over Abe and Beatty's objections, David married his Roman Catholic classmate Gayle Jurenes.

used—she *knew* her Bobby was, at long last, a son of the Commandments. Bob consulted the Written Torah like a scholar. Still, for all the outward trappings of a kosher home, he remained aloof about his convictions.

"I've never felt Jewish," Dylan said.

Indeed, he appeared to place as much faith in the *I Ching* as he did the Bible. "Besides being a great book to believe in," he said, "it's also very fantastic poetry."[196]

"As a child, Bob attended *all* the churches around Hibbing," said Beatty. "He was very interested in religion, and *all* religions, by no means just his own."

But the next LP he delivered to Columbia in the fall of '67 oozed Old Testament allusion, not New Testament gospel or Eastern mysticism. With particular attention to the prophets Isaiah and Ezekiel, *John Wesley Harding*[197] carried none of its messages or meaning in the same obvious and angry way that his earlier albums had. And yet his lyrics would have pleased B. H. and all the rest of his elders back in Hibbing.

"As early as 1967, *John Wesley Harding* sounded an uncustomarily smooth note: modest celebrations, calm questions, tentative answers," observed '60s scholar Todd Gitlin. "The rasp was gone from Dylan's voice, the creeps and geeks banished from his tales."

For the first time, according to Dylan, his words preceded his music. Following Allen Ginsburg's advice, he drafted *John Wesley Harding* like a working poet rather than a drug-inspired mystic. He

---

[196] The ancient Chinese text describes music as "the invisible sound that moves all hearts."

[197] The real-life Texas outlaw ended his last name without a "g." Dylanologists took Dylan's misspelling to signify "God" because the initials JWH are traditional Talmudic shorthand for Yahweh. Dylan later ended the high-minded speculation by saying, "I just thought that was the way he spelled his name."

typed at his desk or scribbled at the kitchen table, drafting spare fables that concluded with a moral . . . or moral ambiguity. Only then did he go searching for a melody.

He still borrowed shamelessly from forebears. "I Dreamed I Saw St. Augustine" takes its cadence directly from the labor standard "I Dreamed I Saw Joe Hill Last Night."[198] But the tales of *John Wesley Harding* were tight, disciplined, and as memorable as Biblical parables. "All Along the Watchtower" stood out, resonant of the eerie night noise of "Visions of Johanna," but with a downbeat beginning, like the opening scene of *Hamlet*. Covered by Jimi Hendrix a year later in a raucous rock version Dylan himself later acknowledged as superior to his own, "All Along the Watchtower"[199] owed its haunting blues to Lonnie Johnson mathematics and became the Dylan standard most frequently featured in future film and TV soundtracks. Though notoriously averse to repeating the same songs from concert to concert, Bob performed "Watchtower" on the road over 2,000 times during the next 45 years, more than any other song.

As with *Blonde on Blonde*, he recorded *John Wesley Harding* in Nashville without the Band. Accompanied by session musicians, he took a step back from rock 'n' roll and told his acoustic fables of Frankie Lee and Judas Priest, Tom Paine and St. Augustine, with a silent nod to the ghosts of Hank Williams, Paul Clayton, and B. H. Edelstein. At a psychedelic moment in time when the Beatles, Stones, and Beach Boys were drowning in Flower Power, *John Wesley Harding* baffled critics. Even ever-faithful Robert Shelton didn't know what to call it: not acid rock or folk rock . . . How about country rock?

---

[198] British folk rocker Billy Bragg continued the tradition in 1990 with the release of "I Dreamed I Saw Phil Ochs Last Night" on his album *The Internationale*.

[199] Allegedly inspired by Mary Shelley's *Frankenstein*, the three stanzas seem to be reversed: a three-act play that begins with Act III.

And yet, even before the punditry got started, Dylan changed course again, dropping further from public view. Over the next year, he virtually disappeared, save for a one-time appearance at Carnegie Hall on January 20, 1968.

Woody Guthrie finally gave up the ghost on October 3, 1967, two weeks before Dylan checked into the Nashville Ramada Inn to begin his *John Wesley Harding* sessions. The title song itself became a sort of unintentional epitaph—homage to a dead outlaw, like Guthrie's own "Pretty Boy Floyd." Woody Guthrie was just 55 years old when he died, leaving his family countless unpublished songs, but very little else.[200]

For the first time since his accident, Bob and the Band publicly performed three Guthrie originals during a memorial benefit[201] in which they joined Woody's son Arlo, Jack Elliott, Pete Seeger, Tom Paxton, Judy Collins, Richie Havens, and Odetta in paying tribute to the fallen patriarch. For those who needed proof Dylan was still alive, he delivered that night. And then he returned to Woodstock and didn't resurface again until the summer of '69.

:: :: ::

Abe Zimmerman died of a heart attack five days after Bob's 27th birthday and only four months following the Guthrie concert. His father was 57—just a year older than Woody. In the space of a few months, Dylan lost both his oracle and his old man.

---

[200] In *Tarantula*, Dylan wrote, "this land is your land & this land is my land— sure—but the world is run by those that never listen to music anyway."

[201] Harold Laventhal, Guthrie's manager and executor, repeated the tribute nearly three years later on Sept. 12, 1970, at the Hollywood Bowl, compiling recordings of both concerts into an album.

"My father had to sweat," he reflected years later. "My father lived in a lot of pain. In this earthly body he didn't transcend the pain . . ."

When he flew home to Hibbing, his uncle Max took him aside. "You're responsible for *kaddish* for him every year as long as you're alive, just like I was for my father." Bob vowed he would indeed honor Abe. For the remainder of his stay, Dylan was once again a Zimmerman.

Seventeen years earlier, long before James Dean ever showed him how to sneer, 10-year-old Bobby wrote Abe a poem that foreshadowed their rocky relationship:

> I know my dad is the best in the world
> Worth more to me than every diamond and pearl
> Though it's hard for him to believe
> That I try each day to please him in every little way
> When sometimes he gets real mad at me
> I think it best to keep quiet
> So that he doesn't get more angry
> I keep his picture on my desk
> And also his handball medal above all the rest
> I'm very lucky to have a Dad this good
> And if all the other kids only could
> You just can't beat him at any cost
> And without my dad, I'd be very lost.
>   Happy Father's Day—Love, Bobby
>   June, 1951

Now Abe was gone and Bobby Zimmerman didn't live in Hibbing anymore. In his latter-day guise as Bob Dylan, such simple sentiment didn't cut it in his hometown. Even close friends and neighbors demanded mystique, wise words, profound protest.

George Fisher, former editor of the *Hibbing Tribune,* once defined "celebrity" in his regular weekly column as "a person who works all his life to become famous—and then goes around in dark glasses so no one will know who he is." And so it was with Bob. After being recognized behind his Ray-Bans at Sammy's Pizza following Abe's funeral, he ducked out the backdoor, but not soon enough. The *Tribune* requested an interview and after Bob politely declined, George Fisher's successor declared war.

"He's dead as far as this newspaper is concerned," fumed *Tribune* editor Ben Ackerman. "His name will never be mentioned."

Nothing new to Bob. Whenever he tried to duck the media, he invited their scorn.

"I wasn't going to fall for being any kind of leader," he told Anthony Scaduto. "And because I wanted out, (the media) all started to rap me. But who could live up to that kind of thing? I wasn't into politics. I didn't want any part of that. But the times are tough. Everybody wants a leader."

The same spring his father died, assassins murdered Martin Luther King Jr. and Robert Kennedy, but perhaps Bob's most sobering moment came on June 3, just days after Abe's fatal heart attack. Valerie Solanas, a former Factory Girl, climbed six stories to Andy Warhol's Manhattan office on Union Square and shot Warhol in the chest. Following five and a half hours of surgery, he got a 50-50 chance of survival. Warhol lived another 20 years, but never fully recovered.

"Probably the main reason Bob hasn't gone back out on the road is just this, the violence," Beatty Zimmerman told Toby Thompson later that year. "He hasn't said too much about it, but I'm sure he's nervous. Assassination isn't so remote a possibility for a figure of Bob's popularity."

Abe left his elder son $1,000,[202] but the bulk of his estate went to Beatty, who put the family home up for sale.[203] She moved in with her younger sister and brother-in-law but continued to clerk at Feldman's Department Store. She rebounded soon enough. Within two years, Beatty had moved to St. Paul and married meat-packing executive Joe Rutman[204]—not exactly Gertrude trysting with Uncle Claudius, but still a bit too soon for Dylan. Inbreeding in the North Country was such that Bob now found himself connected by marriage to his old Camp Herzl pal and fellow Joker Howard Rutman, nephew of his new stepfather.

The mantle of family patriarch now rested squarely on Bob's shoulders. Mindful of his uncle's admonition about honoring Abe's memory, Dylan named his second son for his father. Samuel Abraham Dylan was born on July 30, 1968, and three months didn't pass before Sara was pregnant again.

While Bob continued to avoid the spotlight, his basement mates finally stepped out on the national stage that summer. After Albert Grossman and Capitol Records convinced them to change their name to the Band, the Crackers released *Music from Big Pink*. Their unique if offbeat sound might have wallowed unrecognized below the bottom of the *Billboard* charts were it not for a cover portrait painted by none other than Bob Dylan. The Band covered three of his newest songs on the album inside, including Richard Manuel's plaintive falsetto version of "I Shall Be Released."

---

[202] David got $1,578.

[203] The home sold for $57, 317.

[204] Beatty became Mrs. Rutman on March 21, 1970. At the time, a family friend recalled, "I was feeling her out, friend of a friend, and it didn't sound like she was ready."

Despite his proximity to the Band's instant notoriety, Dylan hunkered down in Woodstock with his growing family while street battles raged outside the 1968 Democratic Convention in Chicago.[205] The rise of Richard Nixon guaranteed four more years of war as the U.S. casualty rate crept past 20,000. Bob watched from Woodstock as a new and radical splinter group of Students for a Democratic Society vowed to prosecute peace, naming themselves Weathermen after a meme from "Subterranean Homesick Blues."[206]

While sympathetic to the cause, Dylan endorsed none of the Weather Underground's implied violence. In a rare interview that autumn, he sounded more like Gandhi than those who had conscripted his songs.

"Well, I'm for the students of course," he said. "They're going to be taking over the world. The people who they're fighting are old people, old ideas. [The students] don't have to fight. They can sit back and wait."

His words went unheeded as the riots of Chicago spread to college campuses across the nation. It took all of '68 and most of the two years that followed for Dylan's friends and colleagues to catch up with his logic.

"The whole *raison d'etre* of the New Left had been exposed as a lot of hot air," observed Dave Van Ronk who, along with Suze Rotolo,[207] Phil Ochs, and dozens of Dylan's former Village peers, had come under FBI investigation. "I mean, these kids thought they were going to change the world, they really did. They were profoundly deluded."

---

[205] By contrast, Phil Ochs was there with the Yippies, satirically nominating a 145-lb. hog named Pigasus as the Democratic candidate.

[206] *You don't need a weatherman to tell which way the wind blows.*

[207] Fed up with the U.S., Suze wed Italian sweetheart Enzo Bartoccioli on Dec. 23, 1967, and moved to Rome.

Dylan was more succinct. "It's all bullshit," he said.

As if underscoring that contempt, he followed *John Wesley Harding* with by far his least political album. He returned to Nashville and the workman-like magic of Grand Ol' Opry session men, keeping his lyrics simple and his music slick. Not only did *Nashville Skyline*[208] deliver Bob's first bona fide *Billboard* hit since "Rainy Day Women No. 12 + 35," the nicotine-free voice with which he crooned "Lay Lady Lay"[209] more closely resembled his natural tenor than any of his previous rants or whines.

By now his close amigo,[210] Johnny Cash wrote the album's liner notes.[211] He also accompanied Bob on the opening duet of "Girl from the North Country" and put him and his family up at his farm near Nashville. Bob and Sara reciprocated, inviting newlyweds Johnny and June Carter to Woodstock where they invested in a second home. After imploding his first marriage, Cash claimed Dr. Billy Graham as a mentor and, like Bob, tapped into the Bible for inspiration, eventually turning his scholarship into a pop biography of St. Paul.

And again like Bob, Cash was subject to regular extortion attempts. The grassroots popularity that made his "Folsom Prison Blues" a hit prompted ABC-TV to offer Cash his own weekly variety show, but it also dredged up crazies. Enough seriously deranged threats smattered his fan mail to warrant a call on the same

---

[208] Bob called it *John Wesley Harding II* and Columbia opted for *Love Is All There Is* before *Skyline* got the nod.

[209] Originally written for *Midnight Cowboy*, but turned in too late for production. Fred Neil's "Everybody's Talking" as covered by Harry Nilsson became the movie's theme song instead.

[210] Dylan sneaked into Manhattan in Sept. 1968 to watch Cash perform at Carnegie Hall and carried on a written correspondence with him for several years.

[211] For which the National Academy of Recording Arts and Sciences awarded Cash a Grammy; Dylan would have to wait another ten years before receiving his first for *Slow Train Coming*.

authorities who'd once arrested, fined, and ultimately scared him sober. According to his FBI file, Cash "was a reformed drinker and had taken the pledge."

Paranoid times called for paranoid reactions. Like Cash, Bob's lyrics were devoid of activism. Critics searched in vain for a single track on *Nashville Skyline* that contained subliminal advice on how to revolutionize the future of the Republic. Nevertheless, record buyers embraced his simple upbeat love songs with sales surpassing any of his previous albums. Following instinct instead of punditry, Dylan once again correctly captured the national mood. While *Hair* dominated Broadway, the Smothers Brothers brought Vietnam protest to CBS, and the Beatles drifted toward dystopia, Dylan tapped into white-bread Americana. Down to the present day, *Nashville Skyline* remains the one Dylan LP that the Country Music Hall of Fame recognizes as a genuine country album.

And while many a former fan remained furious at his failure to lead them into civil war, others recognized his inaction as an endorsement of peace.

"I know a lot of people are knocking Dylan because he's singing songs about love, saying that he's not committed, no more war songs," observed no less an activist than John Lennon. "He's singing about love now, and that's more committed than anything."

8

RETURN TO GREENWICH

Though the growing army of Dylanologists did not yet have a name, a second wave of professional Bob watchers launched a cottage industry during the year between *Nashville Skyline* and *Self Portrait,* deciphering Dylan's words and music while they set new standards for second-guessing pop culture. The first wave, which included slightly older Dylan apostles like Robert Shelton, Nat Hentoff, and *San Francisco Chronicle* pop/jazz critic Ralph J. Gleason, passed the torch to postwar upstarts like *Rolling Stone* publisher Jann Wenner, *Crawdaddy* founder Paul Williams, and pop historian Greil Marcus, who carved out entire careers sifting through Bob's life and lyrics.

"Dylan is a strange, dubious character," wrote Marcus, eventual author of three volumes of Dylan lore. "He has more to do with the Lone Ranger than John Wayne—'*Who was that masked man?*' He keeps his distance. He is from somewhere else. He not only speaks in riddles, he lives in them."

At the beginning of the turbulent summer of '69, a wary Dylan emerged briefly from self-imposed exile to do his first Q & A with Wenner's upstart San Francisco tabloid.[212] Following months of

---

[212] First published on Nov. 9, 1967, with $7,500 in borrowed capital, the biweekly took its name from Dylan's anthem and its credo from Wenner: "*Rolling Stone* is not just about the music, but about the things and attitudes that music embraces."

negotiations, he met the *Rolling Stone* publisher in Manhattan the same week that Mesabi Range native Judy Garland came from London in a casket. Her meteoric drug-laced career ended in a funeral home visible from the New York high-rise where Wenner met Dylan for their interview. Growing up in Minnesota, Bob knew Frances Ethel Gumm as a different sort of girl from the North Country[213] but if Wenner knew their connection, he made no effort to compare the two former Rangers.

While hardly revealing, the *Rolling Stone* Q & A did fill in gaps about Bob's vanishing act since his motorcycle accident: his struggle to turn *Tarantula* into something more than mind doodles; his war with ABC over *Eat the Document*; his relaxed basement music-making with the Band . . . even a glancing reference to his drug abuse.

Wenner: "Did taking drugs influence the songs?"

Dylan: "No, not the writing of them, but it did keep me up there to pump 'em out."

Instead of pressing further, Wenner followed up with an innocuous inquiry about why Bob decided to go "country" on *John Wesley Harding* and *Nashville Skyline*. For the remainder of the interview, Dylan fell back on his "aw shucks" routine, disarming Jann with solicitous familiarity. From the outset, Dylan answered questions with questions, committing to minimal answers or none at all. Some 7,000 words later, readers knew nothing of Sara, his children, his parents, his brother, his renewed passion for painting, or the philandering, drugs, and alcohol that would continue to both plague and pleasure him.

:: :: ::

---

[213] A northern Minnesota icon who'd proven early there was life beyond her Grand Rapids roots, Garland inspired Range youngsters like Dylan to migrate to Hollywood or New York for success. Drugs killed her at 47.

"Sara's a very regal, powerful chick," observed David Blue.

Those few Bob associates whom Mrs. Dylan deigned to meet agreed on her saintliness, but the woman who so deeply influenced his poetry remained invisible most of the time. As Dylan edged his way back into the public eye, his muse hid like the dark lady of Shakespeare's sonnets. Bob menaced any who tried breaching her privacy. "She doesn't have to be on the scene, any scene, to be happy," was the most he would say.

Dylan praised the mother of his children as "madonnalike": big-eyed with the outward frailty of a Modigliani child at seeming odds with her quiet, tensile core. A junkyard angel, Bob once called her in song; a strong, ethereal sylph so burdened with grace that she could only be defined with similes. Eyes like smoke, voice like chimes, flesh like silk, face like glass . . .

"She is not Mother Earth in the heavy way, but she just rolls with nature," concluded Robert Shelton. "She has a low center of gravity, if not quite indestructible, then something close to it."

Beginning with the Woody Guthrie memorial concert, Sara tentatively emerged from Bob's shadow. By the time he guested on the premiere episode of ABC-TV's *The Johnny Cash Show* on June 17, 1969,[214] Sara was appearing with increased frequency, once again cheering Dylan from the wings. Still a raven-haired beauty after bearing four children, Dylan's sad-eyed lady juggled her several roles with skill and an apparent absence of ego: lover, mother of his children, business partner, boon companion.

In July, Bob and Sara left for Minnesota to attend his ten-year high school reunion. Bob characteristically had second thoughts about coming home. Dressed in baggy suit and tie with Sara at his

---

[214] Joni Mitchell was also a guest during the debut broadcast taped six weeks earlier on May 1 in the Grand Ol' Opry's Ryman Auditorium.

side, he didn't materialize upstairs at the Moose Club on Howard Street until after 10 P.M. He stayed for just over an hour while admirers politely mobbed him, armed with reunion programs that required his autograph.

Wearing a miniskirt as if time had stood still, Echo remained shyly at the back of the crowd. When she worked up enough nerve to push forward, Bob brightened.

"Hey, Echo!"

He introduced Sara who flashed the girl from the North Country her beatific smile. All conversation ended there.

The Dylans might have stayed longer if a crocked classmate hadn't tried picking a fight. Jerry Bloomquist suffered from "Mesabi Range Alzheimer's"—bingeing until he'd forgotten everything but imagined grudges. Bob had no idea which grudge that might be, but traded few words and no punches before wrapping a protective arm around Sara and retiring for the evening. He might have expected a little more propriety, even among Range drunks, given that his wife was again pregnant.[215] The reunion marked the last time he'd announce his return to Hibbing. He reportedly jammed with a few old friends in nearby St. Cloud during his brief sojourn, but henceforth whenever he sneaked into town for a visit, he left the same way.

The Dylans did stick around the day after the reunion. Bob drove Sara by his boyhood home and took her to Hibbing High to show her the auditorium where he'd made his showbiz debut. She gaped the way outsiders do when entering a cathedral.

"Oh, I can't believe this place," she told Bob as he hoisted three-year-old Jesse to his shoulders and walked to center stage. "This is absolutely unbelievable!"

---

[215] Jakob, the last of their five children, was born Dec. 9, 1969.

Not so unbelievable that the Dylans felt compelled to remain in northern Minnesota any longer than necessary. A week later, they were flying to England, kids in tow, while half a million of Bob's most ardent admirers descended on Woodstock.

By mid-July, promoters had already sold more than 50,000 tickets for the three-day Woodstock Arts & Music Festival, but they expected 200,000 more—an estimate that turned out to be less than half of the 500,000 that showed up. Boomers poured into the Hudson River Valley, partly on the strength of rumors that the voice of their generation would soon speak once more—this time from a stage at the center of Max Yasgur's farm.

By the time the hordes got to Woodstock, however, Bob was on the other side of the Atlantic, dismissing their celebration. He sniped at the festival as "just an excuse to sell tie dye," but his fans still held out hope. During the previous year, Bob had inched back into public view, occasionally performing unbilled or using a pseudonym.[216] His surprise appearance on Johnny Cash's TV debut fueled hope he'd step further into the spotlight. With the announcement that both Joan Baez and the Band would perform at Woodstock, Dylan loyalists by the thousands naturally assumed Bob himself would grace them with his unheralded presence. They would be wrong.

Instead, he showed up in an ice-cream suit at the Isle of Wight Festival the week following the collapse of the Woodstock Nation. After months of breathless buildup surrounding the American rock spectacle, 200,000 British fans expected something even grander,[217] but they came away as disappointed as their colonial counterparts. With no encores and the tersest of stage banter, Dylan doomed to

---

[216] As Elmer Johnson, he jammed with the Band during a swing through Illinois in July.

[217] UK journalists wrote an estimated 250,000 words about Bob in the weeks leading up to the festival.

anticlimax his first major concert appearance in three years. Once he took the stage, wrote the *Los Angeles Times'* Geoffrey Cannon, "he looked and acted like a Hasidic scholar." As if it were a bland "greatest hits" road show, Bob nervously concluded an hour's worth of his mid-60s with a mumbled, "It's great to be here. Sure is." And then he and the Band left the stage.

"What I saw was a good-looking boy in a nice shiny-white suit, accompanied by skilled but uninspired musicians, singing a Bob Dylan medley á la Sinatra," summed up Christopher Logue of *The Times of London*. For his hour on stage, Dylan reportedly earned $84,000.

And yet, for all his chintzy stage presence, Bob had lost none of his capacity to spin tantalizing half-truths in the media. In explaining the presence of his wife and children backstage before the concert, he told one interviewer, "Sara and I grew up as kids together in Minnesota. Then some years back we met again in a New York restaurant where Sara was working as a waitress. We fell in love— although it was not love at first sight, and five years ago we were married in New York State."

If bullshit and a flat stage presence were all he had to offer, the summer of '69 might have been a bust for Bob, but as it turned out, it was also the summer *Easy Rider* blew away conventional moviemaking, breaking box-office records at the same time its rebel cast and rock 'n' roll soundtrack declared war on what remained of Hollywood's creaky studio system.

Easy Rider's nihilistic story line, combined with Roger McGuinn's omnibus pop score, set a pattern for a new generation of filmmaker, and the *auteur* behind *Eat the Document* reluctantly stumbled right into the thick of the revolution.

After Peter Fonda and Dennis Hopper drafted McGuinn to score their film, he urged Fonda to give Dylan a private screening if they wanted permission to use "It's Alright, Ma." All Bob saw was another cheap biker exploitation flick. He did not want to contribute his voice, but pressed further, scribbled some lines on a cocktail napkin, and handed it to Fonda:

> The river flows
> It flows to the sea
> Wherever that river goes
> That's where I want to be
> Flow river flow.

"Here, give this to McGuinn," he said. "He'll know what to do with it."

Not only did McGuinn turn Dylan's doggerel into "Ballad of Easy Rider," he also covered "It's Alright, Ma" and encouraged Bob's basement buddies to lend their hit single "The Weight"[218] to his score. Moviegoers who might have forgotten why Dylan mattered suddenly remembered that Bob was the first to tell them they had nothing to live up to.

"About a month later," said McGuinn, "when the soundtrack album was out and the credit (for "Ballad of Easy Rider") read Bob Dylan and Roger McGuinn, I got a call from Dylan at three o'clock in the morning. . . . 'What is this? I don't want the credit. Take it off. I don't need the money.' He didn't want it. So I said okay. The thing generated half a million."

Thus, Bob's profile rose in spite of his absence from Woodstock, his mediocre return to live performing on the Isle of Wight or his inability to spot a hit movie. *Easy Rider* made international stars of Fonda, Jack Nicholson, and Dennis Hopper, but it also reinforced

---

[218] Because Dwarf Music owned the Band's publishing, Dylan and Grossman shared in the profits.

Dylan's image as *the* counterculture prophet, whether he meant to be or not. It also gave him a renewed taste for filmmaking.

⠶ ⠶ ⠶

In the autumn of 1969, Dylan bought a refurbished nineteenth-century brownstone at 94 MacDougal Street just two blocks from the Fourth Street hovel he once shared with Suze. Later admitting it was "a stupid thing to do," he moved his family back to Manhattan in hopes of recapturing some of his old Village magic.

"The worst times of my life were when I tried to find something in the past," he reflected a few years after his botched experiment. "I didn't know what to do. Everything had changed."

Six months earlier, the Dylans sold Hi Lo Ha after their every effort to remain hidden had failed. They moved to another manse on Ohayo Mountain Road north of the town of Woodstock,[219] but the music festival and attendant publicity robbed them of sanctuary there, too. Protective neighbors and the local constabulary misdirected or discouraged wayfaring strangers, but no one could protect the Dylans against their most ardent admirers.

Bob remembered, "people living in trees outside my house, fans trying to batter down my door, cars following me up dark mountain roads . . ." He literally found the uninvited in his living room, his kitchen, even in his bed. Privacy was out of the question.

By moving back to New York, he reasoned that he'd at least be closer to the pulse of American pop and his kids would have access to good schools. He took a basement studio on Houston Street a block away from his Village condo to jump-start his landscape and portrait painting as well as have a quiet place to write. About the

---

[219] Davasee Enterprises continues to own property there to the present day.

same time, he bought a beach house on pricey Lily Pond Lane in East Hampton for summer getaways. He counted on Manhattan's blasé attitude toward its celebrities to give him privacy.

"I'm completely uptight," he confided in Terri Thal, who'd never left the Village. "Got all this money and don't know what to do with myself. Got a great wife, great kids, but don't know what to do. Can't perform any more. I hate performing in front of big audiences. But I guess I'll have to 'cause I don't have anything else to do. Ain't done any writing in a while. Can't seem to write."

Didn't mean he wasn't trying. In addition to painting and drafting new songs, he started an autobiography.

"I think back sometimes to all those people I once did know," he said. "It's an incredible story, putting together the pieces. It's like a puzzle, as far as stories go. I meditate on it sometimes, all that craziness. . . . I really like to work on it."

But the relaxed new arrangement was doomed before it began. As cynical and guarded as fame had made him, even Dylan didn't foresee a three-year siege at the hands of his single most fanatic apostle.

An angry caricature of New Left lunacy with a vague resemblance to Allen Ginsberg, Alan Jules Weberman was a bearded Michigan State dropout who'd dedicated his life to an active, avid pursuit of all things Bob. Robert Shelton called Weberman "The Scavenger," but he preferred to think of himself as Bob's conscience. The world's first full-time Dylanologist fit Greil Marcus's arcane definition of a "weird": an alter ego so deeply obsessed with his imagined blood brother that he tries to *become* the obsession.

Broadside, the tabloid that first published "Blowin' in the Wind" and once listed Dylan as a contributing editor, had passed through several hands by the late '60s, but its core audience remained folkies. Thus, its newest publisher decided that an oddball like

Weberman might appeal to readers by turning his encyclopedic knowledge into a regular Bob column. It didn't take long for *Broadside* to get its fill of Weberman's strange commentary, so the self-styled journalist migrated to the *East Village Other* where he continued to mine Dylan songs for subtext and radical ideas. Coining the term "Dylanologist," Weberman tinkered with Talmudic interpretation of Bob's most nonsensical lyrics and played songs backward to extract hidden meaning.[220]

"I discovered backward masking years ago," he said. "I'd play a line like 'If dogs run free, so it may flow and be,' run it backwards, and it was 'If Mars invades us,' and there was another line that says 'don't expose me.' So I had everybody playing Dylan backwards. I found hidden pictures in the *John Wesley Harding* album cover[221] too. I had everybody looking at Dylan's hair and the guy standing next to him holding the rifle."

Like many of the more highbrow Bob scholars, Weberman would eventually publish multiple volumes interpreting Dylan songs, including a 536-page *Dylan to English Dictionary* (2005) that purported to decode every lyric Bob ever wrote.

"Dylanology requires a working knowledge of the life and times of Bob Dylan," Weberman said. Putting himself in the same league as Greil Marcus and such latter-day Dylan academics as Princeton

---

[220] Inspired by Jefferson Airplane's "White Rabbit" ("the White Knight is talking backwards . . .") a fad evolved in the late '60s of listening to LPs in reverse for hidden, often Satanic messages. The most egregious urban myth to arise from this practice was the popular notion that Paul McCartney died in an auto accident. "Revolution 9" from the *White Album* played backward yields a garbled voice that supposedly says "Paul is dead."

[221] In the cover photo, Dylan is flanked by a pair of Bengali musicians and a stonemason Bob befriended in Woodstock. Searching for a connection with *Sgt. Pepper's Lonely Hearts Club Band*, fans less obsessed than Weberman imagined the faces of the Fab Four as well as Dylan himself embedded among the trees in the background.

history professor Sean Wilentz and British literary critic Sir Christopher Ricks, Weberman beseeched his fellow Dylanologists to "confirm the validity of the Dylanological method because, to put it quite succinctly, they have some motherfuckin' brains!"

From the start, Dylan harbored doubts about Weberman's gray matter. After reading several of his *East Village Other* columns, he damned him with faint praise:

"Well, he oughta take a rest. He's way off," he told *Rolling Stone* a few months before moving back to Greenwich. Tongue planted firmly in cheek, Bob suggested Weberman could better spend his time explicating Dostoevsky or Freud, "doing a really big analysis of somebody who has countless volumes of writings."

Weberman took Bob's repudiation as serious challenge. Combining tenacity with nerve, he carried the art of Bob stalking to strange and dizzying new heights. "I drove him out of New York City, drove him out of Greenwich Village," he boasted 40 years after the fact.

But in the beginning, Weberman claimed he merely wanted to force a dialogue on the one subject that Dylan had no interest in discussing. As self-appointed surrogate for the thousands who came to Woodstock to hear the words of their prophet, Weberman demanded to know why Dylan went MIA at the height of Vietnam; why he would not rejoin Joan[222] and John and Yoko in nonviolent protest; why he retreated from the times he helped to change, even as those times seemed about to change again.

At first, Dylan ignored him. He owed Columbia another album and poured his time and energy into satisfying his contract obligation. While Weberman sniped, Bob climaxed the 1960s with the

---

[222] An unabashed attempt to shame Dylan out of his cocoon and back into the protest mainstream, Baez wrote "To Bobby": "Do you hear the voices in the night, Bobby? They're crying for you. See the children in the morning light, Bobby? They're dying."

unveiling of his *Self Portrait,* easily the most excoriated record he ever made. *Rolling Stone* famously attacked the double-LP with a review that began, "What is this shit?" Weberman's *East Village Other* shrieked "This album sucks!" Showing slightly more decorum, the British underground *International Times* concluded that Bob had become "complacent, uncaring, and seemingly dedicated to a solid conservative way of life . . ."

When Roger McGuinn asked if he'd written any new songs the Byrds might cover, "he said no, that he was kind of hard up, that he hadn't been writing as much as he used to. And I mentioned that we all get fat and lazy, and he laughed."

Never mind that *Self Portrait* was precisely what it purported to be: a straightforward anthology—some pop standards, some folk, a smattering of choir-backed instrumentals, and a handful of tributes to contemporary singer-songwriters who had influenced his career. Dylan may literally have tipped his hat on the cover of *Nashville Skyline*, but *Self Portrait* represented a grander homage to those who came before: Elvis, Frankie Laine, Rodgers & Hart, Charlie Rich, and such Bob contemporaries[223] as Gordon Lightfoot[224] and the two Pauls—Simon and Clayton.[225] The only Dylan originals on *Self Portrait* were a pair of instrumentals,[226] a honky-tonk version of "Like a Rolling Stone," and his basement tape of "Quinn the Eskimo," which Manfred Mann had already charted as a *Billboard* hit.

---

[223] He also covered Joni Mitchell's "Big Yellow Taxi" and "The Ballad of Ira Hayes," signature song of Peter La Farge, but Columbia didn't release them until three years later on an omnibus collection called simply *Dylan.*

[224] Yet another Albert Grossman client.

[225] At the nadir of his death spiral, Clayton sold the copyright of his best-known song "Gotta Travel On" for $500 to buy drugs and food. Several critics cited Dylan's rendition as the best track on *Self Portrait.*

[226] An upbeat bluegrass number called "Wigwam," and a set of soprano voices repeating "All the Tired Horses" as if in rehearsal for Dylan's greatest dirge, "Knockin' on Heaven's Door."

At the time, Bob called *Self Portrait* "my own bootleg record," though he later dismissed the entire album as a practical joke released for no other reason than to satisfy Columbia. Weberman called it further proof that Dylan had sold out; that the voice of a generation had become a bourgeois whore.

And he intended to prove it.

▪ ▪ ▪

Just four months after the universal scorn he suffered for *Self Portrait*, Dylan resurrected his reputation with a dozen lightweight but wholly self-composed originals. Accompanied by a simple head shot of a relaxed, bearded Bob on its cover,[227] *New Morning* was no return to *Blonde on Blonde* or even the stylized complexity of *John Wesley Harding*, but in the immediate wake of *Self Portrait*, critics fell all over themselves praising its thimble-deep poetry.

"*New Morning* began the 1970s with a statement of serenity, even as *Self Portrait* had ended the 1960s with nostalgic pastiche," rhapsodized Robert Shelton.

Rolling Stone's Ralph Gleason concluded just the opposite. "He's coming out again. Come on, Bob! We need you. That's the truth, man, we really do. Come out, Bob, come out!"

Crawdaddy's Paul Williams, a cheerleader who praised Bob's every jot and scribble, was nearly alone in his dissent. "*New Morning* is Bob Dylan pretending to be Bob Dylan," he said, calling the entire LP "inauthentic."

The New Yorker's Ellen Willis struck a neutral chord, praising the music if not the message: "Dylan is still very much preoccupied

---

[227] On the back cover, a much younger Bob appeared with Victoria Spivey in a 1961 photo probably shot during her studio session with Lonnie Johnson.

with finding happiness in the pastoral life. The title song[228] is his definitive statement on the subject."

His smooth *Self Portrait* tenor intact, Bob half-crooned the opening track "If Not for You" as a jazzy talking blues, almost like a Vegas lounge singer, but it was "Sign on the Window," another lyric deeper in the album, that summarized his post-Woodstock reverie:

> Build me a cabin in Utah
> Marry me a wife, catch rainbow trout
> Have a bunch of kids who call me "Pa"
> That must be what it's all about.

He trilled the worshipful "If Not For You" for Sara, forecasting none of their future domestic upheaval. Indeed, his ever-supportive muse coaxed him into stepping out into public again and accepting an honorary doctorate from Princeton during its 223rd commencement. The result was "Day of the Locusts," yet another *New Morning* track he wrote reflecting the same escapist theme as "Sign of the Times," but with a slightly different destination: he and his lady would hide out in the Black Hills of Dakota instead of an idyllic cabin in Utah.

During the short limo ride from Manhattan to Princeton, Bob eased his anxiety with a spliff he shared with former Byrd David Crosby, whom he and Sara had invited along to witness the ceremony. But cannabis alone couldn't sedate Bob. Crosby and Sara

---

[228] "New Morning" was one of three tracks (including "Time Passes Slowly" and "Father of Night") he originally wrote for Archibald MacLeish's Broadway production of *Scratch*, a stage adaptation of *The Devil and Daniel Webster*. In *Chronicles*, Dylan characterized the former Librarian of Congress as he had MacLeish contemporary Carl Sandburg: both were cranky old geezers. MacLeish rejected Bob's songs, *Scratch* failed, and the 78-year-old poet faded from public life, but his poetry was honored with three Pulitzers during his long career; Dylan won once, for *Chronicles*.

tried bolstering his spirits, but he just got jumpier. His old restless leg syndrome returned with a vengeance as he donned his robe. When he settled among the graduating elite, Bob fell to silence.

"I don't like it," he confided to Sara. "They're asking questions."

The Minnesota dropout did become an honorary Doctor of Music that day, but at a visible cost. His grim, straight-line frown matched his feral, darting eyes. If he smiled, it was only in obligatory and superficial flashes. Had he been drunk instead of merely stoned, he might have rattled off a list of offenses at his valediction the way he did six and a half years earlier at the Emergency Civil Liberties Committee dinner. But an older and more subdued Dylan kept it together long enough not to turn contempt into public spectacle. He delivered no speech; just accepted his sheepskin and ducked out the back way. As he concluded in the final verse of "Day of the Locusts"—"Sure was glad to get out of there alive."

The Doors' Jim Morrison[229] didn't, nor did Albert Grossman's newest client, Janis Joplin.[230] On September 18, 1970, Jimi Hendrix also died, choking on his own vomit in a London hotel room. In memoriam, Dylan sketched Hendrix's portrait.[231]

Bob's acute sensitivity to the ravages of excess had been renewed a year earlier when the Rolling Stones' Brian Jones was found dead at the bottom of his swimming pool.[232] From Paul Clayton to Judy Garland, the victims of drug abuse kept mounting.

---

[229] Dead at 27 of an apparent drug overdose, July 3, 1971.

[230] Dead at 27 of heroin overdose Oct. 4, 1970.

[231] "The day after Jimi Hendrix died I found a photo of Jimi that somebody had mailed to Dylan," said A. J. Weberman after going through Bob's trash. "It was ripped to pieces."

[232] Once one of Dylan's midnight rambling buddies during his and Neuwirth's Andy Warhol partying period, Jones also died at 27—"death by misadventure," according to the coroner who also noted an enlarged heart and liver from drug and alcohol abuse.

"The drugs at the end of the '60s were artificial," Dylan reflected years later. They were also lethal.

John Lennon, who'd once done everything from weed to heroin with Bob, maintained at the dawn of the '70s that the entire culture had fallen into a "Post-Drug Depression." Those who survived sobered up one way or another. Bob once again was at the leading edge.

"In the '60s, there was a certain bunch of us who came through the wars," he said. "There was a lot of death during that time. The '60s were filled with it. It has helped me to grow up. The '70s are more realistic, but the '60s exposed the roots of that realism."

A. J. Weberman didn't believe a word of it.

▪▪ ▪▪ ▪▪

The world's premier Dylanologist first made off with Bob's garbage on December 17, 1970, but he'd been fascinated with rubbish since he first learned to walk.

"My mother wasn't an Orthodox Jew and my father was, so he'd go through the garbage in the house to see if she was buying non-kosher food," he recalled.

Weberman had been stopping by regularly at Bob's Village brownstone for months, but even when he spotted Dylan on the street, the most he got was a grunt and the stink eye. It was in the wake of one of these frustrating moments that Weberman remembered his old man's trash obsession. He beamed when the maid set a black plastic bag out on the Dylans' front stoop.

"I just reached into the garbage and kinda pulled a letter out," he said. "It was to Johnny Cash! I say to myself: 'This is a gold mine!' So I came back and got his garbage for weeks and weeks."

Weberman theorized that Dylan had become a clandestine junkie and thus, turned his back on the counterculture to indulge his habit. His objective was to find the hypodermic proof he needed among the dog crap and disposable diapers,[233] save Bob from himself, and return him to his proper role as Pied Piper to the Woodstock Nation. To that end, Weberman became a one-man rehab strike force. He called himself and his occasional followers the Dylan Liberation Front.

Each trash day, Weberman scooped up Bob's garbage before the trucks arrived. He spirited it ten blocks away to DLF headquarters on Bleecker Street[234] where he scrupulously sifted through the dregs and came up with a corollary to Dylanology. Indeed, his first full-length book on the subject was titled *My Life in Garbology*—the interpretive science of mining celebrity trash for clues to lifestyle.

Bob soon wised up and began expurgating his refuse before setting it out at the curb, but before the curtain came down Weberman was able to piece together a snapshot of the Dylans' daily routine. The clues did not bear out his junkie theory, but were intriguing nonetheless, for Bob and Sara Dylan turned out to be precisely what they purported to be: Yuppies raising a large family while living the good life in the heart of New York City.

Sara was a member of the Book-of-the-Month club and shopped at Bloomingdales while the children attended the exclusive Little Red School House in the Village. Recently remarried and now Mrs. Beatty Rutman, Bob's mother sent the grandkids postcards and candy from Florida. The family's diet consisted of granola, cookies, liverwurst, and milk products, with no indication that they kept a kosher pantry.

---

[233] According to Jewish law, opening the adhesive tabs of such diapers on the Sabbath constitutes work and is therefore verboten.

[234] Current home of the Yippie Museum, Café & Gift Shop.

Bob's life was just as bland and secular. The unrevealing letter he'd started to Johnny Cash contained no hint of either musician's lifelong struggle with addiction. Indeed, the best Weberman could find to bolster his theory was a doctor's prescription for a muscle relaxant.

Weberman knew Bob was on to him when the quality of the garbage changed. While loaded with more diapers and gooey deposits from Sasha,[235] the family dog, there were fewer and fewer receipts, discarded letters, or other telling bits. By January, Weberman countered Bob's gambit by offering classes in Dylanology. He took students on field trips to Dylan's town house where they stood outside and chanted at Bob to give up his millions and rejoin the cause. Finally, there was a confrontation.

"Al, why'd you bring all these people around my house for?" Bob asked from his front porch.

"It's a demonstration against you and all you've come to represent in rock music!" shouted Weberman.

Dylan escorted him down the street, out of his students' earshot.

"You know, Al, a lot of people have been asking me about your theories. They're going around saying that you're telling people I'm a junkie."

"Are you?"

To which Bob rolled up his sleeves and held out his arms. "Clean. No track marks."

Weberman was unappeased. He switched his argument from drugs to Zionism, accusing Dylan of sending money to Israel instead of donating to antiwar causes. Dylan had indeed donated $5,000 in his late father's name to Rabbi Meir Kahane's newly created Jewish

---

[235] Despite a diet of Ken-L Ration and Gainsburgers, she paid visits to the vet for an upset stomach.

Defense League[236]—a generous contribution that amounted to nearly 10 percent of the JDL's annual operating budget. Starting in the summer of '69, the Dylans visited Israel annually. At one point, Bob even gave serious consideration to moving his besieged family to a kibbutz. But he felt no need to apologize for any of this.

He switched tactics and offered Weberman Victor Maymudes's[237] old job as his bodyguard/chauffeur. It was a tried and true strategy. Bob let the overly inquisitive into his life by cautious, co-opting degrees—a maneuver that seemed to work with journalists. To ensure access to his subject, Robert Shelton censored himself each and every time he wrote about Dylan. When it became clear that Anthony Scaduto would publish the first book-length Dylan biography with or without Bob's cooperation, Dylan finally granted him full and unfettered access. As Scaduto later acknowledged, that last-minute ploy was designed to soften his reporting. As it turned out, his access was neither full nor unfettered. Bob gave him an audience, but he still lied, shaded the truth, declared parts of his life off limits, and steered Scaduto away from uncomfortable questions.

Weberman was canny enough to decline Bob's consolation prize. He preferred street theater to a chauffer's cap, especially after he'd gone public with his garbage revelations. His Dylan Liberation Front swelled in numbers and, during the February premiere of *Eat the Document* at a Manhattan benefit for Pike County coal miners, Weberman and his DLF loyalists demonstrated outside the theater, carrying placards condemning Bob's lack of charity. Instead of applauding his effort to help coal miners, they distributed handbills

---

[236] Before founding the JDL in 1968, Kahane was neighborhood rabbi to Woody Guthrie's half-Jewish family in Howard Beach. "He's a really sincere guy," Dylan told *Time* magazine. Kahane was assassinated by an Arab gunman in 1990.

[237] Maymudes left both Manhattan and Bob in 1968 to start a construction business in New Mexico.

that claimed "Dylan has *at least* $5 million!" Weberman's idea of appeasement was a sizable donation to a cause of his choice, preferably with Weberman in a paid supervisory role.

And their war escalated.

When Bob finally phoned him, Weberman taped the call and made it public. He exploited Bob's trash by writing about garbology for *Rolling Stone* and *Esquire*. When Bob begged him to stop, he demanded more information, more access, more contributions to the Cause.

On Bob's 30th birthday, Weberman and his entourage showed up outside the town house with a cake decorated with hypodermic needles, but Bob wasn't there to hear them sing "Happy Birthday." He was in Israel where he celebrated by taking Sara to see a Gregory Peck movie.

"I'm quite a fan of his," he told the *Jerusalem Post*. The *Post* photographer captured Dylan standing at the Wailing Wall but missed a photo of Bob purchasing a bootleg record[238] from a street vendor—irony that Weberman would have broadcast far and wide, had he known.

By late summer, Weberman's trash picking had made him notorious. He moved his operations to the upper Eastside and more upscale garbage: Jackie Kennedy, Gloria Vanderbilt, Bella Abzug . . .

For the sake of an Associated Press reporter who wanted to witness the ritual firsthand, Weberman did concede to dig through Bob's garbage one more time. No sooner did he help himself to some slop than a banshee descended from the Dylans' brownstone.

---

[238] "I like the Egyptian singer Om Kalsoum," Dylan sheepishly explained years later. The "Star of the Orient" as she was known was widely recognized as the Edith Piaf of Cairo. Millions turned out for her funeral in 1975, but Kalsoum's music was often counterfeit and/or contraband on the streets of Jerusalem.

"Get the hell out of my garbage!" shrieked Sara Dylan from her front door. "You filthy animal! I can't throw anything away without you pawing through it! Get out of the garbage you leech!"

She chased him down MacDougal Street, but that wasn't the end of it. Later that afternoon, Weberman loitered across the street from DLF headquarters when a man on a bicycle zipped up behind him. Inches shorter and far thinner than Weberman, Dylan nonetheless grabbed him around the neck and wrestled Weberman to the ground.

"He began to knock my head against the pavement," Weberman recalled.

He'd seen Dylan shooting hoops at the park across the street from his condo and knew him to be in pretty good shape, but had no idea how strong Bob really was. It took a couple of Samaritans to come to his aid before Weberman could shake him off. Outnumbered, Dylan climbed back on his bicycle and pedaled home.

One of Weberman's rescuers asked if the mugger got away with much money. Weberman shook his head "no."

Still hyperventilating, he said, "*That* was Bob Dylan!"

9

CALIFORNIA

I'm used to four seasons,
California's got but one.
  —Dylan's "California"[239]

The din over Dylan's ongoing vanishing act rose to the top of the *Billboard* chart with the release of Don McLean's "American Pie." A Pete Seeger protégé, McLean encapsulated in surreal verse the history of rock since the 1959 plane crash that killed Buddy Holly, identifying Bob as the Jester who sat out the '60s "on the sidelines in a cast." Four weeks at No. 1 during the summer of 1971, "American Pie" not only charted higher than "Like a Rolling Stone," it also clocked in at two and a half minutes longer, demonstrating just how far rock and radio had advanced in the five years since Dylan's motorcycle accident.

Indeed, the entire culture had shifted outside of his domestic cocoon. AM became the hoary venue for talk radio while transistorized FM "underground" deejays ruled the exploding youth market. Singles were out; LPs were in. Music evolved from garage bands, hootenannies, soul and surf sounds to a $2 billion annual business—twice what it was when Dylan had first arrived in New York.

---

[239] Probably written in Hollywood's Thunderbird Motel (now the Standard) during Dylan's taping of *The Steve Allen Show* in winter '63, but unreleased until 2010 on the soundtrack of the CBS-TV series *NCIS*.

Fast-changing multitrack recording technology made Garth Hudson's primitive setup in the basement of Big Pink quaint at best, passé at worst. Whole albums were created one track at a time. The warring Beatles recorded much of their final LP, *Let It Be,* without having to set foot in the same studio together at the same time. The old movie-making cliché—"we'll fix it in post"—now applied to records as readily as it did to TV and film. Stereo replaced high fidelity as the essence of commercial sound, and America's pop epicenter, shifted from East to West.

Johnny Carson led TV's Eastern exodus when he moved *The Tonight Show* in 1972 from Rockefeller Center to beautiful downtown Burbank. The previous year, CBS canceled the venerable *Ed Sullivan Show,* which had so offended young America by refusing to let Dylan eviscerate the John Birch Society. Ironically, the Band[240] was among Sullivan's final guests. Like Johnny Carson, the Big Pink fraternity would soon abandon New York for California.

But a simple change in geography didn't change television. East or West, TV couldn't—or wouldn't—capture rock's outlaw spirit. Dick Clark's *American Bandstand,* pop's one televised through-line from the dawn of the Golden Chords to Dylan's *New Morning* and beyond, remained safe and homogenized throughout its long national run, whether the broadcast emanated from Philadelphia or L.A.[241] Dylan's songs might get covered on *Bandstand* by lesser-known artists, but he never set foot on its antiseptic soundstage. Except for his single appearance on *The Johnny Cash Show*, he spurned TV altogether, and rarely did radio interviews.

"To Woody Guthrie, see, the airwaves were sacred," Dylan explained in a 1991 interview. "And when he'd hear something

---

[240] Sullivan also hosted the Byrds whom he introduced as "Mr. Tambourine Man."

[241] First aired over ABC in 1952, the show moved in Hollywood in 1964 and continued there through 1989.

false, it was on airwaves that were sacred to him. His songs weren't false. Now we know the airwaves aren't sacred. But to him, they were."

Network TV's concept of cool was *The Monkees, Happy Days, The Partridge Family,* and *The Brady Bunch.* Ed Sullivan's heirs were déclassé tastemakers like Sonny and Cher, Donny and Marie, Tony Orlando and Dawn. Emcees with the power to break exciting new music acts on national TV didn't, and the "cool medium" as defined by Canadian media guru Marshall McLuhan remained anything but.

And yet Dylan himself straddled the uneasy generation gap between Woody and Woodstock. As a husband and father, he no longer encouraged everyone to get stoned. He might toke and drink on occasion, but privately and in moderation. Following the Rolling Stones' catastrophe at Altamont,[242] panicky politicians and their graying constituencies bought into Richard Nixon's Drug War, stifling the possibility of another Woodstock. Too many kids smoking too much weed in a rock-and-roll meadow instilled dread among the Silent Majority.

Nonetheless, the 1970 release of the *Woodstock* movie expanded its original audience exponentially so that millions came to share the festival experience. They demanded bigger and better concerts, assuring the growth of arena rock. However tepid Dylan's reception on the Isle of Wight, his final concert of the '60s was a guidepost to pop's commercial future. Intimate Village venues and small-time

---

[242] Four months after Woodstock, 300,000 gathered in the Altamont hills southeast of San Francisco for a free concert headlined by the Stones, but unlike the peace and love of the Eastern conclave, the media played up the beating death of a fan at the hands of Hell's Angels. Two died at Woodstock, both of natural causes, while four died at Altamont. In addition to the beating victim, there were two hit-and-runs and a drowning. In its defense, Altamont recorded four births—twice that of Woodstock.

college or high school playdates did a fast fade as rock promoters filled football stadiums and hippodromes with paying customers hungry for Woodstock redux.

And still, Dylan was a no-show.

"I'm concerned about him," said Roger McGuinn told an interviewer that spring. "I'm concerned as a friend. Does a performer have an obligation to the public? If so, he has shaken that obligation."

On August 1, 1971, Dylan finally met his obligation. He made his first public appearance in nearly two years at Madison Square Garden, taking the stage as George Harrison's unannounced guest during a benefit for flood and famine victims half a world away in Bangladesh. Dylan performed a medley of golden oldies with Harrison, Eric Clapton, Leon Russell, and Ringo playing backup. Garden fans delivered a shrieking 10-minute ovation following "Hard Rain." Postmortems were unanimous: Dylan hadn't lost a step during his absence nor had he abandoned compassion for the less fortunate. Ticket sales alone for the two concerts raised more than $250,000 for UNICEF while album sales and film rights eventually brought in $5 million.

Dylan also returned to the studio that fall, recording at least one upbeat original[243] to supplement a double LP of his *Greatest Hits Vol. II*.[244] Still wary of Weberman, he routinely camouflaged himself before visiting Blue Rock Studios in nearby SoHo. He hid in plain sight on the streets of New York, covering up with hooded parka or a hunter's hat whose side flaps hid his face like a North Korean border guard.[245] Once he was safely indoors, he abandoned the disguise and got down to business.

---

[243] "Watching the River Flow."

[244] Five times platinum, his all-time bestselling album.

[245] His various getups also included false mustaches, head bandanas, and a large Panama hat.

Paranoia would seem to have made Dylan a perfect candidate for the new technology. All he had to do was lay down a vocal track in the solitary safety of his basement office on Houston Street and messenger the tape to Columbia for mixing, but Bob insisted on recording live in studio where *he* controlled the sound, not the engineer or producer.

As further proof that the old Dylan was back, in November he released his first pointed political song since the early '60s: an angry lament for black activist George Jackson who'd been shot dead by San Quentin prison guards just three weeks after the concerts for Bangladesh.

Still steeped in controversy today, Jackson's killing was either a botched escape attempt or a political assassination, depending on who tells the tale. Dylan's version leaned toward murder and seemed to pick up where he'd left off with Hattie Carroll, Emmett Till, Medgar Evers, and other martyrs of the civil rights movement. He recorded two versions—one acoustic, the other with electrified backing—and Columbia released them both as A and B sides of a single that climbed to No. 33 on the *Billboard* chart.

But "George Jackson" came and went as quickly as the dead inmate's legend. Bob's first bona fide protest song since "The Times They Are a-Changin'," the lyrics resonated anthemic anger à la "Blowin' in the Wind," yet still managed to strike a sour note. Columbia rebuffed Jackson's mother when she asked for a share of the royalties, and the song was not included on any subsequent American LP,[246] nor did Dylan play it in concert. His protest renaissance ended before it began, raising questions as to his motivation. No less a critic than America's former Poet Laureate Stephen Spender suggested his inspiration might be money: "Bob Dylan

---

[246] "George Jackson" was included on Dylan's 1978 collection *Masterpieces* released in Australia and Japan where U.S. copyright law is not recognized.

may be sincere in every line he sings, but the atmosphere of the (recording) industry soaks through an awful lot of this, like incontinent urine through pants."

Dylan could not be blamed for heeding the bottom line. He and Grossman had recently parted ways after nearly eight years. As with so many he'd once called "friend," Bob shut the door on his former manager after discovering the 50/50 Dwarf Music deal, prompting him to question every transaction, negotiation, and accounting that Grossman had ever performed on behalf of his No. 1 client.

"I haven't seen him in years," was all Bob had to say to Scaduto on the subject.

The kid from Hibbing who'd once told Nat Hentoff and Studs Terkel that he didn't care about money had come to care about it a lot.

"A cynical observer might say that Dylan no longer needed the shark since his own teeth were now sharp enough to handle any exigency," observed former Journeyman Dick Weissman, another Bob amigo from Village days.

His *laissez-faire* approach to business behind him, Bob became practical if not litigious, especially over bootlegs. *The Great White Wonder*[247] was Exhibit A. Combining several pirated Big Pink recordings along with some of his earliest demos, the album began surfacing in the backrooms of record stores as early as 1969. The first bona fide bootleg LP in a growing sub rosa industry, *The Great White Wonder* cut into Dylan's profit margin while simultaneously boosting his mystique. Trafficking in unreleased Dylan[248] material became both a badge of honor and the mark of a true fan.

---

[247] Apparently referring to the ice-cream suit he had worn at the Isle of Wight concert.

[248] The original acetate of *Highway 61*, which included "Can You Please Crawl Out Your Window" and "Sitting on a Barbed Wire Fence," was also bootlegged as *I Never Talked to Bruce Springsteen.*

He also lost royalties from the sale of so-called "booklegs": unedited early texts of his stillborn *Tarantula*. Among other buccaneers, A. J. Weberman financed his Dylan Liberation Front by running off copies of stolen *Tarantula* galleys and selling them on the street for $2 apiece.

To put an end to profiteering, Dylan gave Macmillan the go-ahead to publish an official *Tarantula*[249] in 1971 and four years later, he belatedly authorized Columbia to officially release *The Basement Tapes*.

Despite such unforeseen setbacks, Dylan managed his career just fine without Grossman. Abe Zimmerman once guessed the boy had a head for figures and it turned out he was right. But like some aging graduate student, Bob's heart remained vested in expanding his horizons, not making more money—especially when it came to music.

"I'd be doing what I'm doing if I was a millionaire or not, whether I was getting paid for it or not," he maintained.

At 30, Dylan struck an uneasy balance between art and commerce.[250] Most days he quested after his muse like a trust-fund baby, but sooner or later he had to start thinking about returning to the stage.

Invited to help them ring in 1972, Dylan joined the Band in four songs that closed out their New Year's Eve performance at New York's Academy of Music. As with Bangladesh, his appearance was

---

[249] In 2003, *Spin* magazine awarded Dylan's *Tarantula* the dubious honor of containing the single-most unintelligible sentence ever penned by a rock star: "Now's not the time to get silly, so wear your big boots and jump on the garbage clowns."

[250] Dustin Hoffman parodied Bob as suicidal George Soloway in *Who Is Harry Kellerman and Why Is He Saying Terrible Things About Me?* (1971), a long-forgotten black comedy that centers on the huge but vacuous success of a schizoid Jewish singer-songwriter.

unheralded and the lucky crowd could not get enough. Bob rewarded them with songs he hadn't played before in public, including his final contribution for the evening and the year—a very apropos "When I Paint My Masterpiece."

■ ■ ■

Since first rolling into Greenwich back in 1961, Bob regularly kept tabs on rivals, measuring his achievement against that of Phil Ochs, Tom Paxton, Paul Simon, et al. Theirs became a self-conscious fraternity reminiscent of nineteenth-century English Romantic poets. Like Lord Byron bitching over the latest from Shelley or Keats, Dylan freaked when he first heard Neil Young's "Heart of Gold." The Canadian carpetbagger stole his act, down to the harmonica bridge.

"I think it was up at No. 1 for a long time," Dylan recalled, "and I'd say, 'Shit, that's me! If it *sounds* like me it should as well *be* me.'"

The late '60s produced a bumper crop of singer-songwriters, some of whom rivaled Dylan both in quality and popularity. Like Neil Young, fellow Canadians Gordon Lightfoot and Joni Mitchell rose high on the *Billboard* charts while Dylan continued playing hide-and-seek in Greenwich Village. One Canadian in particular threatened to fill Bob's vacuum, dogging his every footstep on the road to success. Albert Grossman's secretary Mary Martin even quit her job around the time of Dylan's motorcycle accident in order to manage Leonard Cohen.

A Canadian herself, Martin dated her friendship with Dylan from his earliest Village incarnation. It was her fat gray Persian[251] that

---

[251] Lord Growling.

Bob cuddled on the cover of *Bringing It All Back Home,* and they once did laps together in Grossman's Bearsville swimming pool. Dylan knew Martin to have a proven, visceral feel for pop poetry. She spotted the Band when they played for peanuts in the bars along Toronto's Yonge Street. She introduced the Hawks to Bob while Grossman was still absorbed with Peter, Paul and Mary.[252] She'd been right about the Band; her intuition looked spot on again with this promising new minstrel from Montreal.

Seven years Bob's senior, Leonard Cohen was a tall, slack-jawed French Canadian with the gaze of a haunted whooping crane who had already established himself as a published poet and novelist[253] before he arrived in Manhattan.[254] Like Dylan, Cohen found his home away from home at the Chelsea Hotel[255] where he surrounded himself with fellow bohemians and wrote one of his most touching elegies ("Chelsea Hotel No. 2") about the night Janis Joplin[256] gave him a blow job.

"I was on speed, I weighed about 116 pounds," Cohen recalled. "It was a very crazy time. That's when I found out about everything that was going on in New York."

---

[252] The Band didn't come to Grossman's attention until they stopped crisscrossing the country with Ronnie Hawkins long enough to back up John Hammond's son John Hammond Jr. on his 1963 debut album *So Many Roads.*

[253] His second novel, *Beautiful Losers,* was a hit upon publication in 1966 and went on to sell more than 3 million copies in 20 languages despite reviews that labeled it "a tirade of obscene poetry" and "the most revolting book ever written in Canada." Cohen suffered a nervous breakdown and contemplated suicide.

[254] In the mid-50s, he did graduate work at Columbia University during which he devoured the somber romanticism of Spanish poet Federico García Lorca the way Dylan had once glommed on to Arthur Rimbaud.

[255] Joni Mitchell also wrote her own popular ode to her stay there—"Chelsea Morning."

[256] She also coauthored "Mercedes Benz" with Bob Neuwirth during his stay at the Chelsea.

Mary Martin introduced Cohen to John Hammond who did for Cohen what he'd done for Dylan six years earlier. Hammond signed him to Columbia and produced his first LP, *Songs of Leonard Cohen*. He further championed Cohen with the suits who heard no sales potential in Cohen's whispery baritone. As they'd done with "Hammond's Folly," the Columbia marketing department gave Cohen his very own pejorative: "the Sentry of Solitude."

"Whereas Mr. Dylan is alienated from society and mad about it, Mr. Cohen is alienated and merely sad about it,"[257] concluded the *New York Times'* chief music critic Donal Henahan.

And yet Cohen's gut ambition matched Bob's. According to biographer David Boucher, "Cohen is something like the Jean-Jacques Rousseau in *Confessions* who is absorbed by the pleasures of the flesh yet ridden with guilt, and desperate for absolution and redemption."

Like Dylan, his father had died young and his mother remarried. He saw women as "a means to an end, rather than an end in themselves," wrote Boucher. "They provide direct lines to something else, and connect men by plugging in their penises."

Further mimicking Dylan's path to stardom, Cohen courted a pitch-perfect muse who brought him on stage during her New York concerts and introduced him to her burgeoning audience. Just as Joan Baez made listeners forgive Dylan's nasality, Judy Collins insured that Cohen's gravelly drone could not be dismissed out of hand. She covered his songs and made her version of "Suzanne" his signature composition, thrusting him further into the spotlight.

But Leonard Cohen's love affair with Manhattan ended with the '60s. At the dawn of the new decade, like most of Dylan's fellow singer-songwriters, he deserted New York. He took his act on the

---

[257] Cohen came clean in 2001 about his lifelong bipolar battle, confessing obsessions with drugs, sex, and religion to deal with depression.

road for a while, sampling every drug he could get his hands on,[258] but ultimately landed in California where film director Robert Altman used Cohen's hypnotic vocals to score the offbeat Western *McCabe & Mrs. Miller* (1971).[259]

"Ever since the Gold Rush was augmented by Hollywood and John Steinbeck's Depression, California has been the golden wet dream for Americans imagining new identities," observed *New York Daily News* music critic Gene Santoro.

Still, Dylan resisted leaving New York. Influenced by his mother's recent move to Arizona, he did move temporarily to Phoenix and rented another place in Malibu for family vacations, but he remained wary of any permanent move. California had sun, beaches, and great-looking women on the one hand, but pervasive vacuity and naked ambition on the other. Blinded by his own ambivalence, Dylan couldn't see that the Greenwich he once knew was a ghost town.

"Dylan was surrounded by all these guys who couldn't play, couldn't sing, had no imagination," said Phil Ochs biographer Marc Eliot. "Those are the guys who finally drove him out of New York. Dylan couldn't stand that stuff."

Bob was a loner—always had been, always would be. But he needed his Golden Chords, his Band, his "anvils off which he could flash his verbal pyrotechnics," as Anthony Scaduto described Bob's musical peers.

Talented confreres like John Phillips, John Sebastian, and Roger McGuinn had vacated the Village early, years before the exodus. By 1972, all those who remained along MacDougal Street were

---

[258] For a time, his band nicknamed him Captain Mandrax, a British synonym for Quaaludes.

[259] The "Sisters of Mercy" serenade for the prostitutes in the movie was originally written for a pair of women Cohen had met during a Canadian snowstorm and invited to spend the night with him in his hotel room.

self-conscious poseurs or parasites like A. J. Weberman. Ironically, it was another Cohen—one free of talent or melancholy—who finally persuaded Dylan that it was time to leave.

"David Blue was a good-time guy," recalled Marc Eliot. "He liked to party and had a lot of stamina the way Dylan had."

Like Bob Neuwirth, Victor Maymudes, and other constants from Dylan's earliest entourage, Blue (a.k.a. Stuart Cohen) cultivated Bob's addictions and tried mightily to match his poetry, though he had neither the words nor the music to do much more than sit in the control booth and down Beaujolais whenever Dylan cut a new LP.

Blue told a British tabloid during the 1966 *Blonde on Blonde* tour, "we were friends and at one point he encouraged me." But as Bob's fame exploded and the relationship shifted, Blue struggled with his own identity.

"I didn't feel it was Dylan and me, two guys going places. It was him, and I'd go out and get a cab if he needed a cab. Not like a lackey," he rationalized, "but just [because] *he* couldn't go out and get a cab."

Blue had movie-star good looks, magnetic charm, and a seemingly unlimited supply of pharmaceuticals. He liked to party, and even during Dylan's post-accident sobriety, their nocturnal friendship flourished.

When Blue moved to L.A., it was because of Joni Mitchell. They'd met in Detroit in 1965 when she was still the shy, unknown wife of Canadian folkie Chuck Mitchell. Though she later would deny it, the title track from her chart-topping album *Blue* seemed to point directly at her affair[260] with Stuart David Cohen:

---

[260] "Joni Mitchell had taken care of David for years," recalled Eric Andersen. "She told me once that she was going over her books, and there were more checks made out to David than there were to the phone company."

Acid, booze, and ass
Needles, guns, and grass
Lots of laughs, lots of laughs . . .

By 1971, Joni Mitchell had abandoned New York for another David: a brilliant young refugee from the William Morris mailroom who promised to transform her from a mere success into a superstar, as he'd done for several other Village expatriates.

"David Geffen used to tell me that I was the only star he ever met who wanted to be ordinary," said Mitchell.

Perhaps—but like Leonard Cohen, Mitchell's extraordinary lyrics and poetic sensibility hit a commercial chord in the early '70s that rivaled Dylan's high-water mark five years earlier, and Geffen nurtured her talent the way Grossman had once nurtured Bob's.

"(Dylan) used to be better off when he was younger and an angry young man," Mitchell observed. "He would scream at you and diminish you if he thought your questions were stupid or unartistic. Now he knows he can't be an angry young kid anymore. He can't growl. Instead, he stays silent and explodes inside. Instead of taking it out on you, he takes it out internally."

As Albert Grossman faded, David Geffen rose to become the next decade's pop Svengali. Joined by fellow William Morris alumnus Eliot Roberts, Geffen formed a management firm based on a philosophy of benevolent protectionism: as long as clients delivered, they were protected, indulged, and enabled like errant livestock. Geffen and Roberts pulled together remnants of the defunct Byrds and Buffalo Springfield, threw in Joni Mitchell's new boyfriend Graham Nash, and created Crosby, Stills, Nash (and occasionally Young), just in time for Woodstock. The first supergroup of the '70s, each member was a capable singer-songwriter in his own right, but together they formed a megaforce that helped fill the vacuum left by the Beatles while simultaneously defining the direction of pop for the new decade. On their first 24-city concert tour following the release of the hit single "Suite: Judy Blue Eyes,"[261] CSN&Y grossed $9.3 million.

"This was the beginning of the end of the love-groove in American music," lamented CSN&Y's first producer Paul Rothchild in an interview he gave 20 years later.

Advising his new clients that they were perfectly capable of producing their own records, Geffen eased Rothchild out while pocketing the producer's fee for himself.

"To me, that's the moment," said Rothchild. "When David Geffen enters the California waters as a manager. The sharks have entered the lagoon and the entire vibe changes. It used to be 'Let's make music, money is a byproduct.' Then it becomes, 'Let's make money, music is a byproduct.'"

Like Grossman's using Peter, Paul and Mary to leverage Dylan during his Village days, Geffen used CSN&Y to introduce new acts. Joni Mitchell's "Woodstock" became one of the first hits that CSN&Y did not write themselves. West Hollywood nightclubs where the four musicians dropped by to jam with other East Coast refugees became the new hunting ground for talent. Like the Gaslight, Café Wha?, and Gerdes Folk City 10 years earlier, Doug Weston's Troubadour, Ed Pearl's Ash Grove, Ciro's, and the Whiskey A Go Go showcased promising young musicians. Jackson Browne. Linda Ronstadt. Glenn Frey. Don Henley. Geffen signed them all. Who wouldn't want to join the same management firm that made millionaires out of Crosby, Stills, Nash & Young?

---

[261]   Written for Leonard Cohen's muse, Judy Collins.

But even Geffen could do nothing with the talent-free David Blue. In 1971, Geffen founded Asylum Records and put out four David Blue albums over each of the next four years, none of which sold more than a few thousand copies. Going with Geffen was not a complete bust, however. Blue did hook up with Asylum's newest and by far Geffen's most lucrative act. In 1973, the Eagles recorded Blue's "Outlaw Man" on their second studio album, *Desperado*, and the income that one track generated was enough to keep Blue in drugs, booze, and women for the rest of his short life.

But he was still very much Dylan's pal and good-time Charlie. Blue wanted to share the wealth. He kept up the tattoo every time they spoke. Blue echoed Hollywood screenwriter Herman Mankiewicz's famous 1926 telegram to Ben Hecht in New York: "Millions are to be grabbed out here and your only competition is idiots." There was a party going on out in L.A. and Bob owed it to himself and to his family to cut the cord, get on the next plane, and join in.

Dylan was finally persuaded and bought an undeveloped lot in Point Dume overlooking the Pacific in 1971. There he and Sara planned to build their dream house, but not before making a detour through Durango.

⁘　⁘　⁘

Indulging his long-gestating interest in film, Dylan joined the cast of *Pat Garrett and Billy the Kid* in the autumn of 1972. Director Sam Peckinpah and producer Gordon Carroll hired him for marquee value, casting Bob as Billy's oddball sidekick Alias. In so doing, they ceded Dylan the media spotlight and, eventually, the film's score.

One of the legendary alcoholics in a profession teeming with them, Peckinpah peaked in 1969 with *The Wild Bunch*, a benchmark Western that celebrated violent death in visual premonition of twenty-first-century video games. Heroes and villains didn't just die; they exploded, the gorier the better. And while he took his lumps for multicamera close-ups of bullet-riddled cowpokes, extolling what became known as "the ballet of death," Peckinpah's box-office prowess spoke the language Hollywood understands best.

Generating buckets of cash did not exempt the director from studio politics. The atmosphere Dylan entered when he agreed to third billing behind James Coburn (Pat Garrett) and Kris Kristofferson (Billy the Kid) had already been poisoned by the same executive who oversaw *The Ed Sullivan Show* back in '63 when Dylan got the boot for talking the John Birch paranoia blues.

Former CBS president James Aubrey lost his job in a 1965 kickback scandal, but landed on his feet four years later at MGM. The studio's new owner, arbitrage pioneer Kirk Kirkorian, needed cash to build his MGM Grand Hotel, the biggest casino on the Vegas Strip, and hired Aubrey to make it happen. Combining Cary Grant charisma with Gordon Gecko ethics, Aubrey was "the Smiling Cobra" while at CBS. He never let quality get in the way of profit margins. He brought similar ruthlessness to MGM, accelerating production schedules, tightening budgets, and putting prima donnas like Peckinpah on a short leash.

Dylan knew nothing of this impending war when screenwriter Rudy Wurlitzer sent him his script the previous autumn in hopes of convincing Bob to compose a title song for the movie.

"So I wrote that song 'Billy' really quick," recalled Dylan.

But at the same time, he put himself in contention for the supporting role of Alias, a stuttering printer's devil and surviving member of Billy's gang. The salary was $6,500 for a total of three scenes. After ruling out a dozen others,[262] Peckinpah cast Dylan. Alias promptly lost his stutter and wound up in Wurlitzer's rewrite with more screen time than any other actor except the two leads. It didn't seem to matter that Bob couldn't act.

"You see (Dylan) on screen and all eyes are on him," said Kristofferson, who knew Bob through their mutual friendship with Johnny Cash. "There's something about him that's magnetic."

Bob did have screen presence. In person, his head seemed too big for his body, giving the startling effect "of a kid wearing a Bob Dylan mask," as author Paul Zollo would later describe his own first impression. As seen through a camera lens, Dylan's big head and outsized facial features pulled all eyes in his direction. Even at his clumsiest, he mesmerized.

"He doesn't even have to move," said Kristofferson. "He's a natural . . ."

Furthermore, Dylan's reputation preceded him. Everyone from day players to makeup artists wanted to step into his orbit. His influence even crept into Wurlitzer's dialogue:

Billy the Kid: "How does it feel?"

Pat Garrett: "It feels like times have changed."

Billy the Kid: "Times maybe. Not me."

Before he graduated to leading man, Kristofferson followed Bob into show business. Back in '65, the former Rhodes Scholar took a job as janitor at Columbia's Nashville recording studio to kick-start his own career. He once swept up after the *Blonde on Blonde* recording sessions, but didn't approach the wunderkind for fear of being fired.

---

[262] Among those passed over in favor of Dylan: Randy Quaid, Ed Begley Jr., Charles Martin Smith, Gary Busey, and Jackson Browne.

"I have never been that comfortable around him," Kristofferson said. "I have the greatest love and respect for him, but I have no idea what's going on in his head. He's a very nervous guy."

Not so nervous that they didn't mesh on location in Durango. By 1973, Kristofferson was a bona fide member of the singer-song-writer fraternity. During a boozy all-nighter, a relaxed Dylan helped Kristofferson mangle the lyrics of his 1970 hit, "Help Me Make It Through the Night":

Kristofferson: "Come and lay down on my face."

Dylan: "Come 'til the morning light."

Kristofferson: "You got your own disgrace."

Dylan: "But I know that it's all right."

Larry Kegan visited the set, but didn't leave when production wrapped. By now a quadriplegic following an auto accident that left him further paralyzed, the disabled Joker from Camp Herzl liked what he saw in Durango and remained behind to manage a resort for returning Vietnam vets. A model for Willem Dafoe's wheelchair-bound character in Oliver Stone's *Born on the Fourth of July,* Kegan held that disability and sex were not mutually exclusive. He made lust part of the resort's agenda.

To Bob, however, Kegan stood out once again as a reminder that by comparison, Dylan's had been a singularly blessed life . . . so far, at any rate.

Bob brought Sara, the kids, and Rover the dog with him to Mexico, but the public perception of Dylan as Family Man was already fraying. Sara told Kristofferson they'd often go weeks without speaking. During a Christmas production break, the Dylans visited George and Patti Harrison in London, but when Bob returned to Durango in January, Sara did not. Following weeks of isolation in the desert and bouts with the same influenza that sidelined Peckinpah, Sara packed up the children and headed to L.A.

Meanwhile, Peckinpah's war with MGM intensified. James Aubrey wanted him to hire cheap Mexican crews; Peckinpah insisted on importing Hollywood's best. Aubrey forbade reshooting out-of-focus scenes; Peckinpah reshot anyway. Alternately sick, hung over, or raving like a lunatic, Peckinpah roared at Aubrey's minions and whipped out his Johnson to literally piss all over the screen whenever he was displeased with the dailies.

Dylan remained as stoic around Peckinpah as Alias. His character was agreeable, impenetrable, respectful, even shy, but the real Bob was late to the set when it suited him and privately critical of Sam's ravings. While Dylan's acting never threatened James Dean's legacy, his style grew on Peckinpah, who blamed himself for Dylan's inability to hit a mark, ride a horse, or follow direction.

"Bobby Dylan was coming out with his cane and hat and his Chaplin act, and we need stuff like that to bring money in," he told producer Gordon Carroll, "but there's no way we can use any of it."

Peckinpah shot Dylan's quirky Chaplin improvisation, but labeled it "a bad take" and ordered it reshot. Somewhere in the MGM vaults, Bob's Little Tramp is preserved for posterity, but comedy had no place in Peckinpah's ponderous horse opera.

While he might have failed as an actor, Bob's cinematic appetite only increased. He studied Peckinpah's storytelling technique the way he once studied Guthrie's cadence and Mike Seeger's finger-picking style.

"I want now to *make* movies," Dylan told Kristofferson. "I've never been this close to movies before. I'll make a hell of a movie after this."

As with Pennebaker, Dylan believed he might better Peckinpah, and jumped at the chance to further his education when Gordon Carroll asked him to help score *Pat Garrett and Billy the Kid.* Two months after production wrapped, Dylan supplemented the "Billy" theme song with several bluegrass arrangements and a haunting dirge he called "Knockin' on Heaven's Door."

Back in L.A., he clashed with Peckinpah's handpicked soundtrack collaborator. Twice nominated for Oscars, once for *The Wild Bunch* and again for Peckinpah's *Straw Dogs*, composer Jerry Fielding saw Dylan as a rank amateur who would not subordinate his music to the story. Instead of complementing a death scene with a gutshot Slim Pickens, Dylan's vocal dominated like the Mormon Tabernacle Choir. Disgusted, the veteran Fielding walked out and turned the whole project over to Bobby the Kid.

And yet "Knockin' on Heaven's Door" succeeded where the movie failed, capturing boomer imagination as well as their cash. Ironically, Dylan contributed as much to the Smiling Cobra's bottom line as Peckinpah. The movie floundered and took a shellacking from critics, but "Knockin' on Heaven's Door" climbed to No. 12 on the *Billboard* singles chart while the soundtrack topped out at No. 16 among the year's bestselling LPs.

Fielding was correct about Hollywood's old guard though. AMPAS refused to even nominate "Knockin' on Heaven's Door" [263] or Bob's score. Dylan would have to wait another 30 years for Oscar recognition, even though his exquisite elegy about the death of the Old West went a long way toward reassuring fans that he still had his poetic chops. With more than 50 cover versions ranging from Boy

---

[263] "The Way We Were" by Marvin Hamlisch won the Oscar. The competition included "All That Love Went to Waste," lyrics by Sammy Cahn, from *A Touch of Class*; "Nice to Be Around," lyrics by Paul Williams from *Cinderella Liberty*; "Love," lyrics by Floyd Huddleston, from *Robin Hood;* and "Live and Let Die," lyrics and music by Paul and Linda McCartney. Hamlisch also won Best Dramatic Score. *Pat Garrett and Billy the Kid* received no nominations at all.

George to the Red Army Chorus, "Knockin' on Heaven's Door" continued to resonate well into the next century.[264]

Not so with *Pat Garrett and Billy the Kid.* James Aubrey wrested away Peckinpah's director's cut and recut the film, lopping off the opening scene which explains every plot point that follows. Aubrey's movie ends with a grinning still of Pat and Billy moments after one murders the other. Even Dylan was appalled.

"Sam himself just didn't have final control and that was the problem," he said. "I saw it in a movie house one cut away from his and I could tell that it had been chopped to pieces."

Peckinpah died in 1985 and did not live to see his version released three years later. MGM's new owner Ted Turner sanctioned the restoration of 16 minutes to *Pat Garrett and Billy the Kid*, including the crucial opening scene. No less a fan than Martin Scorsese declared Sam's cut a masterpiece.

The lesson wasn't lost on Bob. He vowed he'd never let studio bosses do to his film what Aubrey had done to Peckinpah's. The only way to ensure integrity was to stay away from the suits and control everything from principal photography to craft services. Of course, having a coherent storyline and a sober editor would also be a big help.

⸬ ⸬ ⸬

Dylan reunited with the Band in November 1973 for sessions that evolved into *Planet Waves.*[265] He and his basement mates had moved

---

[264] Many Generation X'ers would be surprised to learn it was not a Guns N' Roses original.

[265] Originally titled *Love Songs,* he switched to *Ceremonies of the Horseman,* then *Wedding Song* before finally settling on *Planet Waves* for his 14th studio album.

to Malibu the previous summer, convening once more under new management and a new label.

"When they went to Malibu, everything changed," Ronnie Hawkins recalled of his former Hawks. "Hollywood will change anybody. Drugs messed up so much. Their records were so great."

In a coup felt all the way to Columbia's executive suites, David Geffen added Dylan to his pop stable, signing him to Asylum Records while Bob and the Band prepped for their first national concert tour since the summer of his motorcycle accident.

Publicly, Dylan blamed Saturn[266] for his eight-year absence from the concert circuit. "It came into my chart a few years ago, and just flew off again a few months ago," he explained to *Rolling Stone*.

But money had as much to do with ending his early retirement as astrology. Travel, dabbling in moviemaking and other pricey self-indulgences, plus supporting a growing family and compulsively investing in real estate got to be expensive. In addition to buying a seaside lot in Point Dume and as many surrounding parcels as possible to assure isolation from the neighbors, Dylan also acquired an 80-acre farm in the village of Andover, about an hour north of Minneapolis–St. Paul. He intended to turn both into gated, self-sufficient compounds where the uninvited wouldn't get past the fences. Geffen promised him both the ways and means.

When word went forth that Dylan and the Band[267] would kick off 1974 with a six-week "Before the Flood" odyssey to 21 North American cities, a mail-order scramble for 650,000 tickets yielded $9.3 million in a matter of days. Geffen grossed $5 million while Dylan netted $2 million before even playing a note.

---

[266] In astrology, the ringed planet rules sobriety, discipline, and responsibility. Saturn restricts and enforces a sense of duty, floating in and out of lives for a period of about seven and a half years.

[267] Like Bob, the Band switched to Geffen, paying Grossman $625,000 to get out of their contract.

L.A. turned out to be a great place to rehearse, offering eternal sunshine along with freeway anonymity. Dylan no longer had to don a fright wig to catch a cab in a snowstorm. He could just drive himself, as he'd done back in Woodstock when weather permitted. His California transition complete, he settled Sara and family into rented digs on Pacific Coast Highway while laying plans for their idyllic estate overlooking the Pacific. At the same time, his marriage crumbled.

"Dylan has always tended to get sticky about women," observed *The New Yorker*'s Ellen Willis, "to classify them as goddesses to be idolized or bitches to be mercilessly trashed."

Sara had bucked the odds for almost ten years, holding on to her man through mood swing and dalliance, anchoring his affection with a passel of children who adored him as deeply as he cared for them. But when Dylan hit the road again, all bets were off. Marriage suited him well enough inside his domestic shelter, whether it be Byrdcliffe or his Village brownstone, but once he and his band—any band—climbed on board a leased 707 or booked in under assumed names at hotel after anonymous hotel, groupies materialized. As fellow party animal David Blue once observed, Dylan operated from his cock—especially after lacing his frontal lobes with weed or alcohol.

But Dylan preferred to stay hitched—an impossible duality even for a self-described Gemini who struggled constantly with split personality. Getting back to the concert circuit resurrected the conflict between laid-back countrypolitan and restless romantic *poète maudit* who maxed out life as a road warrior. That duality surfaced in largely forgettable songs he recorded for *Planet Waves*. On the one hand he asserted that "I love you more than blood" and "your love cuts like a knife" ("Wedding Song"), while on the other, Dylan snarled that "I hate myself for lovin' you and the weakness that it showed" ("Dirge").

Sara might be his muse but she also held his leash. The years, the vows, the children that he treasured didn't add up to monogamy or memorable music. *Planet Waves* struck a hollow note. A restless heart like Bob's might swing from sweet sentiment to acerbic lyrics, but clever words alone didn't chill the gut or thrill the soul. While Band leader Robbie Robertson praised Dylan for resurrecting the spirit of Hank Williams, he just as quickly condemned his failed poetry.

"It can get a little blabby, and I wish that it could say something, and be very moving and very soulful at the same time," he said. "When something tends to *ramble* on, that's not the train that I came in on."

Rambling *Planet Waves* did produce one deeply moving classic which Dylan wrote the previous year during the family's sojourn in Tucson. Inspired by his children, "Forever Young" came to him instantly as in the old doped-up days before *Blonde on Blonde*. Without his even having to think about it, the song materialized "in a minute."

"I don't know. Sometimes that's what you're given," he said. "You're given something like that. You don't know what it is exactly that you want but this is what comes. That's how the song came out. . . . I was going for something else, the song wrote itself."

He liked "Forever Young" so much he recorded two versions— one a waltz, the other more up tempo. Was it too syrupy? Too maudlin? A chance comment from an old pal's tootsie nearly derailed its inclusion in *Planet Waves* all together.

After securing millions in his family's lucrative Lake Superior fishery, Dylan's Camp Herzl amigo Lou Kemp moved to L.A. and reclaimed their friendship. Kemp joined Bob Neuwirth and David

Blue as part of Bob's inner circle. During the *Planet Waves* sessions, he dropped by the Shangri-La Studio[268] in Zuma Beach as much to impress his girlfriend as to support his old friend.

"You're getting mushy in your old age, Bob," she teased after a playback of "Forever Young."

Her throwaway line stung. Dylan had already recorded "Forever Young" in a half dozen different styles, showing a deep insecurity that never plagued him before. "One-Take" Bob once commandeered a studio for a couple of graveyard shifts and—presto!—a new LP was born. Not this time. A flip remark from a stranger could do to Dylan what *glissendorf* did to the bongs of Hibbing High.

His producer Rob Fraboni talked him out of deep-sixing "Forever Young," but Dylan tinkered with *Planet Waves* for weeks, shifting the track sequence eight times and aborting the cover photo at the last minute. He substituted a crude charcoal drawing[269] that made as much sense as the technically perfect but largely stillborn contents of the album itself.

His long-suffering fan base didn't seem to care. Without waiting for reviews, they snapped up the album the same way they purchased tickets for the upcoming tour. *Planet Waves* shot to No. 1 on the *Billboard* chart just in time for the opening show in Chicago. And while the album tended to disappoint and faded quickly, the concerts did not. Bob and the Band were greeted by fans and critics alike as the Second Coming. Tour impresario Bill Graham's army of sound engineers captured it all for Asylum, assuring a one-two punch following *Planet Waves*. Asylum released *Before the Flood* in June—Bob's first double LP since *Blonde on Blonde*. It was both a

---

[268] A one-time brothel converted first to a school and then a studio.

[269] In addition to a trio of Picasso-esque figures and a peace sign, the sketch bears the subtitles "Moonglow" and "Cast-iron songs & torch ballads" and no further explanation.

commemorative must-have for the thousands who witnessed the performances and an enduring souvenir for those who never got to see the Bob/Band alchemy in person.

And while those performances met and exceeded expectation, Dylan revealed none of his inner turmoil. Levon Helm remembered "tons of white powder" getting them through set after set and Bob found accommodating ladies at every stop. But the most he had to say to his worshipful public was a one-line promise with which he climaxed the final concert at the Los Angeles Forum in his new hometown.

"See ya next year."

10

ON THE ROAD AGAIN

In a deposition delivered before a small battery of lawyers nearly two decades later, Ruth Tyrangiel recalled with *Chronicles* clarity sitting on a Queen Anne chair in a lavishly appointed suite at San Francisco's posh Fairmont Hotel on February 10, 1974. It was the day before Dylan and the Band played the Oakland Coliseum in one of their climactic "Before the Flood" concerts, and Ruth remembered snuggling up beside Bob as he introduced her as his wife to *Rolling Stone* publisher Jann Wenner.

Never mind that they were both married at the time to other people, or that Ruth would exchange vows twice again in the ensuing years while Bob would divorce, remarry, and divorce once more. For the next 20 years, Ruth Tyrangiel waltzed in and out of Dylan's life like the gypsy girl she was, and Bob promised someday he'd make good on his marriage proposal.

"He waved a very long, sick carrot for too many years and that's sick," she declared when she filed for $5 million in palimony.

Ruth became one of several friends with benefits during the "Before the Flood" concert tour, decades before that polite term for easy coupling came into vogue. Most backstage gal pals remained anonymous, satisfied to have made Dylan's intimate acquaintance once or twice before quietly letting themselves out the bedroom door the following morning. But there were trysts with more staying power, and they were occasionally commemorated in song.

One enduring hookup was a 24-year-old publicist for Columbia Records who influenced Bob's return to his former label later that same year. Ellen Bernstein stayed up all night playing backgammon in Dylan's hotel room, making so deep an impression that he immortalized her as the girl from Ashtabula in "You're Gonna Make Me Lonesome When You Go."

"To put it in a song is so ridiculous, but it was very touching," Bernstein told Dylan biographer Clinton Heylin. She characterized her on-again, off-again companion as "a very caring, loving person and lots of fun to be with, so I didn't tend to sit around and analyze what his state of mind was . . ."

Neither Bernstein nor Tyrangiel gave much thought to Sara or the children, which was not surprising in that Bob seldom dwelled on family life while on the road.

At 32, Dylan wrestled with a condition that Georgia governor Jimmy Carter would refer to as "lust in my heart" during a *Playboy* interview he gave two years later. In that same interview, the future president recalled Dylan visiting the governor's mansion during the Atlanta stop of the "Before the Flood" tour.

"He didn't have any inclination to change the world," Carter told *Playboy*. "He wasn't crusading."

And yet Dylan would become as much a centerpiece of Carter's presidential campaign as peanut farming or post-Watergate moralizing. Every president thereafter would invoke a line from the growing Dylan oeuvre at least once during his White House tenure, either to illustrate an oratorical point or to rally the populous to his particular administration's cause *du jour*.

But in the spring of 1974, Bob Dylan wasn't interested in presidential politics, the impending collapse of the Richard Milhous

Nixon Administration, or the rise of Jimmy Carter. Bob Dylan was once again intent on finding Bob Dylan.

"There is no answer to who Bob Dylan is," he told an interviewer. "It's a meaningless question . . . Socrates said, 'Know thyself.' We spend a lifetime finding that out. But the names don't necessarily mean something. We are underneath the name what we really are. Back there where the soul is, is who we really are . . . and like Woody Guthrie said, 'We're all one soul, anyhow.' So it doesn't matter."

On reflection years later, Dylan would scorn the Me Decade as it was dubbed by journalist Tom Wolfe, calling the '70s an era of "take, take, take." While living through those years, Dylan was as self-involved and grasping as any navel-gazing EST-hole. He never announced his intent to become some sort of twentieth-century Renaissance man, yet he left no doubt that he wanted to conquer culture beyond mere music and poetry.

While *Tarantula* confirmed his severely limited ability to sustain prose narrative, Dylan bounced back from that initial debacle with *Writings & Drawings*—a 1974 assemblage of song lyrics, free verse from concert programs, and rambling album liner notes. He accompanied his songbook with line drawings and cubist doodles akin to those that Guthrie had scattered through the pages of *Bound for Glory*, but unlike Woody's autobiography, *Writings & Drawings* contained no storyline.

Though hardly a bestseller, *Writings & Drawings* did re-ignite Bob's artistic aspirations. Following the dubious precedents set by his kindergarten-style album covers for *Self Portrait, Music from Big Pink,* and *Planet Waves*, he decided to take art more seriously. Ten years earlier, fanzine journalist Laurie Henshaw punctuated a typical Dylan interview by timidly asking, "Do you paint?"

"Yeah, sure," he answered.

"What sort of painting?" she persisted.

"I painted my house," he answered, after which he stood and left the room.

Pictures never came to Dylan as easily as words. Even his most ardent apologists didn't see Dylan as a threat to Andy Warhol, let alone Picasso. Back in Bob's countrypolitan phase, his Woodstock neighbor and fellow amateur artist Bruce Dorfman encouraged Bob's hobby and gave him a deeper appreciation of abstract impressionism and the circus dreamscapes of Marc Chagall. But Dylan displayed none of the talent or ambition to duplicate a Chagall or Van Gogh. If he ever stood a chance of producing paintings that matched his poetry, he had to apprentice himself to as patient and talented an artist as Woody had been a songwriter.

"I was convinced I wasn't going to do anything else," Dylan recalled, "and I had the good fortune to meet a man in New York City who taught me how to see."

In the weeks following his triumphant concert tour, Dylan returned to New York and indentured himself to artist Norman Raeben.

"He came to this country from Russia in the '20s, started out as a boxer and ended up painting portraits of women," said Bob.

The crusty 73-year-old son of celebrated turn-of-the-century Yiddish storyteller Sholem Aleichem,[270] Raeben auditioned students at his 11th-floor studio above Carnegie Hall before he'd allow them to join his classes. Despite an introduction from Robin Fertik, one of Sara's friends, Dylan almost didn't make the cut. No fan of Top 40 radio, Raeben knew Dylan only as a bad artist with bad habits badly executed on bad canvases.

---

[270] A Ukrainian émigré who gave his adopted nation the Yiddish cast of characters that would populate *Fiddler on the Roof*, Aleichem was a Hasidic Jew whose New York City funeral in 1916 attracted more than 100,000 mourners. "Life," he said, "is a dream for the wise, a game for the fool, a comedy for the rich, a tragedy for the poor."

Fellow student John Amato once overheard Raeben slam Dylan's clumsy painting of a vase as "tangled up in blue." Nevertheless, Bob left his ego at the door and suffered Raeben's dismissive scolds and abuse for months, breaking old habits while learning to see the world anew as a visual artist.

"He put my mind and my hand and my eye together in a way that allowed me to do consciously what I unconsciously felt," said Dylan.

But painting alone didn't pull Bob out of his funk. Along with loose women, he also indulged once more in the mind-numbing excesses of weed, white powder, and wine. Two weeks before his 33rd birthday, Dylan got falling-down drunk with Phil Ochs and Dave Van Ronk before a benefit concert at Madison Square Garden. Just as in the old Village days when he'd tank up before a civil rights hoot, he lent his name and presence to the Friends of Chile, and subsequently embarrassed himself on and off stage.

Dylan joined an eclectic lineup that included Pete Seeger, Dennis Hopper, Arlo Guthrie, and Beach Boys Mike Love and Dennis Wilson in singing out against the murderous right-wing dictatorship of Chilean general Augusto Pinochet. It is frequently cited as his single-worst public performance. Years after swearing off protest, Bob the apolitical country squire stumbled back on stage with an incomprehensible version of "Blowin' in the Wind" that he sang from a cheat sheet taped to a microphone stand while Von Ronk steadied him from behind to keep him from toppling over.

He didn't sober up after the concert either. Dylan misplaced his Gibson backstage and whined to his fellow drunks: "My guitar! My guitar! What would I do without my guitar?" Once he relocated his instrument, he joined half a dozen others outside the Garden where they all piled into a cab for the short ride to Central Park West and a concert afterparty. But too many guitars and too many drunks spooked the driver.

Didn't the cabbie know who Bob Dylan was? Apparently not. He ordered everyone out. Dylan punched his window as he drove way, screaming "You motherfucker!"

Sara joined her husband at the party and took charge of his sobriety. She still had her haunting eyes and auburn mane, but Mrs. Dylan's halo had slipped. The Woodstock earth mother who once calmed chaos by simply stepping into its midst now had a nicotine addiction that rivaled her husband's. She bummed cigarettes all night long and had an irritating habit of leaping in front of Bob during cocktail conversation in order to pull him away to meet somebody new. As the evening wore on, Bob began ignoring her.

Shortly after that bacchanal, he and Sara quietly separated. During an interview 15 years later, long after she'd vanished from his life for good, Bob waxed rhetorical over the uneasy balance between men and women: "God of the self or goddess of the self? Somebody told me it was goddess of the self. Somebody told me that the goddess rules over the self. Gods don't concern themselves with such earthly matters. Only goddesses . . . would stoop so low or bend down so low."

Sara made it clear she was finished stooping. Bob took the kids and retreated to the family's new 80-acre spread on the Crow River in the hamlet of Hanover, an hour's drive north of Minneapolis. There he would convert a barn into an artist's studio and build residences for Beatty, his brother David and his family, and for David's mother-in-law. In the coming years, there would be a gym, tennis and basketball courts, a pool, and a general aura of secrecy about the compound's very existence—a sanctuary where Dylan could hide whenever he needed to recharge in the same way he'd once been able to hide at Hi Lo Ha. Ellen Bernstein joined him there that summer and watched him wrestle his demons firsthand.

"He would do his writing early in the morning and then kinda materialize around midday, come downstairs, and eventually, during the day, share what he had written," she recalled.

Bernstein sewed for him and fed him homemade granola the way Sara once had done, and all the while he was synthesizing something new in a small red notebook that he carried with him everywhere.

■ ■ ■

"A man is married to a woman who has made him a home, in every sense of the word," wrote *New Yorker* pop critic Ellen Willis. "He assumes that she is as content as he is. Suddenly, she declares that their marriage is intolerable. She reveals needs, expectations, bitter resentments that he never suspected; makes demands that he doesn't know how to meet. He reacts with love and hate, guilt and self-pity, fear and despair. He is angry that she has disrupted not only his comfort but his sense of reality, that she is not what she represented herself to be; and at the same time, he is deeply wounded that she has guarded her secret self from him. Eventually, the marriage ends or survives, and he learns something about himself and women, or doesn't."

While Willis made these general observations about the mid-70s feminist revolution and not specifically about *Blood on the Tracks*, a better summation of the underlying theme of Bob's mid-70s masterwork would be hard to find. The bittersweet concept album that reclaimed his mantle as undisputed poet of his generation became *the* original breakup album. As such, the LP both met and surpassed the test of enduring art[271]: *Blood on the Tracks* stopped time.

From "Tangled Up in Blue" to the nostalgic farewell of "You're Gonna Make Me Lonesome When You Go," Bob's audience not only had to suspend disbelief; they were asked to surrender all expectation about the linear nature of time itself. There is no beginning, middle, or end to *Blood on the Tracks.* Dylanologists by the dozens have parsed the geography and shifts in tense that take Bob from past to future and back again with stops along the way in Italy, Delacroix, Montague Street, and a hundred other destinations. The simple wonder of *Blood on the Tracks* is that it remains as enigmatic as it is engaging from its first trip round the turntable to its five-hundredth. A decade after *Highway 61*, Dylan had answered precisely how it felt to be on his own; to have loved and lost and learned to love again. His confession of profound disillusionment with his dying marriage rings as true today as it did when he first recorded it in the autumn and winter of 1974, in New York and Minneapolis.

Kevin Odegard, who played guitar during the Minneapolis sessions, summed up Dylan's alchemy 30 years later in the dedication of *A Simple Twist of Fate,* his 2005 memoir about the making of *Blood on the Tracks:* "This book is for all who believe that for one brief heart-breaking moment, the guitars were in tune, the voice was on the mark, and every song on the album was a fine, polished diamond."

Blood on the Tracks struck a deep chord with thousands upon thousands of '60s survivors who married for love just like Bob and Sara, advanced from collegiate poverty to middle-class stability,

---

[271] As defined by novelist Henry Miller, a favorite of Dylan, "The role of an artist is to inoculate the word with disillusionment." Miller, who once played Ping-Pong with Dylan, also advised that the only three things to be done with a woman were to love her, suffer for her, or turn her into literature.

established families along the way, and still arrived at a point in their lives where "happily ever after" seemed inadequate at best, hollow at worst. In her 1974 bestselling examination of the tectonic shifts that age imposes on American lives, *Passages* author Gail Sheehy first popularized the idea of midlife crisis. Dylan took the concept a step further, merging his own year of soul-searching with what he regarded as the mystical climax of Saturn's seven-year visit to his birth sign of Gemini. Echoing a line from John Lennon, his dream seemed over, and his angst spilled out on each of the 10 tracks of his 15th studio album.

But it was not an easy birth. He later claimed to have written all of the songs "in about a month," but *Blood on the Tracks* took months to get down on vinyl.

For the original New York sessions, he recruited Eric Weissberg's bluegrass band Deliverance, but they couldn't keep up with Bob's unaccommodating style. Rather than rehearse to work out the kinks, Dylan dumped most of Deliverance after two sessions and added new sidemen in his search for just the right sound. Three months later, with the album's release only weeks away, he tossed half the tracks and returned to the studio—this time in Minneapolis, courtesy of his kid brother.

David both worshiped and feared Bob. He tried mightily to follow in his brother's musical footsteps, stopping just short of openly trafficking on the Dylan name. After finishing college, he managed a folk group called the Greenwood Singers, wrote and produced local TV and radio advertising jingles, and began Bernard Productions to manage new pop acts in and around Dinkytown.

David Zimmerman was a self-promoter with the husky nebbish appearance of his father and the pleasant effervescence of his mother. He directed a Broadway-type musical in the mid-70s called *Growing Pains* and invited his brother back home to Minnesota for the premiere. David's coming-of-age story was set in Hibbing but that made little difference. Bob left the theater 20 minutes before the curtain came down. He did not suffer mediocrity, even if it came from his own flesh and blood. *Growing Pains* closed soon after it opened—the first and last time David would try emulating Bob's penchant for turning autobiography into art.

In the week before the new year of 1975, David did find a way to please his big brother. Bob made an annual tradition of coming home for the holidays to his farm, but during this first December in the new family compound, he spent Christmas kvetching over *Blood on the Tracks*. David picked up his cue, pulled together a crew of local musicians, and ran through Bob's tunes one more time.

The resulting tracks replaced half those produced in New York, including the haunting opener "Tangled Up in Blue,"[272] and while neither David nor his Minneapolis musicians got album credit or royalties, their efforts shared in Bob's immortality. The band members continue to commemorate their roles well into the twenty-first century with a *Blood on the Tracks* benefit concert staged each August in Minneapolis.

When the album topped the *Billboard* chart during the early months of 1975, Dylan did not share the band's satisfaction of a job well done. To him, *Blood on the Tracks* was private catharsis tailored for mass commercial appeal. In a rare radio interview he gave later that year to PP&M's Mary Travers, he acknowledged that the album brimmed with personal pain, but denied it had anything to do with his crumbling marriage. Years later, Jakob Dylan would beg to differ, declaring that he heard the echo of his parents' pitched battles

---

[272] He revised the lyrics ten years later in an Amsterdam hotel room. "That was another of those songs where you're writing and you've got it, you know what it's about, but half of it you just don't get the way you wanted to," he explained to *Musician* magazine.

in the haunted hallways of their Malibu home each time he listened to the album.

⊞ ⊞ ⊞

While Dylan remained married for the time being, *Blood on the Tracks* did represent his divorce from David Geffen. Dylan's tour with the Band netted nearly $13 million, but all U.S. record sales topped $2.36 billion during 1975. Bob's share of the exploding pop market should have been substantial, yet he never seemed to have enough money, and Geffen got the blame. For better or worse, Dylan's return to Columbia coincided with his determination to be his own business manager as well as his own producer, promoter, and music publisher.

If he'd learned nothing else from Albert Grossman, it was that publishing was where the real money lay. Expenses, overhead, and outright corporate theft often devoured touring and retail profits, but royalties *always* paid off. Following his bitter break with his former manager, Bob created Ram's Horn Music,[273] the first repository for his songs without Grossman as partner.[274] Bob alone controlled his ever-increasing cash flow. He also controlled his burgeoning real estate portfolio.

In addition to the farm in Minnesota, the ranch in Tucson, and the Dylans' remaining real estate in Woodstock, Montauk, and

---

[273] Named for the shofar, the sacred instrument sounded by rabbis during the so-called Days of Awe between Rosh Hashanah and Yom Kippur, his music publishing arm seemed to belie Bob's public denial of his Jewish roots. Its British counterpart was Big Ben Music, Ltd.

[274] In addition to Dwarf Music, he and Grossman created Big Sky Music after their break with Witmark, and royalties from most of Bob's earliest and best-known songs flowed through one or the other for the next 20 years.

Manhattan,[275] Bob poured his nouveau riches into a dream home overlooking the Pacific. He and Sara systematically bought up adjoining property around the Point Dume mansion[276] and over the next two years, the compound grew to 12 acres.

In record time, the house mushroomed into a hotel. A simple remodel that began as an additional bedroom for one of the children evolved into a $5 million overhaul, transforming the existing building into a 6,000-square-foot multi-themed, split-level Kremlin complete with copper-skinned onion dome, a grotto swimming pool with bridge, and a Great Hall large enough to suspend one of Bob's first automobiles from the ceiling. Artisans and contractors came and went by the dozens. Some camped for months in tepees on the property while they designed and manufactured everything from custom doors to individually fired tiles. The Greenwich minstrel who once spurned cash spared no expense. His home literally became his castle.

Completing the fairy tale, Sara became as profligate as any princess imagined by the Brothers Grimm. Her passive-aggressive husband went along with every new expense, adding his own free-spending fantasies from time to time. But when the bills came due, trouble brewed. The money pit expanded in direct proportion with their marital discord.

Indeed, the long-delayed release of *The Basement Tapes* in the spring of '75 was as much about earning extra income as it was chronicling Bob's shift from acid to country rock. Staged in the

---

[275] Tempered by the Weberman episode, the Dylans moved to anonymous quarters Midtown on 49th Street, far from the neighborhood where they had met, started their family, and tried unsuccessfully to resettle following their Woodstock retreat.

[276] As an additional investment, they also purchased an undeveloped tract miles away, higher up in a remote section of the Santa Monica Mountains straddling the Los Angeles–Ventura County line.

boiler room of a Y.M.C.A., the cover photo was meant to resemble the cluttered basement of Big Pink. The album Greil Marcus labeled Dylan's most subversive featured old-timey Bob and the Band on the cover flanked by David Blue, Neil Young, and Ringo Starr. Inside, were the missing links that connected *Blonde on Blonde* with *John Wesley Harding*. *The Basement Tapes* was his second *Billboard*-hit LP in less than a year.

But increasing his income didn't defuse domestic strife. Bob's remedy was to run away. After a brief reconciliation between *Blood on the Tracks* and *The Basement Tapes*, he left his family and resumed his role as wayfaring *schnorrer*, moving from couch to couch the way Woody once did when he abandoned Arlo and his sisters.

Late in the spring, Dylan took off to Europe where he roomed for a while in Paris with artist David Oppenheim, who praised "his amazing self-confidence." He added that Bob was "the most egotistical person I know."

Dylan celebrated his 34th birthday at a gypsy festival at Saintes-Marie-de-la-Mer along the Côte d'Azur, absorbing the flamenco rhythms of the natives the way he had once absorbed the *Anthology of American Folk Music*, salting each tune away as the foundation for future composition.

By the end of June, he'd returned to Greenwich and moved into a friend's loft. He reconnected with old friends like Ramblin' Jack, Bob Neuwirth, and David Blue, but also cultivated new acquaintances like composer Jacques Levy.

Dylan had met Levy a year earlier through Roger McGuinn. Best known for concocting the off-Broadway revue *Oh! Calcutta!*, Levy held a PhD in psychology, but climaxed his own midlife crisis by abandoning a career in counseling to take up musical theater. Following the minor success of *Oh! Calcutta!,* Levy persuaded

McGuinn to help transform the gloomy Norwegian satire *Peer Gynt* into a musical comedy. While their project never got off the ground, it did yield several McGuinn-Levy songs that were among the last ever recorded by the Byrds.

When Dylan bumped into Levy on Bleecker Street that July, Levy invited him up to his apartment. Bob got right to the point.

"I really like the stuff you do with Roger," he said. "How about if you and I do something together?"

It wasn't Dylan's first collaboration. He and the Band's Richard Manuel and Rick Danko had written together in the basement of Big Pink, notably "Tears of Rage" (Manuel) and "This Wheel's on Fire" (Danko). But beginning with the tomb-raiding saga "Isis"[277] and the rollicking *meringue* "Mozambique,"[278] he and Levy embarked on a new style of storytelling reminiscent of Bob's earliest polemics about Hattie Carroll, Davey Moore, and, more recently, George Jackson.

Levy spent three weeks with Dylan at his East Hampton retreat, piecing together most of the songs for Bob's follow-up to *Blood on the Tracks*. Summarizing Dylan's genius, Levy compared his spare lyrics to stage directions: "You know, Bob loves movies, and he can write these movies that take place in eight or ten minutes, yet seem as full or fuller than regular movies."

Indeed, one Dylan-Levy ballad became a movie a quarter century later. Based on the life of middleweight boxer Rubin "Hurricane" Carter, director Norman Jewison's 1999 biopic evolved out

---

[277] "A song about marriage," according to Dylan, he dedicated "Isis" to Leonard Cohen for delivering his own ironic definition of wedded bliss—"the hottest furnace of the spirit."

[278] Begun as oneupsmanship to see who could rhyme the most words with the name of the South African nation, the song evolved into a flirtatious reggae suited to the disco era.

of Bob's hit single about the 1966 murders that landed Carter in a New Jersey prison.

In eleven tight stanzas, Dylan and Levy made a convincing case for the wrongful conviction of "The Hurricane," based in part on Bob's prison visit with Carter that summer after he'd read the boxer's autobiography. As with George Jackson, Carter could not have found a more effective advocate. Whereas Jackson was mythologized as a martyr, however, Carter remained very much alive, and anxious for Bob to help arrange a pardon "for something that he never done."

Bob believed, and yet doubt lingered. Carter won a new trial following the release of "Hurricane" and was convicted for the triple murder a second time. When a federal judge finally ordered the 48-year-old convict's release in 1985, it was based on the prosecution's alleged racism during his first two trials. Now in his 70s, the former middleweight "who coulda been the champion of the world"[279] lives in Toronto where he is a motivational speaker and outspoken advocate for the wrongly convicted though his own innocence was never proved.

What is clear is that Carter grew up a violent young petty criminal not unlike George Jackson, quite capable of homicide until he sobered during his time in jail and mellowed further as he passed into middle age. Carter maintained he was not guilty and was repeatedly honored for championing other convicts in the years since his release, but his prosecutors never stopped contending that Dylan's ballad merely succeeded in exonerating a killer.

---

[279] Peaking a year before his arrest, Carter scored 27 wins with 19 knockouts in a 40-fight professional career, once climbing as high as No. 3 among contenders, but he'd declined by the time police fingered him and his friend John Artis for the triple murder at Paterson's Lafayette Grill.

Equally controversial if not nearly so ambiguous, another Dylan-Levy ballad exalted the life and death of Mafioso Joey Gallo. In the tradition of Woody's "Pretty Boy Floyd," Levy's lyrics rehabilitated the memory of a Brooklyn sociopath by transforming him into a deeply misunderstood street philosopher with a penchant for Kafka, Tolstoy, and Camus.

Crazy Joe got his nickname for adopting the persona of actor Richard Widmark's giggling assassin in the 1947 noir classic *Kiss of Death,* but Gallo was never a matinee idol. Before his enemies gunned him down in front of his family at a Little Italy restaurant in 1972, Gallo initiated New York's bloodiest mob war since the Roaring Twenties, dispatching rivals with everything from bullets to strychnine.

But those who listened to Dylan mourn the death of "Joey" only heard about a wry, articulate, and much-maligned intellectual from Red Hook who never got a break. Missing in totem from "Joey" was the scabrous douche who executed with cold-blooded impunity while introducing crack to Harlem. As pop critic Lester Bangs wrote after its release, Dylan's 11-minute paean to "Joey" was "one of the most mindlessly amoral pieces of repellently romanticist bullshit ever recorded . . ."

"His chief literary virtue—sensitivity to psychological nuance—belongs to fiction more than poetry," said *The New Yorker*'s Ellen Willis.

In rewriting the lives of real-life characters,[280] Dylan's myth-making reflected a dark tendency to embrace the thrill of being an

---

[280] They also wrote "Catfish," a tribute to New York Yankees pitcher Jim "Cat-fish" Hunter, but it didn't make the album and wasn't released until 1991.

outlaw without actually having to cross the line himself.[281] The other miniscreenplays he and Levy wrote that summer weren't as loaded with lies or as partisan as "Joey" and "Hurricane." The rabbinical chant of "One More Cup of Coffee" resonated with elongated gypsy vowels straight out of the Casbah while the Caribbean fantasy "Black Diamond Bay" had the fantastic sweep of a James Bond movie. When Dylan entered the studio that fall, he was armed with a collection of well-crafted ballads and no less a backup vocalist than Emmylou Harris. The result was *Desire*, for which Allen Ginsberg wrote the liner notes and violinist Scarlett Rivera made her debut as the fiery fiddler backing Bob on "Hurricane."

While most *Desire* tracks were Dylan-Levy collaborations, one stood out as Dylan's naked plea to his estranged wife. Allen Ginsberg called it "ancient blood singing."

With none of his equivocating over the breaking-up-is-hard-to-do content of *Blood on the Tracks,* the climactic song of *Desire* was replete with specific reference to domestic bliss: the Dylan kids playing together on the beach at Malibu and Montauk, the trysts in Portugal, Jamaica, and the Chelsea Hotel, and Bob's first flat-out confession that Sara was indeed his sad-eyed lady. He invited her to the studio to hear him record "Sara," and one more time his magic worked.

The Rolling Thunder Revue was about to leave the station, and Mrs. Dylan was on board.

---

[281] Alternatively, "The Lonesome Death of Hattie Carroll" was based on an actual murder. The real William Zantzinger later considered suing Dylan for distorting the facts, but because he was indeed guilty of manslaughter, nobody rallied to his cause.

11

RENALDO AND SARA

The Rolling Thunder Revue coincided with the release of *Desire* in much the same way that the "Before the Flood" tour had hyped *Planet Waves,* but without a David Geffen or Bill Graham orchestrating the itinerary or collecting the cash. Under the loose control of Zebra Concerts Inc., Dylan ran his own musical odyssey from start to finish.

"I don't like to feel controlled by others," he said. "I choose people. They don't choose me."

He later suggested that he had hatched his plan for a rock 'n' roll blitz across America during the 61st birthday celebration of Gerdes Folk City founder Mike Porco,[282] but Dylan had already hired camera crews to capture the event on film, implying a far grander scheme than the mere feting of an old friend.

Bob had long incubated a fantasy of a *laissez-faire* musical circus to match the Art B. Thomas traveling carnival of his youth. More than a year earlier, Phil Ochs discussed the possibility over many, many drinks before and after the Friends of Chile concert, and Ramblin' Jack had prodded Bob for years to gather together a caravan and hit the road.

---

[282] Among the first of many Village elders to take pity on Bob, Porco turned 61 on Oct. 23, 1975. He sponsored Dylan for a cabaret card while he was still a minor so that he could legally perform, joking forever after that he was Bob's stepfather.

Porco's birthday gave Dylan the necessary focal point to assemble old friends and new for a semispontaneous road show set to the soundtrack of *Desire,* though Bob's idea of spontaneity differed considerably from that of his peers. Impulse demanded an impresario. Bob appointed himself.

While teary-eyed Porco blew out the candles, Dylan quietly auditioned the ragtag gathering of old folkies, Hollywood groupies, and bona fide rockers who'd returned to the Folk City stage. Phil Ochs was one of the last up, wearing shades and the same fedora that Dylan had worn during his own performance earlier in the evening. Bob's old Village rival sang five songs and then yelled from the stage, "Bobby, Bobby, Bobby—this is for you!" Ochs then launched into "Changes," his aching elegy to lost youth.

"I felt so sorry for both of them," recalled the evening's emcee. "I'd never seen Phil Ochs act that humble or want something that much. He was a loner that night. He sang 'Changes,' and you would have tears in your eyes. Some people who were just getting up to leave sat back down."

Dylan stood at the bar smoking an unfiltered Gitano, but wouldn't look at Ochs. After Phil stumbled from the stage, Bob sent David Blue to fetch his fedora.

When Bob's thunder began rolling through New England a week later, Ochs wasn't part of the brigade. A cast of cronies ranging from Joan Baez to Ramblin' Jack to Bobby Neuwirth joined Rolling Thunder—more than 30 acts in all during the 31 stops from Plymouth Rock to Madison Square Garden. A host of new talent, some of whom Dylan had only heard perform once, was also invited to perform.

But Phil Ochs wasn't among them.

Like Paul Clayton, Peter La Farge, and a growing list of '60s casualties, Phil Ochs stalled at the end of the decade and never recovered. Haunted by commercial failure, booze, drugs, depression, and a very real paranoia over G-men dogging him after his angry protests outside the 1968 Democratic National Convention in Chicago,[283] Ochs first lost his record label, then his confidence, and finally, his audience. By 1975, he'd also lost his mind, squandering his hard-earned reputation as a baby boomer Pied Piper who was second only to Dylan.

But when he reached out for a hand, Bob gave him the cold shoulder. It hadn't always been so. During the brief time Ochs wrote such classics as "There But For Fortune" and "Power and the Glory," even Dylan acknowledged his genius. During the 1965 *Dont Look Back* tour, Bob told a British journalist: "I just can't keep up with Phil, and he just keeps getting better and better and better."

"He was a little threatened somebody was coming onto the scene, writing political protest songs," recalled Sam Hood who ran the Gaslight just down MacDougal Street from Gerdes Folk City. "It was probably the last time Dylan felt threatened until Springsteen."

But when he returned from England, Dylan reversed his opinion. He famously ejected Ochs from his limo on a New York City street after Phil had the temerity to critique "Can You Please Crawl Out Your Window?" as a lame follow-up to "Like a Rolling Stone." Dylan shot back that Ochs was just a singing journalist who'd never rise to the level of poet, then told him to get out of the car. Hurt and confused, Ochs complied.

---

[283] In the years following his death, the FBI released two volumes containing 447 pages of surveillance dating from 1964. "The truth is I have much less sense of career than I did a year ago," Ochs said during the '68 antiwar protests. "To have a career, you need a society to have it in. You go off and you make works of art and you present them. . . . America doesn't provide that society anymore."

"Phil could never play the game," said David Blue. "He always told Dylan what he thought and when Dylan struck back, Phil just took it. He didn't stand up to him at all."

While they were cut from the same cloth, their friendship had been rocky from the start. Both were middle-class Jewish rebels born in the gentile heartland, steeped in rock, and drawn to Greenwich by a curious combination of youthful optimism and Beat malaise. But their paths diverged once Dylan renounced politics, retreated to Woodstock, and "took the cure"[284] for his drinking and drug abuse.

Ochs rode out the '60s as cofounder of the radical Youth International Party, ratcheting up his antiwar rage, all the while continuing to binge. Between rants over Vietnam, the FBI, CIA, and Watergate, Ochs descended into fits of rage, alternately threatening murder or suicide. He beat up acquaintances with scant provocation. He once ripped a sink from the Troubadour men's room because Van Morrison put on a mediocre performance.

In the months prior to Porco's birthday, he symbolically "killed" Phil Ochs and took on a new identity. John Butler Train was a paranoid street bard who carried a shiv with him at all times. For months, he was literally homeless.

Ochs abandoned his alter ego for Porco's celebration. It was a final chance to shine, and for that one evening, power and glory returned to his voice. He made his case with keening clarity for a spot on the Rolling Thunder caravan.

But the invitation never came. His public performance at Folk City was his last.

■■ ■■ ■■

---

[284] Dylan finally confessed as much in the lyrics of "Sara."

From Greenwich to Malibu, musicians and fans alike guessed that the Eagles' "New Kid in Town" was Bruce Springsteen:

> There's talk on the street; it sounds so familiar
> Great expectations, everybody's watching you . . .

Dylan scoffed at titles like "king" of pop or rock or folk, but always tuned in early to the competition. Whether it was Phil Ochs or the Beatles, Paul Simon,[285] or the Eagles,[286] he'd feign disinterest while paying close attention. So it was with the new Springsteen kid at Columbia.

Eagle-in-chief Don Henley made no bones about his interest in the phenom from Asbury Park. Though L.A.'s peaceful, easy answer to the Beatles dominated the *Billboard* charts through the early '70s, *Born to Run* threatened the Eagles primacy. Springsteen's third LP ignited a seismic shift throughout the entire industry. The Boss was a game changer and everyone knew it, especially Dylan whose long-time label unveiled a marketing blitz for Springsteen like none it had ever delivered for Dylan. During the same week as Mike Porco's birthday party, Bruce occupied the covers of both *Time* and *Newsweek*. Columbia's P.R. triumph muffled Bob's thunder while boosting *Born to Run* to the top of the charts in an LP rollout that remains unmatched to the present day.

The coastal opposite of the Eagles, the Boss's E Street Band performed raw urban balladry with none of the harmony or countrified rhythm of California rock, but with all the complexity and anthemic

---

[285] Simon deliberately avoided Dylan's style except for parody: "A Simple Desultory Philippic (or How I Was Robert McNamara'd into Submission)" wove cultural allusion into nonsense lyrics punctuated by a whiny drawl, harmonica solo, and the apologetic line, "It's all right ma, everybody must get stoned."

[286] "You see, my records take a week or two to make," he pontificated in one interview. "The Eagles go in and make a record, they take a year. And me, I don't do that, 'cause I don't have a producer."

anger of early Dylan. Bruce's debt was indelible, but he inspired in Bob the same insecurities Phil Ochs and Leonard Cohen once provoked. In Bob's eyes, it didn't help that Springsteen also turned out to be John Hammond's last great discovery.

Bob was neither gracious nor willing to acknowledge his newest rival. When Springsteen's name buzzed through the Rolling Thunder caravan, Dylan behaved as if he didn't give a shit. "Who's this guy Springfield?" he asked Bobby Neuwirth.

As Dylan's longest-surviving sidekick, Neuwirth was expert at massaging Bob's thin skin. When a timid fan approached them in public, burbling some embarrassed ice breaker like "Say, aren't you one of the Supremes?" it was always Neuwirth who laughed like a hyena while Bob glowered in silence. Like a good court jester, he protected his liege and still got excited about hitting the road.

Neuwirth described Rolling Thunder as the world's first existential concert tour. "It's gonna be a new living room every night!" he effused. "It's rock and roll heaven and it's historical . . ."

Bob Dylan did *not* need hacks like Phil Ochs or upstarts like Bruce Springsteen to achieve his goal.

The first and most famous leg of Rolling Thunder began the night before Halloween in Massachusetts and climaxed six weeks later in Manhattan: 40 days of high energy, high-decibel rock and ramble through the blue highways of New England all the way to Montreal and Quebec City, and then back to Madison Square Garden for an all-star "Night of the Hurricane" with proceeds earmarked for Rubin Carter's defense fund.

The journey was well documented. Besides 240,000 feet of film Dylan ordered shot along the way, journalists slipped in and out at every stop, giving varying accounts of a roving, manic rave fueled by equal parts hubris and camaraderie. Sara came along for part of the tour and agreed to star in the formless quasi-documentary her husband had percolating in the back of his head since he first sat through *Children of Paradise*.

Norman Raeben turned Dylan on to the marathon French melodrama. Set in the seedy world of Parisian street theater circa 1820–1830, *Children of Paradise* was shot in occupied Paris during the waning days of World War II. A classic among New Wave auteurs, *Paradise* influenced Bob's own filmmaking as much as Truffaut's tragicomic gangster tale *Shoot the Piano Player.* The chief distinction between Dylan's movie and *Paradise* or *Piano Player* was that both French films actually had plots, identifiable characters, and a beginning, middle, and end.

Based on a noir classic by hardboiled American novelist David Goodis, *Piano Player* tracked the life of a slack-jawed cabaret pianist (Charles Aznavour) caught up in his brothers' criminal capers until his girl winds up dead during a snowstorm in crossfire with another gang.

"I saw that movie a bunch of times because the snow part of it reminded me of back where I come from," said Dylan.

Children of Paradise followed the lives of a French courtesan and her four lovers, one of whom bore a striking resemblance to the lovesick mime Dylan aped on stage during Rolling Thunder.[287]

Renaldo and Clara had no story, no structure or theme. Bob's directorial debut smacked of self-indulgent doodling given permanence by a limitless checkbook. Those who sat through its nearly four hours left baffled or angry or both.

---

[287] In a tip of the hat to Watergate, he kicked off Rolling Thunder in a Richard Nixon mask, only revealing his whiteface after performing the first number. Bob said the greasepaint forced his audience to hear his words and not see his face. "A walking, talking Kachina doll," remarked Anne Waldman who joined Ginsberg as unofficial poet in residence during the tour.

Like Dennis Hopper who'd been given the chance to direct a dream project in the wake of *Easy Rider*'s success, Dylan shot more than 100 hours of film with no real script. Unlike Hopper, Dylan didn't have a studio to foot the bill. When *The Last Movie* (1971) crashed along with Hopper's career, MCA/Universal still had to pay the $1 million price tag. By contrast, *Renaldo and Clara* was underwritten solely by Bob's Lombard Street Films.[288]

Soured by his *Eat the Document* experience and the drubbing he'd witnessed Sam Peckinpah take at the hands of MGM, Dylan opted out of Hollywood. He summoned *Eat the Document* co-conspirator Howard Alk to oversee filming. Similarly, he drafted Camp Herzl alumnus Lou Kemp[289] as chief roadie and made Jacque Levy the Rolling Thunder stage manager. He also hired four independent camera crews to simultaneously shoot concert footage and stagey "scenes" to later cobble into the narrative.

"They were filming with more crew and lights than Cecil B. DeMille," recalled Ronnie Hawkins, one of the earliest Rolling Thunder volunteers.

Before taking cinema verité to its dreadful extreme, Dylan did bring in a capable screenwriter. Like many others who dropped in and out of the caravan, off-Broadway playwright Sam Shepard tried giving shape to Bob's movie, but the future Pulitzer Prize–winning playwright gave up by the end of the first leg of the journey. Instead, he wrote an *Esquire* essay about his experience, followed by a more complete account in his *Rolling Thunder Logbook*. Despite Shepard's best efforts, the real Bob remained inscrutable.

"If a mystery is solved, the case is dropped," he concluded. "In this case, in the case of Dylan, the mystery is never solved, so the

---

[288] Named for the Wilmington, Delaware, street where Sara grew up.

[289] A sign on the side of a camper Dylan drove from venue to venue through much of the tour read "Kemp Fisheries."

case keeps on. It keeps coming up again, over and over the years. Who is this character anyway?"

To keep his mystique intact, Dylan held off most journalists. Despite—or perhaps *because* of their history—he wouldn't let Nat Hentoff[290] near him. On assignment for *Rolling Stone,* the one-time Bob booster had to make do with impressions from Thunder participants likes Joan Baez and Allen Ginsberg. When a Bob gofer contacted Hentoff near the end of the tour to let him know Mr. Dylan would finally see him, Hentoff said (with great pleasure, he later added), "It's too late . . . I don't need him."

Larry "Ratso" Sloman, a *Rolling Stone* reporter who'd earned as much of Bob's wary trust as any, did win limited backstage access, but when Dylan wanted no scrutiny, he ordered bodyguards to bar the door—even going so far as to put writers like Sloman under temporary house arrest.

Musicians, family, and fellow travelers were treated only slightly better. All who showed fealty by contributing to Bob's impulsive showmanship generally had free range. The entire enterprise reflected Dylan's whims. Nicknamed "The Shaman," Dylan had mood swings measured by chain-smoking and binges. He was back to a couple packs of Camels or Gitanos a day and lubricated himself

---

[290] For Dylan's 1966 *Playboy* Q&A, Hentoff grudgingly watched his editors cave to Bob's demand that he rewrite his own interview, allowing Dylan to turn fact into flippant fiction:

Q: What made you decide to go the rock and roll route?

A: Carelessness. I lost my one true love. I started drinking. I wind up in Phoenix. I get a job as a Chinaman. I start working in a dime store, and move in with a 13-year-old girl. Then this big Mexican lady from Philadelphia comes in and burns the house down. I go down to Dallas. I get a job as a 'before' in a Charles Atlas 'before and after' ad. I move in with a delivery boy who can cook fantastic chili and hot dogs. Then this 13-year-old girl from Phoenix comes and burns the house down. The delivery boy—he ain't so mild: He gives her the knife, and the next thing I know I'm in Omaha.

with everything from Courvoisier and vino to as much as a fifth of bourbon a day.

As a Rolling Thunder participant through the autumn of '75 and part of the spring of '76, Joan Baez characterized the first leg of the tour as "monumentally silly," "loads of fun," and "a complete circus." Whatever rancor remained from their broken romance disappeared once she and Bob hit the road again. On stage, they resurrected their roles as the King and Queen of Folk, swapping identities as easily as they did songs. Nearly all who joined the revue did some role playing and "that's putting it very mildly," said Baez.

On the pretext of creating fiction, Dylan cast Joan as the Woman in White, pairing her in several *Renaldo and Clara* scenes opposite Sara. Upping the irony, he disingenuously cast his girlfriend Ruth Tyrangiel in the minor role of Girlfriend.[291] Despite his clumsy orchestration of a male fantasy with no identifiable storyline, Bob's women never let him down. Sara spoke her pretentious if prophetic lines flawlessly: "I'd stay if you found the right way to ask me," and "I don't want you to chase me. If I go, I go."

While his wife indulged his psychodrama,[292] Joan saw the entire subterfuge as amusing lunacy. Whatever his "actors" thought of his manipulation mattered little. All hands deferred to Cap'n Bob.

"Hey, you know Dylan's wife Sara is gonna show up in Niagara?" effused David Blue two weeks into the tour.[293] "You wanna see a

---

[291] Another girlfriend Dylan cast as Girlfriend was punk guitarist Denise Mercedes, who would find limited notoriety in the twenty-first century as founder of "the world's first and only all-girl Judas Priest tribute band."

[292] Like Joan who once wore an Egyptian ring that sparkled in accordance with a Dylan lyric, Sara wore an Isis amulet during Rolling Thunder that she designed herself.

[293] Tapped by Bob to narrate while playing a game of pinball in what passed as a frame story for *Renaldo and Clara,* recalling the glory days of Greenwich Village.

heavy chick? Just wait till her and Joni Mitchell get around each other. You'll get some shit on camera then, I can guarantee it. Sara's a very regal, powerful chick, and Joni's getting into her empress bag now. . . . You just wait until they get in front of the camera!"

But the wait was in vain. Sara's performance was wooden while Joni's was worse. Only Baez really got into the spirit, frugging on stage like a go-go girl while mimicking the Man himself off stage. When Sara arrived in Niagara Falls, Joan dressed like Bob to greet her.

"A couple of times I fooled his wife and kids," she recalled.[294] "I thought that was pretty good. I also fooled his kids (by) doing *her*."

Fooling would have been a better title than *Renaldo*[295] *and Clara.* On the road and in the movie, most everybody was fooling or fooling around with everybody else. According to the film's advance publicity, Renaldo and Clara were a fictitious dance team. With few exceptions, every female character was some sort of whore while every male was looking to get laid, chief among them being Neuwirth who was billed in the credits as The Masked Tortilla.[296] In a further bit of bizarre casting, Dylan gave Ronnie Hawkins the role of Bob Dylan. When Hawkins asked for direction when seducing a young girl in a motel room, Dylan said "wing it." Nobody, least of all Dylan, had any idea what they were doing.

Meanwhile, offstage and out of camera range, Rolling Thunder took on the trappings of a French bedroom farce. Right under Sara's nose, Bob rutted frequently and with minimal discretion. Rolling

---

[294] Baez also brought her mother and son along on the tour.

[295] A possible source for the name of Bob's title character was Duncan Renaldo, a.k.a. "The Cisco Kid" of 1950s TV fame who made a brief pop reappearance in 1974 when the band War released an album with the 70-year-old actor's picture on the cover.

[296] A reference to "Tacos-to-Go," Neuwirth's nickname during Village days when Bob got the Mexican munchies.

Thunder publicity coordinator Chris O'Dell described her seduction as a low-key take-it-or-leave-it encounter that followed a night of close dancing and too much booze. She submitted, but came away less than dazzled, while Bob's morning after often throbbed with guilt.

"He told me he was so ashamed because he was with one of the women managing us on the road," recalled Ruth Tyrangiel. "And I said, 'You can't do that kind of stuff. You need to be discreet.' So here I am telling *him* to be discreet! If he did that today, it'd be all over the Internet."

Figures from his past kept popping up along the way, ranging from Roger McGuinn to Larry Kegan, Albert Grossman to Mama Beatty Rutman. Even Bruce "Springfield" stopped backstage to pay his respects. He offered to join the show, but Dylan didn't want the E Street Band upstaging him and the pop summit ended before it began.

The bonhomie began to sour after the first of the year. Following a one-month layoff over Christmas, the second leg of the tour kicked off at the Houston Astrodome on January 25, 1976, coinciding with the national release of *Desire.* From the outset, there were problems. Unlike the climactic and profitable "Night of the Hurricane" at Madison Square Garden in December, this "Night of the Hurricane II" subbed Stevie Wonder for Joan Baez and had a distinctly commercial feel about it, even though it earned just $50,000 in contributions for Rubin Carter's defense fund.

The carnival atmosphere of the first leg of Rolling Thunder gave way to the sheer financial crush of the enterprise. Bob could no longer subsidize both *Renaldo and Clara* and the stage production, which had depended on spotty revenue from underpriced tickets at spontaneous small-town gatherings. Following Houston, Rolling Thunder II played only arenas. The national juggernaut rolled from

East to West, but never got farther than Utah. Ticket sales faded. As *Rolling Stone*'s Janet Maslin saw it, the show "had just plain run out of steam."

Drugs dissipated the magic among cast and crew. Most everyone either coked or drank themselves into a stupor at least part of the time. Even nondruggies like Scarlett Rivera found her drink spiked before she went on stage and powered through "Hurricane" high as a kite. Bob stalwart Ramblin' Jack got so wired he had to abandon the tour.

Dylan's depravity spiked during a rainstorm at a Colorado dude ranch where the remaining Revue cast members holed up before their May appearance at Fort Collins's Hughes Stadium. As bassist Rob Stoner recalled his boss, "He was confused and he was searching. He tried a lot of chicks. He tried one chick. He tried (every) kind of chick."

Sara again showed up, kids and Grandma Beatty in tow. Joan Baez remembered a "mad woman, carrying baskets of wrinkled clothes, her hair wild and dark rings around her eyes.

"Bob was ignoring her," said Baez. "(He) had picked up a curly-headed Mopsy who perched on the piano during his rehearsals in a ballroom off the main hotel lobby. Sara appeared airily at the front door dressed in deerskin, wearing her emerald green necklace and some oppressively strong and sweet oils. She greeted me with a reserved hello and talked distantly about nothing in particular, all the while eyeing the closed door to the ballroom."

After a blowout with Bob in the hotel parking lot, Sara absented herself from the second half of Rolling Thunder. She lit out for Mexico. What ought to have been a clear portent of impending doom escaped everyone's attention, including Bob's inner circle.

His circus ground to a halt two days later on May 25, 1976, in Salt Lake City, the day after his 35th birthday. SRO audiences may have clamored for tickets in the beginning but by Utah, fans had grown as jaded as Bob himself. Fewer than half the 17,000 seats were filled.

■ ■ ■

After battling booze and depression for over a decade, Phil Ochs hanged himself at his sister's home in Queens on April 9, 1976. He was 35 years old. Sonny Ochs staged a memorial concert the following month, shortly before Dylan's own 35th birthday.

"It was destructive for Phil to worship Dylan, because Dylan was not a nice person," she said. "I don't think he just put Phil down; I think he was actually cruel. When we did the memorial benefit for Phil a lot of people were invited, and against my wishes Dylan was invited. Dylan *never, ever* responded."

When his brother Michael Ochs confronted Bob Neuwirth at the Troubadour weeks later, Dylan's apologist-in-chief said Dylan didn't get his invitation in time. Ochs was not mollified.

"I talked to a person who said he was too coked up[297] to make the flight," he said.

"Where the fuck did you hear *that!*" said Neuwirth. "Don't spread those kinds of stories about Dylan!"

To be fair, Bob had his hands full. In addition to his movie and the full weight of the Thunder debacle, his roller-coaster marriage had begun its final plunge.

---

[297] During a break in the disintegrating Rolling Thunder schedule two weeks before Ochs's suicide, a stoned Dylan played bass for Eric Clapton at Shangri-la Studio in Malibu, but was so wired he made a tent out of bedsheets and slept outdoors with a girlfriend rather than make the short trek home to Point Dume.

During a rare interview with *TV Guide* that autumn, reporter Neil Hickey let the tape recorder roll with no inkling that Bob might be rambling on about his breakup with Sara.

"Anger is often directed at oneself," Dylan moralized. "It all depends on where you are in place and time. A person's body chemistry changes every seven years. No one on earth is the same now as he was seven years ago, or will be seven years from today. It doesn't take a whole lot of brains to know that if you don't grow you die. You have to burst out; you have to find the sunlight."

In predictable Dylan fashion, Bob let the magazine with the nation's highest circulation believe that domestic life was peachy. Hickey wrote of Sara and the children nestled around the Dylan hearth with no proof beyond Bob's word that anything was amiss. Unrecognizable in a *Lawrence of Arabia* burnoose, Dylan shared beers with Hickey at the beach near his Malibu compound while he waxed grandly on the nature of the universe.

"I can see God in a daisy," he said. "I can see God at night in the wind and rain. I see creation just about everywhere. The highest form of song is prayer. King David's, Solomon's, the wailing of a coyote, the rumble of the earth. It must be wonderful to be God. There's so much going on out there that you can't get to it all. It would take longer than forever."

Bob no longer flat-out lied the way he once did, but he had become expert at misdirection. He played Hickey like Scarlett Rivera's violin.

"You're talking to somebody who doesn't comprehend the values most people operate under," he said. "Greed and lust I can understand, but I can't understand the values of definition and confinement. Definition destroys. Besides, there's nothing definite in this world."

Hot air served its purpose. *TV Guide*'s audience had to tune in to his first TV special to get a further dose of Dylan. NBC aired *Hard Rain* a week later to modest ratings. The special documented a Colorado State University concert near the end of Rolling Thunder. While NBC's licensing fee and a subsequent live record album helped defray expenses, Dylan remained on the hook for both the tour and *Renaldo and Clara.*

Perhaps his most revealing comment to Hickey was delivered as a non sequitur. Popping open a can and leaning back to enjoy a classic Pacific sunset, Dylan grinned behind his shades and said, "I hope there's not a snake in my beer."

■■ ■■ ■■

Two months later, Dylan joined the Band for their giddy swan song—a stoned soul farewell before the quintet broke up forever, captured on film by director Martin Scorsese. Still regarded as the best concert movie ever made, *The Last Waltz* featured Bob and several other guest stars[298] performing a handful of chestnuts, but it was Dylan's behavior off camera that hinted at underlying angst.

Stoned much of the time (Band members also fessed up to coking themselves to the gills), Dylan pulled a peculiarly coquettish star turn by refusing to let Scorsese film him, and then reversing himself and changing his mind once again. Caught in the middle were loyalists like Howard Alk, who believed Scorsese might upstage *Renaldo and Clara*, and Louis Kemp, who had strict orders from Bob to keep the cameras off of him. Kemp and producer Bill Graham nearly came to blows over the on-again, off-again filming while Bob shifted

---

[298]   Joni Mitchell sang "Coyote," her subtle tribute to Bob's horny Rolling Thunder incarnation.

from diva to insecure nerd and back again. Scorsese ignored the flip-flops, let the cameras roll, and created an enduring record of Dylan and the Band's final performance.

Like many functional addicts, Bob indulged in private, covering his tracks.

"Bob goes through changes," said Eric Clapton, who suffered through his own well-documented bouts with drugs. "Sometimes he's a heavy drinker, sometimes he's not. Sometimes he's into dope, then not. He can disappear with a carload of Mexicans. No phase is the final one."

Dylan could quit any time he liked. As long as the applause continued, he was just fine. It took the long-suppressed outrage of his soul mate to finally blow his cover. To fans and friends alike, the news came as a jolt. Six months after the *TV Guide* interview, Sara accused her husband of flagrant adultery, emotional torture, and physical abuse while she made a grand display of suing him for divorce.

In a five-page affidavit accompanying her March 1, 1977, petition, Sara described the straw that broke their marriage contract: one February morning, she came downstairs for breakfast to find Bob and the children gathered around the table with an itinerant poetess identified only as "Malka."[299] Apparently Malka had spent the night. When Sara objected, Bob allegedly hit her and ordered her back upstairs.

Bob's pattern of serial philandering, getting caught, and groveling for forgiveness—whether privately or globally in the form of confessional love songs—ended abruptly. Sara moved the children to rented quarters in the gated Malibu Colony a few miles south of

[299] Later identified as Malka Marom, the Israeli-born Canadian artist had been introduced to Dylan by Leonard Cohen.

Point Dume and—at the suggestion of fellow Colony resident David Geffen—hired celebrity divorce attorney Marvin Mitchelson to sue for half of the Dylan empire, including real estate, record royalties, and a 50 percent share of the rights to every song her husband had written during their 12-year marriage.

Sara had become what *Passages* author Gail Sheehy called "a runaway wife": a rational woman in her mid-30s content in her role as mother and homemaker who wakes up one morning and realizes her husband has no idea who she is. Add to that disturbing revelation the license to philander granted by *Open Marriage,*[300] another '70s bestseller, and the Dylans' marriage was doomed to failure like those of thousands upon thousands of Bob's devoted fans. By the end of the decade, couples who'd climaxed the free-loving '60s at the altar began divorcing in droves. Bob blamed L.A.

"California is hard on married people," he said a year later. "It's tough to be married here because life is pretty loose."

Within days of Sara's filing, both petitioner and respondent could agree on just one thing: sealing the court record. The pretense was protecting the children but, in truth, the children were the battlefield on which their protracted war was waged. Within weeks, both sides agreed to separate issues of property and alimony from the far more contentious question, "Who gets the kids?" Bob girded for battle, showing a breathtaking capacity for fighting dirty, beginning with the ballad of Faridi McFree.

---

[300] *Open Marriage* sold over 1.5 million copies and advanced the lingering Flower Power fallacy that consensual adultery could be a tool for wedded bliss, even though authors Nena and George O'Neill devoted a mere three pages to the tentative idea (later recanted) that sex outside of marriage could be beneficial in some cases. The media hyped that one racy notion in the O'Neill's 1972 manual on New Age marriage and forever after, their otherwise thoughtful academic argument for greater gender equality became a catchphrase for indiscriminate rutting.

A proponent of New Age mysticism and holistic remedy since she had first nested in Woodstock, Sara believed art therapy might minimize her kids' divorce trauma. The theory was that even the youngest Dylan could express his or her frustration over the family breakup by painting anguish and sculpting anger, thus preventing future visits to a psychiatrist. At the behest of a friend, Sara hired a free-spirited artist from Woodstock named Faridi McFree to supervise the art project.

The two women clashed immediately. Sara's sad-eyed hippie grace had ossified over the years into a matronly sense of entitlement while McFree remained strictly a mystical working-class girl. McFree resented being treated like a servant but was good with the children, so she and the missus overcame their differences until Sara whisked her family off to Hawaii for vacation and left McFree to house-sit.

According to McFree, she bolted upright in bed one morning after waking from a vivid dream of Dylan agonizing over his divorce. On impulse, she cold-called. Bob blubbered that her dream had been spot on: he was in dire need of consolation. In short order, McFree moved into the Point Dume compound where consolation ensued. In what appeared to be a lifelong pattern, Dylan turned McFree from mistress to muse. She nursed him through his summer of discontent, including the night Elvis Presley expired.

"It was in August,"[301] McFree recalled to Dylan biographer Clinton Heylin. "He really took it very bad. He didn't speak for a couple of days."

---

[301] Aug. 16, 1977.

Dead at 42, Presley had reportedly met Dylan just once in Las Vegas,[302] but covered several Bob songs.[303]

"When I first heard Elvis's voice, I just knew that I wasn't going to work for anybody and nobody was gonna be my boss," Bob reflected ten years after the King's death. "Hearing him for the first time was like busting out of jail."

In his meticulously detailed history of Dylan's Hibbing years,[304] Mesabi Range historian Dave Engel made the inevitable comparison of one megastar to another: "Elvis is actually a shy, polite, religious, white, small-town boy who favors his mother and lives with his grandmother, just like Bob Zimmerman."

Bob's Elvis funk stood in stark contrast to his nonreaction a year earlier to Phil Ochs's suicide, but the message Dylan took from both deaths was the same—clean up your act and get back to work.

"I almost didn't have a friend in the world," Bob recalled. "I was under a lot of pressure, so I figured I better get busy working."

Bob took the kids with him and McFree to Minnesota that summer. He relished the role of patriarch, fell into a clean-and-sober routine, and renewed his regimen of composing poetry in the company of a muse—a blueprint that began with Echo, Suze, Joan, and then Sara, and continued when Ellen Bernstein inspired *Blood on the Tracks*.

"He started to write *Street Legal* when we were together," recalled McFree. "He would show me some of the songs that he was writing . . . practically the entire album . . ."

---

[302] Dylan's tribute to that summit meeting was allegedly *New Morning*'s "Went to See the Gypsy," but 30 years hence, he claimed he'd never met Presley, adding cryptically, "That's what I'm *supposed* to say."

[303] "Tomorrow Is a Long Time," "Don't Think Twice, It's All Right," "Blowin' in the Wind" and "I Shall Be Released."

[304] *Just Like Bob Zimmerman's Blues: Dylan in Minnesota*. Rudolph, Wis.: River City Memoirs-Mesabi, 1997

Dylan poured himself into his movie as well as his music. He took a long-term lease on a one-time rifle factory that he renamed Rundown Studio. There he and Howard Alk continued piecing together *Renaldo and Clara* while Bob also began rehearsing his new material. He spent so much time at Rundown he installed sleeping quarters upstairs.

He also redoubled his custody battle. Fearing Sara would move the children out of state, Bob pulled out all the stops. According to Sara's old friend Sally Grossman, the war escalated to a point where Bob persuaded stepdaughter Maria to testify against her own mother. Early in the school year, Sara's rage gave Bob an unexpected boost.

Flanked by three beefy private eyes, Mrs. Dylan strode into her children's elementary school one morning. After rounding up two kids, she tried dragging a third from his classroom. When the teacher objected, Sara punched and choked him until he released the terrified child. She later defended herself on grounds that Bob had brainwashed her children, but wound up with a six-month suspended sentence and a $125 fine. She threw in the towel on seeking sole custody.

■ ■ ■

The creative turmoil that conjured *Blood on the Tracks* during his first split with Sara did not yield similar dividends during their divorce.

"It is an interesting historical fact," observed Dylanologist Paul Williams, "that Dylan did not lose his mass audience with *Self Portrait* and six years of largely mediocre albums and no touring. Instead he lost it, or began to lose it, immediately after three consecutive No.1 albums . . . and two hugely successful tours."

Dylan began auditioning backup for a new world tour at the same time he started to rehearse *Street Legal*. During the first six months of 1978, he played both Australia and Japan where Columbia recorded a double-sided live LP released later that summer as *Bob Dylan at Budokan,* shortly after the release of *Street Legal.* Critics excoriated both albums. The record-buying public agreed.

While no review repeated *Rolling Stone*'s memorable *Self Portrait* query ("What is this shit?"), *Street Legal*[305] suffered universal damnation with the faintest of praise. The musicianship and production values reflected the name of the studio where it was recorded.[306] Beyond the uneven sound, Bob's songs paled in comparison to those on previous albums. Loaded with self-pitying questions ("Do you understand my pain?" "Will I be able to count on you?" "Are you willing to risk it all?" "Will you let me be myself?"), he delivered few answers.

Street Legal did yield three memorable gems: the epic "Changing of the Guards"; the gypsy jeremiad "Señor (Tales of Yankee Power)"; and a lover's portent, "Is Your Love in Vain?" His live show, however, was a mess. He introduced an annoying new habit of switching arrangements, tempos, and even lyrics, seldom with positive results. Those who came to hear "Blowin' in the Wind" or "Just Like a Woman" couldn't figure out what the band was playing as Bob warbled and slurred like a stroke survivor.

"As the show progressed," wrote *US* magazine's Martha Hume, "it turned into an annoying game of 'Name That Tune.'"

Despite a polished stage presence and a tight backup band, he alienated more fans than he pleased. Dylan wasn't the only '60s survivor to lose his audience when the zeitgeist shifted. As Yippies

---

[305] He dedicated the album to heroin addict Emmett Grogan, a founder of San Francisco's Digger movement, who suffered a fatal heart attack on the New York subway on Apr. 6, 1978. Grogan was 35.

[306] It did not help that frugal Bob hired a mobile recording van to do the actual recording so that the music being played *inside* Rundown was not the same that his sound engineers were recording out in the truck.

became Yuppies, the purchasing power of the American Dream made a stunning comeback, but they weren't spending it on middle-aged rockers. As Bob sorted out his personal life, his music got caught in the consumer riptide of the Me Decade. Dylan likened the assembly line pace for the release of new LPs to the production of Saran Wrap.

Disco and punk began to supersede singer-songwriters. The children of Flower Children wallowed in heavy metal. Stadium rock belonged to elaborate road shows from the likes of KISS and Led Zeppelin while glam entertainers like David Bowie,[307] Elton John, and Alice Cooper infected the young with walls of sound and frequent costume changes.

Bob tried to keep pace. He mounted his own sophisticated stage production that took eight hours to set up and four to tear down. He hired an 11-piece backup ensemble that included violin, flute, grand piano, mandolin, and a sax player who sounded suspiciously like E Street's Clarence Clemons. Patterning himself after Elvis, he added a black female gospel trio[308] he called "my cousin, my fiancée, and my ex-girlfriend."

"When you introduce the singers onstage as your childhood sweethearts, your present girlfriend, your former girlfriend—is that literal?" asked *Rolling Stone*'s Jonathan Cott.

"Oh, of course," deadpanned Dylan.

Dressed more like a lounge lizard than a late-model hippie, he swapped Rolling Thunder's blue denim for black leather jacket,

---

[307] "Dylan taught my generation that it was okay to write pop songs about your worst nightmares," said Bowie, who imitated Bob's curtsy to Woody by performing "Song for Bob Dylan" on 1971's *Hunky Dory*.

[308] Presley's version of Ray Charles's Raelettes called themselves the Sweet Inspirations.

white penny loafers, and tight white trousers. When he introduced his band, he looked and sounded like he stepped out of the Rat Pack:

"On violin, we have Bob Mansfield. He don't drink or smoke marijuana. Keeps us all in line. And my name's Bob Dylan and I'd like to do one of my favorites for you now . . ."

If Rolling Thunder taught Bob nothing else, it was that he was no manager. To fulfill that role, he hired Jerry Weintraub's Management III, which also managed Frank Sinatra and John Denver.

"He was a god to his fans, but to me he was just another smart Jewish kid from the provinces," recalled Weintraub.

The quintessential 10-percenter, Weintraub was Col. Tom Parker with a Brooklyn accent. He spangled Bob the same way he'd successfully repackaged former Brill Building denizen Neil Diamond, another "smart Jewish kid." Under Weintraub's tutelage, Diamond went from modestly successful songsmith to superstar. He pledged to work similar magic for Bob.

"Yes, he is brilliant," said Weintraub. "I don't think he has any idea just how brilliant. The man can break your heart with a turn of phrase. But to him it is just another day of work, which is how I treated it too."

As executive producer of Robert Altman's triumphant 1975 country music satire *Nashville*, Weintraub might have been the right man to keep the books on *Renaldo and Clara*, but he didn't arrive soon enough to impact Bob's biggest bomb since *Tarantula*.

Dylan micromanaged *Renaldo and Clara* throughout postproduction, never fully grasping the nuts and bolts of the filmmaking process. Despite a long and expensive learning curve, he continued to fancy himself an *auteur*, ignoring the heavy lifting until it was too late.

"All the people on the Rolling Thunder Revue were supposed to sign something," recalled Ronnie Hawkins. "I forgot to sign the clearance. Then this lawyer calls me and is carrying on, saying, 'You gotta do this, do that.' The lawyer pissed me off so I said, 'Take me out of this!'"

Five minutes later, Bob was on the phone.

"We need you to sign this," Dylan pleaded. "You're going to get $25,000!"

Hawkins stiffened. He didn't like pressure, but appreciated even less Bob's assumption that he could be bought.

"I would have done the film for nothing," said Hawkins.

He knew he had Dylan, so he played him. When Bob offered to fly him first class to L.A., send a limo to pick him up and put him up at the Beverly Hills Hotel, Hawkins said that sounded okay. Only after he'd taken in L.A. like visiting royalty, eating out on Bob's dime, and ordering the limo driver to haul him all over the city, did he finally get around to signing the release.

Dylan's imperious manner rubbed others the wrong way, too, and cost him accordingly. The final price tag for *Renaldo and Clara* was reportedly $1.25 million with at least another $400,000 for advertising and distribution. When he had a four-hour rough cut, he sought the advice of David Carradine, who had just been nominated for an Oscar for his portrayal of Woody Guthrie.[309] Carradine suggested cutting the film by half, but Dylan just sniffed. He told the actor he obviously didn't know what he was talking about.

---

[309] Portrayed by six-foot-tall Carradine in *Bound for Glory*, Guthrie got the full Hollywood treatment in director Hal Ashby's 1976 biopic, but in real life he stood just 5'4". Down to the present, Guthrie's heirs discount Ashby's account of Woody's life as pure fiction.

Carradine knew. Despite a last minute media blitz, the stillborn *Renaldo and Clara* opened and closed the same week and has seldom been seen since.[310]

Dylan tried jump-starting his movie with a spate of promotional interviews that oozed pretense: "It's about naked alienation of the inner self against the outer self. It's like life exactly but not an imitation of it. It transcends life and it's not like life."

The media wasn't as malleable as it once was. Reporters remarked on Bob's fidgeting and his perpetually crimson, dripping nose. He seemed always to just be getting over the flu. When he tried snowing the *Minneapolis Star Tribune*'s Jon Bream the way he had *TV Guide*'s Neil Hickey, Bream paid attention instead to his rehearsed style. "He would seem to be contemplating something," said Bream. "But then he would stop speaking and wait for a reaction or another question. At times, he would speak very slowly with long, contemplative pauses between words. At other times, he would complete his sentences seemingly without contemplation."

Dylan told Bream his movie was about "the dream filtering into daily life." He spoke of himself as a "conscious artist"—a term he borrowed from Norman Raeben. Bob insisted that he manipulated the very concept of time in *Renaldo and Clara*, just as he'd done with "Tangled Up in Blue."

What worked on vinyl, however, fell flat on film and Bob's psychobabble came off as self-serving bullshit. When Bob gazed into the middle distance like a stoned monk, journalists weren't buying it.

---

[310] When he failed to get a Hollywood studio or independent distributor interested, Bob turned to kid brother David who set up his own network, Circuit Films, with sad results. A larger number turned out for the Dinkytown premiere at the Varsity Theater, but the film closed in short order. Bob's movie played just once in Hibbing with only one patron and the projectionist reportedly at the screening.

"The movie creates and holds time," he told *Rolling Stone*'s Jonathan Cott. "That's what it should do—it should hold that time, breathe in that time and stop time in doing that. It's like if you look at a painting by Cézanne, you get lost in that painting for that period of time. And you breathe—yet time is going by and you wouldn't know it. You're spellbound."

The New Yorker's Pauline Kael was spellbound, but in the manner of a witness to a train wreck. She compared him to Norman Mailer who, like Dylan, arrogantly believed his success on the page would automatically translate to the screen. Dylan came off as a "surly, mystic tease" and "a sour messiah" with "more tight close-ups than any actor can have had in the whole history of movies."

Most fans never got a chance to see *Renaldo and Clara*. Belatedly, Dylan caved to investors who wanted *Renaldo and Clara* whittled down to two hours, but the chop job was worse than the original. After short runs in Europe, both versions vanished along with Bob's tortured explications.

"The key line of the movie is, 'What comes is gone forever every time,'" Dylan told Allen Ginsberg who indulged Bob with a postmortem Q&A about *Renaldo and Clara*. When Bob insisted that *Renaldo and Clara* was Bob Dylan's epitaph, Ginsberg told him the movie was too little too late. Dylan had put philosophy in a jukebox and was doomed to immortality. As the Me Decade coasted to a close, Zimmy, Elston Gunn, Blind Boy Grunt, and all his other aliases were a long time gone, but Bob Dylan lived on and on and on.

⁙ ⁙ ⁙

Dylan began digging out of debt in earnest, salvaging his reputation, and licking the wounds of divorce. The court finalized the interlocutory judgment in April, putting him on the hook for alimony, child support, and an estimated $36 million of the Dylans' community assets, but with the final decree, he also won Sara's silence. She never spoke publicly of her ex again.

Sara moved out of Malibu Colony and into a venerable five-bedroom manse at 727 Bedford Avenue in the heart of Beverly Hills. She conceded the Point Dume compound to Bob, but took title of their remote retreat in the Malibu hills, along the Ventura County line. She eventually took in boyfriends who would make any ex-husband grind his molars. Shelby Gregory was a male model, stuntman, and TV actor whom Sara met during Rolling Thunder. After he moved out, others replaced him, including a shady New Age botanist, sometimes DEA informant and dealer to the stars whose wealth evolved out of his development of a seedless strain of marijuana. David Wheeler[311] was the kind of fast-talking operator that a much younger Bob had scourged in "She's Your Lover Now."[312]

Commenting on the divorce, a chastened Dylan regretted breaking a long Zimmerman tradition of staying married no matter what, as had his own parents. He declared that their split didn't mean he'd stopped caring about Sara.

"It really doesn't affect that," he said. "Divorce is just a game of the material world. It doesn't really affect the reality of love one way or the other to me."

In a tongue-in-cheek homage to both the divorce and Dylan's indiscriminate rutting, the Rolling Stones released *Some Girls* that

---

[311]   Adding ironic insult to injury, Wheeler and his own ex-wife had named their first son Dylan.

[312]   Allegedly about another triangle: Bob, Edie Sedgwick, and Bob Neuwirth.

spring with a title song that refers to a Lothario who buys his girl a house in Zuma Beach[313] and gives her half of all he owns.

In May, Jerry Weintraub launched the summer leg of Dylan's *Street Legal* tour, taking him to Europe through July. After a late summer break, Bob climaxed the year with a 62-city blitz across the U.S. While playing to sell-out crowds in France, Germany, Scandinavia, and England, stateside his so-called "Alimony Tour" petered out following the tepid reviews of *Street Legal* and *Renaldo and Clara.* Still, an estimated 885,000 fans paid $7 to $10 apiece to see their musical hero.

The week before Thanksgiving, the Alimony Tour ground to its weary end and so did Bob. Exhausted, strung out, and playing to dwindling audiences, he merely went through the motions. At one of the final stops, in San Diego, someone tossed a silver cross on the stage.

"Now usually I don't pick things up in front of the stage," Dylan recalled. "Once in a while I do. Sometimes I don't. But I looked down at that cross. I said, 'I gotta pick that up.' So I picked up the cross and I put it in my pocket."

By the time he got to Phoenix, he felt even more low-down.

"I said, 'Well, I need something tonight,'" he remembered. "I didn't know what it was. I was used to all kinds of things. I said, 'I need something tonight that I didn't have before.' And I looked in my pocket and I had this cross."

He wore it on a chain around his neck in Fort Worth, Houston, Nashville, Atlanta, and all the way to the end of the forced march to Hollywood, Florida. At the last stop, even as paying customers continued to drift away, Dylan felt reinvigorated. Something told him his luck was about to change.

---

[313] Located at the base of the Point Dume peninsula, the surf-and-bikini symbol of all that is Southern California lies just beneath Dylan's Malibu compound. But when quizzed by *Rolling Stone*'s Jonathan Cott about the damning lyrics in Mick Jagger and Keith Richards's ode to lechery, Dylan snapped way too quickly: "I've never lived in Zuma Beach."

Abe & Beatty Zimmerman in early '40s Duluth, before Abe contracted polio and had to move the family to Hibbing where he became the accountant for his older brothers' business, Micka Electric. (Courtesy Hibbing Public Library)

Bobby Zimmerman, about age five, at lower right. (Courtesy Hibbing Public Library)

Winter on Howard Street, downtown Hibbing. (Courtesy Zimmy's Café)

Bob's senior picture. He announced that his postgrad ambition was to emulate Little Richard. (Hibbing Hematite, 1959)

Echo Helstrom, Bob's high school steady and inspiration for "Girl From the North Country." (Hibbing Hematite, 1959)

Bob's boyhood home, now located on Bob Dylan Drive. Current owners commissioned a rendering of the album cover for "Blood on the Tracks" on their garage door. (Photo by Dennis McDougal)

Dylan and girlfriend Suze Rotolo, with fellow Greenwich Village folkie Dave Van Ronk. (Photo by Jim Marshall)

Bob with bodyguard/companion Victor Maymudes. (Photo by Edward Chavez, courtesy of Maia Chavez Larkin)

Bob and Albert Grossman, architect and manager of Dylan's early career. (Photo by Jan Persson, Getty)

Bob and Joan Baez, the King and Queen of Folk, at 1963 Newport Folk Festival. (Photo by Rowland Scherman)

Bob astride motorcycle he would crack up during the summer of '66 in the spill heard 'round the world. (© Douglas R Gilbert)

Bob at home with Sara Dylan and son Jesse during his Woodstock retreat in the late '60s. (Photo by Elliott Landy)

Dylan chugs wine backstage at the Friends of Chile Benefit in 1974. (© Bob Gruen / www .bobgruen.com)

Dylan and friends following a performance by Ronee Blakely at the Roxy in 1976. From left to right: David Blue, Lainie Kaza, Dylan, Robert De Niro, Blakely and Martine Getty. At center is Sally Kirkland. Many of the same faces would also appear in the seldom-seen Bob epic, *Renaldo and Clara*. (Photo by Brad Elterman)

Pope John Paul II meets Dylan, 1997. (AP Photo/ Arturo Mari)

Dylan admitted to the Songwriters' Hall of Fame, 1982. (Time and Life, Photo by Getty Images)

Bob honored during the 2011 Grammys. (Photo by Getty Images)

Abe and Beatty reunited in the Jewish section of Tifereth Israel Cemetery north of Duluth. Though she remarried following Abe's death in 1968, Beatty was interred beside her first husband following her passing in 2000. (Photo by Dennis McDougal)

President Obama awards the Presidential Medal of Freedom to Bob, 2012. (Rex Features via AP Images)

Bob honored during the 2011 Grammys. (Photo by Getty Images)

Zimmy's nightclub, home of the annual Dylan Days festival in downtown Hibbing. (Photo by Dennis McDougal)

Permanent Dylan exhibit in the basement of the Hibbing Public Library. (Photo by Dennis McDougal)

The original Golden Chords, 50 years after their debut at the Hibbing High Jacket Jamboree. From left: drummer LeRoy Hoikkala; rhythm guitar, keyboards, and vocalist Robert Zimmerman; and lead guitar Monte Edwardson. (Photo by Dennis McDougal)

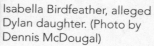

Will DeVogue, alleged Dylan son. (Photo by Will DeVogue)

Isabella Birdfeather, alleged Dylan daughter. (Photo by Dennis McDougal)

PART III

GET ON BOARD, LIL' CHILDREN

1978–1989

Midway upon the journey of our life

I found myself within a forest dark,

For the straight-forward pathway had been lost.

—Dante Alighieri

12

SLOW TRAIN

On that lonesome ribbon of highway where Bob felt most at home, he'd bargained for salvation much of his adult life before meeting Jesus face-to-face. Out in the parking lot at every concert stop, there seemed to be a Hare Krishna selling illuminated Hindi artwork, a New Age zealot dealing tarot cards, or a gaggle of evangelicals brandishing placards that read "Jehovah is God, Jesus His Messiah. Tell Dylan."

The Me Decade delivered a thousand methods new and old for making contact with the godhead. Restless and probing as ever, Bob dabbled in them all—usually with early enthusiasm that eroded fast. From the *I Ching* to the *Tibetan Book of the Dead;* the teachings of George Gurdjieff[314] to personalized readings given by psychics like Tamara Rand[315]; the world according to Norman Raeben to Sara's herbal-tinged macrobiotic fads, Dylan kept finding and then losing his way, often with the help of a joint, a beer, or a woman . . . or all three at once.

---

[314] A spiritualist who promoted pragmatism akin to that of Norman Raeben, the early-twentieth-century Russian teacher, and his disciple P. D. Ouspensky together preached that humans live in a daydream and rarely break free of their cradle-to-grave hypnosis without constant, dedicated work on their higher selves.

[315] Bob consulted the L.A. psychic during his divorce because (as he explained at the time) when things fall apart, "you need someone who can tell you how to crawl out, which way to take." In 1981, Rand claimed to have forecast John Hinckley's attempt to assassinate Ronald Reagan, but her prediction later proved to be a hoax.

"What is it that attracts people to Christ?" he demanded of *Play-boy*'s Ron Rosenbaum at the outset of his *Renaldo and Clara* publicity blitz. Answering his own question, he concluded that the fascinating tragedy and continuing mystery of the Crucifixion was reason enough, and yet Bob remained skeptical.

"Who does Christ become when he lives inside a certain person?" he asked. "Many people say that Christ lives inside them. Well, what does that mean? I've talked to many people whom Christ lives inside. I haven't met one who would want to trade places with Christ. Not one of his people put himself on the line when it came down to the final hour. What would Christ be in this day and age if he came back? What would he be? What would he be to fulfill his function and purpose? He would have to be a leader, I suppose."

Like Bob, perhaps—a roving, charismatic Jew in need of a trim, with chin whiskers and piercing cobalt eyes straight out of a Renaissance oil portrait. He'd have loyal if frequently confounded disciples, an instantly recognizable voice that summoned true believers by the thousands, and a pocket full of parables set to ancient rhyme. But Dylan wasn't even the Voice of his Generation, let alone its Messiah.

"If anything, I'm a pagan Jew," he extolled. "Existentialist Jew. Buddhist Jew. . . . I mean, I don't know what these things mean. Pure Jew? I don't know. I doubt it."

Check out the eyes, he advised. Thoroughbred Ashkenazis don't have baby blues. He was far more likely the mongrel descendant of a Cossack who raped his great-great-great grandmother.

As his 1978 Alimony Tour dissipated to its weary end, basic questions of identity plagued Dylan as often as the bigger ones about the meaning of life. He was not alone in his brooding. Jimmy Carter diagnosed the entire country as suffering from malaise.

As the first politician in a century to declare his born-again bona fides before rising to the national stage, Carter appealed as much to Dylan as Dylan appealed to Carter.[316] At his 1977 Inauguration, the Baptist president declared a new beginning following the trauma of Watergate and told America that "he who is not busy being born is busy dying."

But the times were still changing as the global paradox of Cold War switched America's focus from Vietnam to uneasy peace in the Middle East. Two years into his presidency, with the OPEC oil crisis forcing millions to queue up at the pump, Carter seemed to lose his cheery disposition as well as his grip.

Dylan too descended into malaise . . . until the night he found the silver cross. Still half-skeptic during the concert in Phoenix, at the next whistle-stop his cross evoked epiphany. After checking in at a Tucson hotel, he felt what he later described as an overwhelming presence in his room.

"Jesus put his hand on me," Dylan told the *Los Angeles Times'* Robert Hilburn. "It was a physical thing. I felt it. I felt it all over me. I felt my whole body tremble. The glory of the Lord knocked me down and picked me up."

His wrestling match with Jesus didn't just happen in a vacuum. His own hand-picked celestial choir—the consorts he only half-jokingly referred to as his girlfriends—had been offering him sweet inspiration since the first *Street Legal* rehearsals a year earlier. Many who rotated in and out of Bob's backup trio—Helena Springs, Mary Alice Artes, Clydie King, Mona Lisa Young, Jo Ann Harris, Carolyn Dennis—had gospel backgrounds. Like his early heartthrob Mavis Staples, these women also stood their ground as strong, proud

---

[316] His favorite Dylan song was "Maggie's Farm."

Christians. They cared not a whit if the white boys in the band scoffed at their love of the Lord.

"Don't you ever pray?" Helena Springs once asked Dylan at a particularly low point in his ongoing domestic drama.

"Pray?" he asked.

"Don't you ever do that?"

"When I have trouble, I pray," said Bob.

But following his electric moment with Jesus, Dylan put prayer into overdrive. He broke out his notebook and toiled over couplets the way he'd once done when moved to song by Suze or Sara.

By the end of the Alimony Tour, Dylan had written the first of several apocalyptic admonitions inspired as much by the national mood as by his bitter break with Sara. In addition to warning of "foreign oil controlling American soil" and "sheiks running around like kings," Bob set his newest anthem aboard a slow-moving train to eternity, ending with a bitter lament over a very mortal ex who'd jilted him for a guy Bob described as "a real suicide case."

This time, however, Sara wasn't doing the inspiring. Jesus was his muse. He unveiled "Slow Train Coming" at the last stop on the Alimony Tour, signaling a new round of songs that found broad appeal among a whole new Christian constituency. Simultaneously, he shut the door on his secular audience.

"Gospel music is about the love of God and commercial music is about the love of sex," he announced.

The break between Bard and Bible thumper was as sharp and unsparing as his shift from acoustic to electric. Not that songs of Armageddon were anything new with Dylan.

Abe Zimmerman's boy had been steeped in the blood and guts of the Hebrew Bible from birth, but dating from his earliest Village days, Dylan expanded well beyond the Old Testament into the New. A fan of "The Nazz," the standup comic Lord Buckley's bebop reprise of the life of Christ, young Dylan also soaked up Sunday gospel shows at Madison Square Garden, listening to the likes of the Soul Stirrers, Clara Ward, and the Mighty Clouds of Joy.

Dylan's 3-line, 12-bar rhyme scheme he absorbed from Robert Johnson and Harry Smith's *Anthology of American Folk Music* captured a cadence similar to that of the King James Bible. As far back as "A Hard Rain's a-Gonna Fall" and "When the Ship Comes In," Bob twinned prophesy with Biblical catastrophe. On a more comforting note, "I Shall Be Released" resonated penitent joy, "Chimes of Freedom" pealed hope from inside an imagined cathedral, and "Lay Down Your Weary Tune" affirmed faith as soothingly as the 23rd Psalm.

By the late '60s, even "Blowin' in the Wind" was a staple at Sunday Mass. In 1969, pop impresario Lou Adler (The Mamas and The Papas, *Rocky Horror Picture Show*, etc.) hired a choir to cover his spiritual-tinged songs and released them as *Dylan's Gospel.*[317]

To those who'd been paying attention, Dylan's conversion came as no shock, but the accompanying fire and brimstone did. It was one thing to croon about a stillness in the wind before a hurricane; it was quite another to rant like Elmer Gantry from the stage, pledging hellfire to all who failed to heed Christ's message.

Ironically, it was the weakest link in his gospel choir who steered Dylan to a three-month crash course in proselytizing. Her stage sisters maintained Mary Alice Artes[318] had neither the pipes nor the stage moves to back up Bob, but she had other talents—enough to catch and hold Bob's eye and ear. At the end of the Alimony Tour,

---

[317] A frequently un-Christian collection performed a cappella by the Brothers and Sisters, the collection included lusty "Lay Lady Lay" and "I'll Be Your Baby Tonight." The album found few takers at the time, but eventually became a prized possession among Dylanologists.

[318] At one time, Artes was also roommates with former Factory Girl Sally Kirkland, another member of Dylan's extensive harem.

Artes told him of a new church in the San Fernando Valley just a few miles from his Point Dume hermitage. She suggested he take his questions there during the winter of 1979.

■■ ■■ ■■

The Vineyard Fellowship evolved out of an Orange County ministry rooted in that peculiarly California theological tradition that mixes charismatic evangelism with showbiz. As stern but forgiving as Father Junipero Serra, yet steeped in the showmanship of Sister Aimee Semple McPherson,[319] California pioneered such hybrid institutions as Christian rock and superstar televangelism, running the gambit from Jim and Tammy Faye Bakker and their Trinity Broadcasting Network to the Reverend Robert Schuller and his Crystal Cathedral.

Indeed, Vineyard founder Kenn Gulliksen cut his reverential teeth on a branch of Sister Aimee's Foursquare Church. He believed in accepting all comers, regardless of their baggage, as long as they read the gospel to mean that Jesus was the absolute and only way into heaven. Gulliksen also recruited to his flock music industry professionals[320] who knew exactly how to handle a born-again celebrity like Dylan.

---

[319] The mother of alternative methods of getting in touch with Jesus, Mrs. McPherson staged revivals from coast to coast before settling in Hollywood during the Roaring Twenties. She launched her own evangelical radio station (forerunner of the Trinity Broadcasting Network) and established Angelus Temple, where she developed extravagant Christian pageants that became the forerunners of multimillion-dollar spectacles staged by Robert Schuller in his Crystal Cathedral. She died of a drug overdose at 54.

[320] Debby Boone was another Vineyard regular who struck an acquaintance with Dylan, prompting a persistent rumor that he'd been baptized in Pat Boone's backyard swimming pool.

After Artes introduced them, Gulliksen dispatched a pair of youth ministers to go over the Bible with Bob, after which Dylan sat in on a crash course on how to interpret the gospel. His indoctrination included the fundamentalist belief that intense scriptural study bypasses the mind all together and asserts the Holy Spirit directly to the heart—a process Dylan described with the Islamic term *raima,* loosely translated as "embedded happiness."

One of the sect's previous converts, former Columbia record producer and songsmith Al Kasha, recognized the spiritual quandary divorce had visited upon Dylan, and volunteered to shepherd Bob through Bible study.

"The deeper the pain, the better the witness," declared Kasha.

A two-time Oscar winner for Best Song,[321] Kasha suffered his own emotional pain as a housebound agoraphobic. Success did not banish irrational fear. He had to look beyond the movies just as Dylan had to look beyond the music. Following a Sunday morning telecast of Robert Schuller's "Hour of Power," Kasha felt the same born-again surge Dylan experienced in Tucson. With the help of Jesus, he once again ventured out of his Beverly Hills home and eventually found himself preaching the Word at the Vineyard. As a fellow songwriter, Kasha shared his story with Bob and adopted him as his personal project.

The Kashas gave Dylan a key to their home where he would often show up unannounced after the couple went to bed. "I heard the guitar playing some nights, but I wouldn't bother him," Kasha recalled. "He wrote his whole entire *Slow Train Coming* album in front of our fireplace."

---

[321] "The Morning After" from *The Poseidon Adventure* (1972) and "We May Never Love Like This Again" from *The Towering Inferno* (1974).

"I didn't like writing them," Bob recalled. "I didn't want to write them." He sensed the firestorm his gospel would ignite.

Kasha and Dylan found they had common ground. During Bob's first year in the Village, Kasha was a John Hammond protégé and producer for Aretha Franklin, and yet it wasn't Kasha he asked to produce his next LP. Dylan turned instead to a heretic.

"I liked the irony of Bob coming to me, the Wandering Jew, to get the Jesus feel," Jerry Wexler recalled to Dylan biographer Clinton Heylin.

A former Atlantic Records vice president,[322] Wexler wanted to record *Slow Train Coming*[323] in the Muscle Shoals Sound Studio where Aretha, Otis Redding, and other '60s soul singers created some of their biggest hits. It wasn't until they arrived in northern Alabama that he learned what the songs were about.

"Born-again Christians in the old corral," said Wexler.

When Dylan tried converting him, he just smiled and shook his head.

"Bob, you're dealing with a 62-year-old confirmed Jewish atheist," said Wexler. "I'm hopeless. Let's just make an album."

The LP they made was an engineering triumph—easily Dylan's best effort since his Nashville period when Bob Johnston was at the control board. *Slow Train Coming* contrasted sharply with *Street Legal*'s uneven "live" sound, delivering a smoother, more disciplined quality on every cut. Backed by his gospel girls and the lead guitar of Dire Straits' Mark Knopfler, the bluesy "Gotta Serve Somebody" set the tone. From the reggae of "Man Gave Names to All the

---

[322] Wexler began his career as a staff writer for *Billboard*. In 1948, he was credited with coining the term "rhythm and blues" as an alternative to "race records."

[323] Foreshadowing the LP's evangelistic title by nearly 15 years, Dylan began the gibberish liner notes of *Highway 61 Revisited* with, "On the slow train time does not interfere . . ."

Animals" to the urgent backbeat of "When He Returns," the music was flawless, but Dylan's all-or-nothing Christian lyrics weren't.

While *Slow Train Coming* sold quickly into gold on the *Billboard* charts, it alienated the secular faithful looking for another *Blood on the Tracks*. Once they listened to Bob's Heaven-or-Hell preachments, *Slow Train Coming* rarely got a replay.

It didn't help that Dylan's first gospel LP landed in record stores on the heels of the Jonestown massacre. At the very moment Bob began demanding absolute obedience to Jesus, the Reverend Jim Jones demanded that 909[324] members of his Peoples Temple drink cyanide-laced Kool-Aid. Besides shocking the nation, the mass suicide ignited suspicion over any religious leader calling for blind faith from his followers.

"You can find anything you want in the Bible," Dylan would later protest to Robert Shelton. "You can twist it around and a lot of people do that."

But caught up in his newfound fervor during the autumn of 1979, Dylan didn't care how deeply his Bible-thumping joy might foul his fan base. He harangued against adultery in free-loving L.A., the vainglorious idolatry of New York, and the "ungodly vice" of homosexuality among the newly uncloseted in San Francisco. True-blue Dylan disciples like Jann Wenner and Paul Williams lauded *Slow Train,* but most reviewers damned Bob with faint praise. One wrote that Dylan spoke from "a mysterious, dangerous and often hilarious place where life was experienced to the full in all its horror and ecstasy."

But others gagged over his hard-sell lyrics. Loyal Dylanista Greil Marcus turned on Bob, calling him "arrogant, intolerant and smug."

---

[324] Four more members died in Georgetown, while five visitors and would-be defectors were gunned down while attempting to board a plane at nearby Port Kaituma.

"There's no sense of his own sin on *Slow Train,* no humility," wrote Marcus. "Jesus is the answer and if you don't believe it, you're fucked."

The truest test of how he'd be taken on his upcoming *Slow Train* tour came during a surprise appearance on NBC's *Saturday Night Live*. Millions who tuned in for a rare dose of televised Dylan heard "Gotta Serve Somebody" followed by "I Believe in You" and "When You Gonna Wake Up," confirming reports that had been filtering out of Santa Monica, Malibu, and Muscle Shoals for months: The old Dylan was history. The new one was a cross between Jimmy Swaggert and Tennessee Ernie Ford.

■ ■ ■

Larry Cragg, Bob's guitar technician since Rolling Thunder, sensed a sea change the first time Dylan asked him to ready his instruments for the *Slow Train* concerts.

"Everything was different," Cragg recalled as he stepped into Rundown Studio. "There were a lot of people in suits hanging around, and the coffee tables had religious literature on them. I thought, 'Wow, that's different.' And I went into the back room and started working on the guitars. But when I lit up a joint, some guy in a suit came rushing in, saying, 'No, you can't do that.' A year before it had been okay, but suddenly I had really screwed up."

Dylan once again swore off drugs and demon liquor. When he met with old Village pal Maria Muldaur, who'd experienced her own Christian conversion, she offered him a glass of burgundy.

"No, no, no," he said. "I don't want it."

"What are you talking about?" she said. "You love wine."

"Not anymore. The Lord delivered me from drinking about six weeks ago. He just lifted any desire."

Muldaur took a sip and said, "Gee, I wish he'd do that for me."

Dylan had a long history of doing nothing by half measures. While others might be in for a dime or a dollar, Bob bet the bank. No Sunday morning penitent back to sinning on Saturday night, Dylan didn't just pay lip service to the Lord. He was *all* in, and that included his conviction that the Apocalypse was just around the corner. The Vineyard Fellowship's attention to prophecy had special appeal to the author of "A Hard Rain's A-Gonna Fall."

Besides the New Testament, the other manual his Vineyard peers recommended during Bob's biblical boot camp was *The Late Great Planet Earth*.[325] Its author, Texas evangelist Hal Lindsey, identified the USSR and Iran as the twin combatants the Book of Revelation predicted would lead the Earth to perdition in the little town of Armageddon, a few miles south of the Lebanese border. The End Times were on their way, according to Lindsey. The Rapture would separate the fake from the faithful. Like millions of others, Dylan read and believed.

The latest in a millennium loaded with self-styled prophets who pulled quotes from Isaiah, Daniel, Jeremiah, Ezekiel, and Revelation to match current events, Lindsey came from a soothsaying tradition that ranged from Nostradamus to Sydney Omarr. The former Campus Crusade for Christ preacher offered the future for the price of a paperback. He assembled his dire sermons and published them in 1970 as an overnight bestseller.

Like the singer-songwriter he influenced, Lindsey became a wealthy man. He parlayed *The Late Great Planet Earth* into more

---

[325] Eventually selling more than 30 million copies, Lindsey's slim volume would inspire fellow evangelicals Tim Lahaye and Jerry Jenkins during the 1990s, prompting the hugely popular and profitable *Left Behind* chronicles of adventure in a post-Rapture world.

than a dozen sequels. When the Soviet Union collapsed, he simply modified his prophecy. "Iran could ignite catastrophe," he warned.

Lindsey divorced twice heading into the twenty-first century. He found a new church and a third wife, both of whom gave him the boot after he allegedly committed adultery. Still, Lindsey never gave up reinterpreting Revelation and his evangelical base never gave up on him. Despite his faltering predictions, he moved into the digital age with a TV program and a widely read website, confirming his one irrefutable prophecy: "'The Future' is big business."[326]

When *Slow Train* left the station, Bob remained in Lindsey's thrall, blind to the arrogance of preaching the one, true, and only way into heaven. The stone-faced rock star who rarely spoke to his audience began to evangelize a homophobic, chauvinistic,[327] apocalyptic fundamentalism. Over the next year, he spouted enough hope and fear from the stage to literally fill a book.

> How many people here are aware that we're living in the end of times right now? How many people are aware of that? Anybody interested to know that we're living in the end times? How many people *do* know that? Well, we are. We're living in the end times. That's right. I told you that 'The Times They Are A Changin' 20 years ago, and I don't believe I've ever lied to you. I don't think I told you anything that was a lie. Never told you to vote for nobody; never told you to follow nobody . . .[328]

---

[326] On the 10th anniversary of 9/11, Lindsey published *The Everlasting Hatred: The Roots of Jihad* (2011) indicting Islam as the engine driving the world toward the Apocalypse.

[327] He told *Rolling Stone*'s Kurt Loder he disapproved of "chicks" performing out front on stage "because they whore themselves, especially the ones that don't wear anything."

[328] *Saved! The Gospel Speeches of Bob Dylan* (New York: Hanuman Books, 1990).

The first stop on the *Slow Train* tour was San Francisco's 2,200-seat Warfield Theater, setting a pace over the next year for small, intimate venues where Bob could get up close and personal with his flock. During his two-week stand, he performed none of his pre-gospel catalog, ignoring the jeers from disappointed fans the same way he once ignored shouts of "Judas!" following his conversion from acoustic to electric guitar. The *San Francisco Examiner* and *Chronicle* spread their own gospel during his Warfield stand, reporting that many walked out and demanded their money back.

"Dylan has written some of the most banal, uninspired and inventionless songs of his career for his Jesus phase," charged *Chronicle* pop critic Joel Selvin. "Years from now, when social historians look back over these years, Dylan's conversion will serve as a concise metaphor for the vast emptiness of the era."

Not necessarily. Some, like fervent Dylanologist Paul Williams, did not demand their money back, stayed for the music, and eventually got right with Jesus, in part because Dylan's sound and stagecraft provided what his clumsy poetry could not. As theologian Stephen Webb would point out in *Dylan Redeemed* (2006), "Rock and roll is sacred music precisely because it provides a modern analogue to medieval mystical passion." Ironically, Dylan's live mystic sound peaked at the same moment his lyrics tanked.

In an attempt to explain Bob's Christian conversion, Williams published *Dylan—What Happened?,* concluding that the excesses of the Me Decade transformed him into a mature performing artist in the Sinatra-Presley mould. Phrasing, enunciation, changeups, staging . . . everything mattered, and those turned off by his preaching missed out on some of the finest performances of Bob's career.

"What I do is so immediate it changes the nature, the concept of art to me," Dylan said, comparing each of his concerts to acting out a stage play.

Nevertheless, word spread that Bob had lost his mojo. He preached in the wilderness; audiences dwindled and few listened. On a Minneapolis visit, Dylan ran into his old girlfriend Judy Rubin who invited him to meet her boyfriend. Bob showed up with Bible in hand.

"He told me that he had found a better way," she recalled to author Bob Spitz. "Worse, lightning would strike me because I hadn't found the way. At first, I didn't know what he was talking about. Then it dawned on me that he meant I was divorced and living in sin with a man. *That hypocrite!*"

Those who did get on board with Bob did so with Pentecostal delight. After hearing of his conversion, the Hibbing High classmate who'd introduced Bob to Echo Helstrom 20 years earlier praised Jesus.

"I was hoping and praying that he would accept the Lord, so it's no surprise to me," said Dee Dee Seward. "God gave him a fantastic talent and I think He'll bless him sevenfold."

He kept the faith and was rewarded with his first Grammy the following February.[329] In accepting the award for best male rock vocal on "Gotta Serve Somebody," Dylan thanked God and Jerry Wexler.[330]

As his *Slow Train* chugged into a new decade, Dylan doubled down with another album. He and Wexler returned to Muscle Shoals, delivering his 20th studio LP three months later. Filled with more fire and brimstone, the cover art of the unambiguously titled *Saved* said it all: a hand from on high with only its middle finger coyly curled into its palm, reaching down to the outstretched fingers of the

---

[329] *Slow Train* also won best inspirational album of the year from the Gospel Music Association.

[330] Wexler's mother later took exception, claiming that Bob got the order reversed.

masses. Perhaps it was the hand of God, but the name writ large across the bottom was "Bob Dylan."

■ ■ ■

By 1980, boomers traded in their bell-bottoms and tie-dye for three-piece business suits, stock options, and adjustable-rate mortgages. Yuppies began to supplant the Greatest Generation. VW microbuses that once carried bumper stickers that read "Question Authority" gave way to BMWs announcing "He who dies with the most toys wins." Greed wasn't good yet but got a little better all the time.

Born-again Bob alienated his boomer base just as they began cashing in on the American Dream and losing interest in music—his and everyone else's. While Dylan barnstormed for Jesus, disco died, punk evolved into new wave, and the Top 40 splintered into Album-Oriented Rock (AOR), Adult Contemporary, and a dozen other radio formats, diluting deejays' power to generate hits.

An air of panic rippled through the music industry. Record sales began sliding in 1977 and three years later the numbers had fallen more than 10 percent. Consumers still bought more than 1 billion LPs annually, but the total dwindled a little with each passing year. Television helped fill pop's power vacuum by creating a new kind of rock royalty with MTV, but choreography and mugging for the camera began to matter more than the music. Celebrity trumped substance while all that glittered turned to gold. A wandering Jew with a penchant for preaching had no place in the new world order.

In retrospect, replacing Dylan-quoting Jimmy Carter with a luxury-loving former movie star seemed oddly appropriate. By the time Ronald Reagan commenced Morning in America, the era of the singer-songwriter had ended and the age of the moonwalk began. The decade in pop would belong to Michael Jackson, Madonna, and another Minnesota troubadour who went only by his royal first name. Before the '80s ended, Prince[331] would supersede Dylan as the biggest noise to come out of the Twin Cities, and Michael Jackson's *Thriller* would outsell Bob's entire catalog.

Slow Train did go platinum in 1980, but it would be Dylan's last hit album for more than 15 years. *Saved* wouldn't even sell enough copies to go gold.[332] Three days shy of his 39th birthday, Bob had to cancel the final concert of his Gospel Tour because of poor ticket sales. That spring, his slow train ground to a halt.

Dylan hadn't given up on Jesus, but neither had he abandoned Mammon. Answering the blunt inquiry of a Fleet Street reporter, Bob went deadpan:

"I'm worth $1.5 million. The cost of a supersonic plane. Maybe a bit less."

He was spotted in a Seattle jewelry store near the end of the tour buying a $25,000 diamond engagement ring. Speculation as to who his covenant woman might be centered on Clydie King, who seemed Bob's perfect foil. One of Ray Charles's earliest Raelettes, King sang backup for Joe Cocker and the Rolling Stones before hooking up with Dylan.

"Two different people you couldn't hope to meet," recalled Rolling Stone guitarist Ron Wood. "Her a black, outrageous, hamburger-eating soul singer and Bob all quiet and white, nibbling off the side of her hamburger."

Did they marry? Bob never said and no proof ever surfaced. Asked six years later if he was *still* married, he said "Yes, in a

---

[331]   Dylan called him the "boy wonder."

[332]   At one point Dylan considered investing in an L.A. radio station and starting his own label, Accomplice, which he planned to distribute through CBS. Both plans fell through along with his record sales.

manner of speaking," before correcting himself to, "Yes, as a matter of fact." Moments later he corrected himself again: "I'm not sure."

Many an old friend sensed cynicism in Bob's conversion. Loyalists like David Blue and Bob Neuwirth quit his orbit for good while Mick Jagger sniped and rolled his eyes. Keith Richards took to calling Bob "the prophet of profit."

While carrying the gospel across North America, Dylan quietly commissioned construction of a quarter-million-dollar 63-foot schooner on the tiny Caribbean island of Bequia. His *Water Pearl* launched without him in November 1979, but during the summer of 1980, the elaborately appointed vessel's 12-man crew welcomed the new skipper aboard.

Fellow rockers David Crosby and Neil Young saw no hypocrisy in owning a boat. They used their own to find solitude. Crosby quipped that his frequent voyages were "my way of keeping both feet on the ground and mixing a metaphor at the same time."

During the *Water Pearl*'s shakedown, Bob mixed his own metaphors. Out on the water, he began a batch of songs resonant of his best mid-70s poetry. They included the cryptic travelogue "Caribbean Wind," the hard-rocking omen "The Groom's Still Waiting at the Altar," and a reverential hymn he entitled "Every Grain of Sand."[333]

After his return to touring in the fall, Dylan had a whole new repertoire. But unlike the songs he'd written the previous year, his evangelism softened. The fresh material wasn't steeped in Jesus.

---

[333] A synthesis of William Blake's "Auguries of Innocence" and the annual inventory that observant Jews recite every Yom Kippur, the six-minute prayer sung to an unnamed God has less to do with Jesus than it does Yahweh, Allah, or the Great Spirit. According to sociologist Steven Goldberg, Bob was borrowing from Blake's "Auguries" as far back as "The Gates of Eden."

For one thing, he'd learned that his mother didn't care for his Bible-thumping. Beatty called on her own rabbi back in St. Paul to have a word with Bob.

For another, his kids had suffered. Earlier in the year, Bob showed up for Jesse Dylan's bar mitzvah[334] only to return to the Gospel Tour the moment the boy was officially a man. More than one Dylan kid felt betrayed by his father's Christianity.

Whether family pressure, plummeting concert attendance, poor record sales, or his own personal epiphanies aboard the *Water Pearl* made the difference, Dylan returned to San Francisco's Warfield Theater the following November minus sanctimony. He did offer something of a parable on the fourth night of the tour. While tuning up a 12-string between numbers, Bob spoke to the audience with deep reverence, but not about Jesus. He praised Leadbelly:

> He made lots of records. At first he was just doing prison songs, and stuff like that. He'd been out of prison for some time when he decided to do children's songs. And people said, 'Oh wow! Has Leadbelly changed?' Some people liked the older songs. Some people liked the newer ones. But he didn't change. He was the same man.

Dylan took to lacing golden oldies among the gospel so that "Girl from the North Country" might follow "Gotta Serve Somebody" and "Like a Rolling Stone" would lead into "Man Gave Names to All the Animals." To mix it up further, he'd occasionally throw in cover versions of the songs of others.

He and Clydie King harmonized on Dion DiMucci's *Abraham, Martin and John.* When they reached the line about "my old friend

---

[334] All of Sara Dylan's children were bar or bat mitzvahed while Maria became an Orthodox Jew.

Bobby," the crowd burst into applause, but with the next question, "Can you tell me where he's gone?" the faithful rose to their feet roaring approval. Welcome back, Bob.

The point he seemed to want to make was that he hadn't gone anywhere, nor had he betrayed his Jewish roots by embracing Jesus.

"I don't really want to walk around with a sign on me saying 'Christian,'" he complained, struggling to reconcile the credo that Christians and Jews don't mix.

"Jesus is not a religion, is not a religion," he insisted. "I could talk about it for days and days . . ."

But he didn't, at least not to the media. He might have said he empathized with Jesus, who spoke in parables and metaphor; that those who insisted on tailoring Christ's declarations to their own purpose were as misguided as those who manipulated Dylan's lyrics; and that the former Bobby Zimmerman could be a Jew, just like Jesus, and still believe that in the beginning was the Word.

But he knew enough about reporters not to waste his time. His yearlong flirtation with zealotry was finished. That was the only story that needed planting in the press. The revelation didn't bring fans back. Unbelievers stayed away while those who'd listened during the Gospel Tour found no reason for a second revival.

"A lotta people may . . . say, 'Wow,' you know. 'Wow, I can read my *own* Bible. I don't have to get it preached at me,' you know," said Dylan. "That's when they decide not to come."

He did learn who his friends were though. Longstanding Christians Johnny Cash and Charlie Daniels applauded Bob's conversion while Rolling Thunder veterans Roger McGuinn and T-Bone Burnett publicly confessed their own born-again experiences, standing in solidarity with Dylan. McGuinn even made a guest appearance at Warfield to sing "Mr. Tambourine Man" with Bob.

But as with Jerry Wexler, Dylan's friends didn't have to embrace Jesus to prove their loyalty. Bill Graham agreed to promote Bob's concerts even when he couldn't fill a venue the size of the Hibbing High auditorium.

"I am a Jew and I am deeply moved by what this man is doing," said the venerable promoter. "It's a very profound public display of personal convictions."

Graham called in the likes of Carlos Santana and Maria Muldaur to pump up ticket sales, but the biggest catch of all came to Bob's aid on his own volition.

"I want to play," said Jerry Garcia. "I want to go down there and play."

"Do you know what Bob's into now?" said Grateful Dead manager Rock Scully.

"Aaaah fuck that," said Garcia. "I'm there."

When Garcia appeared on stage with guitar in hand, Dylan had no idea he was even going to show up. But as news spread that as notoriously a fallen Catholic as the founder of the Grateful Dead was playing backup, Bob's show became a sellout.

■■ ■■ ■■

"I saw these people that have died, you know," Dylan told Ron Rosenbaum in the weeks leading up to his Christian conversion. "I've seen Buddy Holly play. I've seen Eddie Cochran play. I've seen Sam Cooke. I'd seen all these people that are dead. Not a day goes by when I don't think about all these people."

Howard Alk tied Dylan's Christian rebirth directly to his abject fear of death.[335] He told Paul Williams as much during the Gospel Tour. Bob froze at the news of Elvis Presley's passing and spoke frequently about the triple tragedies of Janis, Jimi, and Jim Morrison. All died of drug abuse at 27, the same age Robert Johnson kept his own appointment with the hereafter.

"You can get away with anything for a while," said Bob. "But it's like Poe's *The Tell-Tale Heart* or Dostoyevsky's *Crime and Punishment:* Somewhere along the line, sooner or later, you're going to have to pay."

In Jesus, he found a get-out-of-jail-free card. At the end of 1980, he'd outlived Christ by half a dozen years. He'd foresworn his low-down ways and once again cleaned up his act. He understood better than most rockers that time was piling up.

"I do believe that things are planned for every one of us," Bob reflected. "But I also believe that we have free will to change it at one time or another, although I'm not so sure about changing the end result."

On the evening of December 8, 1980, with the West Coast leg of his tour wrapped, an upbeat Dylan reportedly scouted New York for a venue similar to the Warfield, planning to pick up there after the first of the year. Four shots from Mark David Chapman's handgun changed all of that and put an end to Bob's evangelism.

"John Lennon had done a great deal of demythologizing his own myth and the myth of the Beatles in the song 'God,'" Jackson

---

[335] One gospel staple that remained on Bob's playlist long after he quit preaching was "Saving Grace":

I've escaped death so many times, I know I'm only living
By the saving grace that's over me
By this time I'd've thought that I'd be sleeping
In a pine box for all eternity . . .

Browne said in the days that followed. "I think we really, in so many ways, have been instructed by his example to be suspicious of anybody who's carrying around the answers or says they have the plan: how to be, how to live, what to do."

Dylan never liked "Imagine," the song by which the ex-Beatle would be forever identified. Perhaps it was Lennon's agnostic speculation that there might be no heaven or hell. No religion, too. Dylan called Lennon's murder "hero worship in a mad kind of way," and reportedly hired a pair of Israeli bodyguards in the wake of the murder. When asked why, he said, "Because they're the best."

Dylan spent the next year dodging reporters' questions about the venerated Beatle. He did not continue his concerts as planned, nor did he resume touring in the spring after a second would-be assassin tried to kill Ronald Reagan.

Instead of heading out for the East Coast, Dylan retreated to the studio following the disturbing winter of '81. He called his new album *Shot of Love*. It would be the worst-selling LP of his career.

13

SOUL TRAIN

One-take Bob who'd once created whole albums overnight, labored for weeks on *Shot of Love*, searching for that thin, elusive sound that used to boogie so effortlessly inside his skull.

"I have to get back to the sound that will bring it all through me," he said as he moved from studio to studio all over L.A., auditioning musicians and producers[336] while simultaneously laying down tracks for the album he called his best since *Blonde on Blonde*. The public disagreed. Of the three so-called Jesus albums, *Shot of Love* would be his last and least popular. And yet, in keeping with the irony that now informed Dylan's every move, it also turned out to be his most redeeming in terms of pure poetry.

In addition to the enduring and masterful "Every Grain of Sand," *Shot of Love* delivered the secular love song "Heart of Mine," cut from the same cloth as "Tomorrow Is a Long Time." There was also a rough-hewn ballad about Lenny Bruce, Dylan's first biographical polemic since "Hurricane." If he hadn't insisted on including "Property of Jesus," *Shot of Love* might have passed as his return to the real world instead of one more reveille in an ongoing Christian crusade.

---

[336] Chuck Plotkin, who engineered Bruce Springsteen's follow-ups to *Born to Run*, got the job on David Geffen's recommendation. "He was late to sessions all the time," Plotkin recalled. "He'd come in two, three hours late and say, 'I took the wrong turn off the freeway and ended up in East L.A.'"

More than three-quarters of the material he recorded that spring never even made it to the album. Originally, he planned an ambitious three-record LP, but Columbia said no. Instead of jumping labels as he'd done eight years earlier, Dylan conceded to narrow his selections to nine tracks.

A decade or more would pass before anyone outside his ever-tightening circle heard all outtakes, first as bootlegs and later, as tracks on Columbia anthologies. Some were slight ("Ah, Ah, Ah," "Fur Slippers," etc.), some were covers (Hank Williams's "Cold, Cold Heart," Junior Parker's "Mystery Train"), and some were genuine Dylan gems ("Angelina," "Caribbean Wind"). He also left out "The Groom's Still Waiting at the Altar," though Columbia released that cryptic rocker as the B-side of a single, and eventually included it as a bonus track on later pressings of *Shot of Love*.

That summer, he refrained from stage evangelizing all together and mixed in more oldies than at any time since his conversion. But Bible-banging Bob was now firmly stuck in the public's craw and he did little to deny it. He gave few interviews, dodged questions about faith, and remained fiercely guarded over his private life.

Spooked by John Lennon's death, he'd acquired his own bona fide stalker by the time he recorded *Shot of Love*. Once she slipped into his life, Carmella Hubbell passed herself off regularly as his Missus, confounding Dylan's every effort to give her the slip. Her zealotry began with unanswered fan mail during the *Slow Train* concerts but quickly escalated to obsession.

Hubbell combed gossip columns and fanzines for clues as to Bob's whereabouts, attempting to insinuate herself into all aspects of his life. She hung around Rundown in Santa Monica, decked out in ball cap, knapsack, and running shoes on the off chance that Dylan might duck down the alleyway. She took up residence at a Malibu motel so she could be within cruising distance of his best-known residence.[337] During a single month in the spring of 1981, she broke inside the chain link surrounding the Point Dume compound 19 times.

Not since A. J. Weberman had a groupie so alarmingly put the "fan" back in fanatic. From L.A. to Minnesota and all points in between, Hubbell convinced newsmen, business associates, and even one of Bob's backup singers that *she* was his woman. Hubbell booked hotel rooms as Mrs. Dylan, ran up tabs on the strength of Bob's name, and tried canceling concerts as the dutiful wife, calling ahead to promoters to report that her husband just wasn't feeling up to performing that night.

In addition to his own growing security detail, Dylan called on local constabularies and even the FBI to help track his tracker. When she finally was caught, Carmella was boarding a flight to Jamaica to greet Bob aboard the *Water Pearl*.

"I've sort of got walls up all over the place," Dylan said after the Carmella episode. "They can only get so far."

He hired P.I.s to track prospective stalkers and develop dossiers that he kept locked in a safe in Minneapolis. Some of his bodyguards carried handcuffs. Hubbell might have been the worst, but she wasn't Dylan's only loony nor was she the last to fake driver's licenses or passports using his name. Groupies staked out elevators in hotels where he stayed, played hide-and-seek in the lobby, and claimed to be outcall masseurs, long-lost relatives, or takeout delivery persons, complete with uniforms.

---

[337] At the time, he stayed much of the time in a Brentwood apartment a few miles from Rundown.

"I have security people around me, only you just can't see them, that's all," said Dylan. "Nobody knows ever who's with me and who's not."

A hooded parka in Greenwich or burnoose on the beach at Malibu no longer guaranteed anonymity. In a post-Watergate world, when even the president was fair game, fans fed more than ever on celebrity. Bob went to extraordinary lengths to dodge them, finding his odds of avoiding detection better when he traveled outside the U.S.

Like Charlie Chaplin and Jerry Lewis, Dylan began seeing himself as *l'artiste,* scorned in his own country. After all, *Renaldo and Clara* reaped praise at Cannes. A quarter-million Brits turned out during the summer of '78 to see him perform at England's Blackbushe Festival. His fame may have faltered a bit after he cozied up to Jesus, but he rebounded in Britain during the summer of '81.

A whole new generation of Anglophile Dylanologists began to promote the Bob legend: encyclopedic Michael Gray, dogged but respectful Clinton Heylin, essayist and chronicler John Bauldie, and no less an academic champion than Oxford Professor of Poetry Christopher Ricks. From England came a new kind of fanzine, dedicated solely to esoterica surrounding the life and times of Bob Dylan. Both *The Telegraph*[338] and *Wanted Man* launched in the '80s, expanding their early UK circulation to the U.S. and beyond before decade's end.

Even Bob's earliest and most venerable defender, former *New York Times* pop critic Robert Shelton, expatriated to Liverpool to

---

[338] The first and most ambitious Bob fanzine was published in Lancashire, England, and dwelt on such minutiae as which sideman wore a spotted shirt during the '65 Newport concert and whether or not Sara's stint as a Playboy bunny referenced the "topless joint" that Bob wrote about in "Tangled Up in Blue."

finish *No Direction Home,* his long-awaited "definitive" biography of Bob that had taken thrice as long to complete as *Tarantula.*

While Dylan might struggle to fill the Warfield, he still drew crowds in Europe, and that's where he chose to unveil *Shot of Love.* He was a hit in France, Germany, Switzerland, Austria, Scandinavia, and England, but Columbia failed to ship the album until the tour was over, widening the gap between America's most successful record label and its most enduring singer-songwriter. Never keen on his Christianity, Columbia poured resources instead into its Epic subsidiary where new pop royalty like Michael Jackson, ABBA, and Cyndi Lauper sold circles around Dylan.

He continued to believe his messianic message, but Bob also believed in record sales. As his most recent five-year contract ground to an end, gaffes like Columbia's late shipping and stingy promotion cut deep.

Following late summer decompression aboard the *Water Pearl* and a visit with his vacationing children at Southfork,[339] Dylan hit the road again in the fall—this time back in the U.S.A. where *Shot of Love* was finally available coast to coast. Whatever problems he'd had with feckless stalkers and prying press, this land was still his land. Like a latter-day Irving Berlin who'd forsworn his European ancestry for an Americanism more apple pie than Tom Sawyer, Bob "got into America harder," according to fellow troubadour Randy Newman. All Jewish singer-songwriters did, from Paul Simon to Leonard Cohen, but Dylan most of all.

"There's this wanting to be part, wanting to be accepted in America," said Newman. "I think sometimes it's why I glom onto whatever Southern background I have so hard."

---

[339] The *Dallas*-inspired nickname the Dylan kids gave Bob's Minnesota farm.

Once embarrassed to admit to being a Jew from the Mesabi Range, Dylan held to those midwestern roots as hard as Newman did New Orleans. Album promotion might carry Bob from the Champs-Élysées to Piccadilly Circus, but he always returned to Highway 61. He saved the best of *Shot of Love* for his own countrymen, and through the autumn of '81, Dylan hyped the new LP in 21 cities across North America, delivering some of the longest and most impassioned concerts of his career. At the final stop in Florida just before Thanksgiving, he performed for more than four hours, returning to the stage for six encores.

But his most inspired moment took place mid-October at the 3,400-seat Holiday Star Music Theater in Merrillville, Indiana—as small-town America as any invention of Frank Capra or Frank Hibbing. Dylan rolled out a special guest that night—a wheelchair-bound quadriplegic who'd attended many concerts as a fan but always had a standing invitation to visit backstage whenever and wherever Bob performed.

"You wanna, you wanna hear something really strange?" Dylan called out from the stage. Once it became clear Bob wasn't going to start preaching again, the groans faded. Instead, he beckoned toward the sidelines. "I got a friend of mine who's gonna sing a song now. Gonna bring him on stage. I wonder if he's gonna sing? This is a friend of mine named Larry!"

Camp Herzl alumnus Larry Kegan was indeed a friend—an old one who predated the Golden Chords, when little Bobby Zimmerman still subdued girls with *glissendorf* and had yet to unfurl his first Little Richard pompadour. Kegan never advertised or traded on their friendship, which guaranteed its permanence. As with Lou Kemp or John Bucklen, who could show up unannounced at any concert and get a backstage pass, the ex-Joker rolled past Bob's ever-tightening security whenever he presented himself.

When he showed for the Merrillville concert, Kegan had his own patriotic point to prove. Just as he'd argued years earlier that sex didn't vanish with a spine injury,[340] Kegan now wanted to demonstrate that a guy in a wheelchair could rock just as loud and long as any able-bodied American. He didn't exactly belt Chuck Berry's "No Money Down" as the evening's final encore, but the chorus still carried the same punch it once did when a pair of Jokers dreamed their Cadillac dreams in the 1950s:

I'm gonna get me a car
And I'll be headed on down the road
Then I won't have to worry
'Bout that broke-down raggedy Ford

Dylan accompanied on tenor sax, punctuating each verse with a blat—not exactly Clarence Clemons, but it would go down in the annals of Dylanology as the only time Bob ever played that instrument in public. The gig went so well that they repeated it two nights later in Boston. This time, however, Kegan collapsed backstage and had to be taken by ambulance to a nearby hospital.

He recovered, and while the Jokers' brief reunion would never happen again, Kegan did form his own band, the Mere Mortals, and would rock on as a regional Minnesota attraction for years to come.

Four days after Boston, Dylan broke character again to sing "Happy Birthday" from the stage to another old friend. One of the few Rolling Thunder alumni still on the road with Bob, Howard Alk turned 51 on October 25.

---

[340] In addition to the Mexican sex resort for Vietnam vets he managed around the time of *Pat Garrett and Billy the Kid*, Kegan's sexual attitude reassessment (SAR) program for the disabled became a staple at the University of Minnesota and other medical schools across the country.

On the off chance Bob might make good on a promise to produce another movie, Alk stayed on the payroll long past *Renaldo and Clara*. He moved onto the grounds of the Point Dume compound and shot stills and film footage during the *Shot of Love* tour, just as he'd been doing off and on for nearly two decades. In a continuing effort to recapture the chemistry of *Dont Look Back*, Alk became Bob's resident documentarian. At the end of 1981, he literally set up housekeeping at Rundown Studio.

A follow-up to *Renaldo and Clara* seemed possible at first. He and Bob initially bonded over film and set out to conquer Hollywood together. During one of his final drunken interviews with *Rolling Stone* before finding Jesus, Dylan himself announced grand plans to make 12 more films.[341] He said his next movie would be based on *The Ringmaster*, novelist Darryl Ponicsan's fantasy travelogue about circus life.

But there would be no *Ringmaster*, no *Renaldo* sequel, no *Eat the Document Deux*, and certainly nothing as iconic as *Dont Look Back*. Once Bob returned to sober stage performing, Alk began losing hope. He divorced, remarried, separated, gained weight, went on prescription antidepressants, descended into heroin,[342] and slowly succumbed to a spiritual dystopia more killing than Larry Kegan's physical paralysis. With an abiding cynicism over Bob's Christian conversion and his own unfulfilled promise as a filmmaker, Alk seemed resigned to his role as Rundown's cinematographer.

---

[341] Jerry Weintraub tried and failed to get Bob to invest in *The Karate Kid* (1984).

[342] As had Mike Bloomfield, Dylan's formidable guitar front man on "Like a Rolling Stone." Though they seldom recorded together after *Highway 61 Revisited*, Bloomfield was the first to hear Dylan play through the entire suite that would become *Blood on the Tracks*, and during the darkest days of his Christian tour in 1980, Bloomfield was one of the few old friends who guested with him at the Warfield. On Feb. 15, 1981, Bloomfield was found in his car in San Francisco, dead of an overdose.

On New Year's Eve 1981, Alk phoned friends and family from the studio and drafted two suicide notes so there would be no mistake about his intentions. Sometime after midnight, he put the needle in his arm. By New Year's Day in 1982, Howard Alk faded to black.

■ ■ ■

Bob disappeared down a rabbit hole during the year that followed. There was no new album, no tour. He surfaced briefly in L.A. to record with Allen Ginsberg late in January and traveled to New York for his induction into the Songwriters Hall of Fame two months later. Mostly he stayed out of the sight.

Following Alk's suicide, the lease ran out on Rundown. During the final months there, he and Clydie King did several sessions together followed by a handful of recordings with stalwarts Al Kooper, ex–Rolling Stone Mick Taylor, and Cream bassist Jack Bruce, but none of the music ever made it to the public's ears, even as bootlegs.

On D-Day, two weeks after his 41st birthday, Bob did his single-stage performance for the year at an antinuke rally at Pasadena's Rose Bowl. Diving deep into post-Christian irony, he sang three duets with Joan Baez—"With God on Our Side" and "Blowin' in the Wind," followed by Jimmy Buffett's "A Pirate Looks at 40."

He spent another sober summer at Southfork, taking in Twins games and listening to rock concerts with his boys at the historic Orpheum Theater in downtown Minneapolis. Dylan quietly invested in the refurbished movie palace and turned it over to his brother, David, to manage. It also served as summer employment for the kids. In addition to David's children, at one time or another Jesse, Jakob, Samuel, and Maria all worked concessions or ticket sales.

Bob's children also accompanied him on Caribbean voyages, sailing to "every island from Martinique to Barbados," according to Dylan. He used the *Water Pearl* to fish for epiphany in Gulf Stream waters. Even before reggae demigod Bob Marley[343] boosted Jamaica higher on the *Billboard* charts than at any time since Harry Belafonte, Bob developed an abiding interest in island song. During the summer of '82, "a bunch of songs just came to me hanging around down in the islands," he said. They included "I and I," a reggae rumination with lyrics that smacked more of randy King David than celibate Jesus. The opening stanza spoke of yet another "strange woman" asleep in his bed.

For all his Christian moralism, Dylan never stopped savoring covenant women in the most basic ways. After his split with Sara, he swapped out his White Goddess for duskier versions, but abstinence was never on his menu. From backup singers to island girls, he sampled The Muse whenever he could. At one point, he allegedly bedded a Maori princess following a concert swing through New Zealand. At another, he pursued an Australian gypsy.[344]

With his sailor's beard, deep cocoa tan, and unkempt hair, he bore a slight resemblance to a Rastafarian. By autumn of '82 he was also back to Marlboros, brandy, and maybe a spliff now and again.

Dylan dropped anchor east of Puerto Rico off the island of Anguilla late that year, dispatching the *Water Pearl*'s captain and co-owner Chris Bowman to search out the author of a gospel-tinged reggae ballad called "Prince of Darkness." Bankie Banx, who already had a regional reputation as a Dylan/Marley hybrid, was not

---

[343] The two Bobs never met, but influenced each other's music in the late 1970s. After hearing that Dylan had attended his Santa Monica concert in the summer of '76, Marley reportedly said, "Him's really say it clear." Marley died of melanoma in 1981. He was 36 years old.

[344] Dancer Emelia Caruna claimed she had a two-week affair with Bob. When tabloids called her Dylan's sex slave, she successfully sued for libel.

hard to locate. He ran a head shop in the Anguillan capital. That's where Bowman found him, selling conch shells, bongs, and music.

"He asked me to come aboard and bring a few guitars," Banx recalled. "We started playing and he was very much interested in 'Prince of Darkness.' He wanted me to write out the lyrics and chord progression."

They lunched aboard *Water Pearl,* snorkeled in the bay, and then adjourned to Banx's home studio where Dylan began noodling at the organ.

"Bankie, I like the sound of this thing," said Dylan, indicating the lyric sheet. "Can you record that?"

Banx, who'd written "Prince of Darkness" five years earlier, answered, "Bob, I've already done that." But he indulged his guest with a reggae bass line and a riff on his rhythm guitar. Dylan wanted more.

"I went and got two girls," Banx recalled. They sang, but without Dylan, who behaved more like an arranger than participant. "He never put his voice on the tape. He just played keyboards and gave us the harmonies."

Like Robert Johnson's "Hellhound on My Trail," Bankie Banx's "Prince of Darkness" harked back to a recurrent Dylan theme: the constancy of Satan, tempting and lurking behind every human endeavor. Bob may have moved beyond Pentecostal rant, but he kept Christ close. As with dozens of other covers recorded in the '80s, Dylan's version of "Prince of Darkness" was never released.[345]

As the year wound to a close, Dylan resumed his process of winnowing potential producers as a first step in planning his next LP. In addition to auditioning the tried and true, he showed up unannounced

---

[345] He did sing "Prince of Darkness" once during a concert more than a decade later.

outside Frank Zappa's door. The lead Mother of Invention knew of Dylan, but had never made his acquaintance. Like any other fan, Zappa was awed. He welcomed *the* Bob Dylan into his home and gladly let him play 11 of his new songs. Zappa liked what he heard but, like Jerry Wexler, couldn't resist poking gentle fun at the idea of an agnostic producing a Christian recording artist. After a tight courtesy laugh Bob left and never returned.

Dylan could be forgiven his thin skin. His year of living anonymously closed out on as lethal a note as it had begun. Howard Alk overdosed on New Year's Day and David Blue's heart failed just as the year ended. In very different ways, heroin killed them both.

Following Rolling Thunder, Blue finally found his métier. His performance as *Renaldo and Clara*'s quasi-narrator brought him more film offers including a minor role in Wim Wenders's German-language *The American Friend* (1977),[346] which Dylan made a point of seeing after its release.

Following years wasted shadowing Bob, Blue found acting to be his new lease on life. He turned his back on eight failed LPs and successfully auditioned for roles in *The Ordeal of Patty Hearst* (1979) and Neil Young's directorial debut, *Human Highway* (1983). What was more, the actor David Blue finally kicked alcohol and drugs, but the musician David Blue had already sustained permanent physical damage.

As part of his new clean and sober regimen, Blue was jogging through Washington Square on December 2, 1982. He didn't make it past the Arch. He carried no ID, so he lay in St. Vincent's hospital morgue for three days until friends tracked him down.

---

[346] Like *Shoot the Piano Player*, the quirky gangster tale was based on an American noir novel and starred Dennis Hopper, another addict. In his adaptation, Wenders quoted several lines from Dylan songs including "One More Cup of Coffee" and "I Pity the Poor Immigrant."

No one sat Shiva for David Blue, least of all Dylan, but many a friend showed for his memorial. Mourners included Joni Mitchell, Bob Neuwirth, Kris Kristofferson, and Leonard Cohen, who delivered a eulogy for the Dylan doppelganger who never was:

> David Blue was the peer of any singer in this country, and he knew it, and he coveted their audiences and their power. He claimed them as his rightful due, and when he could not have them, his disappointment became so dazzling, his greed assumed such purity, his appetite such honesty, and he stretched his arms so wide, that we were all able to recognize ourselves, and we fell in love with him. And as we grew older, as something in the public realm corrupted itself into irrelevance, the integrity of his ambition, the integrity of his failure, became for those who knew him, increasingly appealing, and he moved swiftly, with effortless intimacy, into the private life of anyone who recognized him, and our private lives became for him the theaters that no one would book for him, and he sang for us in hotel rooms and kitchens, and he became that poet and that gambler, and he established a defiant style to revive those soiled archetypes.

⊞ ⊞ ⊞

Like Dylan, Leonard Cohen fell from grace during the '80s.

"I was living, in a certain sense, in the same kind of universe that he was living in," said Cohen. "When I heard him, I recognized his genius, but I also recognized a certain brotherhood in his work."

A brotherhood that took a dive on the *Billboard* charts. Leonard and Bob both descended into limbo as their boomer base became *The Big Chill* generation. In 1980, Columbia rejected *Field Commander Cohen,* a concert LP that didn't get released for another 20 years. In fact, the entire singer-songwriting fraternity lost momentum. Even tireless Paul Simon didn't have a hit for half a decade. With a single exception, troubadours tanked in Ronald Reagan's America. Of John Hammond's many discoveries, only Bruce Springsteen's star continued to rise.

Born to Run established Springsteen's bona fides as a Dylan disciple in much the same way Bob's earliest LPs had resonated Woody. Springsteen deified Dylan for having the "guts to take on the whole world and make me feel like I had to, too." If imitation is the sincerest form of flattery, then *Nebraska* ought to have knocked Dylan back on his heels. At a time when unemployment topped 12 percent, Bruce's bleak, acoustic paean to working class America earned *Nebraska* both the No. 3 spot on *Billboard*'s 1982 album chart and Best Album honors from *Rolling Stone.* As they'd once done with Dylan, crowds and critics clamored to know what Bruce would do next.

"Maybe the idea is gonna be to just keep the thing real stripped down right now, almost like a *John Wesley Harding* type of thing," Springsteen drawled before heading back into the studio.

Few asked Dylan what was next. When they did, Bob snarled that '80s music was "soulless and commercial," marching to the beat of drum machines.

"When you go into a department store to buy an umbrella, your mind is attacked by fictitious sound—the B52s, the Pretenders or somebody—and you kind of end up drifting in and out while the cash registers ring," said Dylan.

As one year rolled into another and Bob faded further from view, he also returned to the studio, but with zero fanfare. He elevated lead guitarist Mark Knopfler to producer in the spring of '83. His new album was to be his comeback, but the outtakes would become more venerated than the material that made the final cut.

Among the rejects was a eulogy loosely based on the unsung life and times of Blind Willie McTell. Moaned to the downbeat melody of "St. James Infirmary," the ballad was less a tribute to an obscure Roaring Twenties bluesman than it was a searing indictment of America's original sin. As harrowing as Billie Holliday's "Strange Fruit," the dirge answered the bitter questions first posed in "Blowin' in the Wind." In nine carefully crafted quatrains, Dylan outlined in vivid black and white the entire shameful legacy of American slavery.

Dylan first referred to McTell 20 years earlier in "Highway 61," though his boomer audience had no idea that Georgia Sam[347] was one of Blind Willie's several nicknames.[348] The closest most Yuppies got to hearing any of McTell's impressive canon was an Allman Brothers cover of his "Statesboro Blues." Like his better-known contemporary Huddy "Leadbelly" Ledbetter, McTell played every genre from ragtime to gospel on the 12-string guitar, though he faded forever into anonymity the same year that Bobby Zimmerman graduated from Hibbing High. Despite a recording career extending over four decades, he died an alcoholic at 61 playing for change on the streets of Atlanta.

If "Blind Willie McTell" was not proof enough that Dylan had returned to angry protest, there was also the ballad of Julius and Ethel Rosenberg—"sacrificial lambs" at the dawn of the Cold War.

---

[347] *Well Georgia Sam he had a bloody nose*
Welfare Department they wouldn't give him no clothes . . .

[348] Dylan called him "the Van Gogh of country blues."

In "Julius and Ethel," Bob recast the couple executed for treason in 1953 as Jewish martyrs, and for the first time, made direct reference to the Third Reich in one of his songs. Just as guilt or innocence became secondary—even irrelevant—in his ballads about Ruben Carter and Joey Gallo, "Julius and Ethel" dodged the issue of passing nuclear secrets to the Soviet Union. Instead, Dylan indicted McCarthyism and saved his venom for the blind conformity of his parents' generation. In their final portrait together, the Rosenbergs bore an uncanny resemblance to Abe and Beatty—an ironic alchemy that could not have escaped Dylan, who slammed the Eisenhower Administration as an era "when fear had you in a trance."

But Bob wasn't about to revert to his unbidden role as the Voice of the '60s.

"I don't write political songs," he told reporter Martin Keller.[349] Likening honest politicians to sanctified whores, he continued: "Politics could be useful if it was used for good purposes. For instance, like feeding the hungry and taking care of orphans. But it's not. It's like the snake with its tail in its mouth: a merry-go-round of sin."

Reanimating Political Bob was a risk he was unwilling to take. If he'd learned nothing more from his brief flirtation with public declarations of faith, it was to avoid easy labels. He made no apologies for his recent zealotry, but neither would he unveil Blind Willie or the Rosenbergs for years to come.

"Religion is a dirty word," he told Keller. "It doesn't mean anything. Coca-Cola is a religion. Oil and steel are a religion. In the name of religion, people have been raped, killed, and defiled. Today's religion is tomorrow's bondage."

---

[349] Keller scored his exclusive for the *Minneapolis City Pages* after getting into Southfork by dating Maria Dylan. Only after publication did he reveal that the interview, not Bob's stepdaughter, had been his real target, souring Bob even further on the press.

He and Knopfler worked on the new LP through the summer. Tentatively called *Man of Peace*, the final title was *Infidels*[350]—a fitting declaration of independence from the Vineyard Fellowship.

As Columbia prepared *Infidels* for market, Dylan was spotted in Crown Heights leaving a Chabad Lubavitch shul, triggering speculation he'd dumped Jesus for ultraorthodox Judaism. The following year, photographers captured him in prayer shawl, phylacteries, and yarmulke on the occasion of his youngest son's bar mitzvah at Jerusalem's Wailing Wall. Confronted with these heresies, Dylan refused to identify himself as Christian or Jew. Two decades later, he went so far as to say the whole charade was a pose to throw off the media.

"There's really no difference between any of it in my mind," he said. "Some people say they're Jews and they never go to the synagogue or anything. I know some gangsters who say they're Jews. I don't know what that's got to do with anything. Judaism is really the laws of Moses. If you follow the laws of Moses you're automatically a Jew I would think."

Released that November, *Infidels* was hailed as Bob's first secular LP since *Street Legal*. Simplistic come-to-Jesus lyrics gave way to a newer hybrid—edgy, eloquent, surreal. "I and I" returned to the dark side of the road with a reggae beat while "Sweetheart Like You" was as backhanded a love song as "Mama, You've Been on My Mind." He wasn't all the way back yet, but he was on his way. The adolescent Joker from Camp Herzl transcended boundaries of time and space once again, this time as the Jokerman.

---

[350] "I wanted to call it *Surviving in a Ruthless World*, but someone pointed out to me that the last bunch of albums I'd made all started with the letter 's,'" he said. "So I said, 'Well, I don't wanna get bogged down in the letters.'"

14

LOVE TRAIN

Five years after *Saturday Night Live* gave Born-Again Bob the national stage he needed to unveil *Slow Train Coming,* TV cool came to be fixed permanently in late night and it was here—not in primetime or over prefab MTV—where the Jokerman began to reconnect with his earliest fans.

No distant cousin of the decidedly uncool Les Crane, David Letterman treated his invaluable March 22, 1984, booking[351] with cautious camaraderie. No hype. No light banter. No worshipful introduction. A simple "Here's Bob Dylan" followed by a handshake at the end of the set and a tongue-in-cheek invitation to return each Thursday night as the *Late Night* house band.

Dylan's poker face remained a studied scowl throughout his first network appearance in half a decade. He refused to be interviewed and said as much to Letterman's audience by opening with a sloppy cover of Sonny Boy Williamson's "Don't Start Me to Talkin'." "License to Kill" from *Infidels* followed, Bob fumbling for his harmonica as if he were drunk and/or just didn't give a shit. It might have been a mildly interesting but uninspired performance by

---

[351] Following the taping, Dylan attended an NBA game at nearby Madison Square Garden where he watched fellow Hibbing High graduate Kevin McHale lead Boston to a 108–100 victory over the Knicks. Born the year Bobby Zimmerman was a sophomore, McHale dedicated the game to Dylan. "I walked up to him and said, 'Dylan,' and Bob Dylan smiled at me and said, 'Hibbing.' Now that was really neat."

another rock relic from the stoned age if Dylan hadn't capped the evening with his *pièce de résistance*.

"'Jokerman' kinda came to me in the islands," Dylan told *Rolling Stone*. "It's very mystical. The shapes there, and shadows, seem to be so ancient. The song was sorta inspired by these spirits they call jumbis."[352]

Smattered with images of Armageddon but grounded in buoyant cynicism, "Jokerman" was an edgy hallucination worthy of the best of *Blonde on Blonde*. Twenty years of fooling had taught him how to shape-shift. The centerpiece of *Infidels* gave Bob pundits as much to chew on as "Visions of Johanna." Was it about Jesus? Lucifer? God? Bob?

Didn't matter. For the remainder of the decade, Dylan was the Jokerman by default, shedding off layers of skin during every public appearance. He was past his holier-than-thou period. Dylan might refuse to sit in Letterman's hot seat to answer the inevitable born-again questions, but later that year he declared, "Whoever said I was Christian? I am a humanist!"

A humanist perhaps, but apparently not of the secular variety. In an exchange with *Rolling Stone*'s Kurt Loder in which he kidded that he'd joined the Church of the Poisoned Mind, Dylan claimed he still read the Bible as literally as he had during his Vineyard phase.

"I believe in the Book of Revelation," he said. "The leaders of this world are eventually going to play God, if they're not already playing God, and eventually a man will come that everybody will think is God. He'll do things, and they'll say, 'Well, only God can do those things. It must be him.'"

---

[352] An Afro-Caribbean demon loosed by a Voodoo curse.

"Jokerman" became Bob's third[353] official music video. He might grumble over the newfangled, but wasn't averse if it sold records. With his gravelly voice[354] and grim visage as its focus, the slickly produced marketing device featured stills of the martyred Kennedy brothers, Martin Luther King Jr., Ronald Reagan, and Adolf Hitler alongside images ranging from a Minoan snake goddess and a squatting Aztec earth mother to Albrecht Dürer's *Redeemer* and Michelangelo's iconic statues of Moses and David. Bob's lyrics flashed at the bottom of the screen so Yuppies could sing along: "oh-oh-oh-oh-oh Jokerman."

The *Infidels* rollout that spring included a "Jokerman" single as well as the routine tour, stretching from May through July across Europe. In another first, Dylan added a second act. Santana and Joan Baez[355] sweetened the ticket and helped fill arenas from Italy to Ireland, playing to as many as 100,000 a night and grossing a reported $21 million by tour's end. Back in the U.S., however, he had competition from the new kid in town.

With the release of *Born in the U.S.A.,* Springsteen dominated the charts[356] for a year. His worldwide tour dwarfed Dylan's. Far from a dour remake of *John Wesley Harding, Born in the U.S.A.* resonated with defiant optimism in Ronald Reagan's America where a trickle-down double standard had left more than two million homeless. Swapping his now-familiar trinity—the car, the girl, and the night— for the red, the white, and the blue collar, Springsteen presented a

---

[353] His first official MTV offering was a pedestrian lip-synch of "Sweetheart Like You," but his unofficial debut was a reissue of "Subterranean Homesick Blues" over the flash-card opening of *Dont Look Back.*

[354] "The sound of my own voice . . . I can't get used to it," he said. "Never have gotten used to it. Makes you wanna *hide.*"

[355] Baez tiffed with Bob, quit after five shows but kept her $250,000 fee. She was replaced by Van Halen.

[356] *Infidels* climbed no higher than No. 20.

critique that was subtle but effective. Unlike Bob, he never preached apocalypse, never disparaged women, and never tried to convert anybody. He so embraced his audience that a Springsteen concert could—and frequently did—last well beyond midnight.

He also embraced his E Street Band mates. Springsteen might be the front man, but he never pretended to act alone. Blood brothers all, they shared the stage, the credit, the tour bus, and the profits.

"My best friends?" Dylan answered in surprise during Kurt Loder's interview. "Jeez." He laughed. "Let me try to think of one."

"There must be a few," Loder coaxed.

"Best friends? Jesus, I mean, that's . . ."

"You've got to have a best friend."

"Whew! Boy, there's a question that'll really make you think. Best friend? Jesus, I think I'd go into a deep, dark depression if I were to think about who's my best friend."

"There have to be one or two, don't there?" Loder persisted.

"Well, there has to be . . . there must be . . . there's gotta be. But hey, you know, a best friend is someone who's gonna die for you. I mean, that's your best friend, really. I'd be miserable trying to think who my best friend is."

Ever the put-on artist, Dylan never answered the question, but in fact his friends were few and frequently so beholden that they dared not speak their mind. When Dylan ended a relationship, reviving it was near impossible. Friends tended to talk; talk could lead to revelation, but not the sort that a mystic Jokerman could condone. If Dylan kept everyone off balance, then nothing was delivered. Even those who knew him best were never best friends.

He had come to hate recording ("It's like working in a coal mine"), but that's the first thing he did once the tour ended. While the rest of L.A. celebrated the 23rd Summer Olympics, Dylan tinkered with tunes at Hollywood's Cherokee Studios, laying down the initial tracks for what would be his 23rd studio album.

"I only make records because people see me live," he declared. "So as long as they're coming along to see me live, I'll just make some more records."

The cycle had become rote: a new LP every year or two followed by a publicity blitz, print, radio interviews, a single release for maximum airplay, and a promotional concert tour. Dylan said he loathed the process but could ill afford to ignore it. He earned far more from concerts than record sales, and much of his catalog belonged to others.

For years he and Albert Grossman had grappled over ownership of his earliest and most valuable copyrights. Their lawsuit generated so much paper that some said it took the dubious title of most voluminous in the annals of New York jurisprudence. Ultimately, Dylan lost more than he gained. Without specifying whether his ex-manager or his ex-wife were the bigger siphons on his income, Dylan did reveal to *Rolling Stone* that he owned none of his songs prior to *Blood on the Tracks*.

As to his recordings, Columbia held the purse strings. In 1978, Congress enacted a new copyright statute that required labels to turn recording rights over to an artist after 35 years, but that meant Dylan would be 71 before Columbia was legally required to begin dribbling out everything the label released after *Desire*.

Technology diluted his revenue stream further. Tape cassettes supplanted vinyl in the 1980s as medium of choice; a third option, the compact disc, was just being introduced. Every new innovation called for royalty renegotiation. Dylan had lawyers and accountants to keep up, but so did Columbia, and with each iteration, Bob's clout slipped a little more compared to a Springsteen, Madonna, or Michael Jackson.

Dylan still had mortgages to pay, children to support, and payroll to meet. He had to keep the cycle going.

■ ■ ■

Children were starving in the horn of Africa, but had been for generations. What made the difference in 1984 was an accretion of TV, music video, and a broad, brief appeal to the First World's guilty conscience. The compassion explosion began with the surprise British charity hit "Do They Know It's Christmas?" that spawned the African relief organization Band Aid.

Harry Belafonte couldn't let the Brits upstage the Colonies. Within weeks, he spearheaded an American clone. Long absent from the pop charts, the Calypso King who'd given Dylan his first professional gig graduated to Blaxploitation movies and Vegas by the 1980s, but his sentiment for the downtrodden remained strong. An early underwriter of Martin Luther King Jr., Belafonte juggled showbiz ethics with personal scruples. Thus, when Nelson Mandela's war on Apartheid gained global attention, he embraced his African roots. Similarly, when newsfeeds of skeletal infants became commonplace on the nightly news, he cofounded USA for Africa.

Aided by producer Quincy Jones and Hollywood talent wrangler Ken Kragen, Belafonte organized an American equivalent of "Do They Know It's Christmas?" Following the broadcast of ABC-TV's annual American Music Awards on the evening of January 28, 1985, rock royalty gathered in the green room at West Hollywood's A&M Studios. With no real expectation Dylan would accept, Kragen included him on the invite list. To the surprise of everyone, Bob came.

Before recording the one-shot chorale, Quincy Jones ordered all egos checked at the door. Melding easily among pop's plutocracy,

Bob sampled the $15,000 buffet, awkwardly accepted hugs from Springsteen and Billy Joel, and let Diana Ross sit on his lap. He behaved like a regular guy, hitting his mark and harmonizing as just another member of the "We Are the World" choir.

As one of the soloists, Dylan stayed behind for some postproduction looping. He relaxed, smiled, nibbled, slouched, and hung with the likes of Willie Nelson who made chitchat about a planned golf vacation.

"I've heard you had to study it," said Dylan.[357]

"You can't think of hardly anything else!" enthused Nelson.

However briefly, Bob Dylan got to be Zimmy again. No one asked to kiss his ring. Nobody wanted his autograph for a kid sister. All went well until some time after 5 A.M. when Stevie Wonder called Dylan to the microphone for his solo. Wonder coached him for 20 minutes, encouraging Bob to sing-speak in a Woody whine. After several takes, Dylan obediently exaggerated, twanging like the 20-year-old folkie he'd been so many years before. Quincy rewarded him with a bear hug.

"That's it! That's the statement!"

"That wasn't any good," said Dylan.

"It's great," whispered Quincy.

"Well, if you say so."

He lingered a little longer to listen to Springsteen croon his one-take Jersey solo. Bruce needed no coaching from Stevie Wonder. Dylan sat alone brooding at a piano, the Jokerman scowl creeping back across his face. Like a timid fan, jazz artist Al Jarreau sidled up from behind.

---

[357] Bob eventually did take up the study, achieving a bogey handicap of 17 by the end of the century.

"Bobby, in my own stupid way I just want to tell you I love you." Jarreau choked up, gazing into Bob's myopic baby blues.

Faux pas. Jarreau broke the Zimmy spell. Dylan returned the blankest stare when Jarreau burst into tears and left the studio, sobbing "My idol." Jarreau later recalled the experience as basking in the supernatural presence of an inspired Renaissance magid.[358]

Dylan saw his own cue to exit, but not before Bette Midler flung her arms around him. She made no pretense over her brand of worship. Three years earlier Midler had told a Fleet Street tabloid she'd almost nailed Dylan in the front seat of his Cadillac. This time, she seemed in a mood to close the deal.

"Good night, dearest," she vamped as Bob cut for the door.

The dawn was breaking as Dylan donned shades, hoisted the collar of his leather jacket, and stared at the ground as inconspicuously as possible until his ride appeared. For a while, Bobby Zimmerman had made a comeback, but Bob Dylan returned with a vengeance in the light of day. Even on this most unusual of nights, when everyone within the sound of Quincy's voice were under strict orders to behave like regular working stiffs, Dylan could not get away from a basic truth. Even among peers, women wanted to fuck him and men wanted to be him.

❚❚ ❚❚ ❚❚

"We Are the World" shot to the top of the *Billboard* charts a month later and maintained maximum MTV rotation for the rest of the year, raising Bob's profile once more. For those boomers who hadn't caught him on Letterman, Bob was now in their line of vision as regularly as the flyblown faces of Ethiopian waifs.

---

[358] An itinerant sixteenth-century Jewish storyteller steeped in Torah mysticism.

For the next several months, Dylan labored incognito as best he could at New York City's Power Station, laying down the rest of *Empire Burlesque* ahead of its June release date. Not a great album, *Empire Burlesque* had its moments. "Dark Eyes"[359] and "I'll Remember You" were among the durable gems that found lasting popularity when covered by others. Mostly, the LP took its mood as well as its name from the Delancey Street strip joint that young Bob had frequented when he first hit Greenwich Village: a teaser here, a peek-a-boo there, but generally more titillation than satisfaction. Worth little more than a jaded listen or two, *Empire Burlesque* prompted fans to move on quickly to something more substantial from the likes of Springsteen, Paul Simon, or Neil Young.

Steeped in uncredited dialogue from Humphrey Bogart movies, even the *Empire* lyrics represented either strained homage or evidence of an exhausted palette. Bob stole shamelessly from the Great Lisper, borrowing line after line from *Key Largo, The Big Sleep,* and *The Maltese Falcon.*[360] As with his other recent albums, the best was left on the cutting-room floor, including a film tribute that succeeded where most of the lifted Bogart lines did not.

"New Danville Girl" was an 11-minute joint effort cowritten with playwright Sam Shepard. Winner of the 1979 Pulitzer for drama and nominated for an Oscar,[361] Shepard had rolled on to success after success following Rolling Thunder, but when called on to collaborate with Bob one more time, he didn't balk. In laconic defense of Bob's on-again, off-again evangelizing, Shepard said, "People don't do what they believe in; they just do what's most convenient. Then they repent."

---

[359] Based on Bob's encounter with a Plaza Hotel call girl.
[360] Also *Shane*, Clint Eastwood's *Bronco Billy,* and an episode of TV's *Star Trek.*
[361] As test pilot Chuck Yeager in *The Right Stuff* (1983).

Opening with a half-spoken reminiscence of Gregory Peck riding across the screen as Johnny Ringo in *The Gunfighter* (1950), "New Danville Girl" devolved into a tender spoof of Bob's Saturday afternoon adolescence inside the darkened interior of the Lybba Theater. Much like the storytelling in "Tangled Up in Blue" or "Just Like Tom Thumb Blues," a typical Dylan protagonist shambles from one iconic American outpost to another in "New Danville Girl." Through his popcorn memory, Bob pursues an elusive ladylove, mixing his own identity with that of an imagined Western hero. In its final form, "New Danville Girl" became "Brownsville Girl." Despite some slaphappy antics along the way, the mini-epic ends as a poignant lament for the vanishing matinee of "a long time ago, before the stars were torn down."

Yet, as with "Angelina," "Blind Willie McTell," and a host of other intriguing ballads from the first half of the '80s, "Brownsville Girl" got shelved without explanation. Instead, the breakout single from *Empire Burlesque* was the slight and seldom remembered "Tight Connection to My Heart (Has Anyone Seen My Love)."[362]

Three *Empire Burlesque* promotional videos followed, none rising to the level of "Jokerman." Bob flaunted rollout protocol by scheduling no tour. He banked instead on the career momentum he'd regained from "We Are the World."

By July, the extraordinary fanfare for both "Do They Know It's Christmas" and "We Are the World" whipped the novelty of so-called pop charities into a new and growing industry. In addition to USA for Africa, the movement spawned every sort of "Aid" imaginable, from Hear 'n Aid (a heavy metal version of "We Are the World") to Fashion Aid (18 supermodels walking the runway for

---

[362] Its most telling line a Eucharistic clue to his evolving faith: "Never could learn to drink that blood and call it wine."

Africa) to Sport Aid (millions of amateurs running simultaneous 10Ks all over the world).

Live Aid was the next logical progression. Billed as the biggest benefit ever broadcast to the largest single TV audience in history, dual concerts at London's Wembley Stadium and Philadelphia's JFK Stadium on July 13, 1985, drew nearly 2 billion viewers. Featuring the largest pop-star roster since Woodstock, the final act didn't duck his American fans this time by slinking off to the Isle of Wight. Whether Live Aid producer Bill Graham decided alone or got a little nudge from Bob, the Voice of a Generation climaxed a daylong parade of superstars. Just to make sure everyone understood the magnitude, Hollywood film icon[363] Jack Nicholson built audience anticipation to a fare-thee-well with a flurry of superlatives: "ONE OF THE GREAT VOICES OF FREEDOM—THE TRANSCENDENT BOB DYLAN!"

Transcendent perhaps, but intoxicated along with accompanists Keith Richards and Ronnie Wood. Together they turned three of Dylan's better-known chestnuts—"When the Ship Comes In," "Blowin' in the Wind," and "Ballad of Hollis Brown"—into chuckle-fucking anticlimax. His tipsy sidemen didn't even know what songs they were playing.

"I thought, Hollis Brown? That's cough medicine, isn't it?" said Wood.

When Dylan broke a string, Wood offered his instrument. He played air guitar until a stagehand hustled up a substitute. Afterward, Bob complained that the sound system was so bad he couldn't hear himself sing.

But any doubt Dylan misunderstood the impact of his own voice vanished with "Hollis Brown." He seized the moment to exercise

---

[363] And Bob's sometimes weed, wine, and cocaine compadre throughout the 1980s.

moral authority while denying he was being political. If the murder-suicide tale of a destitute Dakota farmer and his family wasn't message enough, Dylan suggested in his best Woody twang that American family farmers deserved as much charity as victims of African famine. The singular power of his few words televised to the masses demonstrated that Bob's power to launch crusades had not diminished.[364]

Two months later, Farm Aid joined the growing crop of pop charities,[365] infuriating Band Aid founder Bob Geldof, who wanted all attention vectored toward the Ethiopian desert. Dylan's answer was little different from the message he delivered 22 years earlier to the National Emergency Civil Liberties Committee: "What are they *really* doing to alleviate poverty? To me, it's guilt money, a way to clear your conscience."

Which didn't mean he was above using Farm Aid to keep his own reemerging career on track. When organizers Willie Nelson, Neil Young, and John Cougar Mellencamp hosted the first of many annual benefits for the nation's Hollis Browns, Dylan headlined, joined on stage with the all-girl chorale he now called the Queens of Rhythm,[366] and no less a backup band than Tom Petty and the Heartbreakers.

---

[364] Within the month, Bob would materialize on the other side of the globe at an international poetry festival, guest of glasnost hero Yevgeny Yevtushenko. Throngs of youthful Muscovites clambered for an autograph, somehow producing hundreds of ancient LPs that had penetrated the Iron Curtain. Bob obliged.

[365] Bob also participated in Artists United Against Apartheid, which put out its own all-star recording, "Sun City." Peaking at No. 38 on the *Billboard* charts, it was the first such single to mark pop charity's diminishing returns, fading in post–"Me Decade" America along with interest in famine, pestilence, or altruism.

[366] Indeed, one of them was named Queen Esther Morrow. The remaining members were Elisecia Wright, Carolyn Dennis, and her mother, Madelyn Quebec.

This time, there were no broken strings, no forgotten lyrics, no air guitars. A semi-sober Bob clearly heard his own voice thundering "Maggie's Farm." His poker face turned into a satisfied grin half-way through and the crowd roared its approval.

He still wore a crucifix, but now it dangled upside down from his left earlobe. His teased and lacquered bouffant hiked higher on his skull than Little Richard's ever did. And as for Jesus, the Messiah got left in the dust along with his Father and the Holy Ghost. Meanwhile, Jokerman mutated once more—this time into a matinee idol.

■ ■ ■

As Ronald Reagan steered a zombie nation past Luke Skywalker and Indiana Jones, ever forward unto the thrall of Gordon Gecko, Dylan began to find renewed equilibrium during the summer of '85. He paid attention where most did not, and didn't like what he saw.

"People are so asleep," he told the *L.A. Times'* Robert Hilburn.

He watched and waited like a reluctant prophet while the American Majority moved inexorably from silent to moral to greedy. From his lonesome outpost in the backwoods of Malibu, he too cashed in on the burgeoning American Dream, yet saw no irony in remaining ever-vigilant for signs of the Second Coming.

"When you get high and then your bubble busts and you get down low again, lower than you were when you started, you have to have values," he preached.

Dylan granted his first formal network TV interview to ABC's *20/20* in September, inviting correspondent Bob Brown as well as MTV and several print journalists out to his oddball Point Dume compound. The *Times'* Hilburn charitably described the pricey property as "rural." Once past the cyclone fencing, the tall stands of bamboo, and the guard shack, chickens and dogs roamed free. A vegetable patch stood off to one side of the dirt driveway that led to the main house. An array of dead rolling stock littered the grounds—an ancient green-and-white ambulance, a trailer without tires, a battered Buick Roadmaster that would never see the road again. Sara's influence was long gone; Dylan lived inside *Green Acres* without Eva Gabor. Despite the million-dollar homes surrounding the Dylan garrison, Hollis Brown would have felt right at home.

Bob had resumed self-medicating, consuming a fairly steady diet of Kools and beer, but he remained restless, demonstrating the attention span of a dyslexic adolescent. He sketched everything, including interviewers, and thought he might compile the caricatures into a book one day, along with snatches of prose, or maybe some short stories. He fancied himself Jack Kerouac's heir, writing vicariously of the lives of acquaintances whose names he changed. He wrote songs that way. Why not a *roman a clef*?

"A while back I started writing a novel called *Ho Chi Minh in Harlem*," he told *Time*'s Denise Worrell. "He was a short-order cook there in the '20s before he went back to Vietnam—it's a documented fact. It excited me there for a minute."

Dylan presented himself unshaven, unkempt, with bags beneath his eyes. A diamond stud replaced the cross that dangled from his left ear during stage performances. He wore week-old sleeveless T-shirts, aromatic jeans, and shitkicker boots. His clothes were dirty but his hands were manicured. His guitarist's nails were shorter on the left hand for fretting, long and pointed on the right.

He met the press either on a deck overlooking the Pacific or in a bare-bones cabin behind the main house. A patio, Jacuzzi, and satellite dish were visible through a window, but there was no gas or electricity inside. A kerosene lamp provided the only illumination and a wood-burning fireplace offered the only heat. An interview became a pioneer game of who could handle the failing evening light and shivery ocean breeze the longest. Holding home advantage, Zimmy inevitably won.

A Q&A was never simple with Bob. He preferred verbal chess, revealing as little as possible until his opponent called stalemate. He parried the inevitable Christian questions with flights of secular philosophizing that smacked more of Buddhist yin and yang than Jesus. Up one day, down the next. What goes around comes around. Those who don't learn the lessons of history are condemned to repeat them.

To career inquiries about what he planned to do next, Dylan waxed eloquent. Maybe a children's album or a collection of Tin Pan Alley standards . . . maybe he'd just record an entire LP of instrumentals.

"My favorite songs of all time aren't anything I've written," he said. "I like stuff like 'Pastures of Plenty' and 'That's All' and 'I Get a Kick Out of You.'"

Questions about his children, his family, or his love life were verboten and grounds for immediate dismissal. The now familiar Dylan scowl was barometer enough when an interview strayed too far into privacy. Even the most inquisitive rock critic knew when to retreat. Trigger a genuine Bob peeve that was *not* personal, however, and he could opine until the chickens came home to roost. Literally.

"Pop music on the radio?" asked Dylan. "I don't know. I listen mostly to preacher stations and the country music stations and maybe the oldies stations . . . that's about it."

Rock as a tool for enlightened dissidence ended with Woodstock Nation, according to Bob. He likened Yuppies to steers: "Have you ever seen a slaughterhouse where they bring in a herd of cattle? They round them all up, put them in one area, pacify 'em and slaughter them . . ." He paused before condescension. "Big business brings in lots of bucks, heavy energy."

For one who seemed to have a lot of it, energy had become a dirty word. His corporate keepers at CBS Records Group were far less interested in talent and musicianship than energy, whatever the hell that meant. "Incredible energy, man," Dylan spat contemptuously.

In a long, breathless epitaph, he excoriated the passing of pop as he'd once known it: "The corporate world, when they figured out what it was and how to use it, they snuffed the breath out of it and killed it. What do they care? Anything that's in the way, they run over like a bulldozer. Once they understood it they killed it and made it a thing of the past, put up a monument to it and now that's what you're hearing, the headstone—it's a billion-dollar business."

Multibillion-dollar actually, and rock wasn't the only casualty. FM radio, which had once been the underground's weapon of mass conscription, now broadcast "country club music." Instead of revolution, radio sold soap, blue jeans, Kentucky Fried Chicken.

"You know, things go better with Coke because Aretha Franklin told you so and Maxwell House coffee must be okay because Ray Charles is singing about it," said Dylan. "Everybody's singing about ketchup and headache medicine or something. In the beginning it wasn't anything like that, had nothing to do with pantyhose and perfume and barbeque sauce . . ."

Under Ronald Reagan, FCC ownership restrictions relaxed so that a single corporation, Clear Channel, could gobble up most music stations from coast to coast, robotizing Top 40 while instilling a mall mentality on the rebel sounds of youth. Bob Dylan, for one, wanted none of it.

"I'm not selling breakfast cereal or razor blades or whatever," he said.

He was selling records. While *Empire Burlesque* sold a respectable half-million copies, Dylan's entire catalog represented 35 million record sales[367] over the course of his 25-year[368] association with Columbia. For three years, the company had been angling to parlay all that latent boomer intrigue into cash, but Bob would not cooperate.

"It concerns me to the point where I was thinking about regrouping my whole thought on making records," he told music writer Mikal Gilmore. "If the records I make are only going to sell a certain amount, then why do I have to spend a lot of time putting them together?"

The answer for both Columbia and Bob was *Biograph,* a boxed set[369] of five LPs containing 53 tracks from Bob's long career, including 18 recordings never before released—and all just in time for Christmas. With sleeve notes, candid photos, and a 36-page booklet based on Dylan interviews conducted by former *Rolling Stone* writer Cameron Crowe, *Biograph* was the brainchild of Jeff Rosen, a young hire in Dylan's New York business headquarters. Also available as three CDs,[370] *Biograph* got an uneasy nonendorsement from its subject.

"I haven't been very excited about this thing," Dylan said. "All it is is repackaging really, and it'll just cost a lot of money."

But Rosen and Columbia correctly guessed that expensive keepsakes in the latest digital format would appeal to Yuppies. Unlike the other lackluster albums he'd put out during the '80s, *Biograph*

---

[367] Michael Jackson's *Thriller* sold more than twice that number following its 1984 release, and leaped to an estimated 110 million following the singer's death in 2009.

[368] Except the yearlong Asylum aberration that CBS corrected, later acquiring rights to *Planet Waves*.

[369] Some called it the first boxed set, making it yet another in the ongoing Dylan legacy of firsts.

[370] The latest iteration in the ongoing technological game of newer, better, and more expensive.

zoomed up the *Billboard* charts to No. 33 despite its hefty price. Analog was fast becoming analogous to buggy whips. At a time when Microsoft and Apple were firmly taking hold of the American imagination, *Biograph* went platinum.

Not a moment too soon, according to CBS lawyers. At the same time *Biograph* hit stores, bootleggers released their own slick, well-produced box set. *Zimmerman: Ten of Swords*[371] rivaled *Biograph* with 134 tracks on 10 LPs. Peddled sub rosa behind the counters of many of the very stores where legitimate albums sold, *Ten of Swords* contained demos, privately recorded performances, unreleased nightclub sessions, and outtakes that dated all the way back to Dinky-town. More than three thousand of the contraband *Zimmerman* collections sold before attorneys shut the operation down.

"It's like the dope business," Dylan complained. "It's supposed to be illegal, but a lot of people make their livelihood off it."

The corporate world Dylan so despised threw a very exclusive party for him a week and a half before Thanksgiving, ostensibly to mark his first 25 years in the music business. Columbia underwrote an uptown reception at the Whitney Museum of American Art the same week *Biograph* hit the stores. *Entertainment Tonight* and MTV were there; bootleggers, Dylanologists, groupies, and the general public were not. Martin Scorsese and Robert De Niro got invited, along with Yoko Ono and Lou Reed and David Bowie; Ruben "Hur-ricane" Carter, who'd finally been released from prison that very week, was not.[372]

---

[371] A tarot card depicting a corpse with ten swords in its back. Considered worse than death by tarot readers, the card represents absolute destruction.

[372] Rather than retrying the twice-convicted boxer a third time, prosecutors gave up trying to buck public opinion. Dylan continued giving Carter a shout-out at concerts, portraying him as a victim of New Jersey justice until 1988 when a federal judge pronounced the case officially over.

And neither was Ralph Edwards, though Columbia had clearly staged a special Bob Dylan edition of *This Is Your Life*. At a trés trendy soiree worthy of Leonard Bernstein or the late Truman Capote, guests were encouraged to loiter upstairs before banks of TV monitors that played clips of Bob's chameleon career: protest folkie, rock icon, country poet, anguished shaman, avenging evangelist. Here was smart-ass Dylan, putting on the media at a press conference; there was tormented Dylan, getting all acoustic and heartbroken for the masses; over there was Bob in white-face thundering sans God while right next to him was sanctified Bob praising Jesus, and over there just one monitor beyond was bebop Bob going electric one more time . . . and screw all those establishment toadies who didn't like the noise.

Downstairs, Manhattan's artistic elite awaited the man himself as they mingled with such Village people as Judy Collins, Arlo Guthrie, and Jim (Roger) McGuinn. Old hands John Hammond and Jerry Wexler drank with the new wave's Iggy Pop and John Cale. Both members of the Band and its E Street facsimile were present, along with Roy Orbison, who openly regretted his decision not to record "Don't Think Twice" way back when nobody knew who Dylan was. Orbison looked squarely into *Entertainment Tonight*'s camera and asked Bob for a second chance. Billy Joel told those same cameras that Dylan was America's greatest songwriter. Joni Mitchell called him a pop Messiah.

"When I head Bob Dylan sing, 'You got a lotta nerve,' I thought, 'Hallelujah, man, the American pop song has grown up!'" said Mitchell. "It's wide open. Now you can write about anything that literature can write about. Up until that time rock-and-roll songs were pretty much limited to, 'I'm a fool for ya, baby.'"

Sara wasn't there, but Dylan brought his latest girlfriend. Carole Childs, a former Elektra Records executive Bob met during Jakob's bar mitzvah, had as much of a hold on Dylan as any female could. She basked in his aura but knew not to cling. Bob hated crowds but loved the one-on-one, especially with women. When it came his time to speak, the gathering hushed.

Resplendent in a vanilla two-piece reminiscent of his *Great White Wonder* incarnation, a clean-shaven Dylan wore an open shirt with a neckline that plunged to the navel, exposing more chest than Elvis at the MGM Grand. Hidden behind a pair of bee-lens goggles, he cleared his throat and thanked all who'd come. He also thanked his record label for honoring him, but wasn't gonna let adulation con him into thinking that he was The One.

If the crowd hoped for sagacity or wit, they'd come to the wrong place. Bob Dylan didn't spew on demand. He was happy to be there for sure; to have survived 25 years in a brutal business and lived to tell the tale. But he wasn't at the microphone for more than a minute or two before Bobby Zimmerman started looking for an exit. No point in staying too long at a memorial to a compromised revolution if deep down inside you still felt like Napoleon in rags.

15
MYSTERY TRAIN

On January 25, 1986, Albert Grossman suffered a heart attack aboard the Concorde, lurched forward in his first-class seat, and died. The 59-year-old Baron of Bearsville was on his annual trek to Cannes for the international MIDEM conference, where he and other industry heavyweights would plot the multibillion-dollar course of pop music for the coming year. His peers registered no surprise that Grossman's hedonistic lifestyle had caught up with him; they tussled instead over who'd claim his seat on Concorde's return flight.

Albert was a bear of a man, "a teddy or a grizzly, depending on your point of view," wrote Robert Shelton in his long-gestating Dylan biography. Dylan saw his ex-manager as the grizzly, ignoring Grossman's role in transforming him from Hibbing upstart to Voice of a Generation.

"He only had me for 20 percent," Dylan told Shelton. "There were others who had to give him 50 percent." Never mind Albert's contribution; Bob paid for it.

"He made everybody move up to Woodstock, then lost his heart for the music and started getting into restaurants and real estate," recalled Band road manager Jonathan Taplin. "As far as Bob goes, Albert just got too greedy."

Mary Travers labeled Grossman a chauvinist who'd earned more from PP&M than all three of its members combined. Nevertheless, Mary joined her partners at his funeral where Peter Yarrow and

Robbie Robertson both delivered eulogies. Sally Grossman recalled during his memorial that her husband had had a premonition his time was up. They all remembered Albert as innovative, perceptive, and shrewd, with a gourmand's abiding love of sensual pleasure, ranging from eclectic music and fine wine to finer food. Finding no decent Chinese, Grossman imported a chef from Manhattan after he and Sally moved to Woodstock. They opened the Little Bear restaurant next to their gourmet Bear Café so Albert could have his choice of exotic eats as well as decent Kung Pao takeout on Christmas Day.

Sally committed her husband's ashes to a grassy oval behind his Bearsville Studios, marking the plot with a simple stone. Backed by his Band mates, Richard Manuel closed the funeral with a keening rendition of "I Shall Be Released," and tears fell over Albert's grave.

Two months later, Manuel hanged himself with his own belt in a Quality Inn just outside of Orlando. Like Howard Alk, Paul Clayton, Phil Ochs, and so many others who'd lost their way dogging Dylan's footsteps, he committed suicide around 3 A.M. on March 4, 1986. The rest of the Band found him hanging from a bathroom shower rod. According to the coroner, his last meal consisted of cocaine and Grand Marnier.

The Band sans Robbie Robertson had been playing their way from club to club across Florida in much the same way they'd begun: a ragged quartet doing one-night stands at dives like Orlando's Cheek-to-Cheek Lounge. Levon Helm, Rick Danko, Garth Hudson, and Richard Manuel hadn't been on the road with Dylan for more than a decade. Strapped for cash, they reassembled seven years after *The Last Waltz,* soldiering on without Bob or Robbie, who held most of the copyrights on the Band's backlist. They had no record label, no career trajectory, no place in the MTV rotation. They just made music.

Dylan attended neither funeral. He'd already left for New Zealand to prep for his upcoming True Confessions tour with Tom Petty and the Heartbreakers. When asked by reporters why he was returning to touring after three years, he said, "The money."

Dylan settled the Grossmans' long-running lawsuit for $2 million shortly after Albert's funeral. He was bound to funnel much of True Confessions' profits toward paying off Sally. As income-obsessed as his ex-manager, Bob remained preoccupied with cash flow for the rest of the decade. Nearly a dozen homes or apartments, a yacht, college-bound children, lawyers, accountants, investments, relatives, girlfriends, and a security apparatus that rivaled that of Howard Hughes did not come cheap.

The tour promised to deliver as big a bankroll as the lucrative Before the Flood bonanza back in '74. Indeed, Dylan and Petty were a match for the Dylan–Robbie Robertson collaboration before the Band finally blew apart. Not only did persnickety Bob rock splendidly to the extemporaneous beat of the Heartbreakers, he and Petty even *sounded* alike, droppin' nasal g's so often that it was often hard to tell them apart.

HBO smelled bonanza in True Confessions. The pioneering premium cable channel paid $500,000 for the rights to trail Dylan across the Far East with a camera crew that winter. Dylan seemed noticeably warmer, funnier, and even humble in the resulting TV special. *Hard to Handle* featured a Rick Nelson "Lonesome Town" tribute as well as a generous helping of Bob's greatest hits.

During a winter fraught with death, Nelson's plane had crashed on New Year's Eve near DeKalb, Texas. Once reviled as an Elvis pretender with a phony TV family, Nelson had earned Bob's respect as a craftsman and a troubadour after generating a Top 40 cover of "She Belongs to Me." Like Dylan, Nelson wearied of playing his own greatest hits and wrote his last one, "Garden Party," about the downside of feeding a fickle public an unwavering diet of golden oldies.

Nelson's wasn't Bob's only shout-out during True Confessions.

"Everybody's got a hero," he preached from the stage. "Some people got a hero, lots of different heroes. Money is a hero. Success is a hero. To lots of people Michael Jackson's a hero. Bruce Springsteen, John Wayne, everybody's got a hero. . . .[373] Well, I wanna sing about *my* hero. I don't care about *those* heroes. I have my *own* hero."

With that, he and the Heartbreakers erupted into "In the Garden," publicly exalting Jesus one more time.

He also broke customary stage silence to remember Tennessee Williams. Reciting from *Sweet Bird of Youth,* he made the playwright's words his own:

"'I'm not looking for your pity. I just want your understanding. And no, not even that, but just your recognition—of me in you—and time, the enemy in us all.'"

He lamented the loss of Williams who "kind of died all by himself in a New York City hotel room[374] without a friend in the world.

"Another man died like that," Dylan continued. "This man didn't have too much success, but he started a lot of people off—people who came, picked up on what he did and took it someplace else and made a lot of money and became very successful. And he died in a lonely grave."

No, not Jesus nor Woody Guthrie. Not even Tennessee Williams. Dylan closed out the set with his *Shot of Love* elegy to Lenny Bruce.

---

[373] At a similar rant in Tokyo, he threw in heroes d'jour Boris Karloff, Henry Winkler, Ronald Reagan, and Richard Nixon for good measure.

[374] Williams died at 71 on Feb. 25, 1983, choking on a bottle cap. A lifelong alcoholic, he apparently laced booze with barbiturates, suppressing his gag reflex.

■ ■ ■

Dylan took a break from True Confessions to crank out another studio album that spring. Recorded in L.A., *Knocked Out Loaded* would be released in August with the resurrected "Brownsville Girl" taking up one whole side. Garnering what little praise critics were willing to concede, "Brownsville Girl" was the one track Dylan didn't slap together to satisfy his Columbia contract. The hopeful phrase "return to form" began creeping into record reviews, most critics agreeing that he hadn't. *Knocked Out Loaded*[375] was a disappointment. Peaking at No. 55 on the *Billboard* chart, it dropped like a failed punch line.

"Back then I wasn't bringing anything at all into the studio," Dylan admitted later. "I was completely disillusioned."

Outwardly, he tried not to appear jaded. He kept moving—an imposter on the run. The Dylan/Zimmerman duality metastasized during the '80s, manifesting in everything from frequent costume changes to quirky offstage behavior.

Who was that masked man? On any given day, Bob had trouble answering the question himself. His latest incarnation was Pirate Bob, appearing in public as if he'd just stepped off of an E-ticket ride. He refused televised interviews unless he was filmed standing still; no questions permitted as he walked or sat. Candid shots? No way.

"Now, Little Richard says if you don't want your picture taken, you got no business being a star, and he's right, he's absolutely

---

[375] In a long list of acknowledgments, Bob thanked everyone from his acupuncturist to a nineteenth-century Russian rabbi. The cover was cribbed from an old movie poster for Gregory Peck's *Duel in the Sun* (MGM, 1946). When his manager suggested they secure reproduction rights, Dylan reportedly told him to let them sue.

right," said Dylan. "But I don't like my picture being taken by people I don't know. . . . I'm a star, but I can shine for who I want to shine for. You know what I mean?"

A personal acupuncturist joined his entourage, presumably to help with residual back and neck pain from that long-ago motorcycle spill. He took up boxing and bicycling to stay in shape, but booze and babes remained a constant, especially on the road. His health ricocheted between sanguine and horrendous. His True Confessions contract rider[376] spelled out the dichotomy. Lemon slices, tea bags, and hot water must be waiting for him backstage at every stop, but so did a jug of Courvoisier.

During Dylan's extended break from touring, ASCAP honored him with its Founders Award for lifetime achievement in songwriting. He showed up at Hollywood's Chasen's Restaurant the night of the ceremony in tight black leather pants and an Oriental shirt carelessly thrown open at the throat. Sporting a generous crop of *Miami Vice* face fuzz, a Little Steven head scarf, and a single gold earring, Pirate Bob settled into a banquette beside Elizabeth Taylor and lit a cigarette. He hunkered down like Jett Rink and flirted with one of the last genuine movie stars, ordering one drink and another, and then another. Taylor later reported that she found him utterly delightful.

Dylan did not get so loaded that he didn't appreciate the irony. Donnie Osmond, Sammy Cahn, Leonard Cohen, Marilyn Bergman, Neil Young, Chrissie Hynde, Bernie Taupin, and George Michael were among an oddball assemblage of songsmiths, old and new, all there to pay homage to the elusive voice of a generation. Osmond

---

[376] By contrast, U2's touring demands called for four cases of Heineken, one of Rolling Rock, half a case of Guinness, two-fifths of Moet White Star champagne, one fifth each of Cuervo, Jack Daniel's, and port or sherry, three bottles each of Chardonnay and Bordeaux, two each of Mouton Cadet red, and Jacob's Creek or Black Opal Australian white.

testified from the dais that "Blowin' in the Wind" had raised his political consciousness while Tin Pan Alley's Hal David oozed praise for the original Village outsider who'd shown the best of the Brill Building how it was done. Richie Havens showed up in tuxedo, carrying his guitar. Dylan stopped the chitchat with Liz long enough to give his old Village confrere a long and heartfelt hug.[377]

"We used to play together for what we could collect in our hats, and Richie's hat always had more," Bob graciously announced. He leaned across the table to confide to Chrissie Hynde: "*Nobody* plays like Richie."

In the end, sentiment, nostalgia, and a lot of tequila loosened Bob's defenses, trumping all irony. When accepting his award, he spoke from the heart, quoting Broadway Billy Rose: "Without a song, the day never ends. Without a song, the road never bends. When things go wrong, man ain't got a friend. Without a song."

■ ■ ■

Before the U.S. leg of True Confessions got underway, Lorimar Productions proudly announced *the* "get" of the season: Renaldo would return to the big screen as aging rock star Billy Parker in *Hearts of Fire*, an eternal triangle saga set to a Bob beat.

"Somebody called me from the William Morris Agency," said Dylan. "I just read (Joe Eszterhas's script) and it seemed like I knew that character, whoever it was. It's a guy who plays oldie shows. I could relate to that. I've done all those things, really."

Director Richard Marquand (*Jagged Edge*) cinched the deal in the kitchen at Bob's beachfront compound, matching his host's

---

[377] He also showed up unannounced at Len Chandler's 50th birthday party. Chandler embraced his old friend, but made him smoke outside on the deck; everyone else in his circle had given up tobacco.

prodigious capacity for Cabernet glass for glass. Commenting later on the experience, Marquand marveled at Dylan's hollow leg, quick wit, and broad span of knowledge. He also met Bob's chickens, which became a running joke in the movie. At one point, the character Billy Parker opens his kitchen refrigerator, which is stocked with nothing but egg cartons, and asks his girlfriend, "Do you want some eggs?"

Casting Bob as Bob, Marquand developed a cynical Billy Parker who cares as little about the outcome of the plot as . . . well, Bob Dylan. If the original script had a redeeming theme explaining why Bob signed on, it was the false and fleeting allure of fame. Billy Parker scorns celebrity, only venturing from his chicken ranch when he needs female companionship or spending money.

Lorimar's other big announcement should have been a red flag: Bob would compose six new songs for the soundtrack. Had he paid closer attention, Dylan might have recognized enough *Pat Garrett and Billy the Kid* hype in *Hearts of Fire* to think twice before joining the cast.

But Bob was a busy man and not given to the lessons of history. Before True Confessions recommenced, he found even more opportunities to increase cash flow. When rap pioneer Kurtis Blow asked him to collaborate on a duet called "Street Rock" for his *Kingdom Blow* LP, Bob accepted the paycheck. His off-kilter verbosity contrasted with Blow's machine-gun delivery and served as Dylan's introduction to a whole new audience. "I'm chillin' like Bob Dylan" became an early rap meme.

The grind of True Confessions allowed scant chillin' during the summer of '86. He reminded the media again and again that he was "cutting costs on this tour, and maximizing profits" as he and the Heartbreakers blitzed across America playing as many as six arenas a week. As if prepping for his upcoming star turn as burned-out

Billy Parker, Dylan seldom changed his stage persona. Pirate Bob regularly wore sleeveless shirts, leather vests, amulets, and his ever-present eardrop, sticking close to a routine that allowed him to get in and out of a city in a hurry.

In a surprise change-up in the Akron-through-Washington, D.C., segment, the Grateful Dead opened the show. In many ways, the quintessential American traveling band was an even better fit for Bob than the Heartbreakers. Jerry Garcia was Dylan's contemporary and co-equal, not a deferential up-and-comer like Tom Petty. Bob and the Dead chieftain had been acquainted since Woodstock. Garcia was one of the first to step up and stand by born again Bob when others fled. During True Confessions, their friendship solidified.

But following the Washington, D.C., gig, Garcia fell off the wagon as hard as Richard Manuel, descending into a diabetic coma that abruptly ended the Dead/Dylan collaboration. Garcia cheated death, recovered, and pledged to clean up his act for the umpteenth time, but True Confessions had already moved on. Once again Petty and the Heartbreakers were Bob's sole backup.

Coming home to Minneapolis, Dylan dedicated "a song that can't be taken but one way" to his mother. Newly widowed for the second time, Beatty Rutman[378] watched from a private box at the brand-new Hubert Humphrey Metrodome as Dylan crooned "Seeing the Real You at Last." She beamed, hands aflutter. A mahjongg partner who'd been invited along to watch her son perform thought that Beatty might lift off and fly away. "Look at Bob! Look at this place!" she blurted. "He is God and everybody's here to worship him!"

Of course, Mrs. Rutman knew better. If ever God needed a reality check, all he had to do was pay a visit to his Yiddish Momma.

---

[378] Beatty had just buried Joe Rutman.

"Bobby gives me such *naches*," she said. "He's a good boy, a regular mensch. He calls, he writes, he listens to his mother. Every mother should have such a son."

Columbia Records chief Walter Yetnikoff could attest to Bob's maternal attachment. His jaw dropped to his knees when he met Bob and Beatty for dinner once in New York, recording their dialogue for posterity in his memoir *Howling at the Moon:*

"You're not eating, Bobby."

"Please, Ma. You're embarrassing me."

"I saw you ate nothing for lunch. You're skin and bones."

"I'm eating, Ma, I'm eating."

"And have you thanked Mr. Yetnikoff for this lovely dinner?"

"Thank you, Walter."

"You're mumbling, Bobby. I don't think Mr. Yetnikoff heard you."

"He heard me."

"Bobby, be nice."

While Yetnikoff continued to gawk, Dylan's current girlfriend, Carole Childs, leaned in from the opposite side and cut up the food on his plate. Also Jewish, Childs filled in the gaps whenever Beatty let up her harangue.

"The mysterious poet suddenly turned into little Bobby Zimmerman," recalled Yetnikoff. When he called Dylan on his fraud, Bob smiled defiantly.

"Is it okay with you if I love my mother?"

:: :: ::

As True Confessions finished its breakneck race across the U.S., Dylan ate badly, drank too much, and looked worse than he felt. By August, he and the Heartbreakers had slowed their gravy train to a halt at the Mid State Fairgrounds in Paso Robles, California, just west of where James Dean met his end. Now nearly twice the age Dean was when he died, Dylan knew precisely where the film legend ran his high-performance Porsche into eternity.

"I was there at the spot," he later told Sam Shepard. "On the spot. A windy kinda place. The curve where he had the accident. I mean, the place where he died is as powerful as the place he lived. It's on this broad expanse of land. It's like the place made James Dean who he is. If he hadn't've died there, he wouldn't've been James Dean."

Perhaps in deference to his first movie hero, Dylan sang "Brownsville Girl" for the first and last time in public that night. He cast the long ballad's matinee spell over an audience who'd come of age somewhere east of Eden, but ended the evening as well as the tour with coming attractions.

"All right, I'm gonna play these last few songs I guess and hit the road," he said. "I'm going off to make a movie now. Wish me good luck. Ha ha. I'm gonna need it."

After the press conference that launched *Hearts of Fire*'s principal photography a few weeks later, the movie that was supposed to relaunch Dylan's film career descended from mediocre to swill before his name ever made it to the marquee. His soundtrack contributions dropped from six to three originals and, while hardly his finest work, the songs turned out to be the best thing in a movie that delivered little beyond a brief moonlit glimpse of his skinny-dipping costar's naked buttocks.

"I think she could be the next Joan Crawford," Dylan deadpanned.

For all its myriad flaws, *Hearts of Fire* belonged to Fiona Flanagan, not Bob Dylan. Whether master-manipulating Bob knew or even cared, his name and mystique were meant to sell yet another *A Star Is Born*[379] retread designed to turn the pert young ingenue into a film goddess. Twenty years Bob's junior, Flanagan was cute as the dickens but had no charisma beyond a chipmunk overbite. Completing the abysmal miscasting, Bob's young rival for Fiona's affections was slithery Rupert Everett, an accomplished British stage actor best known in the twenty-first century as the voice of Prince Charming in *Shrek* and Madonna's openly gay sidekick.

From the outset, director Richard Marquand warred with Lorimar, echoing Sam Peckinpah's battles with MGM.[380] Final cut in both cases fell to the studio, but at least Peckinpah coaxed a quirky performance from Dylan before surrendering to the suits. Under Marquand's laissez-faire direction, Bob mugged for the camera like a shelter animal, thinking too long before speaking and translating his notorious impermeability to the screen—method acting without much method. Those who believed they'd meet the real Bob in *Hearts of Fire* got stiffed.

They weren't the only ones. During the three months of production, BBC producer Christopher Sykes dogged the cast of *Hearts of Fire* for a hopeful documentary entitled *Getting to Dylan*. It didn't. While Sykes strove mightily to ply Bob with empathy and honesty, Dylan responded with *glissendorf*. During one session, he blithely sketched the producer's likeness on a pad of paper while they played duck-and-parry.

---

[379] Kris Kristofferson starred opposite Barbra Streisand in the 1976 version, taking the role of aging rocker that fell to Bob in *Hearts of Fire*.

[380] In a *Hearts of Fire* getaway scene, Dylan and Flanagan motorcycle past a theater showing *Pat Garrett and Billy the Kid*.

"How do you decide when to talk to people and when not to?" asked Sykes.

Dylan laughed. "Do you think I'm talking now?" He continued sketching while suggesting Sykes speak to Roger Daltrey or Peter Townsend, maybe Paul McCartney.

"Well of course I *would* if I'd been commissioned to make a movie that involved *them*," said Sykes.

"You would have to, wouldn't you?" asked Bob, glancing from Sykes to his pad and back at Sykes.

"Yeah," he answered.

"Well, you know, I'm not going to say anything that you're gonna get any revelations about," said Bob. "It's not gonna happen."

True to his word, he spoke with Sykes frequently over a period of weeks, never once hinting at his true identity. Years in the spotlight only heightened Bob's scorn for the media. The Jokerman rewarded persistence with contempt—behavior that might be forgiven in a 20-year-old naïf, but not a 45-year-old con artist. The most Sykes got for his efforts was a pretty good charcoal sketch of himself.

Hearts of Fire wrapped before Christmas and Sykes's documentary aired soon thereafter to universal yawns. Nothing was revealed. Sykes and his BBC audience would have been thunderstruck to know that Bob had married and fathered a child during the previous year. In fact, for all the microscopic scrutiny given Bob's life and career during the late 1980s, he managed to secretly wed not just one of his Queens of Rhythm but possibly two others[381] to boot.

After years of dalliance with rotating members of his all-female chorus, Dylan impregnated Carolyn Dennis around the time of the "We Are the World" recording session. She bore him a daughter in

---

[381] In addition to Clydie King, Dylan was also reported to have tied the knot for a time with backup singer Carol Woods.

January 1986 and six months later, they wed during a True Confessions break. He installed wife and child in their own household in a gated community at the west end of the San Fernando Valley and then went on about his career.

More than ever, Bob Dylan and Robert Zimmerman led two separate lives—maybe more—but fans, friends, even intimates never had a clue. Dylan moved from tryst to tryst, compartmentalizing with firewalls that separated one sleepover cell from another. Going public was punishable by Old Testament ostracism, divorce, or disinheritance. Cross Bob once and all Christian mercy evaporated.

Calculating precisely when Dylan began stashing women is vexing, but at some point following Rolling Thunder, he took to behaving like a latter-day King David, taking mistresses at will—sometimes for a night, sometimes a season, occasionally longer—then moving on. To some degree, he and his ladies co-conspired. The girlfriends didn't even know or professed not to care all that much about their rivals.

"He's amusing, he's spiritual. As for the promiscuity, at least he's honest," said Dana Gillespie, a British blues singer Bob first hooked during the mid-60s when she was Donovan's underage girlfriend. "Women prefer to be seduced by a brain (rather) than a bullock. Brains go a helluva long way."

Carole Childs didn't seem to mind. Around the same time that Carolyn Dennis-Dylan and daughter Gabrielle were settling into the flatlands of Tarzana, his most public girlfriend during the late '80s moved into Dylan's secluded ridge-top hideaway on Oak Pass Road[382] above Beverly Hills.

---

[382] Dylan set up the Oak Pass Trust using Childs's address as his base of operations for real estate transactions throughout the 1990s, the idea being that his name wouldn't appear on any public records.

Meanwhile in New York, Bob maintained similar crash pads. At various times, he boasted to his on-again, off-again girlfriend Ruth Tyrangiel of having three different Manhattan flats—a brownstone on East 49th Street,[383] a place up in Harlem, and a suite in Trump[384] Towers that his business managers Ben and Naomi Saltzman occupied when Bob wasn't in town. On occasion he also stayed with Tyrangiel, who had lived in the same second-floor apartment on East 82nd Street for more than ten years. She had married, divorced, and had a son by a Dylan imitator[385] since Rolling Thunder, but never ended her relationship with Bob whom she characterized as her common-law husband. Dylan spent the night often, according to Ruth, but by the late '80s, he was also staying over at another rent-controlled apartment across town occupied by ex-groupie Susan Ross.

One of the few Dylan women who ever dared go public, Ross wrote an unpublished tell-all in the late '90s detailing their relationship, which she dated from the *Biograph* retrospective Columbia Records staged at the Whitney in November 1985. Dylan showed for that testimonial with Carole Childs on his arm, but met and made overtures to Ross during that same evening. Six months later, at the outset of the U.S. leg of True Confessions and within weeks of wedding Carolyn Dennis, Dylan dropped by Ross's apartment for a visit and, by her own recollection, consummated their relationship "across my big brass bed."

"If he wants to have sex with a woman in another city when he is on tour that is up to him," Ross later told the *London Daily Mail*.

---

[383] Katharine Hepburn was his next-door neighbor.

[384] He once checked into a hotel in San Sebastian, Spain, under the name Donald Pump.

[385] A former caretaker at Hi Lo Ha during the late '60s, Bob Miles "made his living ever since mimicking his reclusive boss," according to Bob Spitz. After he and Tyrangiel divorced, Miles starred in a Dylan-sanctioned musical, *Bob Dylan, Words & Music,* which opened and closed in the fall of 1986.

"He has never been able to get the big picture from one woman. We are not, either of us, conventional people. I always know when he has slept with another woman. What I care about is that when I am with him, I am queen. I want to be accorded respect."

■ ■ ■

Dylan took the winter off but returned to the annual drudgery of cranking out another LP in the spring. *Down in the Groove,* a mix of originals, collaborations, and covers, would become his 25th studio album. Savaged by *Rolling Stone* as the worst bilge Dylan had ever recorded,[386] *Down in the Groove* had a single saving grace—"Silvio," co-credited to Grateful Dead lyricist Robert Hunter. Even as the album tanked, the single charted and gained significant airplay in the fast-fragmenting FM radio market.

Hunter wrote the words while Dylan provided the music, but just who was "Silvio"?[387] Was he an "old boll weevil looking for a home" or some oddball shaman only dead men know? Critics speculated Hunter had Bob's own erratic behavior in mind when he began his barrelhouse blues, "Stake my future on a hell of a past . . ."

In and out of the studio, Bob's past was still and always close behind. The Dylan/Zimmy duality tipped precariously toward multiple personality disorder as he blundered toward the summer of '87. He ricocheted from Jokerman to Pirate Bob to Billy Parker and all alter egos in between. He began showing up in the strangest places:

---

[386] According to a special 2007 edition detailing the 15 worst LPs produced by major rock acts, *Down in the Groove* outranked *Self Portrait* in the rank derby.

[387] Paul Williams maintained that Hunter was inspired by a Carlos Castaneda character, Silvio Manuel who "seemed like a character from another time. He was friendly and warm during the daytime, but as soon as the twilight set in, he would become unfathomable."

Elizabeth Taylor's 55th birthday party; U2 and Taj Mahal concerts in L.A.; Graceland[388] and Sam Phillips's legendary Sun Studio[389] in Memphis.

During a George Gershwin retrospective for PBS, Bob materialized on a bare Brooklyn stage accompanied only by his own acoustic guitar. In appearance, he seemed to channel Woody from a quarter century earlier, but the lyrics of Gershwin's "Soon"[390] smacked more of Country Bob. He had come to prefer the poetry of others to his own.

Dylan described his life's work as "a package of heavy, rotting meat" that he lugged with him from concert to concert. As the months dragged on, he postponed the inevitable touring in which he'd have to perform the same old lineup all over again, night after night, town after town.

"The public had been fed a steady diet of my complete recordings on disc for years, but my live performances never seemed to capture the inner spirit of the songs—had failed to put the spin on them" he recalled in *Chronicles*. "The intimacy, among a lot of other things, was gone."

He seriously began thinking about retiring. "I wasn't getting any thrill out of performing," he told *60 Minutes'* Ed Bradley nearly 20 years later. "I sorta (thought) it might be time to close it up, you know."

Like Billy Parker, he hunkered down on his chicken ranch by the sea. And then one day he got a call from the Grateful Dead.

---

[388] "It was just awesome and it was very clear that Elvis was going to be a religion in a lot of different ways," said Bob.

[389] Dylan allegedly kissed the very spot on the concrete floor where Elvis, Johnny Cash, Carl Perkins, and Jerry Lee Lewis launched the rockabilly revolution.

[390] An obscure Gershwin love song from the 1927 Broadway musical *Strike Up the Band*. "It sounds like sophisticated city stuff," mused Dylan, "but there's a country, backwood, Alley cat element to it."

On the strength of their brief True Confessions collaboration the previous year, Jerry Garcia invited Dylan to join the band during their travels that summer. Bob arrived at their San Rafael headquarters, bodyguard in tow, but found that he was just another schlub working through his probation.

"He loved it," recalled Len Dell'Amico, the Dead's resident videographer. "He'd come in there and the crew would go, 'Hey, Bob,' and then turn their backs on him."

A good dose of humility seemed at first to be just what the doctor ordered. Because they already had their own Bob,[391] the Dead nicknamed Dylan "Spike." After that first visit, Spike dismissed his bodyguard and regressed to Elston Gunn jonesing for a spot in Bobby Vee's band.

But he sucked and he knew it. Dylan hated his old songs and performed them badly. When urged to sing, he'd forget the words. One rainy afternoon, he quit early and went for a walk.

"I wasn't planning on going back," he recalled.

A half dozen blocks away he heard music filtering out of a hole-in-the-wall lounge. Ducking inside, Bob found a four-piece combo playing jazz at the back of the bar. He ordered a gin and tonic and stayed awhile. Clad in mohair suit, shiny tie, and a porkpie hat, the aging lead singer reminding Bob of 1940s balladeer Billy Eckstine. Dylan studied his baritone phrasing, his effortless breathing, his careful enunciation as he ran through jazz standards like "Time on My Hands" and "Gloomy Sunday." The bar might be empty, but the music mesmerized.

"If I could in any way get close to handling this technique," he decided, "I could get off this marathon stunt ride."

---

[391] Bob Weir who, along with Garcia, bassist Phil Lesh, keyboardist Ron "Pigpen" McKernan, and drummer Bill Kreutzmann, cofounded the Dead in 1964.

An hour later, Bob returned to the Dead's Front Street rehearsal hall, ready to roll, with all thoughts of retiring behind him.

▪▪ ▪▪ ▪▪

However much he'd grown to admire Jerry Garcia over the years, Dylan's respect surged that summer. At death's door a year earlier, the Dead's nominal leader had cleaned up his act again and "was his old self," according to Dell'Amico.

"I remember everybody just more or less beaming about it," he said. "He'd done it completely by himself and he was proud of himself and everything was going great."

Though a year younger than Bob, Garcia became Dylan's role model. Just as fans and fellow songwriters longed to *be* Bob, Bob wanted to *be* Jerry. They shared addictive appetites for wine, women, and song, but Garcia sustained his equilibrium through his band. By the '80s, the Dead were a self-supporting institution—a multimillion-dollar refuge where Garcia could retreat from speed and heroin, recharge among brethren, and live to fight another day. The one place both Jerry and Bob truly felt alive was on stage, but only Garcia had nurtured a support group for coping with the pressures.

Among other things, Garcia taught Dylan to shut up. No more sermonizing, crowd banter, or Tennessee Williams quotes. The Dead came to town to play music, period. Second, Jerry told Bob to toss his set list. Following his born-again period, Dylan's concerts had slowly ossified into golden oldies showcases. He mollified audiences, but came away feeling like a yodeling drone.

"He'd say, 'Come on, man, you know, this is the way it goes. Let's play it, it goes like this.' And I'd say, "Man, he's right, you know? How's he getting' there and I can't get there?'" said Dylan.

Third, Garcia urged Bob to dig through his backlist for long-forgotten gems. While the Dead covered more Dylan songs than any other act in the world, there were never enough. The band demanded more. Under Garcia's tutelage, Bob sifted through dozens of compositions he'd never played before in public. Never mind "All Along the Watchtower" or "The Times They Are a-Changin.'" How about "The Wicked Messenger" or "The Ballad of Frankie Lee and Judas Priest"?

"Jerry Garcia could hear the song in all my bad recordings, the song that was buried there," said Dylan.

The Dead played what they wanted to play, not what the crowd demanded—a sentiment Dylan shared but had long forgotten. He followed their lead, but found their tight, hypnotic riffs difficult to follow. Even with established bands like the Heartbreakers, Bob had always been the boss. His sidemen followed *him*, not the other way around. Not so with the Dead.

"When they went out on the road that summer Dylan had trouble with the Dead," recalled Dell'Amico. "Compared to his garage bands, the Dead were like an orchestra, and so I think he was very intimidated. When they rehearsed, it was looser, but once they got on with the shows, it was probably hard for Dylan to go out in front of 70,000 or 80,000 fans who were there for the Dead, and then try to fit his thing into this wall of sound."

After just six shows, Dylan had had enough. He took the rest of the summer off to be with his children and his chickens. In the fall, he rejoined the Heartbreakers and launched another road show under a different name.

The Temples in Flames Tour kicked off in Jerusalem the same week *Hearts of Fire* opened in London. Dylan did not attend the premiere. It was just as well. The movie closed days after the director died of a stroke at age 49.

Richard Marquand had edited holes in the plot big enough to drive a tour bus through. With Lorimar angling for a PG rating, the director even cut a nude love scene that might have at least brought voyeurs into theaters. Instead of getting to watch Bob and Fiona[392] rut, audiences saw faux groupies hang their panties from Rupert Everett's aquiline nose. The pièce de cheesy résistance was a scene featuring a blind female stalker who confronts Billy Parker with a pistol and the words "I've always wanted to see you," just before she blows her brains out. Lorimar cancelled its U.S. release, perhaps dreading reviews that began, "So bad it killed the director . . ."

While *Hearts* came and went, Dylan busied himself road testing all that he'd learned from the Dead.

"In these first four shows, I sang 80 different songs, never repeating one, just to see if I could do it," he recalled.

And, yes, he could. Bob and the Heartbreakers spent the remainder of the year crisscrossing Europe, putting Garcia's advice to the test: no stage banter, no set list, no predictability. Despite his time with the Dead, however, audiences continued to elude him. He could not seem to connect the way the Billy Eckstine clone had done so easily back at that San Rafael cocktail lounge. More than once, Bob suppressed the urge to cut and run. Before panic set in, he always deferred to the Queens of Rhythm: "They were good-looking girls, you know? And like I say, I had them up there so I wouldn't feel so bad."

Reviews across Europe were mixed, but for the first time in a while Dylan seemed up to the task until a stormy night in the Alpine village of Locarno, on the banks of Lake Maggiore.

"For an instant, I fell into a black hole," he recalled.

---

[392] Her next role was as a groupie in Oliver Stone's *The Doors,* after which she vanished into New Jersey, never to be heard from again.

In a far-ranging interview he gave ten years later to *Newsweek* and again in the pages of *Chronicles*, Dylan described an epiphany that marked a new beginning to his stage career. Most Dylanistas trace the spark for his Never Ending Tour to that evening, and more specifically, to his keening rendition of "Tomorrow Is a Long Time."

For the 21st show on the Temples tour, roadies erected a stage in the middle of Locarno's market square. Thirty thousand fans—twice the population of the village—filled the medieval streets. From the stage, his audience looked like "cutouts from a shooting gallery," and during the first few numbers, he went through the motions. And then . . .

"I opened my mouth to sing and the air tightened up," he said. Nothing came out.

As with his motel meet-up with Jesus in Tucson nearly a decade earlier, he heard a voice in that awful silence, only this time it came from within: *I'm determined to stand, whether God will deliver me or not.*

"No one would have noticed that a metamorphosis had taken place," he said.

The weather and the setting were both appropriate for revelation. Buckets of rain; thunder from the Alps; fog and wind that howled across the surface of Lake Maggiore. No one but Bob heard his declaration, but the effect was both miraculous and immediate. He reclaimed his own voice at the same moment he reconnected with his audience. The heavy, rotting words he'd written so many years before suddenly had renewed meaning: there *is* beauty in the silver, singing river and the sunrise in the sky.

In that instant, his blind faith in Jesus gave way to a deeper confidence in himself, and his late-life music ministry began.

But not without a little boost from Jerry Garcia's favorite elixir. A week following Locarno, at a concert stop in Birmingham, England, a security guard reported coming up to Dylan backstage at the National Exhibition Center. He found Bob alone in a dressing room bent over a "mountain of cocaine." While never corroborated, the story seemed a match for Bob's erratic stage presence—up one night, down the next.

At tour's end, Dylan was decidedly up. He got positively giddy with Elliot Roberts, the manager he'd hired to replace Jerry Weintraub. David Geffen's ex-partner listened patiently in a London pub while Bob feverishly laid out his plan to rebuild and reconnect with an all-new audience over the next three years.

Dylan was determined to stand. He flew back to Malibu flush with tour money, hubris, and a renewed faith in his future.

16
MONEY TRAIN

In the winter of 1987, Dylan ripped and mangled his hand "to the bone." Weeks after the freak accident, he got reports that his *Water Pearl* lost her rudder and hit a reef off of Panama. While he recuperated back home in Malibu, he followed the daily salvage bulletins. He still had no feeling in his fingers when word came that his schooner had foundered and sunk.

"This loss paled somewhat compared to the use of my hand," he recalled in *Chronicles*, "but I had been grateful for the boat, and the news came as an unwelcomed shock."

His stitched and wounded hand in a plaster cast, all the effusive touring plans he'd laid out for Eliot Roberts suddenly seemed a mirage. Dylan feared he'd never play again.

"I didn't know what had befallen me, and this was a bizarre shift of fate," he said. "All potentialities had gone to pieces."

And yet, in the earliest stages of convalescence, he learned that he'd been voted into the Rock and Roll Hall of Fame. Clearly, not *all* potentialities had faded. In fact, he miraculously recovered enough to perform "All Along the Watchtower" and "Like a Rolling Stone" during induction ceremonies at New York's Waldorf-Astoria. He kidded Muhammad Ali from the podium, thanked Alan Lomax, Little Richard, and Bruce Springsteen who were among his audience, and didn't wince at all when shaking hands. In fact, both hands looked just fine. He'd either exaggerated his injury or, as with other

Chronicles moments, simply made the whole thing up. In retrospect, his wounded self-confidence also seemed suspect.

"I felt done for, an empty burned-out wreck," he insisted in an interview he gave 20 years later to *USA Today*'s Edna Gundersen. "I had horse-whipped myself so bad, and I was critically hurt in so many ways, I really didn't have much more to say at that point."

For the next several months, Dylan went mute, but his pen did not. Carolyn Dennis, his new wife and latest muse, nursed him back to health while he scratched out a brand-new crop of songs at the kitchen table, beginning with "Political World," which skewered politicians the way "Masters of War" had once nailed arms dealers.

"There was a heated presidential race underway," Dylan recalled. "You couldn't avoid hearing about it."

The George Bush–Michael Dukakis campaign for Ronald Reagan's throne was setting new lows in White House politicking. Unprecedented attack ads played on Yuppie fear and loathing, and, despite having long foresworn politics, Dylan paid curiously close attention. He concluded that America had become a "bottomless pit of cultural oblivion," even as he was plunging into the abyss himself.

During a decade that began with *The Cosby Show* and ended with *Dynasty,* the average American TV set was on seven hours a day. At middecade, 60 million U.S. households had cable, but those who could afford to do so like Dylan installed satellite dishes and VCRs so they could capture even more.

"TV is so super powerful," he observed. "It forms people's opinions. When I was growing up, and even in the '60s, that never was the case. You had to go out and experience things to form opinions. Now you don't have to move. You get knowledge brought in to you, you know, without the experience of it. So I think there's something really dangerous in that."

And yet, despite the danger, Dylan took full advantage. When TV reported that NBA star Pete Maravich had dropped dead at 40, Bob didn't have to be on the basketball court to translate tragedy into poetry. The obituary that aired on the nightly news was epiphany enough. Bob wrote "Dignity"[393] as a Maravich tribute. Similarly, breaking news about televangelist Jimmy Swaggart's tryst with a hooker led to "The Disease of Conceit."

By his own count, he composed 20 new songs during his TV-inspired convalescence. Only a few—"Man in the Long Black Coat,"[394] "Ring Them Bells," and "Most of the Time"—rose to the level of his best work, but he still had the nucleus of a new studio album. None of the new crop would appear on his next LP, however. Before recording his own songs, he became a Wilbury.

The five pop pros who called themselves the Traveling Wilburys gathered to make music in Dylan's garage that spring. At first, they were the "Trembling Wilburys,"[395] as George Harrison remembered it. The serendipity sparked when the ex-Beatle needed a B-side for a new single. Hearing that Dylan had jerry-rigged a studio in his garage, he asked to record it there. Roy Orbison, Tom Petty, and Jeff Lynne joined the cause and extemporaneous energy reminiscent of Big Pink descended on Bob's beachfront compound.

"With the Wilburys, it was more like an experimental band, where you didn't show up with anything," said Petty. "There were no songs when you showed up, and then everyone sat down together and had

---

[393] Recorded at the same time as "Political World," but unreleased until *Greatest Hits Vol. 3* (1994). The only new song on the album, "Dignity" charted as a single at a time when no new Dylan songs had been released for several years.

[394] Johnny Cash, the original Man in Black, had had double-bypass surgery followed by double pneumonia when Dylan wrote his gloomy ballad. Cash wasn't expected to survive but lived another 14 years.

[395] Wilbury was a sound engineer's slang for "we'll bury" any recording gaffes during the editing.

to knock out a song. So, you know, some times different people would take the lead and then the others would follow along."

As with the Band, collaboration hastened Bob's recovery. From their very first effort, which took its title from a "Handle with Care" sticker on the side of a cardboard box, the Wilburys snatched ideas from out of thin air. Harrison never did get the B-side for his single, but in a little over a week they'd noodled a whole LP's worth of new tunes. Unlike the standard studio album, *Traveling Wilburys Vol. I* was a labor of pure whimsy, free of lawyers, managers, ego, or record company executives. [396] After its release, the LP went double platinum, even though Bob refused to promote it.

"He has no qualms about taking 20% of the royalties, but he doesn't do interviews," deadpanned Harrison.

Instead, Bob concentrated on publicizing *Down in the Groove*, which Columbia released as the belated kickoff for Dylan's summer concert series. Were it not for "Silvio," dismal *Down in the Groove* might have persuaded more fans to stay away than join Dylan on the first-ever leg of his Never Ending Tour. In addition to awful music, the album oozed manipulation. For the first time, a Dylan LP invited fans to join Bob's "Entertainment Connection,"[397] i.e., his fan club mailing list. Bob meant to duplicate the Grateful Dead's marketing synergy: develop a core audience who will follow wherever and whenever the band performs and purchase official Dylan merchandise along the way. The Dead had their Deadheads; Bob would have his Bobcats.

Meanwhile, he publicly mocked the crass materialism of his peers. No Dylan song would ever sell soap, he boasted.

---

[396] Noel "Paul" Stookey remarked that listening to the Wilburys was "a little like going bowling."

[397] Those who signed up were promised a set of liner notes on each of the album's songs. No notes were ever delivered.

"They'd like to use my tunes for different beer companies and perfumes and automobiles," he said. "I get approached on all that stuff. But, shit, I didn't write them for those reasons. That's never been my scene."

He preferred making money by performing. He cut overhead on what came to be known as the Interstate 88 Tour [398] by firing the Queens of Rhythm and paring his traveling band down to a couple of guitars, a drummer, and a bass. The only vocals were his own. He stayed on the road for most of the year, doing 40 shows before the August break and another 31 in the fall.

During the hiatus, he gave away his stepdaughter Maria to Minneapolis folkie Peter Himmelman. It was an orthodox wedding, but a slightly less born-again Bob seemed to fit right in. So did the rest of his and Sara's kids, all adults by now. Soon, they would all marry and eventually make him a grandfather 14 times over, even as he'd begun his own second family.

"I love children," he said. "I [was] always taught that if you were blessed to have them, you just had more of them."

After the wedding but before resuming his Interstate 88 Tour, Dylan also renewed acquaintance with his oldest roadie. In the 20 years since they'd last worked together, Victor Maymudes's construction business had failed along with several marriages. He moved from New Mexico to Pacific Palisades with little more than hope that Bob would take him back, but slipped right back into his factotum role as if he'd never left.

"I'm looking for a job," said Maymudes.

"You're hired," answered Bob.

Dylan started him off at $750 a week, quickly bumped him up to $1,000 and gave him the title "tour manager."

---

[398] "Interstate" as in the shield shape of the backstage pass; "88" as in the year.

"Flunky was more like it," said Maymudes.

As in their earliest Village days, surly, loyal Victor took care of everything from pimping and plumbing to pizza and beer. He fit perfectly into Bob's master plan, which seemed finally to be succeeding. By year's end, *Traveling Wilburys Vol. I* had topped the charts. Dylan's star crept higher in spite of the quick death of *Down in the Groove*. His Interstate 88 concerts, which began ragged and ill-attended, ended with a four-night SRO engagement at Radio City Music Hall. For one long weekend, he was the darling of Manhattan. His determination to stand seemed finally to have taken hold. With Victor at his side, how could he fail?

■ ■ ■

On the evening of February 12, 1989, Dylan joined the Grateful Dead at L.A.'s Fabulous Forum. He played background on eight songs until Jerry Garcia urged him to step out front and croon an awkward version of "Knockin' on Heaven's Door." Were it not so awful, Bob's guest appearance might have been mistaken as a desperate sales gimmick, for just one week earlier Columbia released *Dylan and the Dead* to universal scorn.

Separately, Bob and the Dead were masters of pop; together, they were disaster. The sure-fire live album recorded during their brief 1987 tour was a critical and commercial dud. As evidenced during their one-night reunion at the Forum, the Dead's symphonic rifts continued to drown Bob's reedy vocals. Drunk or simply befuddled, Dylan often couldn't remember his own lyrics.

Undaunted by the crowd's negative reaction, Bob made an extraordinary request the following morning. He phoned Garcia and asked to join the band. Bob Weir remembered bassist Phil Lesh as the sole "no" vote, but one veto was all it took. The Dead required unanimity on all band decisions. All for one and one for all, they nixed the voice of a generation.

A few weeks later, a chastened Dylan continued his late '80s identity crisis by retreating to New Orleans. He installed his wife and entourage in rented quarters near Audubon Park. On the strength of recommendations from U2's Bono and George Harrison, he hired Canadian producer Daniel Lanois to produce his next LP—the first under a new Columbia contract.

A cut below *Blood on the Tracks* or any of his '60s classics, *Oh Mercy* still hit Bob's highwater mark for the decade now coming to an end. In much the same way *Nashville Skyline* smacked of white-bread country or *Slow Train Coming* sounded like Sunday morning in Muscle Shoals, *Oh Mercy* laid claim to the terrain in which it was recorded. Dylan may have composed most of the songs a year earlier while convalescing in front of his TV set, but the downbeat dirge for "Man in the Long Black Coat" could only have arisen from the bayou.

Lanois set up a makeshift studio in a Victorian mansion on Soniat Street and went to the mat regularly with one-take Bob over sound and style. As usual, Dylan wanted to get in and out quickly while his producer insisted on doing each song over and over until they got it right.

On his way to the studio each day, Dylan recalled passing by Lafayette Cemetery No. 1 where he paused to peruse the epitaphs. Fortified by a daily dose of voodoo, he submitted to his producer's badgering. Chiefly through Lanois's efforts, the magic gloom that hangs over New Orleans like Spanish moss eventually found its way on to *Oh Mercy*.

Dylan made the most of his Louisiana sojourn. He renewed his interest in sketching, rendering the decorative ironwork of French

Quarter balconies and the antebellum porches of the Garden District in both charcoal and pencil landscapes.[399] He purchased a big blue Harley to explore Cajun country and the swamps south of Lake Pontchartrain, escaping the studio the way he'd once escaped warehouse drudgery at Micka Electric by cycling off into the Mesabi Range.

In *Chronicles*, he wrote a travelogue as fanciful as his Village recollections of life with Ray Gooch and Chloe Kiel. Despite very specific *Chronicles* directions, no Dylanista has ever been able to locate King Tut's Museum: a roadside trinket emporium supposedly across a vacant field from "a gas station off Highway 90 near Raceland." Bob recalled hog jowls and cane baskets hanging from the same rafters as voodoo beads and votive candles. He allegedly found a "WORLD'S GREATEST GRANDPA" bumper sticker at the rear of King Tut's that he later slapped on the back of his pickup.

But the museum's oddest attraction was its owner—a slight, bespectacled outback original named Sun Pie. As with Ray Gooch's apartment, Dylan detailed with photographic precision King Tut's multilayered interior as well as his exact dialogue with its grizzled proprietor—"one of the most singular characters you'd ever want to meet." Sun Pie held Bob in thrall with his conviction that Native Americans descended from ancient Chinese who walked across the Bering Straits during the last Ice Age. Those same Chinese would soon return to subsume the West.

"You a praying man?" asked Sun Pie.

"Uh huh," answered Bob.

"Good," he said, "gonna have to be when the Chinese take over."

---

[399] In 2013 the Halcyon Gallery displayed "Mood Swings," a seven-piece series of iron gates welded by Dylan. He credits his Mesabi Range roots for inspiration: "I've been around iron all my life ever since I was a kid. I was born and raised in iron ore country—where you could breath it and smell it every day. And I've always worked with it in one form or another."

A conspiracy theorist to rival A. J. Weberman, Sun Pie was none-theless "the right guy to run into at the right time," according to Dylan. After whiling away an afternoon discussing everything from Bruce Lee to Kitty Wells, Dylan got back on his bike and headed to New Orleans. Fictitious or real, Sun Pie got the credit for inspiring Bob to mend fences with Lanois and finish *Oh Mercy*.

■■ ■■ ■■

The '89 edition of the Never Ending Tour kicked off in Sweden a week after Bob's 48th birthday and didn't pause until September at the Greek Theater in L.A. In all he played 72 dates, tacking on another 27 in the autumn and setting a pattern for breakneck touring over the next 20 years.

"To write is one thing and to sing is something completely differ-ent," said Bob. "One opposes the other and I can't write with the energy with which I perform and I can't perform with the same energy with which I write."

One hundred concerts a year became routine—a grueling pace that could level musicians half Dylan's age. Twenty years earlier, as a young man, he told *Chicago Tribune* reporter Hubert Saal, "If you take a show on the road you might as well be out for six or eight months and the test is if it will hold my interest for that long. To tell you the truth, right now it couldn't. It's hard out there. One plane to another, bad food, motel rooms, they herd you around. Europe is even worse. They have no heat. You have to sleep with hot water bottles to keep warm . . ."

Times had changed. In 1989, an older, wiser Dylan told Edna Gundersen he no longer had any qualms about hitting the road.

"Touring is part of playing," he said. "Anybody can sit in the studio and make records, but that's unrealistic and they can't possibly be a meaningful performer. You have to do it night after night to understand what it's all about. I've always loved to travel and play my songs, meet new people and see different places. I love to roll into town in the early morning and walk the deserted streets before anybody gets up. Love to see the sun come up over the highway."

Touring is also a showcase of dramatic ups and downs. The Dylan on display during the summer of '89 frequently cloaked himself in Unabomber ball cap, shades, and hooded parka, but was just as likely to show up in beret and gold lamé Elvis suit. He ordered the spotlight dimmed or shut off all together when he felt like singing in shadow. On those rare instances when fans did get a clear view, the lines and bags and creases on his face advertised dissipation.

Admission to a Dylan concert became a lottery ticket: one night might be a jackpot; the very next, a dud. Dylan played Atlantic City midsummer, inviting further Presley comparisons. One critic carped, "On the 20th anniversary of Woodstock the man who wrote 'money doesn't talk it swears' and meant it, sang for the first time in capitalism's playground."

John Bucklen caught the show in Wisconsin on one of the better nights. Zimmy's oldest Hibbing running buddy lived an hour north of Madison when he heard the Never Ending chatter on local radio: Bob Dylan was coming to town.

"My two teenage daughters said, 'If you *really* know Bob, how come you never see him?'" Taking up the challenge, Bucklen tracked down Dylan's L.A. booking agent. "I'm John Bucklen, a friend of his," he explained.

Right. So's everybody. Days passed. Bucklen figured that would be the end of it.

"The night of the concert, we were sitting at the table having supper," he said. "I hadn't heard anything. About 6 P.M. this Australian woman called, saying she was Bob's road manager. 'I have some backstage passes for you,' she told me."

Bucklen hustled the girls into the car and sped 70 miles to the Dane County Coliseum, arriving just before curtain time.

"G. E. Smith[400] was there," recalled Bucklen. "My daughter said, 'That's the guy on *SNL*.' She was more impressed meeting him than Bob. All of a sudden, the Australian woman came in. 'The king will see you now.'"

Bob looked tired but centered. He wrapped an arm around Bucklen and introduced him all around: "I've known this guy as long as anybody . . ."

During the mid-60s when Bob's career first kicked into high gear, Bucklen remembered meeting a very different Dylan. It was backstage in London; Bucklen was in England putting in his time with the military.

"He was all strung out, jittery then," he recalled—skinny, punked out, obviously speeding on some substance that controlled him more than he controlled himself.

"This time, he was more like he was in the beginning, more cordial, friendly, good to talk to, very mellow, very warm," said Bucklen. "He seemed very interested in what I had to say. We talked about old times. He was Bob, the old Bob, when Bob was at his best."

During the concert, Bucklen marveled at how far Elston Gunn had come. Bob duckwalked the stage like Chuck Berry. He flexed

---

[400] Dylan's bandleader from 1988 through 1990, George Edward Smith backed Hall and Oates before becoming musical director for *Saturday Night Live* (1985–1995).

his knees and kicked the air like Keith Richards. During a temporary power outage, Dylan kept his band jamming, segueing into "Shelter from the Storm"[401] as if nothing had happened. A consummate pro, he never had to say a word to keep his Bobcats mesmerized. When he sang, he was a North Country ranger who'd caught the last train for the coast and lived to tell the tale.

Bucklen didn't know how he did it, night after night in a different city in front of a different crowd. On the drive home, he shared his awe with his daughters. It was almost as if Bob had discovered the secret of the Fountain of Youth or the portrait of Dorian Gray. Maybe both.

■■ ■■ ■■

"I never got hooked on any drug—not like you'd say, uh, 'Eric Clapton: his drug period,'" Dylan declared as he lit another Marlboro.

By the late '80s, drug and alcohol abuse no longer carried the same stigma it had when Bobby Zimmerman first hit the bottle. Alcohol and Narcotics Anonymous meetings were everywhere. Betty Ford dried out celebrities by the dozens, lending increased credibility to nationally known rehab centers like Minnesota's Hazelden, which had been advertising itself since 1947 as "a sanatorium for curable alcoholics of the professional class." Marianne Faithful cleaned up her act there. Dylan took notice in *Chronicles*, applauding her sobriety. The *shandeh* of being "drunk as a goy" was something he never discussed about himself, however.

In the fall of '89, before setting out once more on his Never Ending Tour, Dylan performed during the annual Lubavitch Telethon

---

[401] Dylan once told Robert Shelton that the lyrics of this song were "the story of my life."

benefitting the drug and alcohol rehab efforts of Chabad House. Three years earlier, he'd taped an antidrug message for Chabad's "L'Chaim To Life," but this time he showed up in person with his new son-in-law, Peter Himmelman, and actor Harry Dean Stanton. The trio called themselves Chopped Liver and performed three Jewish folk tunes, climaxing with "Hava Negilah." Dylan, whom Himmelman introduced as Moishe Rubenstein, wore a yarmulke, played the flute, and spoke not a word.

Dodge and parry. Make up for a bad night by doing better the next. Each performance became another shot at redemption. There were sightings: Dylan on a bicycle, Dylan in a public swimming pool, Dylan ducking into a convenience store. He once rented an entire gym after midnight so he could work out in private. He kept moving: Houston, Norfolk, Poughkeepsie . . .

Late in October, a pair of Brits cornered him in a hotel room in Narragansett, Rhode Island. They were fanzine journalists who made the most of their interview while bemused Bob poured champagne for himself and a blonde he never bothered to introduce. One of Dylan's two Great Danes[402] ("a rhinoceros in a dog suit") carefully eyed the intruders. Like so many who had come before, the intrepid journalists alternately fawned and cajoled, hoping for the key to what made Bobby run, but the best they came away with was that he was a sloppy eater (smear of baked beans on his sweatshirt), liked *The Food Network* (a chunky baker on a soundless widescreen made Swiss rolls throughout the interview), and implied that a '60s Fleet Street gadfly named Max Jones was the inspiration for "Ballad of a Thin Man."

He did give his desperate interrogators what turned out to be the enduring title for his ongoing exercise in stage therapy.

---

[402] Brutus and Baby.

"Tell me about the live thing," said one of the reporters. "The last tour has gone virtually straight into this one."

"Oh, it's all the same tour," said Bob. "The Never Ending Tour . . ."

"What's the motivation to do that?"

"Well, it works out better for me that way. You can pick and choose better when you're just out there all the time and your show is already set up. You know, you just don't have to start it up and end it. It's better just to keep it out there with breaks, you know, with extended breaks."

Dylan acknowledged that one lousy night might follow another filled with magic, but took no responsibility for the difference. His Never Ending Tour relied as heavily on the audience as it did the band. But wasn't Bob the one who controlled the music, the pace, the staging? Distracted by the drama of a Swiss roll rising on the TV screen, Dylan mumbled, "It's hard to say. It's hard to say. It's the crowd that changes the songs."

■ ■ ■

Despite his never-ending efforts to reconnect, by the close of the '80s most early Dylan fans had moved on. Bob's Pied Piper groundswell peaked in '66 and had ebbed ever since with only the occasional flash of brilliance. And yet, despite a string of bad albums, spotty concert appearances, and a closely guarded personal life, those loyalists who truly believed in the cult of Bob transubstantiated their faith into something approaching zeal. *Life* magazine named him among the twentieth century's 100 most important figures. Dylanology found its way into university coursework and scholarly journals where academics fanned metaphor into parable. Cambridge musicologist Wilfrid Mellers labeled Dylan "a shaman in relation to the Global Village's tribe: his songs are ritual as well as art."

A bumper crop of explication, interpretation, and biography appeared. *Isis, On the Tracks,* and *The Bridge* would soon join early fanzines *The Telegraph, The Wicked Messenger,* and *Wanted Man* in dissecting Bob minutiae. Indeed, Bobcats had taken to greeting each other, "In Bob we trust." Had he more megalomania about him, Dylan might have become L. Ron Hubbard, Jim Jones, or Joseph Smith.

Robert Shelton finally published *No Direction Home: The Life and Music of Bob Dylan* to near universal acclaim in the mid-80s: "Absorbing" . . . "a great success" . . . "detailed and perceptive." Even Shelton's stodgy alma mater, *The New York Times* grudgingly called *No Direction Home* a "creditable overview."

"No journalist has covered Mr. Dylan's career longer or with more respect than Robert Shelton," observed the reviewer Don McLeese. Years of fine-tuning put the bio on the bestseller list, but respect turned out to be *No Direction Home*'s biggest flaw.

"A lonely man with money is still lonely," Dylan told Shelton back in 1964 when *No Direction Home* first began taking shape. Two years later, Bob added a personal coda: "It's always lonely where I am."

"It's difficult to recall protracted periods when Dylan has been happy," Shelton concluded. It didn't take readers long to reappraise his exhaustive study as hagiography. The Dylan they met in the pages of *No Direction Home* had no recurring drinking, drug, or women problems. Shelton barely mentioned Bob's tug-of-war between Judaism and Jesus, didn't say how he spent his millions, but did disclose that he surrounded himself with family and friends, some from as far back as Camp Herzl—hardly a revelation.

Above all, *No Direction Home* exalted Bob as a serious artist, not some pop hack out to make a buck. For boomers who hadn't been paying attention because they were cashing in on their own American Dreams, *No Direction Home* reaffirmed Bob's place in their lives. Fans who hadn't picked up a Dylan disc in a decade bought the book. They scoffed at the hero worship, but began to remember once more why Bob mattered.

In England where he'd never stopped mattering, Dylanology had become a cottage industry. Well before A. J. Weberman's first dumpster dive, British chroniclers had been parsing Bob's life and poetry. Music historian Michael Gray launched the movement in 1973 with *Song and Dance Man: The Art of Bob Dylan*, revising each subsequent edition until the book weighed 3.2 pounds and was only superseded in bulk and word count by Gray's exhaustive *Bob Dylan Encyclopedia*.[403]

Gray's great rival Clint Heylin originally wrote his *Bob Dylan: Behind the Shades* as just another biography but transformed later editions into an 800-page oral history. Along the way, Heylin published a half dozen other Dylan studies, including *Revolution in the Air* and *Still on the Road*, a two-volume explication of every known Bob song dating all the way back to 1957.

Back in the U.S., Paul Williams matched Heylin's prodigious output with his own year-by-year, concert-by-concert, song-by-song examination of Dylan's career, eventually publishing a trilogy entitled *Bob Dylan: Performing Artist*. Completing the decade's Dylan deluge was another American biography—this one written by Bob Spitz, a former manager for both Springsteen and Elton John. Taking Anthony Scaduto's withering skepticism up another notch, Spitz tended toward sacrilege. He later admitted his sarcasm went too far

---

[403]   Published in 2008 and revised periodically as more Dylan esoterica comes to light, the latest edition weighed 3.6 pounds and was 756 pages long.

too often, but never regretted his approach. Through luck, circumstance, and design, he argued, Bob had been deified. Among his most ardent admirers, Dylan stood somewhere between Shakespeare and the Dalai Lama. Spitz set out to test his divinity. He came away with a precocious portrait of an artist as a young rebel whose extraordinary capacity for observation, synthesis, and self-promotion put him at the vanguard of boomer cynicism.

On a wall above his desk, the author kept a framed detention sheet that a junior high instructor once made Bobby Zimmerman write. Acquired during one of Spitz's Hibbing expeditions, the handwritten and signed objet d'art proclaimed over and over, some 50 times, that Bobby would no longer lie or misbehave in class. It became a permanent reminder to Spitz that, at an age when young Jesus lectured rabbis in the Temple, Zimmy was fibbing, acting out, and talking back to his own elders.

Bart Simpson or the Messiah? Hard to say.

PART IV

SOMETIMES A MAN MUST BE ALONE

1989–Present

Art is anything you can get away with.

—Marshall McLuhan

17

TROUBLE AHEAD, TROUBLE BEHIND

On the first day of the first February of the new decade, Dylan met Leonard Cohen for coffee at a Parisian café.[404] It was cold and dark and drizzly along the Left Bank, but cozy and anonymous indoors, just as it once had been during the dead of winter at the Kettle of Fish in Greenwich Village or the L&B Café in Hibbing: a quiet cocoon where a couple of Jewish misfits could get a slice of cherry pie, kick back, and chew the fat. The cuisine, locale, and era might have changed, but the conversation remained curiously similar. Both drifters had survived half a century of drugs and loose women,[405] success and failure, and a mutual lust for more experience, more wisdom, more fruit from the twin trees of Knowledge and Life.

Cohen's songs were "almost like prayers," observed Dylan.

Leonard held a similar opinion of Bob's music. Both men had moved from spiritual quest to spiritual quest over a lifetime, their shifting beliefs spilling into verse. Each had dabbled in yoga, Christianity, mystical Judaism, and all manner of drink and mind-altering substances; Cohen once told a *USA Today* reporter it took him a

---

[404] Besides taking his Never Ending Tour to Europe, Dylan was in Paris to become the third American after T. S. Eliot and Lillian Gish honored by the French government with the *Commandeur dans L'Ordre des Arts et des Lettres*.

[405] On Cohen's 1977 album *Death of a Ladies' Man*, Dylan and Allen Ginsberg backed him on "Don't Go Home with Your Hard-On."

decade to recover from his LSD abuse. He would soon quit pop music all together to join a Zen Buddhist monastery.

Extolling the exquisite rhyme of "Hallelujah," Bob wanted to know how long it had taken Cohen to write his masterful hymn to God, sex, and salvation.

"A couple of years," Cohen replied. It had actually taken much longer, but he kept that to himself. He didn't like to boast. In turn, he praised "I and I" and asked Bob how long it took to write.

"Fifteen minutes," said Bob.

Dazzled, Leonard assumed Dylan spoke the truth. What would be the point of exaggerating? He'd never thought of being in any sort of competition with Bob. If anything, he bowed to a master who could compose ballads without a second thought.

"Bob Dylan is a figure that arises every three or four hundred years," he intoned. "He represents and embodies all the finest aspirations of the human heart. He is unparalleled in the world of music and will remain a torch for all singers and all hearts for many generations to come."

Dylan was never so eloquent in praise of Cohen, or any other peer for that matter. In a far-ranging soliloquy, however, he did acknowledge just what sort of person aspires to the lyrical life:

> Poets don't drive cars. Poets don't go to the supermarket. Poets don't empty the garbage. Poets aren't on the PTA. Poets, you know, they don't go picket the Better Housing Bureau, or whatever. Poets don't . . . poets don't even speak on the telephone. Poets don't even talk to anybody. Poets do a lot of listening and . . . and they usually know why they're poets.

Dylan insisted he just entertained for a living. He drove his own Ford and bought his own groceries at the Co-Op. He took out the garbage when there was no maid service. He dutifully showed up at Santa Monica's Wildwood School for parents' meetings. When his kids were younger, he attended soccer practice and recitals. He slept on the couch in his underwear, just like any other dad.

Real poets, on the other hand, "live on the land," he said. "They behave in a gentlemanly way. And die broke. Or drown in lakes. Poets usually have very unhappy endings." Dylan had a very different goal in mind: sell music and survive to sing another day.

"A lot of people want to write Bob Dylan off," said Cohen. "I'm not one of them. Doesn't matter if Bob takes a ten-year rest.[406] Doesn't matter. First of all, if Bob never sang again he's got a catalog of work that will ensure his reputation into the next millennium. But I don't think that's the case anyway. I think he is Picasso.[407] I think he's resting."

He certainly rested after the modest success of *Oh Mercy*. Despite an all-star supporting cast that included George Harrison, Elton John, and Stevie Ray Vaughn,[408] Dylan recorded *Under the Red Sky* in the spring of 1990 to near universal revulsion. The selected single "Wiggle, Wiggle"[409] is still cited as Dylan's worst song ever.

---

[406] Cohen's popularity also tanked in the '70s and didn't recover until the 1988 release of *I'm Your Man*.

[407] In terms of "exuberance, range and assimilation of the whole history of music," Cohen likened Dylan to the Spanish master who plagiarized with glee. "When there is something to steal," said Picasso, "I steal."

[408] Vaughn died in a Wisconsin helicopter crash after a concert that summer, prompting a rare eulogy from Dylan: "He'll probably be revered as much as and in the same way as Hank Williams."

[409] *Wiggle, wiggle, wiggle, like a bowl of soup*
   Wiggle, wiggle, wiggle like a rolling hoop

The usually hypercritical Robert Christgau actually liked *Under the Red Sky,* once he learned that he dedicated it to Dylan's four-year-old daughter Desireé Gabrielle. But Bobcats demanded solemn, not silly. At the time of the album's release, they remained ignorant that their hero had remarried or had a second family.

"The Dylan myth does not conform to silliness," said Christgau. "It does not tolerate the Prophet being silly."

Bob remained at odds with his myth, confounding those who sought an answer to the Meaning of Life. He began the new decade swimming in silly. Absent the late Roy Orbison,[410] Dylan and fellow Wilburys "Spike" (George Harrison), "Muddy" (Tom Petty), and "Clayton" (Jeff Lynne) recorded *Traveling Wilburys Volume III*[411] about the same time that "Boo" Wilbury[412] produced *Under the Red Sky.*[413] The results were equally vapid, though Dylan didn't seem to care. As if to underscore his scorn for Bob the Profound, he even paired up with Michael Bolton that summer.

"I got a phone call from a woman who works with him," recalled Bolton, "and they said, 'We know you're in town. Bob would like to write a song with you.' I thought it was a friend of mine playing a trick on me. It took a moment to sink in."

A '70s rocker who'd reinvented himself as pop lounge lizard, Bolton drove out to the Point Dume compound the following day for what he later described as "an out of body experience."

---

[410] Orbison died of a heart attack two and a half weeks before Christmas in 1988, just as his Traveling Wilbury success revived his long moribund pop career. Gone at 52, Orbison was one more reminder to 49-year-old Dylan that the clock was ticking.

[411] The slight sequel to *Volume One* skipped directly to *Volume Three* because, as Harrison explained it, bootleggers got their hands on outtakes from the original sessions and had already produced *Volume Two.*

[412] Like his fellow Wilburys, Bob switched names on the new LP, from "Lucky" to "Boo."

[413] Using yet another pseudonym, Dylan listed the LP's producer as "Jack Frost."

"He is kind of our musical Shakespeare," said Bolton. "He was such a pleasure to work with. As soon as he started talking to me I went into outer space. I kind of just lost it and thought, 'Oh my God—he really *is* Bob Dylan!'"

A friend warned Bolton to write well or he'd never hear from Bob again. The result of their one-day session was "Steel Bars," which Bolton recorded for Columbia the following year. The slight love anthem achieved modest success as a single in 1991, but apparently not enough for a reprise. Bolton never got a second summons to Xanadu.

⁛ ⁛ ⁛

After nine months on the market, Dylan's two-story boyhood home sold that August for $84,000—twice its appraised value.

"Well, they better check the furnace," quipped Bob.

After long spurning its native son, his hometown once more warmed to Dylan. The new owners of the old Zimmerman place commissioned a portrait of Bob as featured on the cover of *Blood on the Tracks*, using their garage door as a canvas. In honor of his upcoming 50th birthday, old friends, classmates, and neighbors contributed Bob memorabilia to a special Dylan room in the basement of the public library. There were alleged Bob sightings from time to time along Howard Street. Some heard he'd purchased or leased a summer cabin at nearby Side Lake. Echo Helstrom Fernandez Casey, now a divorcée working at a California film studio, got a call from him one day out of the blue. Just checking in, he told her.

"The call of the decade," she said. "He calls each decade."

But true to his myth, he never announced or confirmed any return to the North Country. His Hanover farm remained a secret as did his mother's St. Paul home, where he visited often.

When he wasn't on the road, Malibu remained home base. California was at the dawn of a real estate boom and Dylan was in the thick of it. He began a side business of buying, refurbishing, and reselling properties. Along suburban streets like Alta and Euclid Avenues in Santa Monica, he put Victor Maymudes in charge of flipping houses. The distinguishing characteristic of each remodel was huge hedges that Dylan ordered planted so pedestrians could not peek inside. Among the epithets A. J. Weberman had once flung at him, one in particular now seemed to have stuck—Dylan had, indeed, become "the singing real estate broker."

In Beverly Hills, he reportedly subsidized his cousin Beth Zimmerman's high-end kids' clothing store, Forever Young, while Stan Golden,[414] another cousin, set up a dental practice in Brentwood festooned with photos of his famous relative. Dylan remained generous with family, frugal with friends, and used purse strings to exact silence about his life as a Zimmerman.

He insisted on staying in touch with the common man, but it became harder and harder to separate himself from his persona. During interviews, he often referred to "Bob Dylan" in the third person.

"When you go to a movie with him, he shifts seats all the time," said Ronnie Hawkins.

Hobbled by notoriety, he waited until dark, routinely disguising himself when venturing into Santa Monica blues clubs or cabarets farther north along Pacific Coast Highway.

And yet Dylan constantly looked for signs and runes among the hoi polloi. Reading about something or seeing it on TV or hearing it on radio was never the same as sampling public opinion. Taking

---

[414] Dr. Golden was the one who'd found Howard Alk's body at Rundown Studios, identified him for cops and the coroner, and subsequently assumed many of Alk's gofer duties for Bob throughout the '80s.

what he could gather from coincidence was not just a line from one of his songs. He'd don ball cap or parka and strike up random bus stop conversations now and again along Montana Avenue, taking notes, trolling for another Sun Pie, until a glimmer of recognition ended the conversation.

The topic d'jour that summer was Saddam Hussein's invasion of Kuwait. Just as Hal Lindsey had predicted in *The Late Great Planet Earth*, war loomed again in the Middle East. With the fall of the Berlin Wall, the forecast for the West grew gloomier, not better. A new word began creeping into headlines: terrorism. Dylan adopted a told-ya-so attitude.

"The world is scheduled to go for 7,000 years," he preached. With the first six millennia nearly history, all that remained was the finale when Jesus would return to call the shots. The worst move any mortal could make was to promote his own legacy, according to Bob. Legend and legacy were pure hubris and Biblical synonyms for Satan. He wanted no part of it.

"If [fans] remember me at all, it's devilish, because that means that there's been a legacy left, and you don't want to leave a legacy," he warned in a radio interview with his publicist, Elliot Mintz. "If you try to attain some type of righteousness in this world, you don't want to leave a legacy."

He made no further attempt to save souls. Mostly, he left Jesus off his playlist entirely. The closest Bob came to issuing a public alarm about the coming Messianic Age was a performance of Curtis Mayfield's "People Get Ready" that he had contributed to the soundtrack of a Dennis Hopper movie.[415] Mostly, he let his choice of venue and music deliver his message.[416]

On the occasion of the late Dwight Eisenhower's 100th birthday, he played West Point.[417] The media made much of his visit to the training ground for America's military-industrial establishment, but cadets not yet been born when Bob wrote his first protest songs attached no great significance to "Masters of War."[418] Dylan was just another pop star passing through. Similarly a few weeks later, Ole Miss undergrads heard him perform "Oxford Town" for the first and only time since the '60s, but for them, the civil rights movement was history. They cared less about his passé message than they did his boozy performance.

As the year wound to a close, it became excruciatingly clear that Dylan had slipped off the wagon again. At one stop, handlers had to walk him around the parking lot before a concert. At another, he dropped his guitar twice and wandered offstage in the middle of "Positively Fourth Street." His granite scowl cracked. He slurred and mumbled incoherently when he wasn't babbling out of earshot all together. In the coming months when he sang "Desolation Row," his voice broke twice at the line "he was famous long ago." He had to step away from the microphone to compose himself before continuing.

---

[415] In the action comedy *Flashback* (1990), aging hippie Hopper cons an FBI agent (Kiefer Sutherland) assigned to arrest him for crimes committed during the hallucinogenic '60s. The two find a common enemy in a relentless sheriff bent on putting both in jail.

[416] As with Rick Nelson and "Lonesome Town," he commemorated Stevie Ray Vaughn's death in a helicopter accident with a cover of "Moon River."

[417] Growing up, Dylan briefly flirted with attending West Point following his fascination with military history in Charles Miller's classes at Hibbing High.

[418] Sang without the line "Even Jesus would never forgive what you do," an edit that dated from 1980, shortly after Bob decided Jesus forgave everybody everything.

When Dylan took his N.E.T. to Europe that winter, his behavior worsened. Paul McCartney ran into him at Heathrow and didn't recognize him at first. Beneath his ever-present hoodie, Dylan "was really like a kind of bagman," recalled the ex-Beatle. Even loyalists like Dylan encyclopedist Michael Gray conceded Dylan had been drinking to excess. Following a particularly dismal Glasgow concert, *Melody Maker* critic Allan Jones was even more blunt:

"Dylan now resembles nothing so much as an alcoholic lumberjack on a Saturday night out in some Saskatchewan backwater, staggering around the stage here in a huge plaid jacket and odd little hat. . . . Dylan, hilariously, doesn't seem to give a fuck."

At some gigs he'd play for hours, hitting every note, delighting audiences with old and new compositions, an occasional cover, and a masterful dexterity on guitar, mouth harp, and keyboard; other nights, he garbled everything from words to notes and left the stage before the first hour was over. Alcohol seemed his one common denominator.

What neither fans nor close friends knew was that he'd once again blown up a marriage: Carolyn Dennis-Dylan had just filed for dissolution. [419] Scorched by the media during his first divorce, Dylan ascertained no detail would leak the second time around. Indeed, no one was yet aware he'd even married. Instead, he displayed his angst in bizarre, boozy behavior on stage and off, for all the world to see.

In February 1991, four months shy of his 50th birthday, Dylan received the Lifetime Achievement Award from the National Academy of Recording Arts and Sciences. In the 30 years since his

---

[419] In *Out of the Dark Woods*, his 2011 study of Dylan's ongoing struggle with his Judeo-Christian faith, physician and national British health commissioner Dr. A. T. Bradford concluded Dylan plunged into clinical depression following his divorce and did not fully recover until after the release of *Time Out of Mind* six years later.

eponymous debut album, he'd sold more than 30 million LPs, 21 of them certified gold by the Recording Industry Association of America. More than 2,000 performers had covered his songs. Whether or not he meant to leave a legacy, his devilish work was already done. It was now being ratified on national TV.

Before accepting his Grammy, Dylan and his band delivered an unrecognizable high-speed performance of "Masters of War." Later interpreted as a slam at George H. W. Bush and the first Gulf War, most in the audience didn't even know what he was singing. Some thought he was speaking in Yiddish.

Clad in white fedora and maroon sports coat, Dylan looked a little like a dissipated version of Batman's Joker. Following the incomprehensible "Masters of War," the Joker himself introduced Dylan to the Grammy crowd. As he'd done five years earlier during Live Aid, a slavishly deferential Jack Nicholson piled on the plaudits: Voice of a Generation, Poet and Paradox, Conscience of the World . . .

While Nicholson waxed on, Dylan fidgeted at his side, juggling his Lifetime Achievement plaque. When his moment arrived, he stepped to the microphone and spoke these cryptic words:

> Thank you . . . well . . . all right . . . yeah, well, my daddy he didn't leave me too much . . . you know he was a very simple man and he didn't leave me a lot but what he told me was this . . . what he did say was . . . son . . . he said uh . . . he said so many things ya know . . . he said you know it's possible to become so defiled in this world that your own mother and father will abandon you, and if that happens God will always believe in your own ability to mend your ways. Thank you.

Dissected and interpreted many times thereafter, his Woody-esque declaration seemed unrehearsed, though clearly it was not. Bob biographer Seth Rogovoy traced its origins to a nineteenth-century German rabbi who elaborated on an Old Testament Psalm that promised God's love no matter what:

> Even if I were so depraved that my own mother and father would abandon me to my own devices, God would still gather me up and believe in my ability to mend my ways.[420]

Dylan later declared that the Grammys "felt like attending my own funeral." He blamed his poor performance and odd acceptance speech on the flu: "The inside of my head was feeling like the Grand Canyon or something."

While he might shuffle and twitch like a junkie, Dylan had not yet become so depraved that his own mother abandoned him. Beatty Rutman was his date at the Grammy after-party.[421]

The following day, however, no one could get to him to find out what the hell his acceptance speech meant. Once more playing the media like a coy Pavlov, he instructed Elliott Mintz to tell reporters that he'd retreated to "a tropical island with no telephones."

And nothing was revealed.

■ ■ ■

In a review of Bob's latest album release later that spring, the *San Diego Union*'s George Varga wrote again about Bob's boozing: "A

---

[420] Rabbi Shimshon Rafael Hirsch interpreting Psalm 27:10—"When my father and mother abandon me, God will gather me up."

[421] When Beatty saw a video of her son's performance, she reportedly commented, "That's nice. Bob's wearing a new sport coat."

small but savvy group of music industry insiders, including one musical collaborator, are now privately expressing alarm about Dylan and what they describe as his growing drinking problem."

The LP itself, on the other hand, was a sobering eye-opener. *Bootleg Series Vol. 1–3 Rare and Unreleased 1961–1989* showcased for the first time nearly a dozen original gems that hadn't made the cut on earlier and far more inferior albums. Brilliant ballads like "Blind Willie McTell"[422] and "Angelina" proved hands down that Leonard Cohen was right: Dylan never lost his touch. He simply couldn't judge what was good and what was awful.

Originally recorded for *Oh Mercy,* "Series of Dreams" was one such jewel released as a *Bootleg Series* single and an MTV music video. Prior to his notorious acceptance speech, a few sequences aired during the Grammys. Against a Phil Spector–like baseline akin to the Crystals' "And Then He Kissed Me," the rambling lyrics sounded like a patient confessing to his shrink. In four uneven and barely rhyming stanzas, Bob allowed a brief, harrowing glimpse inside his skull, where "there's no exit in any direction 'cept the one that you can't see with your eyes . . ."

Six years earlier in an interview with author Bill Flanagan, he attempted to articulate the difference between dreams and fantasies:

"When you sit around and you *imagine* things to do and to write and to think—that's fantasy," he said. "I've never been much into that. Anybody can fantasize. Little kids can, old people can; everybody's got the right to their own fantasies. But that's all they are. Fantasies. They're not *dreams*. A dream has more substance to it

---

[422] "I didn't think I recorded it right," he told *Rolling Stone,* his only explanation for dropping the song from *Infidels.*

than a fantasy, because fantasies are usually based on nothing, they're based on what's thrown into your imagination."

Bob's fantasies graduated to dreams, he insisted, because of their moral subtext which he tried to pass on to his audience. "I'm a messenger. I get it. It comes to me so I give it back in my particular style."

His style for the remainder of 1991 was to remain a moving target. He returned to Europe, hopscotched the U.S., and toured South America for the first time, finding his anonymity in Brazil and Argentina especially appealing. He gave few interviews and stayed hidden from view. Bob traveled in one tour bus; his band traveled in another. The sidemen and the boss stayed in different hotels and rarely fraternized.

"This is just where he lives now," Albert Lloyd wrote in *L.A. Weekly*. "It's no act. He walks the walk. He sings like a man who can't sleep at night."

At year's end, Sotheby's auctioned off[423] several of his earliest songs, including "Talkin' New York" and "Talkin' Bear Mountain Picnic Massacre Blues." Typed by Bob himself in various Greenwich haunts at the dawn of the '60s, some had never been recorded. They included titles like "Dope Fiend Robber," "V.D. Seaman's Last Letter," "California Brown-Eyed Baby," "Over the Road," "Crying Holy to the Frost" and "Don't." Like Hank Williams and Woody Guthrie, Dylan seemed destined to leave an unrecorded trove for future generations to sift through. As 1991 rolled over into 1992, no plan emerged to put any of them on a new LP of Bob originals. For all his never-ending stage presence, he removed himself further and further from his fan base.

---

[423] Two years hence, a prerelease copy of *Freewheelin'* containing the banned "Talkin' John Birch Paranoid Blues," sold at auction for more than $10,000.

"It's music as a game of three-card Monte," observed Greil Marcus, who compared Dylan to a Pied Piper leading fans into a forest only to abandon them. "For more than ten years, he has had more in common with a dead blues singer or old-time ballad singer than any contemporary."

Bob had never tried to be pop's flavor of the month. Metallica, Garth Brooks, MC Hammer, even Kenny G sold circles around him. Nirvana hit in '91 with *Nevermind,* eventually selling more than 35 million CDs. By comparison, *Under the Red Sky* topped out at 300,000.

While grunge resurrected rock from a decade of Madonna and Michael Jackson, Nirvana still smelled like a teen sales pitch to Bob. He called most of the new music he heard artless corporate noise.

"People today are still living off the table scraps of the '60s," he said. "They are still being passed around—the music, the ideas."

His old Greenwich guru Dave Van Ronk blamed Bob. "We were sitting around a few years ago, and he was bitching and moaning: 'These kids don't have any classical education,'" he said. "He was talking about the stuff you find on the *Anthology* [*of American Folk Music*]. I kidded him: 'You've got a lot to answer for, Bro.'"

Bob had no stomach for '60s sentiment.

"I'd rather live in the moment than some kind of nostalgia trip, which I feel is a drug, a real drug that people are mainlining. It's outrageous. People are mainlining nostalgia like it was morphine. I don't want to be a drug dealer."

During his sober moments, Dylan agreed. He'd rather channel Alan Lomax than rehash his greatest hits. He launched the "Strikin' It Rich" label with the intent of unearthing rarely heard rhythm and blues, but its only release turned out to be *Christmas Party with Eddie G!,* a bizarre holiday novelty CD equally influenced by Dr. Demento and Harry Smith.

A rising TV gag writer, Eddie Gorodetsky first captured Dylan's attention with an annual mixed tape he distributed each Christmas as a gift among friends.

"People will listen to anything if you put sleigh bells on it," observed Gorodetsky.

A template for Dylan's own future *Theme Time Radio Hour*, the album interspersed Eddie G's running quips among such oddities as Rufus Thomas's "I'll Be Your Santa Baby," Louis Prima's "What Will Santa Claus Say (When He Finds Everybody Swingin')?," and "All I Want for Christmas Is You" by Foghat. Though Dylan coaxed Columbia to distribute *Christmas Party,* it sold *nada*.[424] *Christmas Party* cemented his relationship with Gorodetsky, however. Their twin interests in the peculiar, hilarious, dark and brooding sounds of old, weird America would not fade away.

Bob took another shrewd step into the past with the creation of Special Rider Music, his umbrella publishing arm. He apparently borrowed the name from Mississippi bluesman Skip James's "Special Rider Blues." Best known for "I'm So Glad,"[425] James made as indelible an impression on Dylan as Robert Johnson, Charlie Patton, or any of a dozen other early black troubadours. A year before Bob went electric, the sick and dying James crossed Dylan's path for the first and only time when he was "rediscovered"[426] at the 1964 Newport Folk Festival. Dylan recalled verbatim James's stage advice: "I don't want to entertain," he said. "What I want to do is impress with skill and deaden the minds of my listeners."

---

[424]   . . . as Augie Rios might have put it in *Christmas Party*'s "Donde Esta Santa Claus?"

[425]   Covered by Eric Clapton on *Fresh Cream* (1966).

[426]   First recorded in 1931, James vanished from view for a generation until folk revivalists found him in a Mississippi hospital and brought him to Newport. Testicular cancer killed him five years later at 67.

Designed to hold copyright to all his music, Special Rider was the beginning of Bob consolidating his empire during the early '90s. Longtime business managers Ben and Naomi Saltzman were out and Jeff Rosen was in. With Rosen now firmly at the helm of his New York business headquarters (known among the *Bobnoscenti* as "The Office"), Special Rider became repository for all Dylan compositions, old and new. As copyrights either came up for renewal or were repurchased from Sally Grossman or one of Bob's other early collaborators, Special Rider became official publisher.

∷ ∷ ∷

Vacillating between bathos and alcohol, Bob sparred his way through 1992 either punch-drunk or cold sober but always hard to pin down. Asked during one interview what he'd like to learn from Hank Williams should Hank return from the dead, Dylan deadpanned, "I'd wanna know where he got his drugs from."

Dylan got more deeply into boxing at home as a way to sweat out toxins, stay fit, and relieve aggressions built up on the road. He hired former middleweight Bruce "Mouse" Strauss as a professional opponent. He worked the heavy bag, but didn't say much. He still took whisky with his coffee, but appeared to be eating better and sleeping more hours at the back of his tour bus. Mostly he remained cocooned inside his own head, constantly reviewing a series of dreams as he moved from Australia to Oakland to England, and back again.

In January, backed by Emmylou Harris, Chrissie Hynde, Mavis Staples, Carole King, and Roseanne Cash, he taped "Like a Rolling Stone" for David Letterman's 10th anniversary show. With so stellar a set of Supremes, no one seemed to care that his larynx had thickened and scarred with the varnish of a thousand Marlboros.

In May, a Not-So-Born-Again Bob returned to San Francisco's Warfield Theater for a Jerry Garcia concert. He watched from the sidelines and wouldn't join Garcia on stage, but two nights later when he played the same venue, Jerry snuck out from backstage. Garcia backed a delighted Dylan on "Cat's in the Well" and "Idiot Wind" while a bootlegging fan captured it all on digital video. As with hundreds of other concert tapes, this final performance of a solo Jerry jamming with Bob began circulating within days among hard-core Deadheads and Bobcats.

Through much of the previous decade, Dylan's growing security detail tried with diminishing success to keep recording equipment out of concerts. Like ticket scalpers and counterfeit T-shirt salesmen who worked the outside of each venue, surreptitious bootleggers continued to sneak their cameras and recorders inside. In the generation since the underground release of *The Great White Wonder*, fan-thieves found newer, smaller, more efficient devices with which to steal Bob's thunder. Since John Hammond first recorded "Song to Woody," audio had advanced from analog to digital and beyond.

Uncomfortable with high tech, Dylan owed Columbia a new album and quietly began recording in a fully equipped Chicago studio during a break in the Never Ending Tour. David Bromberg, a folk arranger he'd known since Village days, produced and played on the album, but after two weeks Bob rejected every track and started from scratch. Suspicious of any ear but his own, he laid down solo tracks that summer in the same garage where the Wilburys once convened.

He wanted a simple sound fans could enjoy from a cassette, not multitrack, overdubbed, and digitally mastered high fidelity. He tested the takes himself on his own car stereo. When an engineer suggested that he attach a separate mike to each guitar string, Dylan scoffed at the idea as "the height of insanity."

During his garage sessions, he ignored his own songs, covering instead the same sort of folk ditties that peppered his very first self-titled LP; not since *Self Portrait* had he laid down so many traditional tracks. *Good As I Been To You* represented a giant step backward to Dinkytown, when he first liberated Dave Ray's copy of the *Anthology of American Folk Music* and declared holy the cryptic lyrics of ancient song and celebration. Old weird America was making a comeback.

But those who could afford to attend his 30th anniversary concert at Madison Square Garden that October didn't know he was headed into the past. Tickets for "Columbia Records Celebrates the Music of Bob Dylan" sold from $50 to $150 apiece, and the audience demanded its money's worth.[427] Here was his original fan base all grown up, Yuppified and affluent, but primed to believe that the times still changed for the better. Mostly what they got were tributes from other artists—some connected to Bob, some not at all. Neil Young, Donald Trump, Tom Petty, and Pearl Jam were there; Joan Baez, Bruce Springsteen, and Van Morrison were not.

Friends and strangers performed for more than three hours before Dylan took the stage.

Like Garcia sneaking up at the Warfield, he materialized during the super session finale standing behind Petty, Young, George Harrison, Eric Clapton, and Roger McGuinn, each armed with his own guitar.

Dylan cleaned up well for the event, wearing a dark suit and open-collar dress shirt, hair teased into the instantly recognizable Jewfro of old. Beatty would have been proud. However damaged his voice had been ten months earlier on Letterman, it improved to a reedy

---

[427] Beyond the Hudson, thousands more paid $20 apiece for a pay-per-view version and, the following year, Sony released a double CD and video.

sotto voce on "It's All Right, Ma," "My Back Pages," "Knockin' on Heaven's Door," and a solo "Girl from the North Country."

When wall-to-wall boomers stood for a final ovation, their huzzahs and applause brought out an uncharacteristic smirk on the old stone face. Thirty years and counting, Dylan demonstrated he could still impress and deaden the minds of his audience. Nirvana, Pearl Jam, and Guns N' Roses might sell more records, but none challenged Bob's staying power.

Two weeks after his Madison Square triumph, Columbia released *Good As I Been To You*. Those who rushed to snap up the next chapter in the Never Ending saga came away puzzled and a little disappointed. Conditioned to expect at least one Bob original on every studio LP that had come before, fans found nothing new at all. *Good As I Been To You* conveyed Guthrie, Robert Johnson, the McPeake Family, and Skip James, but there wasn't one line on the album written by the poet laureate of pop.

"Presumably, Dylan did this in tribute to the originals," said Andrew Muir, who compared the contents of *Good As I Been To You* to ballads sung by other artists on previous recordings.

"If so, though," Muir continued, "it seemed strange that there were no credits on the sleeve notes and that the songs were copyrighted—rather laughably—as Dylan originals."

While Dylan acknowledged that the songs were traditional and presumably in the public domain, he copyrighted the arrangements as his own. A meticulous Dylanologist who chronicled the first decade of the Never Ending Tour, Muir tracked down and played the sources for each track on *Good As I Been To You*. Without exception, every one came from a previous recording. As with "House of the Rising Sun" which he lifted directly from Dave Van Ronk's Village stage act for his first album, Dylan cloned the work of others. This time he also claimed ownership.

Irish folkie Paul Brady first popularized the 1840 murder ballad "Arthur McBride" in the 1970s; British session guitarist Nic Jones recorded "Canadee-i-o," a nineteenth-century love song, on his 1980 LP *Penguin Eggs*; 80-year-old Texas minstrel Mance Lipscomb released "You're Gonna Quit Me" years before his death in 1976; the Celtic band De Dannan did a version of Stephen Foster's "Hard Times" that not only became the group's signature song but also sounded note for note the same on *Good As I Been To You . . .* and so on.

"This was a source of some disquiet," said Muir.

18
UNPLUGGING

Thirty years after the March on Washington, a boomer famous for toking without inhaling welcomed Bob back to the Lincoln Memorial for an encore. The times had indeed changed. Bob substituted filtered Camels for weed while Bill Clinton smoked nothing at all, spurning tobacco as had most of his generation. With the Clintons now occupying a healthier White House, the Big Band sound of the Greatest Generation also faded. Rock resonated in the halls of power. Zimmy no longer stood on the outside looking in.

On the occasion of Clinton's Inaugural, Dylan sang "Chimes of Freedom" on the National Mall backed by Quincy Jones and full orchestra, but later that night the nation's 42nd president invited 2,500 of his closest pals to a private "Blue Jeans Bash." Bob joined the four surviving Band members in providing a more down-home mode of entertainment. Denim and string ties superseded Reagan-Bush-era tuxes and gowns. Ice-sculpted Arkansas Razorbacks signaled a new menu for the presidential buffet: barbeque, catfish, hush puppies, and candied yams. Cowboy Bob fit right in.

Underscoring the power shift, Dr. John pounded out "Iko Iko" at the piano while Clarence Clemons praised the new commander-in-chief as a fellow sax player. With "For What It's Worth," Stephen Stills reminded the gathered that Vietnam and Watergate weren't exactly ancient history, but Dylan didn't dwell on the past. He partied down with "To Be Alone With You" and climaxed the whole hopeful evening with "I Shall Be Released."

Some weeks later an inquisitive Italian reporter observed, "For the first time, you have been on stage for a politician. Why?"

Stung by the obvious inconsistency, apolitical Bob stumbled. "It happened when (Clinton) had already been elected," he said. "I didn't help his electoral campaign. . . . Anyway, the fact is no one invited me there before."

Dylan's own constituency had undergone as subtle a shift as his politics. As many teens and college undergrads now attended N.E.T. concerts as Yuppies. While many a Dylan contemporary dismissed Generation X as headbanging losers, Bob saw promise.

"America gives a free license to destroy yourself at an early age," he said, "but what my eyes see and what my ears hear is that the young people aren't going for that . . . there are young people who are fed up with what they hear."

His own son numbered among them. Determined to step into his old man's boots, Jakob Dylan learned the folk basics in Bob's garage. With scant encouragement from his father, he cofounded the folk-rocking Wallflowers[428] in 1989. The group gigged regularly at Canter's Delicatessen in the Fairfax District of L.A. and, on the strength of Jakob's name, signed with Virgin Records. The Wallflowers' first album bombed. Virgin dropped the group just as quickly as they'd been signed. Like Bob, Jakob learned a hard business lesson early: pop is only recognized as art after the coffers are filled.

While the Wallflowers struggled, Bob delivered the final LP on his own most recent contract. Five years earlier, Sony bought Columbia Records for $2 billion. Though no one talked about dumping Dylan,

---

[428]   Bob recorded "Wallflower" by Etta James and Johnny Otis when Jakob was still in diapers. A simple blues about two misfits who find each other on the dance floor, it was the only Dylan song that David Blue ever declared a misfire.

the corporation did have two billion reasons to shed nonperforming assets. Bob needed a hit. Instead, he chose to deliver art.

Encouraged by the modest success of *Good As I Been To You,* he undertook a prequel in *World Gone Wrong*, digging even deeper into the subterranean mythology of America while at the same time praising his forbears.

"These people who originated this music," he declared, "they're all Shakespeares, you know."

Over the years, Dylan had become a big fan of the Bard's uncanny ability to dazzle with a phrase. "One line will come out like a stick of dynamite, and you'll be, 'so-what-was-*that?*'" he said. One girl-friend maintained he listened to Shakespeare on tape when falling asleep at night and put the playwright at the pinnacle of the five poets[429] Dylan held in highest regard.

As dense and thought-provoking as any Shakespearean soliloquy, the hoary folklore that first tantalized young Bobby Zimmerman had fully matured in the imagination of 52-year-old Bob Dylan. *World Gone Wrong* was his tribute to those early memories, conjuring just as much nightmarish magic as the three weird sisters in *Macbeth*. Every cut on the LP was a horror story.

Here, a woman died hideously at the hands of her lover; there, another kissed her man thrice before stabbing him in the heart and nodding off beside the rotting corpse. Ballads about gamblers and addicts and gruesome death haunted the tracks of *World Gone Wrong*.

"A mesmerizing and sanguinary walk down the blood-soaked history of folk and blues," wrote critic Bill Wyman. "Eerie and enticing," concluded Robert Christgau.

---

[429] William Wordsworth, William Blake, Lord Byron, and Percy Shelley were runners-up.

But Bob's back-to-back LPs of old folk ballads represented something more than a mere tribute to America's bluesy past. With *World Gone Wrong,* the Voice of a Generation officially signed off. Paul Williams wrote the epitaph.

"There was an era, famously, when a whole international generation found out who they were by the patterns their psyches perceived, individually and collectively, in Dylan's new batches of song-performances," he said. "That era is gone. . . ."

Critics might applaud his return to roots, but those who came of age humming "Blowin' in the Wind" did not, and the album sold poorly. No new songs from Bob meant no new sales from boomers. At long last, the Pied Piper had abandoned the children of the '60s. They were now on their own, left to fend, forage, and philosophize for themselves.

⸬ ⸬ ⸬

Stung by critics for failing to give proper credit on *Good As I Been To You,* Bob cited Doc Watson, Blind Willie McTell, and the New Lost City Ramblers among his sources for the arrangements on *World Gone Wrong.* Nonetheless, Special Rider again laid claim to the copyrights. As Bob cashed in on royalties, he continued to condemn Yuppie greed.

"Everywhere there are artificial shopping paradises and theme parks," he said.

Consumer goods and services held no such fascination for Dylan. During 1993, his Never Ending Tour would take him 'round the world in 80 shows, but to hear him tell it, he was the same homespun troubadour who once informed Studs Terkel, "My life is the street where I walk. That's my life—music. Guitar—that's my tool."

At the dawn of the Clinton Era, neither his faux romanticism nor his preachy condescension had changed much. According to Bob, most listeners didn't "get" the songs on *World Gone Wrong* because their minds were polluted with advertising.

"People are tied up making important decisions on whether to buy a Coke or a Pepsi," he scoffed.

While Dylan raged against Madison Avenue, the Beatles and the Rolling Stones had already sold out. As early as 1966, the Stones[430] were hawking Rice Krispies. The Beatles held out another 20 years, but by 1985, Ford Motor Co. had licensed "Help" for a TV spot urging car buyers to help themselves to a Mercury.

Two years later, the surviving members of the Fab Four belatedly got religion. It turned out to be Michael Jackson who briefly reunited Bob and the Beatles on the topic of music licensing. Jackson used his *Thriller* millions to buy the Beatles' early catalog and then licensed "Revolution" to sell Nike running shoes. Echoing Dylan's disdain, George Harrison sneered that, "Every Beatles song ever recorded is going to be advertising women's underwear and sausages."

Paul and Ringo concurred, joining George in suing to end Jackson's outrage.

"They don't have any respect for the fact that we wrote and recorded those songs, and it was our lives," lamented Harrison.

But his indignation faded after their injunction failed. Nike aired its commercial and two years later the remaining Beatles[431] settled out of court. Ironic perhaps, but "Spike" Wilbury shared in the

---

[430] Jagger, Richards, & Co. went on to hawk everything from Grey Goose vodka, Chanel perfume, Pepsi, and Corvettes to the Apple iMac ("She's a Rainbow") and Microsoft Windows ("Start Me Up").

[431] Beatles songs have routinely sold goods globally since, from smartphones to disposable diapers.

advertising proceeds while his brother "Lucky" Wilbury continued to swear that he'd *never* pander to Madison Avenue.

"The purpose of music is to elevate the spirit and inspire, not to help push some product down your throat," said Bob.

Dylan stuck to his convictions until the winter of '94, when Special Rider licensed Richie Havens's rendition of "The Times They Are a-Changin'" for a commercial that rhapsodized the accounting services of Coopers & Lybrand. A hue and cry rose among Bobcats. How could Dylan let this happen? It took another musician to point out the obvious.

"Woody Guthrie used to do commercials," said Andrew Cash.[432] "People forget that, but he did it all the time to make a living."

A year hence, Dylan himself would be singing "The Times They Are a-Changin'" on behalf of the Bank of Montreal. After that, he made no further public pretense about the commercial exploitation of his music.

It was hard to fault him. In addition to the times, the recording industry itself had undergone massive change. Even established pop stars had to generate new revenue streams.[433] The big black 33-1/3 LPs with which Bob launched his career now accounted for less than 2 percent of the $11 billion generated each year by the six major record companies.[434] The technology Bob hid from in his garage had taken over the business.

---

[432] A '90s rocker who gave up punk to make a successful run in 2009 for a seat in the Canadian Parliament.

[433] To this end, Jeff Rosen pioneered the prospect of future voicemail and ringtone sales by letting callers listen to "Forever Young" when they were put on hold or called "The Office" after hours.

[434] Time/Warner, Matsushita/MCA, Thorn/EMI, Philips-Polygram/PMG, Bertelsmann Music Group/BMG, and Sony/CBS, which distributed Dylan's venerable Columbia label.

Even audio tape was becoming passé. CDs surpassed cassette sales in 1993—a neon signpost to the twenty-first century.[435]

Up 24 percent from the previous year, music videos looked to be one of the few old-tech ways to make a buck while bucking the techno-trend. Dylan might defy the digital future,[436] but he still knew how to mug for a camera. Wearing top hat and waist coat, he starred as an Edwardian fop in a *World Gone Wrong* video, bringing him back before the all-important MTV audience. The video's success got him to thinking about unplugging.

Five years earlier in 1989, MTV launched a series that reversed Dylan's original logic in going electric. *Unplugged* meant just that: a different pop star went acoustic every week. Eric Clapton, Mariah Carey, Springsteen, McCartney, and Pearl Jam had all successfully unplugged. After *Good As I Been To You* and *World Gone Wrong,* Dylan appeared to be a natural.

In typical fashion, however, he demanded control. To that end, he financed a four-night stand at a New York night club, paying film crews out of his own pocket. He climaxed his *Unplugged* sessions with a surprise appearance on David Letterman's new CBS *Late Show* program, performing a much-praised rendition of "Forever Young." Once again, his music straddled the generations.

But without explanation, the fruits of his four nights in New York never aired. For whatever reason, Bob didn't approve the footage. He rehired the same film crew a year later to shoot three concerts in

---

[435]   In a prophetic analysis published that year in the *Journal of Cultural Economics*, Ohio Wesleyan professor Peter Alexander observed, "These new digital delivery systems may also lead to structural turbulence in a range of other culture-based industries, including newspapers, book publishing, and motion pictures among others."

[436]   The following summer, he sued Apple Computers for trademark infringement when the company released its Dynamic Language software DYLAN. Bob forced an out-of-court settlement.

Rochester, arranging to have a crowd rush the stage each night for a "documentary." Like the *Unplugged* footage, the faux stage rush never aired.

Long ago, D. A. Pennebaker taught him an indelible lesson about manipulating verité. If it's not perfect, burn it or bury it so deep that it would take a steam shovel to unearth. MTV would just have to wait. All that expensive film went into the vault along with *Eat the Document* and *Renaldo and Clara*, never to be seen again.

■ ■ ■

"A lot of people don't like the road, but it's as natural to me as breathing," Bob once told the *New York Times*. "I do it because I'm driven to do it, and I either hate it or love it. I'm mortified to be on the stage, but then again, it's the only place where I'm happy."

Whether a secret stint in rehab, 12-steps, or simply white-knuckling made the difference, Bob's benders went into remission after *World Gone Wrong*. He appeared to spend most of the fifth anniversary year of his Never Ending Tour sober, even triumphant on occasion, ranging the globe once again while performing more than 100 concerts over four continents.

The year's highlight was a three-day stand in Nara, Japan, on behalf of UNESCO where he hunkered down beneath the shadow of Vairocana, the world's largest bronze Buddha, backed by the Tokyo New Philharmonic Orchestra. Others on the bill included Joni Mitchell and INXS, but no one matched Dylan's symphonic omen about a hard rain soon to fall. The steady drone of strings, tympani, and woodwinds at his back, he built his postapocalyptic premonition to a crescendo using only his reedy whine to hammer home his warning.

"[He] really opens his lungs and heart and sings like he's not done for many a year," reported *Q* magazine. "The only word for it is majestic."

Three months later, 10 miles southeast of Max Yasgur's farm, he opened his lungs again and the clouds above responded. As with the original Woodstock Arts & Music Festival a quarter century earlier, the 25th anniversary[437] endured a summer rainstorm, but the 350,000 fans who turned out for the star-studded extravaganza got a special treat when Dylan appeared. Like some Sunday morning portent, the sun cracked through and Bob gave the Woodstock Nation what they'd been waiting decades to hear. One of the dozen songs he belted was, appropriately, "Rainy Day Women No. 12 + 35." When the Red Hot Chili Peppers followed him on stage, the summer deluge resumed.

Dylan unveiled no new LP in 1994, but he did publish a portfolio of sketches. In his forward to *Drawn Blank*, he revealed what he did to relax between concerts from 1989 through 1992, sharing 92 of his charcoal, pencil, and ink drawings[438] that evolved out of his N.E.T. travels.

"You have to commit a lot of time to it," he said.

The studies in black and white were more than a cut above the primitive marginalia Woody Guthrie scribbled on the pages of *Bound for Glory* or the doodling Dylan himself had added to his 1974 songbook, *Writings & Drawings*. From the kindergarten

---

[437] Co-produced by Richie Havens, the pay-per-view festival spawned an album and video and led to latter-day festivals like Lollapalooza, Bonnaroo, and Coachella, but provoked nowhere near the media hysteria of the original Woodstock.

[438] Only existing for public consumption in book form, Exeter's Castle Galleries announced in 2013 they would display 11 *Drawn Blank* pieces, six of them never before seen.

smears of *Big Pink* to *Self Portrait*,[439] he'd made fans vaguely aware
he had artistic aspirations, but after the bizarre album cover for
Planet Waves, no one outside of his ever-tightening circle knew or
cared much about Bob's artistic progress.

Chock-full of portraits, landscapes, and nudes, *Drawn Blank*
showed a serious craftsman at work. Not since he broke out the
sketch pad to draw BBC producer Christopher Sykes during the production of *Hearts of Fire* had Dylan demonstrated just how far he'd
come after his Norman Raeben apprenticeship. At a time when the
public still had no idea Dylan slept through much of the 1980s with
one or more of the Queens of Rhythm, *Drawn Blank* featured several zaftig black women—some clothed, some not—as well as a
series of sterile streetscapes, usually sketched from above as if he'd
worked from a hotel balcony or studied the avenue through the
anonymous safety of a third-floor window.

Critics were quick to cite the influence of Chagall, Van Gogh,
Matisse, and Picasso, though none of those modern maestros
detached themselves the way Bob did. Like a vacation photographer
who waits until everyone's out of his shot, Dylan's streets were as
vacant as the eyes of his human subjects. His still lifes were deadly
sterile.

Before the year was over, Dylan conceded to unplug for MTV.
Over two nights in mid-November, he ran through his greatest hits
at Sony Studios in New York accompanied only by an acoustic guitar and his five-man N.E.T. band. When he showed up for the taping,
he insisted on wearing shades but all trace of alcohol seemed absent.
MTV floor managers moved anyone with gray hair to the back of
the studio.

---

[439] He also painted the cover of *Sing Out!* that featured his interview with Happy
Traum and John Cohen.

The network edited the best of the sessions down to a tight two hours that aired in the U.S. on December 14. The soundtrack became Bob's first bona fide bestseller of the '90s, climbing to No. 23 on the *Billboard* charts. *Dylan Unplugged* not only gave him another gold record, it introduced the '60s folkie spirit to those Gen Xers who'd found no reason to buy *Good As I Been To You* or *World Gone Wrong*.

All in all, 1994 turned out to be the best year in Bob's long comeback from that wobbly Locarno night when he swore to stand, whether God sided with him or not. Like Jerry Garcia, Elvis, and his most recent role model, Frank Sinatra, he'd done it *his* way. In fact, 1994 might have been *the* banner year for Bob at the dawn of the Clinton era if an old girlfriend hadn't hired a familiar lawyer to sue him for $5 million.

:: :: ::

Ruth Tyrangiel characterized herself as a shadow wife, an eternal lady in waiting, a steady, ready companion whenever Robert A. Dylan needed shelter from his various storms. After two decades, she'd had enough.

"Can you cook and sew and make the flowers grow?" she asked, invoking Bob's own rhetorical irony[440] in the palimony suit she filed in November 1994. "Do you understand *my* pain?"

Married four times, but never to Bob, Tyrangiel said she was Dylan's "go-to" companion whenever things went south. Since his marriage proposal the year before she joined his Rolling Thunder caravan, Tyrangiel served his on-again, off-again whims without complaint, but every time she brought up marriage, Bob had an excuse.

---

[440] From "Is Your Love In Vain?" on *Street Legal*.

"Once he was off the road, once the children were grown, once he sold the house, once he was done with the work, once he finished this tour and that tour and the other tour, that we could actually have a life together and it went on promise after promise year after year after year after year," said Ruth.

Whenever she objected, Bob demurred.

"If I would go along with his, so-to-speak 'game plan,' that everything would be cool and fine and that I ought to just chill out," she recalled. "I think 21 years is enough of chilling out."

It was a N.E.T. gig at the Hollywood Bowl in the fall of '93 that pushed her over the edge. Dylan opened with "You're Gonna Quit Me" from *Good As I Been To You*, setting the ironic tone for the evening that followed. Out from New York visiting family in her native L.A., Tyrangiel hadn't told Bob she'd be in town, let alone in the audience. When she scanned the stage with binoculars, she spotted a familiar face sitting near the curtain.

"Carole Childs!" she said. "He'd sworn to me he wasn't seeing her anymore."

Ruth left in tears, retreating to a rented house in North Hollywood to nurse her wounds.

"I'd never felt that way before," she recalled. "Emotionally broken. Hanging by a thread. And then he shows up outside my door in his old Chevy pickup! I don't know how he found me because I was supposed to be in New York. Nobody knew where I was."

Dylan cajoled and apologized and promised things would be different, but this time Ruth was having none of it.

"It wasn't the worst thing he'd ever done, but it was the straw that broke the camel's back," she said.

In the months that followed, she repeatedly warned Dylan she would even the score for two decades of pain and suffering.

According to Tyrangiel, Bob oscillated between sweet talk and veiled threats, pointing out that no one would believe her.

Ruth ultimately hired a pit bull who'd bitten Bob before. With his famous judgment against actor Lee Marvin on behalf of Michelle Triola Marvin, Beverly Hills attorney Marvin Mitchelson had established palimony as a legal precedent in California. But his other claim to fame was even more chilling. Mitchelson had engineered Sara Dylan's huge divorce settlement, setting Bob back by millions for years to come.

Neither fact escaped Dylan or his lawyers. When pretrial depositions began, so did the war outside the courtroom.

"He had Elliot Mintz smear me in the media," said Ruth. "I had a couple telephone books' worth of receipts, but as far as the press was concerned, I was just another kook."

Tyrangiel suffered a further setback when Mitchelson's vaunted career imploded. A cocaine addict through most of the '80s, Mitchelson was convicted of tax fraud and fought a losing battle to stay out of prison just as he was preparing to take Dylan to court. He handed off the case to Cary Goldstein, a young associate who found Ruth likeable and sympathetic, but her story incredible. Nonetheless, there were those receipts signed by Bob Dylan himself that seemed to attest to her truth.

Tyrangiel said she first met Dylan in Greenwich Village during the early '60s, when she was a teen tourist visiting New York with an older relative. It was a brief and innocent encounter, but the impression was permanent. Bob inspired Ruth to pursue a music career. Nearly ten years later, when their paths crossed again during Dylan's Before the Flood tour, they sparked anew and spent the night together in San Francisco, according to Ruth. She was married at the time, but so was he.

In her deposition, Tyrangiel testified that they bonded; that Dylan promised he'd share "his family, his music, his body, his soul, his spirit, his consciousness, his intellectual abilities, his everything." She took him at his word, but after Rolling Thunder the excuses began. Ruth feared he'd never leave Sara.

Frustrated, she moved on. Four days after Elvis died, she married Robert Miles, the Dylans' former Woodstock groundskeeper. Still, she remained in Dylan's thrall. Whenever he called, she was there.

"He actually used to call me his nurse because he said I had very healing hands and I had a very healing touch," she said.

Finally extricated from Sara, Dylan began urging Ruth to dump Miles. In 1980, they divorced, reigniting her campaign to capture Bob. He didn't say no, but now his excuses turned on a new set of concerns.

He feared for Sara. She'd tried suicide, he told Ruth, though he offered no evidence in support. There was the further problem of *halacha*, the Hebrew doctrine governing marriage. Officially, Bob and Sara were divorced, but under Jewish law they remained a couple. The only way to break that bond was for Bob to formally present his ex-wife a rabbinical divorce decree known as a "get."

Dylan enlisted a Lubavitch rabbi in his quest, according to Tyrangiel. He was supposed to "train me in his world," she said. But when she met with the rabbi, he warned her instead against Bob. Dylan could be cruel, feckless, and malicious.

Ruth remained smitten. In 1981, just as *Shot of Love* tanked in the *Billboard* charts, she once again took Dylan at his word. He told her to forget the rabbi, sign a prenuptial agreement, and the wedding would happen. There was just one more thing. She had to pass his test to see if she fully understood his life, career, and philosophy. Thereafter, he quizzed her when he wasn't on the road. She had to answer all questions correctly.

Her ex finally opened her eyes. Bob Miles called to tell her that while she was playing 20 questions, Dylan had hooked up with Clydie King.

"He was a womanizer," Ruth testified during her deposition. While swearing she was his only one, Bob was actually "endangering my life sexually and otherwise, and my integrity and my dignity. And then finding out that he was in fact with other women? He did in fact give me sexually transmitted diseases that I nearly lost my life over because I didn't even know I had anything and I had to go and . . . and . . . and . . ."

Her attorney interrupted.

"Do you need a break?"

"Yes," sputtered Ruth, adding beneath her breath, "To fucking dignify 21 years . . ."

The Bob Dylan she described under oath was a far cry from the prophet of his generation. Here was the niggling effete who offered Ruth a 40 percent commission on his art if she could find a gallery to take it. Here was the reckless buffoon who sat on Ruth's custom-made guitar one drunken night, neither apologizing nor offering to repair the damage. Here was the profligate husband who blurbed the dustcover of a 1989 book on the need of orthodox Jews to exercise monogamy[441] while he juggled multiple affairs, including ongoing trysts with Ruth.[442]

She traveled with him before and after the N.E.T., using the "Mrs." version of whatever alias Dylan happened to be using at the

---

[441] *Doesn't Anyone Blush Anymore? Reclaiming Intimacy, Modesty and Sexuality* by Rabbi Manis Friedman: "Anyone who's either married or thinking of getting married would do well to read this book," wrote Bob.

[442] In the liner notes of *Knocked Out Loaded*, he offers special thanks to "Ruthie," as well as 122 others who helped him along the way, dating back to Mel and Lillian Bailey from his Village days. Far from his only lover on the list, Bob also cited Carole Childs, Clydie King, and a host of others who may have had carnal knowledge, including "Gal Shaped Just Like A Frog."

time. Among other hotels, they checked into Four Seasons in Toronto, the Regency in London, The Ritz-Carlton and The Peninsula in L.A. She counseled him on everything from the nasal intonation of his voice to the prospective purchase of a FM radio station. Above all else, she advised him to reconnect with the world outside his hotel or dressing room, to give up some of his precious privacy, and to quit taking fans for granted.

"I would always encourage him to actually follow through with the wonderful things that he did say in his songs, and have the people have some kind of feeling of contact," she said.

But according to Ruth, Bob dismissed true believers as easily as lovers. All he saw from the lip of the stage was a sea of anonymous faces. He clocked in each night as if he'd drawn the graveyard shift. Occasionally he played from the heart, but more often he just manufactured widgets on a musical assembly line.

"He would always say, 'OK, it's just my work.'"

■■ ■■ ■■

Dylan worked like a sober journeyman through the following year. He preferred espresso over booze. He had to scrub a March concert because of flu, but only canceled one other time in six years of touring. His Never Ending Tour passed the 600 mark. Judging by his energy, he'd chalk up 1,000 concerts long before the turn of the century.

On the road that winter in Japan and Australia, he reportedly began writing a new batch of songs just as *World Gone Wrong* won him another Grammy.[443] He changed things up on stage. Armed only with harmonica and handheld mike, he stood stock still at the keyboard, grimacing at the crowd. He often didn't touch a guitar at all.

---

[443] Best Traditional Folk Album.

With more good nights than bad, both boomers and Gen X converts came away satisfied.

He hooked up with a host of other musicians in the spring: Elvis Costello, Carole King,[444] Van Morrison, and Sheryl Crow among others welcomed him to the stage. In June, he reunited for the first of several concerts with the Grateful Dead, who introduced him as their "very special guest." Dylan was in top form: spectacular sound, tight sets. In addition, there were enough drugs among the Deadheads to float half the audience back to 1968.

"As Bob Dylan played before the Dead took the stage, 10,000 fans without tickets stormed the fences and tore them down, turning the concert into a 'free event,'" chronicled pop historian Robert Greenfield. "Five Porta-Johns actually in use at the time were knocked over. Many people were injured. Many more were drunk. Inside the venue, even as the Grateful Dead played, hundreds of people who had gotten too high to hear any form of music but their own lay passed out in the dirt."

Jerry Garcia didn't make that show or any of the six that followed. At 52, he resembled a graying grizzly with a permanent hangover. Years of yo-yoing in and out of rehab had taken their toll. He'd clean up for a while and then return to speedballs, heroin, and Jack Daniel's. According to peers like fellow guitarist Buddy Cage of the New Riders of the Purple Sage, Dylan tried keeping pace for a time, but saw where Garcia was headed. Bob pulled back and cleaned up.

On June 25, Garcia rejoined Bob and the Dead on stage in Washington, D.C., but couldn't remember which song was which. He turned the volume down on his Stratocaster and went through the

---

444   Dylan also collaborated on a pair of songs with her ex-husband and Brill Building partner Gerry Goffin. Goffin included "Time To End This Masquerade" and "Tragedy Of The Trade" on his 1995 LP *Back Room Blood*.

motions. The last number he and Bob played together was the stoned chorus from "Rainy Day Women."

The following day Dylan headed for Europe while Garcia traveled back to Southern California to check himself into Betty Ford. Two weeks later, he transferred to Serenity Knolls Treatment Center in Marin County, closer to home. On the morning of August 9, 1995, orderlies allegedly found him curled up in bed clutching an apple, a smile frozen on his face. Garcia's heart had stopped eight days after his 53rd birthday.

Dylan got the news shortly after returning from a N.E.T. date in Switzerland. Over the years drugs had claimed dozens of peers and pals, from Paul Clayton and Phil Ochs to Howard Alk, Richard Manuel, Mike Bloomfield, and Elvis, but none shook Bob the way Jerry did. The following day, Dylan issued a press statement:

> There's no way to measure his greatness or magnitude as a person or as a player. I don't think any eulogizing will do him justice. He was that great, much more than a superb musician, with an uncanny ear and dexterity. He's the very spirit personified of whatever is Muddy River country at its core and screams up into the spheres. He really had no equal. To me he wasn't only a musician and friend, he was more like a big brother who taught and showed me more than he'll ever know. There's a lot spaces and advances between the Carter Family, Buddy Holly and, say, Ornette Coleman, a lot of universes, but he filled them all without being a member of any school. His playing was moody, awesome, sophisticated, hypnotic and subtle. There's no way to convey the loss. It just digs down really deep.

Along with Old Glory, a tie-dyed banner flew at half-mast over San Francisco City Hall. Bill Clinton praised his genius while media around the world grieved as if mankind had lost another JFK or Martin Luther King Jr. Deadheads staged an all-night vigil and 25,000 turned out for a public memorial in Golden Gate Park.

Dylan flew in for the funeral. He sat directly behind Garcia's longtime assistant Sue Swanson, who compared his surreal presence to a Dali painting of melting clocks and watches. Bob didn't attend memorials. Time was out of joint.

"Are you thinking what I'm thinking, Mr. Dylan?" Swanson asked herself. "That when you are lying there that these are the words that they're going to be speaking about you?"

In mid-eulogy, Garcia's widow saw Bob rise from the pews. She caught his arm.

"He was really trying to get out of there and she stopped him when he walked by," recalled bluegrass musician Sandy Rothman. "He had his head down. His eyes were really red, and when she came to a momentary pause in what she was saying, he looked at her with those incredibly steely ice blue eyes and said, 'He was there for me when nobody was.' And he walked around her and split out of there as fast as he could."

19
NOT DARK YET

S ometimes you feel like a club fighter who gets off the bus in the middle of nowhere," Dylan once told Cameron Crowe. "No cheers, no admiration, punches his way through ten rounds or whatever, always making someone else look good, vomits up the pain in the back room, picks up his check and gets back on the bus heading for another nowhere."

By 1995, boxing was more than a metaphor. In the ten years between *Biograph* and the private christening of Ruby's Gym, Dylan exalted the sport from sweet science to personal ritual. Despite his sporadic drinking and a nicotine addiction as intractable as his never-ending need to travel, Bob always found the wind to go a few rounds.

"I'm not a fight fan," he said. "I just like to watch guys I know fight."

His interest dated back to Hibbing when he followed Marciano, Archie Moore, and a young Sonny Liston. "Who Killed Davey Moore?" might have looked off-kilter in the era of "Blowin' in the Wind," but Dylan found common ground early with gladiators. By the time he recorded "The Boxer"[445] on *Self Portrait* and apprenticed himself to the former boxer Norman Raeben, Bob's evolution to amateur "Hurricane" seemed natural. After Ruben Carter, he didn't just sit ringside. He climbed in and mixed it up himself.

---

[445] Paul Simon consigned to urban myth the notion that he wrote "The Boxer" about Dylan and that the "lie la lie" chorus was an indictment of Dylan's proclivity for prevarication.

"Most people think Sylvester Stallone is a boxer," he scoffed. Most people were wrong.

It was no act when Dylan put on the gloves. In ever-present hoodie, he inhabited the role: eyes downcast, slack jaw, leonine stride. He had no reach, but danced and dodged and coiled a decent left hook when he sensed an opening. He eventually began taking a pro[446] along with him on the road, jousting each afternoon to focus himself. Of course, no sparring partner ever clocked him. He was Bob Dylan.

Even though punches were pulled, he advanced from fight fan to fully formed sock jockey by the mid-90s. He worked the heavy bag inside a gym tucked away on his Southfork compound and sparred anonymously in Malibu. When he opened his restaurant, adding a private boxing ring seemed perfect.

The 1994 Northridge earthquake temporarily shook real estate prices in Southern California. Always on the lookout for a bargain, Dylan used his Oak Pass Trust[447] to snap up an entire city block late that year. He rented one storefront to a synagogue[448] but turned the Marmalade Café next door into his 18th Street Coffee House. Though he gave Victor Maymudes a $100,000 start-up budget, in its first six months of operation the café lost more than $90,000. In the basement at the back of the property, however, Ruby's Gym thrived.

Nobody was supposed to know about Ruby's. Like his wives, his children, his lovers, and his addictions, the gym was Bob's secret. In fact, the coffeehouse itself was a secret. But once celebrities like

---

[446] "This guy could walk across a football field on his hands," he said in a 2006 interview. "I kept it up. Still do, as much as I can."

[447] In addition to "flipping" houses in the Santa Monica suburbs, the trust was also the instrument for purchasing more exotic real estate. As far afield as Dublin and London, he checked out houses while on tour and bought a pair of $20,000 lots for a Gulf of California retreat near the Baja city of La Paz.

[448] Sha' Arei Am or, more simply, the Santa Monica Synagogue.

Quentin Tarantino and actress Gina Gershon[449] discovered Ruby's, it didn't take long for the rest of the world to catch on. When he played chess at a corner table with his boss, Maymudes could hear customers inquiring at the counter: "Does Bob Dylan own this place?"

Nope, they were told. Whatever gave you that idea?

If he showed any response at all, Dylan merely scrunched lower and pulled his hood higher, adjusting his Ray-Bans while he moved the next pawn. He hated unbidden conversation nearly as much as he hated signing autographs.

Six years after returning to the payroll, Maymudes had again secured both his role as majordomo and Bob's trust. As tour manager, he learned early that the personality he witnessed splitting during the '60s had become two distinct Bobs. Bob Zimmerman played chess, jammed and joked with friends, and poked at punching bags, but Bob Dylan was a brand-name enterprise. All trace of the devil-may-care Bobby from Village days had disappeared, replaced by a labyrinthine corporate structure controlled from Jeff Rosen's Manhattan hub and overseen by suits. Attorney David Braun and accountant Marshall Gelfand were among Bob's über advisers while Elliot Mintz acted as mouthpiece. It took some adjusting, but Victor learned to fit in. At home base in Santa Monica, Maymudes had little trouble dealing with Dylan's dual identities. On the road, things got dicier.

Victor wasn't much into boxing, but like Bob, he fancied himself a ladies' man. Married thrice, he let neither wives nor girlfriends preclude the occasional one-night stand. What was more, Victor liked them young.

Todd Gelfand, Marshall's son and junior partner, warned him against bringing girls backstage. Sex, drugs, and rock 'n' roll was

---

[449] "*Gina Gershon* Got In Shape For 1996 Movie *Bound* By Beating Up Rock Legend *Bob Dylan* In The Gym!" screamed the *New York Post*.

a slogan and a behavior from a different era. On tour in Oakland, Victor learned just how different. When police arrested him for investigation of rape, he made his 2 A.M. phone call to his assistant Linda Jacobs. He told her to get hold of Gelfand or David Braun right away.

He posted $50,000 bail and the rape charges didn't stick, but later, in June 1995, Maymudes met a 17-year-old at a Seattle concert and his female trouble started up again. The girl and her mother were known Dylan groupies who showed up whenever the Never Ending Tour rolled through the Pacific Northwest. After inviting both backstage, Victor asked if they'd like to visit his home in Pacific Palisades. They did. Victor later boasted that he got the girl to give him a hand job. Linda Jacobs told the suits.

Maymudes originally hired Jacobs to help him flip houses for Dylan, but while he toured Japan with Bob the previous year, her loyalties began to shift. The rape charges in Oakland were one thing. Sex with a minor was something else.

Dylan wasn't happy. Zimmy might love Victor like a brother, but brand-name Bob could not risk scandal. In August, days after Jerry Garcia's funeral, Victor lost his job as tour manager. He remained on the payroll, but was relegated to overseeing Bob's real estate and the day-to-day operations of the 18th Street Coffee House. Next time N.E.T. left the station, Victor wasn't on board. He took out his frustration on a speed bag in Ruby's Gym. Dylan might be mollified by the demotion. Victor was not.

⁘ ⁘ ⁘

When Frank Sinatra celebrated his 80th birthday, he invited Bob to the party.

Dean Martin would have come, but he was in the final stages of emphysema.[450] Sammy Davis Jr. had died five years earlier from throat cancer. Drugs killed Peter Lawford in 1984. Judy Garland, a Rat Pack[451] cofounder and Mesabi Ranger like Dylan, was first to go; a quarter century had passed since drugs and drink had claimed her.

But enough of Sinatra's contemporaries survived to host an old-fashioned black-tie bash. At first glance, his well-wishers appeared to have stepped right out of a publicity still from the heyday of the Sands Hotel. Men in tuxes and women in couture sat at cocktail tables evenly spaced across the floor of the Shrine Auditorium. Everyone had a drink, but no one smoked, including Sinatra.

Laugh-In creator George Schlatter filmed the spectacle for an ABC-TV special, inviting an eclectic lineup ranging from the peculiar (Salt-N-Pepa, Hootie and the Blowfish, Little Richard) to the sublime (Tony Bennett, Ray Charles, Natalie Cole). Upping the strange bedfellow factor, Walter Cronkite and John Travolta emceed. Most adhered to the unofficial Rat Pack dress code, including Bruce Springsteen.

But not Dylan.

When his turn came to sing, he stepped to the mike in pale gray sharkskin. No cummerbund, no bow tie. That didn't mean the one-time Village rebel was tweaking the Chairman's nose. Long ago, Bob had come to appreciate that both he and Frank saw music through the same blue eyes.

Dylan planned to sing "That's Life," but Sinatra requested "Restless Farewell." Bob wrote his bittersweet declaration of independence

---

[450] A smoker to the end, he died at 78 on Christmas Day.

[451] Officially vice president to Pack Leader Sinatra, Garland was an original disciple of the late Humphrey Bogart in whose memory the "Clan" was created during the mid-1950s.

for *The Times They Are a-Changin'* at a time when Sinatra surged at the pinnacle of his fame. Dylan was just 22 years old then; Frank was pushing 50.

Like "Bob Dylan's Dream" and "Percy's Song," "Restless Farewell" was a bittersweet kiss-off to those that Dylan had left behind following his *Freewheelin'* triumph. Demonstrating a precocious understanding of the isolating nature of celebrity, the song apologized to friends, foes, and women that fame forced him to abandon. He meant no harm. He would have liked to have stayed past closing time the way Frank used to do, maybe have one more for the road. He pledged they'd meet again someday.

But of course, that never happened.

Dylan hadn't performed the song in public for a generation and "Restless Farewell" was largely forgotten. Even Bobcats who could rattle off whole stanzas from "Subterranean Homesick Blues" or "Like a Rolling Stone" didn't know the words. That Frank knew them spoke volumes; that he asked Bob to deliver the song as a birthday gift transcended another routine performance in another routine Hollywood tribute.

Bruce Springsteen saw how apt "Restless Farewell" was. Sinatra's was the voice of cool but it was also "the sound of hard luck and men late at night with the last $10 in their pockets trying to figure a way out." "Restless Farewell" belonged as much to Bob as "My Way" belonged to Frank.

In some ways, Dylan's tribute rang truer than any of the others delivered that night. As he reached the final stanza, his backup band fell silent. Only Bob's tinny voice argued against "a false clock" that "tries to tick out my time."

The kid in the Huck Finn cap was now as anachronistic as the Sultan of Swoon, but neither Bob nor Frank was ready for the final curtain. Both suffered gossip and rumors and yet remained true to their respective destinies. With the final couplet of "Restless Farewell," a torch was passed: "So I'll make my stand and remain as I am and bid farewell and not give a damn."

Ol' Blue Eyes led the ovation. Already suffering dementia, Sinatra hadn't performed publicly for almost a year. He closed out his night by joining everyone on stage for a rousing "New York, New York" finale. It would be his final televised appearance. Of the many who did perform that evening, only Springsteen, Dylan, Steve Lawrence, and Eydie Gormé got invited back to Frank's place for a nightcap.

Sinatra would live another two and half years. When he died, Bob uncharacteristically attended the funeral, as he had Jerry Garcia's. He also issued a public statement.

> Right from the beginning, he was there with the truth of things in his voice. His music had an influence on me, whether I knew it or not. He was one of the very few singers who sang without a mask. It's a sad day.

The night following the eulogy, Dylan prefaced the end of a N.E.T. concert with a few words about the end of an era.

"I played at the Frank Sinatra tribute show a few years back, and I played this next song," he said. "We had it all worked out and everything, but then they said they wanted to hear this one instead so . . ."

Bob swallowed.

"I hadn't played it up till that time and I haven't played it since. I'll try my best to do it."

As he finished, the crowd was on its feet. The applause echoed long after he quit the stage. The houselights went up. There was no encore. He never played "Restless Farewell" in public again.

■ ■ ■

Uncertain he had anything more to say, Bob renewed his Columbia contract anyway.

"I didn't want to record anymore," he recalled. "I didn't see any point to it, but lo and behold they made me an offer and it was hard to refuse."

When he retreated to his Crow River compound in January, rumors ran rampant across the World Wide Web. Bob was writing again. A new album was on its way. Tentatively titled *Coupe de Ville,* this time there would be no geriatric covers, no creaky folk tunes. It was going to be all originals. Dylan had found his voice again.

Those looking for leaks were out of luck. Not a single title found its way to the Internet. Thirty years of bootlegs taught Bob not to tip his hand. For the rest of the year, no one outside his ever-tightening circle heard a note of the new material. When he rehired Daniel Lanois to produce,[452] demos were dispensed solely on a need-to-know basis; the words, a closely guarded secret.

On the information superhighway, lyrics of a new song could get halfway around the globe before Dylan picked up the phone to call his lawyer.

"I mean, you don't drive a car out of the showroom without paying for it, do you?" he asked. "You don't leave the supermarket without passing through the checkout with your goods. It's called stealing. Why the principle should be thought to be any different when it comes to music, I really don't know."

---

[452] Or co-produce, as Bob took equal credit under the pseudonym Jack Frost.

The World Wide Web had united N.E.T. followers via chat rooms and newsgroups. Bob websites[453] were on the way to becoming clearinghouses for Bob sightings and Bob downloads. Pool.dylantree.com began as a fan attempt to guess Bob's set list before each concert, for example, but by 2006, more than 2,000 Bobcats played regularly. Bob remained unimpressed.

"I know people who've got that online thing and games and things," he grumbled, "but I find it too inhibiting to sit in front of a screen on any level."

His label saw the future even if Dylan didn't. Stereos were history. Tape decks were next. Sony was now in the digital business, putting out the first interactive Dylan CD-ROM[454] the previous year with bonus tracks that could only be played on a PC. Digital rights headed the business agenda. Maria Himmelman became her stepfather's representative in the emerging law surrounding copyright and performance rights.

"I'm frightened of the net," he joked. "I fear that some depraved person may take me somewhere I don't want to go."[455]

Running the risk of irrelevancy, Dylan remained wedded to the past, especially when he was on the road. His Never Ending Tour continued to feed the kitty, albeit with diminishing returns. Except

---

[453] Using Bob's old Woodstock holding company Davasee Enterprises as registered owner, Jeff Rosen launched www.bobdylan.com on Jan. 1, 1997.

[454] Like many digital innovations of the mid-90s, the software didn't work in most computers and the product was a bust.

[455] On Nov. 19, 2013, Dylan acolyte Vania Heymann unveiled an interactive version of "Like a Rolling Stone" that simulated channel surfing. The 27-year-old programming wunderkind videotaped 16 lip-synchs of the anthem so that each time the viewer changed channels, Dylan's voice and lyrics picked up with a different person where it had just left off. For example, Drew Carey could be mouthing "You've gone to the finest school Miss Lonely . . ." on *The Price Is Right* and a BBC newscaster would pick up with ". . . but you know you only used to get juiced in it."

for an occasional addition like the Jerry Garcia tribute "Alabama Getaway," his playlist atrophied. In fact, the biggest Dylan surprise of the year wasn't even Bob.

After climbing out of the hole they dug with their Virgin Records deal, the Wallflowers released *Bringing Down the Horse*. Rolling Thunder graduate T-Bone Burnett produced 26-year-old Jakob's second Wallflowers album for Interscope, resulting in several hits including the No. 1 single "One Headlight."

"I wonder how many Wallflowers fans even know who Bob is," said Burnett.

Bringing Down the Horse sold over 6 million copies. Bob's biggest seller, *Blood on the Tracks,* had only sold half as many. Internet chatter speculated father-son rivalry. For his part, Bob claimed to be "superstitious" about discussing his son and way too busy for idle gossip.

"He's had an amazing amount of success in a short time," he said. "I just don't want to see his heart get broken in this business, that's all."

From April through October, Bob was on tour. When he returned to California, he came home to both a flattering moment and a rude surprise.

A committee of distinguished academics formally nominated him for the Nobel Prize in Literature for the first of several years in a row.

"Dylan, in word and music, has created an almost unlimited universe of art which has permeated the globe and, in fact, changed the history of the world," effused Virginia Military Institute professor Gordon Ball. "In catalyzing whole generations of youths, his *oeuvre* has shown more than any other poet's in this century the power of words to alter lives and destinies."

Adding gravitas and legitimacy to the swelling reputation of a self-described song-and-dance man, the nomination was just the latest honor in a string that began with the French *Commandeur dans L'Ordre des Arts et des Lettres*. Within the year, Richard Avedon would be handing him the Lillian and Dorothy Gish Prize[456] for his "outstanding contribution to the beauty of the world and to mankind's enjoyment and understanding of life."

But Bob also came home that autumn to more red ink at his 18th Street Coffee House. Victor Maymudes had assigned his 24-year-old daughter Aerie to manage with disastrous results. While Victor stood by glowering, Dylan fired her.

"You're outta here," he said.

"Why?" Aerie demanded. "Tell me why?"

He might have said sloppy scheduling, lousy bookkeeping, or the fact that she'd just returned from a week's vacation in New Mexico without bothering to tell anyone she was leaving. Instead, Bob jabbed at her with his cigarette.

"I don't have to," he said. "You're outta here."

She left in tears.

"That's it?" asked Victor.

Dylan nodded.

Maymudes drove his daughter home. A few days later Marshall Gelfand mailed her final check. Bob never spoke of it again. He put Linda Jacobs in charge of the coffeehouse. Victor got past the incident but any remaining illusion that he and Dylan were still road musketeers evaporated. Things had changed.

⁝ ⁝ ⁝

[456] Presented annually since 1994 at the exclusive Lotos Club on Manhattan's Upper East Side, the $200,000 prize has been given to such leading cultural lights as playwright Arthur Miller, actor Robert Redford, director Ingmar Bergman, and architect Frank Gehry.

Originally titled *Stormy Season,* the Columbia album that went to market as *Time Out of Mind* was recorded over 11 days in Miami in January 1997. Dylan could still be a pain, changing keys without warning and refusing do-overs, but Daniel Lanois would not be intimidated. He pulled out all stops, stuffing the studio with tape-looped rhythm tracks and a band of backup musicians—four drummers alone.

When technophobe Bob accused him of overproducing, they conferred in the parking lot. The strung-out icon that Lanois remembered from the *Oh Mercy* sessions seemed less combative but just as intense. Clearly sober, Dylan demanded assurance his words would be presented correctly—a subtle but significant shift from New Orleans where music held priority. They compromised.

"We treated the voice almost like a harmonica, when you overdrive it through a small guitar amplifier," said Lanois.

Neither used the term "comeback," but that clearly was on both of their minds. *Time Out of Mind* climaxed a 25-year period Bob described as his "downward spiral."

"Artistically speaking, it would have to have begun sometime in Woodstock . . . ," he recalled.

Steeped in bleak metaphor and death-defying imagery more familiar in the poetry of Dylan Thomas than Robert Zimmerman, Dylan's 30th studio album demonstrated a startling return to runic rhyme. "Not Dark Yet," the standout on an album hailed as his best since *Blood on the Tracks*, raged against the dying of the light. Like his namesake, Bob was not about to go gentle.

"*Time Out of Mind* recreates some of the somberness and eeriness of *World Gone Wrong*, but also resurrects the morbid fascination with death that so characterized his first album, which faked the world weariness of an aging man worn down and worn out," wrote pop historian David Boucher. "In *Time Out of Mind,* we get the real thing."

From *Bob Dylan* through *World Gone Wrong,* Bob regarded most of his LPs as a showcase for his upcoming concert season, cranking them out less to satisfy fan expectations than to meet contract demands. *Time Out of Mind* represented both an epiphany and a sharp break in that assembly line mindset.

"There wasn't any wasted effort on *Time Out of Mind,*" said Bob, "and I don't think there will be on any more of my records."

Perhaps in deference to the master, Dylan phrased as Sinatra once did, carefully enunciating each iamb, dactyl, and catch phrase. His macadam voice, so easily distracting, provoked empathy. A plea like "Make You Feel My Love"[457] summoned sentiment as profoundly as any love song he'd ever written while "Highlands"[458] reprised the wry cinematic wit and hoary dreamscape of "Brownsville Girl."

"It is a spooky record because I feel spooky," said Dylan. "I don't feel in tune with anything."

Life for Bob had *become* his never-ending tour. He sought satisfaction night after night while contentment always remained just beyond his grasp. Death continued to stalk him as Lanois put the finishing touches on the album.[459] While on the road in Canada, word came that 70-year-old Allen Ginsberg had died in New York. As one of the original angel-headed hipsters, Dylan dedicated a downbeat rendition of "Desolation Row" to the author of "Howl." As he approached the same age as Woody and Abe when they died, Bob still smoldered like Ginsberg's "starry dynamo in the

---

[457] Billy Joel and Garth Brooks both had hits with covers of the song.

[458] Originally 21 minutes long, Lanois talked him down to a 16-and-a-half-minute version.

[459] Switching coasts, he mixed the album at Teatro Studio, an abandoned 1920s movie house in Oxnard 20 minutes north of Point Dume.

machinery of night." He needed one more supernova before he too joined Allen, Jerry, and Elvis on the other side.

Dylan was not so different from the boomers he led out of the '60s. Now beginning to wonder where all that youthful promise had gone, they too faced a geezer future. SUVs with bumper stickers boasting, "I'm spending my children's inheritance" and "He who dies with the most toys wins" smacked of ironic desperation. F. Scott Fitzgerald's famous proclamation that America fostered no second acts didn't even consider a third. Those who grabbed the brass ring in their 20s like Bob had precious little chance of holding on to early success. Those who hit 50 without ever having grabbed it at all were unlikely ever to do so.

Home in Malibu to celebrate his 56th, Dylan kept a stiff upper lip. He had been experiencing chest pains for weeks. The following day, they grew calamitous. He called stepdaughter Maria Himmelman,[460] who rushed him to St. John's Hospital emergency room in Santa Monica.

In typical misdirection, Elliot Mintz let the *Los Angeles Times* and other major media believe that Bob was hospitalized in New York, lessening the chance of a Bobcat vigil. Within hours of the bulletin, Columbia Records fielded more than 500 calls as hard-core fans began circling his Malibu compound.

The European leg of his N.E.T. cancelled, Dylan learned he'd contracted histoplasmosis, a rare heart ailment caused by inhaling mold spores. He later concluded he'd probably picked them up the previous winter following a freak storm along the banks of the Ohio River, though visitors to his dusty digs in Point Dume believed he

---

[460] Jakob was on tour and didn't rush home when he heard Bob's condition wasn't critical.

could just as easily have contracted it breathing the muck kicked up by his chickens.

Stoicism nearly did Dylan in. His doctors said it never would have been so bad had he come in sooner. Dylan did complain about the pain, but it was slight and he ignored it, fearing that it might be his heart. He couldn't sleep, but refused sedatives. The spores grew slowly, but over time the sac around the heart became so infected that cardiac arrest was inevitable. His brush with death turned out to be as much a mitzvah as his 1965 motorcycle accident. There's nothing like an ER visit to revive a long-dormant dialogue with the Deity.

"I really thought I'd be seeing Elvis soon," he joked.

Bedbound for six weeks, by August he was back. He took pills three times a day and had to sit between numbers, but resurrection fervor took over on stage. No more half-assed performances. No more manic ceilings or depression floors. He forged a new pact with heaven.

"Here's the thing with me and the religious thing," he told the *New York Times*' Jon Pareles. "This is the flat-out truth: I find the religiosity and philosophy in the music. I don't find it anywhere else. Songs like 'Let Me Rest on a Peaceful Mountain' or 'I Saw the Light'—that's my religion. I don't adhere to rabbis, preachers, evangelists, all of that. I've learned more from the songs than I've learned from any of this kind of entity. The songs are my lexicon. I believe the songs."

Thus, when Bob got the call to visit Pope John Paul II at the World Eucharistic Congress in September, it was not as a born-again or even a Christian. He needed no cane to stand and play before the Vatican's top gun.[461] Dubbed "the Catholic Woodstock," more than 300,000 showed up to watch Bob meet the Pontiff. He wore a steady

---

[461] He earned $350,000 for his appearance, according to media estimates.

gaze as he doffed his white Stetson and shook the papal hand without kissing his ring. Attending priests may have disapproved, but not John Paul, who had nothing but praise following "Knockin' on Heaven's Door," "Forever Young," and the apocalyptic "A Hard Rain's a-Gonna Fall." The Pope compared the message in "Blowin' in the Wind" to the Gospel itself.

"You say the answer is blowing in the wind my friend." he said. "And so it is true! But it is not the wind that blows everything away into nothingness, it is the wind that is the breath and the life of the Holy Spirit . . . the voice that says 'come!'"

■■   ■■   ■■

With "Not Dark Yet" already a single and getting airplay like no Dylan original in nearly 20 years, Bob returned home from Europe just as *Time Out of Mind* hit the *Billboard* charts. It peaked at No. 10 and remained among the top 100 for the next six months.

"We always knew rock 'n' roll music was a great music about youth," wrote Robert Christgau. "And what we're finding is it isn't *just* a great music about youth. It's a great music about the whole process of aging. It's around the whole process of one's chronology in life. If you associate your chosen form with a celebration of youthful exuberance and you no longer feel youthful exuberance either you fake it or you deal with the fact that you've lost it. It is organic to do that."

Bob hadn't lost it. *Time* magazine shrieked "Dylan Lives!" His disciples now spanned three generations.

"I don't think of myself in the highfalutin' area," he said. "I'm in the burlesque area."

The White House begged to differ. At the end of 1997, Bill Clinton called him to Washington, D.C., as a Kennedy Center Honoree.

Along with Lauren Bacall and Charlton Heston, Bob's lifetime achievement put him several rungs above his peers. The president said as much in his opening remarks:

> As a young boy growing up in Minnesota, Bob Dylan spent a lot of time in his room writing poems. Then at the age of 14 he bought a guitar. With it, he would set his poems to music, striking the chords of American history and infusing American popular music, from rock-and-roll to country, with new depth and emotion. With searing lyrics and unpredictable beats, he captured the mood of a generation. Everything he saw—the pain, the promise, the yearning, the injustice—turned to song. He probably had more impact on the people of my generation than any other creative artist. His voice and lyrics haven't always been easy on the ear, but throughout his career Bob Dylan has never aimed to please. He's disturbed the peace and discomforted the powerful. President Kennedy could easily have been talking about Bob Dylan when he said that, "If sometimes our great artists have been most critical of our society, it is because their concern for justice makes them aware that our Nation falls short of its highest potential." Like a rolling stone, Bob Dylan has kept moving forward, musically and spiritually, challenging all of us to move forward with him. Thank you, Bob Dylan, for a lifetime of stirring the conscience of our Nation.

Gregory Peck[462] stepped out of the stanzas of "Brownsville Girl" to present him his medallion, but Dylan remained as uncomfortable as he'd been nearly 30 years earlier on the "Day of the Locusts,"

---

462 Peck was a 1991 Kennedy honoree.

when Princeton University made him an honorary Doctor of Music. Beatty Rutman sat behind him, alternately fussing and beaming.

"Who is this fellow Bob Dylan?" Peck asked. "He is surprises and disguises; he is a searcher with his songs. In him we hear the echo of old American voices: Whitman and Mark Twain, blues singers, fiddlers and balladeers. Bob Dylan's voice reaches just as high and will linger just as long."

Following the awards, Dylan had little to say and did not perform at the three-hour show staged in his and the other recipients' honor. It was left to Bruce Springsteen to sing that the times were changing, for better or worse.

■■ ■■ ■■

Before year's end, Victor Maymudes collected his final paycheck.

"I thought I had a long-term lifetime deal with him," he said. "I was in shock."

So was Bob when Linda Jacobs told him about Victor's latest peccadillo. Never mind that he'd impregnated one longtime girlfriend and encouraged her to abort; he'd also taken up hiking in an effort to corral more quim.

During an outing in rustic Temescal Canyon on the outskirts of L.A., Victor unzipped and displayed the goods to a 17-year-old waitress from the 18th Street Coffee House. A blow job would be nice, he said. The girl did not agree. She hotfooted it back to civilization where she told Linda Jacobs who, in turn, told Bob. Still recovering from histoplasmosis, Dylan confronted his old friend. Was it true?

Well, what if it was? It wasn't as if Bob was sinless.

But the fuck-anything-that-moves Dylan who once rolled doobies and whored around the Village was long gone. So was Rolling

Thunder Bob, who could hoover a line and drive a train with the best of 'em. Of all the Dylans that Victor once knew, only one remained and he was a survivor. Had Victor been paying attention, he might have been a survivor too.

"I quit!" he shouted and stomped out of Ruby's Gym for the final time.

He expected Bob to follow, to ask him to reconsider. He did not follow. Instead, Dylan had his attorney draft a follow-up letter confirming that Victor had left voluntarily and had not been fired.

Dylan was not heartless. He promised Victor paychecks through the end of the year. But in order to receive them, Maymudes had to drive Bob's pickup back to Point Dume and surrender the keys to his groundskeeper.

He did. And then Victor went looking for a lawyer.

20

MILLENNIUM

More than 400 scholars descended on the campus of Stanford University during the second week of January to explicate, venerate, and celebrate Bob.

"We only think he is the most amazing phenomenon in our lifetime," said Christopher Ricks.

Academics from as far away as Virginia and New York flew in for Stanford's first-ever Bob conference. Ricks set the tone by wading waist deep into the canon. The Oxford Don who moved to Boston University to complete *Dylan's Visions of Sin*[463] dubbed Bob's collected works "the Dyland." While admitting to no sign of illness himself, Ricks warned that "anyone who gets his or her kicks from biographizing Dylan's songs is likely to end up with a medical condition."

Nonetheless, the Bobnoscenti wallowed in a weekend of Zimmy. Ricks's own favorite mix and match was Dylan and John Keats.[464] Comparing "Not Dark Yet" to the tubercular English romantic's "Ode to a Nightingale," Ricks found resonance in rhythm, darkness, and doom.

---

[463] Published in 2003, his 520-page explication of Bob's songs became a national bestseller.

[464] During his European pursuit of Suze Rotolo in the winter of 1962, Dylan stopped at the Spanish Steps where the 25-year-old Keats had rented a room just before dying of tuberculosis in 1821. Then just 22, Dylan eventually incorporated that visit into the lyrics of "When I Paint My Masterpiece."

"Dylan's refrain or burden is 'It's not dark yet, but it's getting there,'" said Ricks. "He bears it and bares it beautifully, with exquisite precision of voice, dry humor and resilience, all these in the cause of fortitude at life's going to be brought to an end by death."

Other conferees weighed in with similar heavy themes and theory, demonstrating their camaraderie by finishing each other's Bob quotes.

"Don't follow leaders . . ."

"Watch the parking meters."

Though biographizing to beat the band, none seemed to suffer any medical condition beyond loss of humor. Conference moderator Susan Dunn suggested a little skepticism and maybe a word or two about Bob's cheesier efforts.

"In the words of those occasionally insightful rock critics Beavis and Butthead," she said, "I want us to think about what sucks about Dylan."

The room fell silent. Christopher Ricks rose to the occasion.

"We're not supposed to fall in love with him?" he asked.

■■ ■■ ■■

Bob himself was on the other side of the country, kicking off the N.E.T. for another year. Whether by design, chance, or some combination, Dylan once again leveraged his small but febrile army of Bobcats to Jeff Rosen's ongoing crusade to rebrand him from rock codger to pop messiah. Venues sold out wherever he went. *Time Out of Mind* went platinum, topped virtually every critic's choice as best album of the year, and took three Grammys—one more than son Jakob Dylan received for *Bringing Down the Horse*.

Bob chose to croak "Love Sick" during the 40th Annual Grammy telecast instead of performing the far more popular "Not Dark Yet."

Ever the contrarian, Dylan bowed neither to convention nor expectation. *He* called the shots, not the Grammy governors, the network, or the audience. *Time Out of Mind* marked Dylan's graduation to Mount Rushmore status. His stone face was unflappable.

Thus, when one of the extras in the mosh pit leapt to his side and began gyrating like an earthworm, Bob never missed a note. He did a double take when the guy tore off his shirt to expose the words "Soy Bomb" across his chest, but kept on playing. Neither did he acknowledge the incident when accepting Album of the Year. He recalled instead standing three feet from Buddy Holly at the Duluth National Guard Armory days before the first rock 'n' roll martyr caught the last plane for the coast.

"And I just have some sort of feeling that he was—I don't know how or why—but I know he was with us all the time we were making this record in some kind of way," he told the hushed crowd.

A scripted speech perhaps, but more substantial than the "Soy Bomb" moment, which fledgling performance artist Michael Portnoy later described as "dense, transformational, explosive life." His spastic dance cost him his $200 extra's fee and got him banned from the Grammys, but spawned parody on late-night TV for weeks thereafter. His 15 seconds of fame guaranteed notoriety for life: nothing Portnoy did before or since carried as much weight as the night he fed off of Dylan's fame.

Meanwhile, Bob returned to trotting the globe. Following two months of touring the heartland, he traveled to South America with the Rolling Stones and then hopscotched Canada and the Pacific Northwest as the centerpiece of an ad hoc superstar trio. For eight shows in May, he played beside Van Morrison[465] and Joni Mitchell.

---

[465] In tribute to Carl Perkins who died at 65 that winter, he and Morrison did a duet of "Blue Suede Shoes."

In June and July he went solo once more, he and his band puddle-jumping through Europe before beginning rehearsals for Australia and New Zealand, moving, always moving.

Ironically, with health restored, his sobered traveling circus ossified. Even a playlist freshened with songs from *Time Out of Mind* didn't help. His most ardent followers sensed distance and detachment. Dylan confirmed suspicions during a London press conference: "When you're up on stage and you're looking at a crowd and you see them looking back at you, you can't help but feel like you're in a burlesque show." Dylan's burlesque sacrificed spontaneity for the safety of routine. Even stage surges were rehearsed. Two-thirds of the way through each concert, security relaxed and a selection of groundlings, preferably photogenic young women, stormed the stage. Bob remained as blasé as if he were being soy-bombed. He spoke not a word, fiddled with his harmonicas, and struck diffident poses between numbers.

"It was as if Dylan was constantly checking his watch to see if it was time for another imitation of Chuck Berry in need of the toilet," complained N.E.T. historian Andrew Muir.

To fight complacency and keep cash flowing, he changed things up the following year. As the twentieth century ground to a close, nostalgia came to dominate pop culture. Retrospectives were everywhere: magazines, Sunday supplements, network specials. In music, "event" tours featured acts from the Woodstock era: Fleetwood Mac, the Eagles, Stones, CSN&Y. Aging Flower children paid top dollar to revisit their rock roots. When Dylan joined Paul Simon for a summer of arena rock, their fans had no trouble coughing up $100 a ticket.

Simon hadn't toured since 1992 and needed a career boost following his well-publicized Broadway debacle *The Capeman*. Both he and Bob were 57. When would two such legends ever tour together again?

"I was right away excited about doing this," Dylan told *USA Today*.

"It appealed to me immediately," echoed Simon.

They reportedly split an average $525,000 per concert, but their mutual admiration wasn't just about money.

"He's like the most mysterious of all the people of our generation," said Simon. "He's sort of impenetrable, really."

While not nearly so reverential, Dylan paid Simon his due.

"I mean, he's written extraordinary songs, hasn't he?" he said. "I consider him one of the preeminent songwriters of the times. Every song he does has a vitality you don't find everywhere."

On stage, Simon remained the respectful foil. He opened for Dylan and deferred to his demands.

"What I do isn't going to change," Bob declared. "I do what I like regardless of what bill I'm on."

Unlike some of his stale performances from the previous year, Bob partied through the summer like it was 1999. Halfway through a set, he'd drop to one knee, wave his left hand á la Al Jolson, and play harmonica with his right just as he once did nightly at Gerde's Folk City. He wasn't averse to displaying a sense of humor again either, grinning at the audience past perfectly capped teeth. He and Simon climaxed each show by swapping duets of "Bridge over Troubled Water" and "Knockin' on Heaven's Door." The faithful sprang to their feet begging "More! More!"

Simon rested at the end of their marathon road show, but not Dylan. He continued touring through the fall, this time with Phil Lesh, the Dead bassist who once vetoed Bob as a member of the band. There was little doubt who dominated the stage ten years later.

Dylan closed out the millennium with more drive and energy than he'd shown in a generation. By the end of November, he tallied 121 concerts—the most he'd ever played in a single year. He also vowed that *Time Out of Mind* would not be his last LP.

"I didn't feel like it was an ending to anything," he told *Guitar World* magazine. "I thought it was more the beginning."

■■ ■■ ■■

As Bob rebounded, the recording business choked.

"Print newspapers and the music industry both started tanking at kind of the same time," recalled singer-songwriter Paul Metsa, a second-generation Mesabi Ranger who grew up in Dylan's shadow. "They had these parallel death trips going on."

Pop peaked in 1999 at $14.6 billion in sales. Over the next decade, the recording industry's annual haul dropped by half to $6.3 billion. The Big Six record labels blamed the Internet. MP3 technology bled hundreds of millions in sales, eroding the bottom line a little more with each passing year. Why buy something you could get for free over the Internet?

The major labels did themselves no favors by cracking down on the very customers who bought the bulk of their product. Switching their antipiracy focus away from counterfeiting hotbeds like Bangkok and China, the Recording Industry Association of America vilified college students. The theft Bob had decried for decades was suddenly front burner. Unlike Dylan's manager, Jeff Rosen, who shrewdly turned the inevitability of bootlegging into a marketing ploy, the RIAA prosecuted all who dared swap MP3s. Adding insult to injury, the major labels also systematically killed off staples like 45s, cassettes, and vinyl LPs in favor of digital discs.

"CDs are *small*. There's no stature to it," Bob observed as pop's death spiral deepened. "I remember when that Napster guy[466] came up across. It was like, 'Everybody's getting music for free.' I was like, 'Well, why not? It ain't *worth* nothing anyway.'"

Labels focus-grouped a mass-produced kind of pop on a scale that left Dylan cold. Asked his opinion of Eminem and Dr. Dre, he said, "No idea. I've never heard of them." With the rise of rap, Britney Spears, and 'N Sync, he began sneering the way Sinatra once did at the likes of Strawberry Alarm Clock or The Monkees.

"The top stars of today, you won't even know their names two years from now," declared Dylan. "Four, five years from now, they'll be obliterated. It's all flaky to me."

And yet, he was not above dipping his toe into the medium that made all those ersatz musical acts possible. The man who once scorned primetime[467] dropped in unbilled on an October 12, 1999, episode of the ABC sitcom *Dharma and Greg*. Dressed in riverboat gambler garb, Bob led his band in a polka on the pretext of audition-ing Dharma (actress Jenna Elfman) as a drummer. Stunt casting never worked so well. His guest shot baffled critics. Closer attention to the show's credits offered an explanation.

Eddie Gorodetsky, the blues archivist and quipster of *Christmas Party with Eddie G!* that Dylan had released eight years earlier on his short-lived "Strikin' It Rich" label, was a *Dharma and Greg* staff writer. Gorodetsky was among a handful of showbiz figures who

---

[466] Shawn Fanning perfected the first peer-to-peer file sharing network in his dorm room at Northeastern University in 1999, teamed with fellow entrepre-neur Sean Parker, and circumvented the RIAA for two crucial years until they were put out of business in 2002. By then, Kazaa, Grokster, and several other P2P networks were effectively gutting the monopoly held by the Big Six for nearly half a century.

[467] He also signed with HBO to do a one-hour musical comedy special. *Seinfeld* director and writer Larry Charles was assigned to develop the show. It never happened, but Charles became a Dylan pal and future collaborator.

learned early that getting to Dylan was a matter of tiptoeing past multiple defense layers overseen by Jeff Rosen. One on one, Bob was a soft touch. That's why he had Rosen.

The son of Albert Grossman's accountant, Rosen said "no" for Bob, making the occasional exception for people like Gorodetsky. They had an archivist's love of ancient pop in common. Both encouraged Bob's penchant for early blues. While Gorodetsky scoured ancient tape and obscure 78s for quirky music, Rosen rounded up rare footage of Skip James, Big Joe Turner, and other names from the Leadbelly–Robert Johnson–Alan Lomax past. He also maintained Dylan's "vault" and dribbled out period pieces as part of Sony's ongoing *Bootleg* series to maximum marketing effect. Increasing Bob's profits while preserving his mystique, Rosen graduated from loyal front man to alter ego, all the while pretending that there was no mystique at all.

"A discreet fellow, to the business born," concluded *Village Voice* critic J. Hoberman.

According to Paul Williams, Rosen screened journalists, blacklisting those who sought personal information or appeared hostile. *USA Today*'s Edna Gundersen and the *Los Angeles Times*'s Bob Hilburn passed muster; biographers Howard Sounes, Bob Spitz, and anyone from *People* magazine did not. Rosen also monitored the Web for stalkers and unsympathetic bloggers. As Bob advanced from elder statesman to national treasure, it was Jeff's job to detect and defeat detractors.

But Rosen did not merely protect the Voice of a Generation. Using his growing arsenal of film, video, and unreleased recordings, Rosen "brilliantly orchestrated" the ongoing Dylan revival, according to Hoberman. As early as 1995, Rosen had begun interviewing early Dylan acolytes like Dave Van Ronk, Allen Ginsberg, and Izzy Young, judiciously editing out criticism or unflattering personal revelation with an eye to eventually creating a bookend to D. A. Pennebaker's *Dont Look Back*.

Though publicly disavowing interest in the project, Dylan himself sat for more than 10 hours of interviews. Rosen focused on Bob's earliest period, prior to his motorcycle accident. Sidestepping years of drug abuse, womanizing, and boozing, he concentrated on the myth of a middle-class Minnesota magpie who blossomed into the greatest American poetic prodigy since Walt Whitman. Rosen had more than enough for a documentary, including a rare on-camera visit with Suze Rotolo and a fawning interview with the usually acerbic Joan Baez.

The project didn't move into high gear however until Martin Scorsese came looking through "the vault" for clips for his own film on the evolution of the blues. An ambitious seven-part series tracing its history from the Mississippi Delta to South Chicago, *The Blues* extended Scorsese's reach as a serious chronicler of American music far beyond his much-celebrated *The Last Waltz*. It also made him Rosen's obvious choice to direct a revisionist Dylan documentary.

■■ ■■ ■■

In December 1999, a morbidly obese Rick Danko went to sleep after decades of drug abuse and never woke up. Two years earlier, the former Band bassist explained to a judge that his addiction began in 1968 when an auto accident left him in constant pain. He got a suspended sentence for smuggling heroin into Japan and lived to celebrate his 56th birthday. He died the following day and was buried in Woodstock a couple miles west of Big Pink.[468]

---

[468] Linda Mesch, a 49-year-old former deejay, bought Big Pink for $144,500 with plans to turn the basement into a recording studio and the three-bedroom living quarters into a rock shrine.

A few weeks later, Beatty Rutman was diagnosed with inoperable cancer. To the end, Dylan's 84-year-old mother remained both loyal and baffled by her beamish Bob.

"People sent her letters, she answered all the letters," recalled her cousin Barbara Fisher. "They'd ask for a picture of Bob Dylan, she'd send it to them. She talked to him after almost every concert."

When strangers asked, "What's it like knowing you gave birth to the Messiah?" Beatty smiled as sweetly as *Seinfeld*'s Estelle Costanza and pretended not to hear. But if a rabbi called to complain about his having been born again, her voice grew as shrill as the sitcom character's: "If you're upset, *you* try to change him!"

Sick and dying, she flew from her winter home in Scottsdale to the Highland Park neighborhood in St. Paul where she'd lived around the corner from Cecil's Jewish Deli for almost 30 years. Beatty Rutman died at a nearby hospital on January 25, 2000. Her sons buried her beside their father in the Jewish section of a cemetery at the northern edge of Duluth.

More than a year later Bob signaled *USA Today*'s Edna Gundersen away from any discussion about Beatty. "Even to talk about my mother just breaks me up," he said.

Dylan worked through his grief by hitting the road. He played 112 concerts during the following year, making one singularly noteworthy addition to his set list.

In February, Sony released the soundtrack album from director Curtis Hanson's *Wonder Boys*. In addition to featuring "Buckets of Rain, "Shooting Star," and "Not Dark Yet," the only new Dylan cut was a wry, upbeat anthem written in the cynical staccato tradition of "Subterranean Homesick Blues." A fan of Hanson's noirish *L.A. Confidential*, Dylan didn't require much convincing to tackle "Things Have Changed" for *Wonder Boys*. Hanson fought his way past Jeff Rosen, screened 90 minutes of the rough cut for Dylan, and made his pitch.

"Who knows more about being a wonder boy and the trap it can be, about the expectations and the fear of repeating yourself?" asked Hanson.

Bob got Hanson's message instantly. Tapping into the boomer zeitgeist, he captured the absurdist angst of middle age, identifying easily with *Wonder Boys* protagonist Michael Douglas—an aging wunderkind gone to seed as a jaded 60-something professor. Both the character and his theme song struck a solid if sour note with Yuppies. Even those who'd given up on Bob long before he found Jesus began greeting each other with the bitter refrain: *I used to care, but things have changed.*

Dylan had come to embrace his inner peeve. Pushing 60, he read no morning paper or tolerated much that was on TV. He preferred black-and-white movies to Technicolor. He disparaged Disney, shopping malls, theme parks, and, of course, politics.

"The government is irrelevant," he said of the Bush-Gore race for the 2000 presidency. "Everybody, everything can be bought and sold."

"Things Have Changed" reflected all of this disillusion and more—"a song that doesn't pussyfoot around nor turn a blind eye to human nature," said Bob.

The Academy agreed. While no match for *Gladiator*, *Titanic*, or any of the other *fin de siècle* blockbusters, *Wonder Boys* performed respectably enough at the box office that "Things Have Changed" got a Best Song nomination—the one Dylan ought to have had a generation earlier for "Knockin' on Heaven's Door." When he won the Oscar,[469] his acceptance was broadcast via satellite from

---

[469] He also won the Golden Globe.

Australia. In performing "Things Have Changed," he discreetly omitted the stanza demeaning Hollywood. Forty-six million viewers did not hear him announce, "Don't get up, gentlemen, I'm only passing through."

Blessing all with peace, tranquility, and goodwill, it mattered little that he resembled Vincent Price after a bout with the flu. Bob thanked Curtis Hanson, Sony and its executives, the brass at Paramount, and, of course, all the AMPAS members "who were bold enough to give me this award . . ."

During a press conference the following year, Dylan described movies as "a second-rate art form,"[470] but saw no hypocrisy in making nice for a night. Over the next several years, he proudly displayed his Oscar from the edge of an amplifier at every concert.

"It's quite something, isn't it?" he said. "There's not a whole lot of people who have them. So that puts me on a different plateau."

■ ■ ■

On the eve of his 60th year, Dylan began recording *Love and Theft* in Midtown Manhattan.

"Well, you know, I stopped counting after 40," he said of his birthday. "I'm sure you would too. A day above the ground is a good day."

Done with Lanois, he did the LP this time on his own. Henceforth, all Bob sound would be engineered by Jack Frost. He also took more care with the process. The new CD took more than two weeks to get right.

---

[470] "Literature leads you into the head and the heart of a fictitious character. No screenplay and no director can achieve that. Film characters always keep their distance, always far away and flat on the screen. I've never seen a movie that would be better than the worst book I've read."

"It's not luck," he said. "Luck's in the early years. In the early years, I was trying to write and perform the sun and the moon. At a certain point, you just realize that nobody can do that."

Dylan half-joked that he'd suffered amnesia after *John Wesley Harding*. Despite *Blood on the Tracks* and occasional sparks of inspiration during the '80s, he'd spent 30 years wandering in the pop wilderness trying to get his groove back. In a lengthy retrospective article on Dylan's 60th birthday, British Bobcat Ian MacDonald speculated on the toll that drugs and drink had taken. Once again sober, Dylan had to relearn "how to do deliberately what he'd once done without conscious effort," concluded MacDonald.

It seemed a fact of creative life that most artists self-medicated at one time or another. During the first half of the twentieth century, not one of America's great novelists stayed away from the bottle. Bob's fellow Minnesotan F. Scott Fitzgerald died drunk at 44 while Faulkner, Hemingway, and Steinbeck kept falling off the wagon throughout their far longer careers.

"There's a temptation, and a desire even, to be able to expand your imagination," concluded Paul Simon. "I mean, a lot of artists try that or do it. Something. Some chemical . . . alcohol, or whatever. And I think sometimes it produces some kind of creativity that wouldn't be there if the chemical wasn't there. And sometimes it produces nothing except the feeling of creativity, which is not the same as creativity."

At a summer press conference during the European leg of his annual N.E.T. trek, Bob revealed he'd begun working on his memoirs, the first volume of which he hoped to publish the following year. What began as liner notes for rereleases of *Freewheelin'*, *Oh Mercy,* and *Blood on the Tracks* evolved into *Chronicles*.

"I'm used to writing songs and songs—I can fill 'em up with symbolism and metaphors," he said. "When you write a book like this, you gotta tell the truth, and it can't be misinterpreted."

A Dylanologist's trove, *Love and Theft* might seem open to misinterpretation, but not if Bob could be taken at his word. "I've never recorded an album with more autobiographical songs," he said.

His follow-up to *Time Out of Mind* smacked of cabaret, rockabilly, jazz, swing, and even hints of rap, but the ancient folk stylings of *As Good As I Been To You* and *World Gone Wrong* still haunted every track.

"The album deals with power, wealth, knowledge and salvation," said Dylan.

Columbia released *Love and Theft* on 9/11. A better day for a pop prophet to address lofty themes would be hard to imagine. In naming the album the best of 2001, *Crawdaddy* critic Matthew Greenwald wrote, "The timeless, in-the-moment quality of this work is so apparent that it sounds as though it was all written and recorded on September 11, 2001."

"Mississippi," the standout single, was originally recorded for *Time Out of Mind,* and made its way to *Billboard* as a hit for Cheryl Crowe two years earlier. Based on a Louisiana prison chant[471] Alan Lomax recorded in 1947, the refrain was a call-and-response that convicts hollered while busting boulders on chain gangs: "Only one thing I did wrong/Stayed in Mississippi a day too long."

The entire album might have been aptly entitled *Mississippi.* Again, if Bob spoke the truth, song after song smacked of the Delta. Southern geography seeped through every cut: Clarksdale,

---

[471] The Lomax song, "Rosie," got a tip of Bob's hat near the end of "Mississippi" with:

I was thinkin' 'bout the things Rosie said
I was dreamin' I was sleepin' in Rosie's bed

Vicksburg, Memphis. Dylan "had to go to Florida dodgin' them Georgia laws . . ." and he dedicated "High Water" to Mississippi bluesman Charley Patton. Levees, southern constellations, boulevards of cypress, trailing moss . . . at every turn Bob's Confederate language evoked agrarian mystique and memories of a mordant culture gone with the wind.

Dylan had certainly put his time in down South, revisiting Highway 61 often. Friends and friends of friends said he owned real estate there. At one point, he purportedly owned 17 houses, but still preferred life on a leased tour bus.

He notarized a deed for a Santa Monica condo during a stay in Monroe, Louisiana, and made a pilgrimage to Jimmie Rodgers's[472] home in Meridian, Mississippi. Bob befriended Memphis bluesman Jim Dickinson who played backup on *Time Out of Mind*.

But there were family references on *Love and Theft* too. In one song, Bob's old man was "like some feudal lord" with more lives than a cat; in another he was a traveling salesman whom blue-eyed Bob had never met. His *Love and Theft* mother was the daughter of a wealthy farmer and his uncle ran a funeral parlor.

There was plenty of fiction among the facts—not like the higher standard to which he promised to hold himself in writing *Chronicles*.

"If it's not too bold, I consider myself to be an innovator, one of very few around," he said of his songwriting.

Two years would pass before a pair of writers for the *Wall Street Journal* discovered the source of some of that innovation.

---

[472] On his own Egyptian label, successor to the early '90s' Strike It Rich Records, Dylan compiled and released the best of the Singing Brakeman's recordings from the 1920s and '30s. He also wrote the foreword to a Rodgers biography. In 2011, Egyptian Records also released *The Lost Notebooks of Hank Williams*, a compilation CD featuring Bob on the theretofore unrecorded "A Love That Faded."

According to the *Journal*, a Bob fan happened upon an obscure oral history of a Japanese gangster while visiting Japan and connected a dozen lines from *Confessions of a Yakuza* to phrases dropped into several songs on *Love and Theft*. After the article broke, Jeff Rosen jumped to his boss's defense. As far as he knew, all 12 songs on the LP were strictly Dylan's. After all, Bob once claimed to have based an entire album on Chekhov stories—though he never revealed which one it was.

Christopher Ricks wasn't quite so forgiving. While Bob was a "very imaginative sponge," his most avid academic supporter said the string of lifted lines represented a strong case for something far beyond just borrowing.

"No one of these instances was very telling," said Ricks, "but when you put together the whole string of them . . . it's quite striking."

▪ ▪ ▪

The same day a pair of jetliners hit the World Trade Towers and Dylan released *Love and Theft*, Larry Kegan collapsed in a Tom Thumb convenience store in Coon Rapids, Minnesota. At 59, he'd already beaten a quadriplegic's odds by more than a decade. On the wall above Kegan's bed were a pair of snapshots: Bob, Larry, and Louis Kemp together at 13 and again at 50—three boyhood buddies who stayed in contact their entire lives. All U.S. flights were grounded for the next week. Dylan didn't make it home for the memorial.

Bob made very few funerals, though they seemed to increase in direct proportion to his age. Victor Maymudes was 65 when he suffered an aneurysm and his heart failed. He died in a Santa Monica hospital five days after "Things Have Changed" won the Golden Globe for Best Song.

"He was next to Bob," recalled Linda Wylie, Maymudes's widow. "He looked out after just about anything. In the beginning, there was just the two of them driving around in a station wagon."

Victor's obituary mentioned nothing about his lawsuit or the accusations of sexual misconduct that had led to his firing. It did mention a memoir he'd written about his halcyon days and nights traveling the world with the Voice of a Generation. Scheduled for publication in 2002, *The Joker and the Thief* was never released.[473]

Bob also outlived a second Beatle. George Harrison succumbed to cancer in November 2001. He was 58. Jeff Rosen put out a press release—a Dylan routine since the death of Jerry Garcia.

> He was a giant, a great, great soul with all of the humanity,
> all of the wit and humor, all the wisdom, the spirituality,
> the common sense of a man and compassion for people.
> He inspired love and had the strength of a hundred men.
> He was like the sun, the flowers and the moon and we will
> miss him enormously. The world is a profoundly emptier
> place without him.

Dylan didn't get to Harrison's memorial either, but sang "Something" for "a good buddy of mine" during a N.E.T. concert the following year.

In 1970 when he recorded *All Things Must Pass*, Harrison wrote "I'd Have You Anytime" as a paean for Dylan. "Let me into your

---

[473] Following a 2013 Kickstarter campaign, Jacob Maymudes resurrected his father's book with a new title and material salvaged from a house fire following Victor's death. *Another Side of Bob Dylan: A Personal History on the Road and Off the Tracks* is scheduled for publication in September 2014.

heart," he sang. "Let me know you. Let me show you. Let me roll it to you."

As the years passed, George despaired that Bob had heard what he tried to say. As a Wilbury, Dylan set himself apart—first among equals. He scorned adulation as weakness, even when it came from a Beatle. That Harrison was one of very few who could empathize with Bob's nagging self-doubt counted for nothing. Dylan never let it show. He was always on the road, heading for another joint.

Harrison once predicted Dylan would still be out front of an audience somewhere, trying to earn their esteem when he turned 90. Bob did not disagree.

"If I'm here at 80, I'll be doing the same thing," he said.

■■ ■■ ■■

The tour rolled on, year after year, state after state, continent after continent. Bob vowed he'd never fade away.

"I didn't want to be a has-been," he said. "I wanted to be somebody who'd never be forgotten. I felt that, one way or another, it's okay now. I've done what I wanted for myself." Laughing, he added: "I think I'm in my middle years now. I've got no retirement plans."

While neither his voice nor his stamina were what they once had been, Dylan refused to give up or give in.

"He's like an old Shakespearean actor," said Paul Williams. "He lives [and finds God] on the boards."

Before "Blowin' in the Wind" first blew him into legend, he bargained with "the chief commander . . . in this earth and in the world we can't see."

"I've had a God-given sense of destiny," he told *Time* magazine at the turn of the twenty-first century. "This is what I was put on Earth to do."

His relationship with the chief commander may have shifted over time, but his bargain never had.

"You hear a lot about God these days," he told *Rolling Stone*'s Mikal Gilmore two weeks after 9/11. "God the beneficent, God the all-great, God the Almighty, God the most powerful, God the giver of life, God the creator of death. I mean, we're hearing about God all the time, so we better learn how to deal with it. But if we know anything about God, God is arbitrary. So people better be able to deal with that too."

21

N.E.T. GAINS & LOSSES

Starting with a concert in upstate New York on August 15, 2002, the announcer introduced *sotto voce*,

> The poet laureate of rock 'n' roll! The voice of the promise of the '60s counterculture. The guy who forced folk into bed with rock, who donned makeup in the '70s and disappeared into a haze of substance abuse, who emerged to "find Jesus," who was written off as a has-been by the end of the '80s, and who suddenly shifted gears and released some of the strongest music of his career beginning in the late '90s. Ladies and gentlemen, Columbia recording artist Bob Dylan!

Adapted from an article that appeared in the August 9 edition of *The Buffalo Tribune*, the simple manifesto of a 40-year career in rock 'n' roll became the standard stage introduction for the Never Ending Tour deep into the twenty-first century. No doubt about it: Dylan was back.

And yet off stage, Dylan faded further and further from view. Some thought he'd retire and make periodic comebacks like Sinatra, lapsing a little more each year away from center stage. Critics who dismissed him or fans who simply forgot who he was mistook his increased anonymity for retreat. While they paid occasional homage as if he were an old quarter horse, Dylan refused to be put out to pasture.

"There's a certain part of you that becomes addicted to a live audience," said Bob. "I wouldn't keep doing it if I was tired of it."

In 1999, director Todd Haynes met with Jeff Rosen and Bob's son Jesse about making a biopic. Haynes wasn't the first, but his proposal was more intriguing than most. It found immediate currency with a middle-aged icon whose entire adult life had been lived behind a facade. Haynes got the nod to develop a script.

"This film would be about change and regeneration," he said, "and there's no more powerful place to look for that than Bob Dylan."

In a single-page synopsis, Haynes called his allegory, "I'm Not There: Suppositions on a Film Concerning Bob Dylan." It took its title from a shrill, indecipherable 1967 requiem[474] that didn't make it out of the basement of Big Pink—more of a yowl than a song.

Haynes's film précis equaled Dylan's inscrutability. He envisioned seven[475] sad characters caroming back and forth across a lifetime with no coherent storyline. Like the annual Dylan Imitators Contest that began as an elaborate joke during the '80s at the Speak Easy disco on MacDougal Street, *I'm Not There* (2007) would feature a mercurial Dylan slipping from one incarnation into another: Folk Bob, Amphetamine Bob, Rolling Thunder Bob, Born-Again Bob, Old West Bob, and Freestyle Bob. Rather than biography, the movie held all the promise of an extended episode of *To Tell the Truth*: Would the *real* Jokerman please step forward?

---

[474] The title "I'm Not There" was allegedly borrowed from Rimbaud's declaration, "I am an other."

[475] Charlie Chaplin Bob, combining the Little Tramp with Borscht Belt humor and talking blues, did not make the final draft of *I'm Not There*.

The Speak Easy imitators contest seemed the clear inspiration for *I'm Not There*. Ragmen, jugglers, clowns, thieves . . . they'd all put in an appearance at the Greenwich Village nightclub at one time or another. Tambourine men escorted covenant women and MacDougal Street masqueraded as Desolation Row, if only for an evening each July. A midget in JewFro might show up alongside a transvestite clad in North Country sheepskin and Huck Finn cap. In the Freestyle competition, contestants sang a song in non-Dylan style. "Like a Rolling Stone" became a lullaby while "Queen Jane Approximately" got reggae treatment. Countrified Jersey boys performed adenoidal versions of "Lay Lady Lay" while a Rolling Thunder mute mouthed "Joey" in white face and Lucite mask.

All the Dylans got their chance to perform, including Bob, as it turned out. According to one former Dylan staffer, Bob's son Jesse filmed the competition one summer[476] and Dylan himself entered under an alias. No one outside his inner circle knew that Robert Allen Zimmerman came in third.

In addition to *I'm Not There*, there were two earlier attempts at Bob biopics in the new millennium, both nontraditional yet true to the Dylan myth. *No Direction Home* (2005) brought Jeff Rosen's own personal gravitas to the legend while *Masked and Anonymous* (2003) reveled in the same dark carnival atmosphere that Todd Haynes had sought to reproduce, but with a lot more slapstick.

Of the three films, *Masked and Anonymous* came closest to approximating a standard two-hour Hollywood entertainment. Filmed over two days in the summer of 2002, the stellar cast (Penélope Cruz, John Goodman, Jessica Lange, Jeff Bridges, et al.) worked for scale just to stand next to Bob. Such was his charisma

---

[476] When the Speak Easy evolved away from Dylan in the early '90s, Nietzsche's nightclub in Buffalo picked up the tradition.

even among celebrities, many of whom were far too young to have visited Greenwich during its prime.

A slight screen confection authored by Dylan[477] and *Seinfeld*'s Larry Charles, *Masked and Anonymous* spoofed the Bob legend, presenting him as an ex-con named Jack Fate whose answer to everything from political malaise to Armageddon was to put on a charity concert. Everything and everyone in *Masked and Anonymous* was deadpan, from the extras dressed as Gandhi, Abraham Lincoln, and Pope John Paul II to Ed Harris costumed as a banjo-playing minstrel spouting dour nonsense. John Goodman was a thinly disguised caricature of Albert Grossman; Christian Slater and Chris Penn wisecracked as dueling roadies; Luke Wilson tended bar; and Mickey Rourke was a power-hungry dictator.

In his first noncameo appearance since *Hearts of Fire*, Bob was a grumpy, anorexic Gene Autry in ten-gallon hat and Vincent Price mustache. His bemused acting style hadn't changed since *Pat Garrett and Billy the Kid*. Summarizing the critical consensus, the *Washington Post* called *Masked and Anonymous* "a fascinating, vexing, indulgent, visionary, pretentious, mesmerizing pop culture curio." Most reviewers recommended skipping the movie and buying the soundtrack. The CD featured fine covers of Bob tunes, including a Spanish version of "Like a Rolling Stone" and a couple star turns from Bob himself, notably his gravelly rendition of "Dixie."

Masked and Anonymous only pulled in half a million at the box office, but it did give Jeff Rosen a chance to try his producing chops in preparation for *No Direction Home*. The three-and-a-half-hour documentary based loosely on the first two-thirds of Robert Shelton's[478] biography would not premiere until 2005, but the timing

---

[477]   Under the pseudonym "Sergei Petrov."

[478]   Shelton suffered a fatal stroke in December of 1995. His was the only biography Bob ever copped to having read.

alone demonstrated once more Rosen's brilliant knack for rebranding. Dylan's Grey Water Park Productions[479] hired Scorsese to give *No Direction Home* cachet without letting the master director near his subject.[480] Simultaneously, Rosen used the synergy of *Chronicles* and a popular traveling museum exhibition to further whet Bobcat curiosity.

During the spring of 2004, Microsoft cofounder Paul Allen launched "Bob Dylan's American Journey, 1956–1966," as part of the billionaire's ongoing Experience Music Project. Moving from museum to museum [481] across the U.S., the multimedia exhibit featured Rosen-approved artifacts from Hibbing, Dinkytown, Greenwich, and Woodstock, focusing on Bob's formative years without revealing anything about the darker side of his appetites. By the time the traveling exhibition came to a halt four years later at L.A.'s Skirball Cultural Center, tens of thousands had paid $10 a head to join Dylan on his American Journey. By then, a companion *Bob Dylan Scrapbook: 1956–1966* was on sale in conjunction with the DVD and CD soundtrack of *No Direction Home*.

But it was *Chronicles* that became the Dylan renaissance *pièce de résistance*. Published in October 2004, the first volume of a promised trilogy landed in the middle of Rosen's revival like a meteorite, demonstrating a narrative skill even Bob's most ardent admirers had never given him credit for possessing. Painstakingly written over three years, according to Dylan, *Chronicles* leaped from the Village to Hibbing to New Orleans, Malibu, San Francisco, and back again

---

[479] Heir to Lombard Films.

[480] In a 2011 interview with author Stacy Schiff, the director said he never met with Dylan or understood what made him tick.

[481] Among other stops, the exhibition traveled to the Rock and Roll Hall of Fame in Cleveland, the Morgan Library in New York, and the Smithsonian in Washington, D.C.

with as little regard for chronology as many of his songs. But unlike *Tarantula*, his only other long-form effort, *Chronicles*[482] actually made sense. It seemed to bear out his long-ago promise to produce a postmodern *Bound for Glory*—exquisitely detailed fiction based loosely on fact. Dylan did indeed carry his readers from page to page with the ease of a seasoned storyteller.[483]

"Lest we forget, while you're writing, you're not living," he said. "What do they call it? Splendid isolation? I don't find it that splendid."

Nor did he find himself bound by the rules of nonfiction, even if that's the bestseller category[484] where *Chronicles* landed in the *New York Times*. "I'll take some of the stuff that people think is true and I'll build a story around that," he said, abandoning his one-time contention that fact ought to trump fiction where history was concerned.

Harking back to his Gaslight days, Dylan claimed to have personally hunted-and-pecked his manuscript in capital letters on a manual typewriter. It was easier for his assistant to read, he explained. Like most writers, he hated the process, but loved the result.

"Whatever you put on the page, it's like making a painting," he exulted. "Nobody can change it. Writing a book is the same way. It's written in *stone*—it might as well be! It's never gonna change. One's not gonna be different in tone than another, you're not gonna have to turn this one up louder to read it."

■ ■ ■

---

[482] *Lyrics*, the update of his 1974 *Writings & Drawings*, was published one week after *Chronicles*.

[483] Some, like Sally Grossman, doubted he wrote the book, believing it to have been ghostwritten by an author with proven narrative skills like Larry Sloman or Al Aronowitz.

[484] Peaking at No. 2, *Chronicles* spent 19 weeks on the list.

Deftly coordinating his appearance with the publication of *Chronicles,* Bob interviewed with correspondent Ed Bradley on *60 Minutes*[485] in 2004. Bradley sat in awe during the one interview he said that he'd lusted after throughout his career. Following a couple minutes of what had become routine veneration, Bradley got down to the central mystery of Bob's mid-60s starburst. From whence came all that exquisite poetry?

"Those early songs were almost magically written," explained Dylan. "Try to sit down and write something like that. There's a magic to that, and it's not Siegfried and Roy kind of magic, you know? It's a different kind of a penetrating magic. And, you know, I did it. I did it at one time . . . and I can do other things now. But I can't do that."

The magic, Dylan said, sprang from a deal he'd made with destiny. He stopped short of elaborating on precisely what sort of deal.

"You know, there was that maddening interview on *60 Minutes*," said Bob's early biographer Toby Thompson. "And Dylan said 'I made this promise to the man upstairs.' And Bradley didn't stop and say 'What promise?'"

Once an outspoken advocate for Jesus, Dylan seldom invoked the Messiah in the new millennium. While born-again Bob had apparently returned to his Jewish roots during the late '80s, by the time he became eligible for Social Security he shunned organized religion all together.

"Faith is degraded by religion," Dylan told *Rolling Stone.* And, to *Newsweek*'s David Gates: "I believe in Hank Williams singing 'I Saw the Light' . . .these old songs are my lexicon, my prayer book."

---

[485] Hitting all demographics, an animated Bob appeared the same night on *The Simpsons.*

Kenn Gulliksen, the born-again pastor who wooed Bob to Christ at the beginning of the '80s, laid his former disciple's insecurities to Satan.

"I wish I had given more of myself because Bob subsequently— because of who he was and the pressures in his life—got caught back into the world," he said. "I believe he is on a greater search than ever and I think he's being so torn and that his life is winding down. He's getting older and he's struggling with what is the most real. Being Bob Dylan, having this acclaim, or having a relationship with God."

Dylan summarized his evolved belief system with New Testament aphorism: "Work while the day lasts, because the night of death cometh when no man can work."

And the work continued: 98 N.E.T. concerts in 2003; 111 in 2004; 112 during 2005 with no letup in sight.

No Direction Home premiered to raves at the Telluride Film Festival in July 2005, followed two months later by its PBS telecast as part of the *American Masters* series. Delivering the network's highest ratings in years, Jeff Rosen's carefully edited documentary was a trifecta: it cost a mere $2 million to make, sealed in amber Bob's apotheosis as a young artist, and skirted the more pointed offscreen cynicism spouted by onscreen amigos.

"Well, he did steal stuff," said Israel Young when the camera wasn't rolling. "Stephen Collins Foster wrote a song in 1851 . . . called 'Hard Times Come Again No More,' and I learned that in public school as a kid. Bob Dylan was born in 1941, 91 years after the song was copyrighted and if you look at the definitive collection of folksongs written by Bob Dylan, there's the song: 'Hard Times Come Again No More,' copyright Bob Dylan."

Taking his cue from Bob, Izzy Young lived his life and never looked back. The founder of the Folklore Center where Dylan first sought refuge during the icy winter of 1961 immigrated with his French girlfriend to Scandinavia in 1973. Young created a similar folk center in Sweden, eking out the spare but comfortable existence he preferred in the Village. He sat for his *No Direction Home* interview in 1995, but didn't get to remake Dylan's acquaintance until a N.E.T. stop at the Globe Arena in Stockholm shortly before the PBS premiere.

"Izzy it's great to see you!" said Bob. "I wrote a chapter on you in my new book!"

"You're full of shit," said Young.

Now well into his 70s but as ornery as the day he and Dylan first met, Young embraced Bob backstage, surrounded by security guards.

"Are you really living on the street?" asked Dylan.

"I'm living on the street but God protects me," said Young.

In the Paul Clayton tradition, Young still sold old-timey music instruments, offbeat LPs, and knickknacks that evoked history over profit. Ironically, the most valuable items in his inventory were a pair of early artifacts he brought with him from the U.S. One manuscript he dubbed "Talkin' Folklore Center"; the other was an anti-nuke polemic, "Go Away You Bomb, Go Away." Both were handwritten by Bob when he was just 22. Both relics could easily command tens of thousands at auction, but Young kept them under lock and key instead. He had no aspiration to move up.

"I'm doing what I have to do," said Young. "I'm fighting, but succeeding in my way without money. Without getting paid. But I have freedom."

"Ya know Izzy, it's boring where I am," said Dylan.

"Boring?" Young replied. "God, I only have the store. I don't even have an apartment. Maybe I can come visit you. . . . Maybe I can come visit your estate."

"Yeah," said Bob. "Listen, I was in it for fun and I'm still having fun."

Young suggested Dylan take a break. Learn to read newspapers again, mingle with the masses, write the sort of song he crafted back in the beginning. Dylan shook his head, but not because he disagreed.

"I don't know why I'm doing this," he sighed. "I should be taking care of my 14 grandchildren." Then he deftly changed the subject. Their exchange lasted all of ten minutes, but Young left content that they'd reconnected.

"He's interested in Italian wines," he said. "He can talk about Iraq also."

A week later, Jeff Rosen called.

"Izzy, Bob Dylan had a great time with you," he said. "He wants your exact address."

Young gave it to him and a short time later, a check arrived for $3,000.

In a 2014 interview with *Tablet Magazine,* Young had only praise for his one-time protégé:

"I get about three to six (Bobcats) in here every week. They've read every single book there is about Dylan so why do they have to come here? Well, they want me to tell them stories about how Dylan fucked somebody here and took drugs there. They want sleaze . . . I've had up to 100 people like that in here this year and none of them have said anything interesting to me. That means they can't get into him."

Still operating his Folklore Centrum in Stockholm, Young hadn't seen Bob in years, but had little trouble imagining how their next encounter might go:

"Maybe the only thing I might tell [Bob] would be 'You know, you and me are the same person.' And he's gonna say, 'What do you mean, Izzy?' So I'll say, 'Well, you do what you want, you've continued with it all your life and you haven't changed, and I do what I want and I haven't changed. So if I'm at the bottom of the economy and you're at the top of the economy, there's still no difference between us.' And he would agree with me."

Like Izzy Young, Suze Rotolo Bartoccioli lived the simple life of an artist. Though the girl on the *Freewheelin'* cover agreed to be in Jeff Rosen's documentary, she remained as radical as the day she and Bob moved in together. In 2004, using the pseudonym Alla Da Pie, Suze joined the Manhattan street-theater group "Billionaires for Bush" to protest the GOP convention. In the editing of *No Direction Home,* her politics got left on the cutting-room floor.

Though it pleased her that Bob survived his fame, she complained that, "he was an elephant in the room of my life." Like Izzy Young, she wasn't so much bitter as disappointed with her first serious boyfriend; unlike Young, she stopped short of accusing him of thievery.

"Imitate, assimilate, innovate," said Mrs. Bartoccioli. "My take on him is as simple as those three words."

Whether his own songs or not, Bob's borrowing was not out of line. Everyone did it. Dylan just did it better. But he was definitely a poseur, she added. Every move he made was calculated. Dylan's cynical preference for appearance over reality iced itself into her memory on that deepfreeze day in 1962 when he mugged for the *Freewheelin'* cover.

"The thing is, I look at that picture and think I look so fat because I had a huge bulky sweater on and a coat," she recalled. "But Dylan, image already was all, and he wore this thin little coat. I was freezing that day. *That's* why we were huddled."

Joan Baez also praised Dylan in *No Direction Home*. On camera, he was her young genius "Bobby" once more. He reciprocated by appearing in Joan's *American Masters* biography five years later.

Off camera, Baez tempered her admiration. Like Dylan, she'd taken to the road again in the twenty-first century and did a mocking nasal imitation of her one-time lover as part of her stage act. Climaxing each concert with "Diamonds and Rust," she lanced their lost romance further with: "and if you're offering me diamonds and rust, *I'll* take the diamonds."

Bruce Langhorne also made a *No Direction Home* appearance, though he left his tambourine at home. In the years since backing Bob on *Bringing It All Back Home*, Langhorne, moved to Hawaii, grew macadamia nuts for a living, returned to California, and begun marketing his own brand of hot sauce.

In the living room of his tiny Santa Monica duplex a mile from Bob's 18th Street Coffee House, Langhorne displayed the huge Turkish tambourine that he bought from Izzy Young's Folklore Center the same year Dylan emigrated from Dinkytown. A stroke he'd suffered kept him from playing it or the guitar, but Langhorne still banged away on his barrelhouse piano. His home was a museum of rare and storied instruments. While Mr. Tambourine Man's tambourine might easily incite as big an eBay frenzy as Izzy Young's early Dylan manuscripts, it was not for sale. Some things were sacred.

When Langhorne was a freshman at NYU, he recalled Dylan as a shy midwestern dropout who materialized one night at Gerde's Folk City and "sang through his nose."

"He didn't talk that much," said Langhorne. "Some people in the coffeehouses come in and they're stand-up comics and they have a long line of patter. . . . Bob really wasn't like that. He just really kinda let his songs speak for themselves, as I remember."

Langhorne had a "blue-sky theory" about Bob's early connection to his audience—a theory that didn't fit with the *No Direction Home* formula. He ascribed Dylan's big bang during the '60s—first at Folk City and very quickly thereafter, around the globe—to telepathy.

"I think that Bob Dylan is a telepath," said Langhorne. "I think he's one of the major telepaths on the planet. And I think however the mechanism of telepathy works that Bob is able to project the contents of his mind to millions of people. I don't know how it works. It might have something to do with quantum signatures of something that's out there someplace. But he was able to project the contents of his mind to millions of people. Millions of people went, 'Oh, Bob Dylan was speaking to *me!*' And he was."

But then, he wasn't.

Offering his own blue-sky theory, Neil Young once described Dylan's burst of mid-60s inspiration as a gift that "keeps on giving and then it goes away and then it comes back and if you're ready to accept it, it's there. I've heard Bob say he doesn't know who wrote ('Like a Rolling Stone'). He doesn't know the guy who wrote those songs any more."

According to Bob, that guy vanished after a motorcycle accident 40 years ago.

■ ■ ■

In the fall of 1966, weeks after the famous accident, young Joyce Carol Oates published "Where Are You Going, Where Have You

Been?" and dedicated it to Bob Dylan. Over the next half century, that short story became the most popular in her mushrooming canon. An author celebrated for inexhaustible output, Oates became to narrative fiction what early Dylan was to songwriting: a virtual word machine. Both novelist and pop poet seemed compelled to create, but with maturity, they had little in common. Domesticated, monogamous, and tenured, Oates taught at Princeton while Dylan remained ever the secretive, seductive vagabond.

And yet Oates continued to acknowledge that it was *his* lyrics that inspired her most famous story: an ambiguous allegory about a teen beauty charmed to death by a serial killer. "Where Are You Going, Where Have You Been?" melded the true life tragedy of Arizona lady-killer Charles Schmid[486] with the melancholy spirit of "It's All Over Now, Baby Blue."

In a 2004 essay about the original '60s antihero who had recently turned 60 himself, Oates praised Dylan as Dionysius writ large for the Aquarian age, able to transubstantiate all he'd gathered from coincidence.

"Like all good poetry, this song of Dylan's can't be paraphrased," said Oates. "Like all good music it is both of its time and timeless."

During her own career, she witnessed America's attention span fade in direct proportion to the quickening pace of TV and the Internet. Despite fickle audiences, Oates marveled at how Dylan "yet retains his stature and something of his original mystery."

---

[486] Short, handsome, talented and troubled, Schmid briefly rose to national notoriety in 1965 for the thrill killing of a Tucson high school coed followed by several more murders that landed him on death row. The Arizona courts overturned the death penalty, but Schmid died anyway, stabbed 47 times by two inmates in 1975.

"When we first heard this raw, very young, and seemingly untrained voice—frankly nasal, as if sandpaper could sing—the effect was dramatic and electrifying," Oates recalled. "Bob Dylan seemed to erupt out of nowhere. The genuine power, originality, and heartrending pathos of 'Blowin' in the Wind,' 'A Hard Rain's a-Gonna Fall,' 'Masters of War,' 'Don't Think Twice, It's All Right' were like nothing we'd encountered before."

In the new millennium, her Princeton students revered Bob anew, but neither recent undergrads nor Oates herself aspired to actually *become* another Jokerman.

"Dylan's music isn't about us any more than it's about the 60-year-old Dylan, but it may be the most purely American music for us," she said.

One of Oates's contemporaries compared Bob's career to that of a Zen master, zigzagging from decade to decade along the route of an Oriental nine-turn bridge—a Buddhist metaphor for abrupt change that a wayfarer endures as he proceeds through the crooked journey of life. Reaching each new switchback, he faces away by 90 degrees and heads off in a new direction. At every turn, another panorama forces him to see the world from a different perspective. In somber understatement, Dylan pondered, "I try not to work in a linear way."

Though Bob never worked on a railroad, plowed pastures of plenty, or traveled lonesome highways in his later years in anything less comfortable than a fully tricked-out Pullman tour bus, he bore poetic witness to the breadth, length, and depth of the American experience. And he wrote about it still, usually alone, often in a trance.

"What I have to do is space out and almost hypnotize myself," he said, adding with a laugh, "without drugs, of course."

As much a professional observer of the human condition as any newsman, Dylan eavesdropped but rarely participated. He deplored journalists, yet they remained closer in temperament and vocation than most of his peers. When he contradicted his most basic convictions, the media were among the first to call him on it.

During his nonsensical KQED press conference in the winter of 1965, he deadpanned that if he ever sold out to TV, it would be to hawk ladies' garments. Forty years later, he kept his word and no reporter let him forget it. In 2004, the lacy ladies' underwear retailer Victoria's Secret became a Special Rider licensee. The man who once declared that music ought to inspire, not "push some product down your throat," stood beside Brazilian supermodel Adriana Lima along a Venetian canal rasping the walkin' lyrics of "Love Sick" in a very effective TV pitch.

The Victoria's Secret spot prompted *Vanity Fair*'s Leslie Bennetts to protest on behalf of her preteen daughter: "When the man who wrote 'Forever Young' starts leering at jailbait during primetime, the result looks like a recruiting tool for a pedophilia advocacy group." Never one to apologize, Dylan upped the ante. He offered a premium "Love Sick" compilation CD in conjunction with the purchase of Victoria's Secret lingerie.

Three years later, he appeared in commercials for the 2008 Cadillac Escalade, cheerfully asking, "What's life without the occasional detour?" When it came to cashing in, Bob's digital distaste for the newfangled did a fast fade. By the following year, he had endorsed Pepsi at Super Bowl XLIII for those who think young, singing "Forever Young"[487] in a duet with the Black Eyed Peas's will.i.am.

---

[487] In 2010, NBC also licensed the song to open each episode of its weekly drama *Parenthood*.

The grandest "sellout" of all, however, came five years later during Super Bowl XLVIII when Dylan blew Bobcat minds around the globe with a Chrysler commercial[488] that reprised the rusting and resurrection of America's auto industry.

Appearing dapper, fluffed, and wrinkle-free, the made-over Dylan advised America in a suspiciously gravel-free voice that "there's nothing more American than America," suggesting that computers and other goods might be produced elsewhere, but automobiles should be made only in the USA. As usual, Dylan took heat from his critics for tacitly approving of iPhone assembly in Asian sweat-shops, but his base constituency—the boomers and beyond—were instantly charmed. With a little (or a lot) of CGI assistance, their enduring '60s standard-bearer arose one more time, preaching the all-American creed[489] during the most widely witnessed television broadcast in history.

In his 2011 biography, Steve Jobs tied the rise of iTunes directly to Dylan. Apple's cofounder recalled meeting the idol of his youth[490] during a N.E.T. stop in Palo Alto. Like Microsoft's Paul Allen, Jobs was awestruck.

"He's one of my all-time heroes," said Jobs. "My love for him has grown over the years. It's ripened. I can't figure out how he did it when he was so young."

Like *60 Minutes*' Ed Bradley, Jobs had to ask about those early songs.

"They just came through me," Dylan told him. "It wasn't like I was having to compose them."

---

[488] Drawing slightly less ire, the night also featured the *Blonde on Blonde* song "I Want You" to sell Chobani yogurt.

[489] Ironically, the company is now a wholly owned subsidiary of Fiat.

[490] He also wanted to—and did—date Joan Baez.

Jobs wanted to offer Dylan's entire catalog over iTunes for $199, but guessing that Apple could be squeezed for more, Sony CEO Andy Lack offered Jeff Rosen $1 million to tell Jobs "no." Rosen took the $1 million, but two years later when Sony's annual revenues were in free fall, Jobs was back. This time, he brought along an iPod loaded with all of Bob's albums. In addition to making them available as a download on iTunes, he argued, Sony could offer the $199 Dylan collection in stores as a boxed set of 773 tracks with an additional 43 unreleased songs dating all the back to Dinkytown. Both CDs and downloads would be available at the release of *Modern Times,* Dylan's follow-up to *Love and Theft.*

Bob agreed.

Breaking with TV ads featuring Dylan singing "Someday Baby" from the new album, Sony sold almost 200,000 copies of *Modern Times* during its first week in release. His latest LP debuted at No. 1—the first time that had happened since *Desire.*

An elegiac collection of laments and love songs laced with apocalyptic warning and Biblical allusion, *Modern Times* marked yet another 90-degree turn. This time, Bob's fans turned with him.

"Even though Dylan has been completely deified, he's taken all the spiritual journeys we plebeians go through," declared Sheryl Crow. "In his search you can see the patterns of humanity."

Like his original audience now pushing 60 themselves, Dylan tapped deep into nostalgia for *Modern Times.* Can't tell where you're goin' unless you know where you been, he once preached. Along with the debut of the *Theme Time Radio Hour* and an ill-conceived Broadway musical based on his earliest songs, the album was another lingering reminder of lessons learned.

More than his two previous albums, the rollicking old-time religion evoked by "Thunder on the Mountain" didn't let up until the dire final notes of "Ain't Talkin.'" Once the infectious walkin' blues faded, index fingers across the land hit replay once, twice, then one more time, as in the halcyon days when *Highway 61 Revisited* or *Blonde on Blonde* first landed on a million turntables and boomers studied each and every word. From California to the New York Island and beyond, *Modern Times* sold more than 4 million units during its first two months in release.

In addition to rallying his core audience, all that close listening raised new charges of plagiarism. Whereas serendipity played the chief role in matching *Confessions of a Yakuza* with *Love and Theft*, search engine technology made matching Bob's newest lyrics with all that had come before very easy. Deconstructing *Modern Times* became a parlor game anyone could play. It took minutes to Google. What turned up on "Expecting Rain" and other fan websites was heresy: Bob Dylan had stolen from a nineteenth-century poet named Henry Timrod.

"If it was anyone else, we'd be stringing them up by their neck," wrote one outraged fan. "But no! It's Bobby Dee and 'the folk process.'"

When another furious Bobcat called Dylan "a thieving little swine," singer-songwriter Suzanne Vega came to his defense.

"I am trying to imagine a Bob Dylan album with footnotes, asterisks, *ibid*'s and nifty little anecdotes about the origins of each song," she said. "It's not going to happen. He's never pretended to be an academic or even a nice guy. He is more likely to present himself as, well, a thief. Renegade, outlaw, artist. That's why we are passionate about him."

As early as "Love Is Just a Four Letter Word,"[491] Bob borrowed from others and incorporated their lines without giving credit—a

---

[491] Lifted from *Cat on a Hot Tin Roof*, which explained in part Dylan's grief when Tennessee Williams died.

practice *New York Times* reporter Motoko Rich ascribed to "magpie tendencies." Dylan shrugged off the indignation. He was far more interested in rhythm and rhyme.

"It gives you a thrill to rhyme something you might think, well, that's never been rhymed before," said Dylan. He managed to rhyme "orphanages" with "sons-of-bitches" in "Thunder on the Mountain," savoring the same poetic pleasure he once derived from combining "juiced in it" with "used to it."

"Words or rhymes that seem gratuitous in print often make good musical sense," observed *The New Yorker*'s Ellen Willis way back when "Like a Rolling Stone" was fresh off Columbia's vinyl assembly line. Words or rhymes from the past always made sense to Dylan.

"My songs, what makes them different is that there's a foundation to them," he explained to the *New York Times*'s Jon Pareles. "They're standing on a strong foundation, and subliminally that's what people are hearing."

Three months before the release of *Modern Times*, his unfamiliar growl began broadcasting over XM Satellite Radio in a weekly testament to that strong foundation. Originating from fictitious Studio D in the equally fictitious Abernathy Building, Dylan delivered deejay patter and an undisguised reverence for the pop poetry of musicians long dead during his *Theme Time Radio Hour*. Located somewhere in the midwest, presumably not far from Garrison Keillor's Lake Woebegone, he resurrected a fiercely independent 1950s radio spirit. WHLB's Jim Dandy came alive once more, reviving the free-form playbook of AM radio along the Mesabi Range.

Produced by *Dharma and Greg*'s Eddie Gorodetsky,[492] each program featured a different theme—baseball, cars, money, weather,

---

[492] His wife, graphic artist Coco Shinomiya, designed the logo for the later CD releases of *Theme Time Radio Hour* as well as the covers for *Together Through Life* and *Christmas in the Heart*.

etc. A total of 50 programs in all, they were 60 minutes long except for two two-hour holiday shows and a tongue-in-cheek broadcast about "time" that ran more than one hour by 17 minutes. Regardless of their obscurity, Dylan lauded each artist and thanked them for making some small difference by recording for posterity.

Traipsing through the past wasn't a complete success, however. After watching her turn Billy Joel's catalog into a successful Broadway musical, Dylan approached choreographer Twyla Tharp to do the same for him. Turned out Bob was a fan.

"I've loved the ballet since my childhood," he said. "I like the atmosphere, the dancer's smooth motions and the staggering sound of an orchestra."

On October 26, 2006, *The Times They Are a-Changin'* opened at the Brooks Atkinson Theater. A familiar fable about a father-son struggle, the musical featured 26 Dylan songs melded with grand visual clichés that included the ceiling of the Sistine Chapel, Michelangelo's Pietà, and the twin pillars of light at Ground Zero. Though *The Times They Are a-Changin'* orchestra managed to make "Dignity"[493] and "Simple Twist of Fate" sound like show tunes, the plot resembled something out of *Tarantula*.

Dylan might have had better luck collaborating once more with Jacques Levy, but the librettist who successfully staged *Oh! Calcutta!* before teaming with Dylan on *Desire* had died two years earlier. Johnny Cash, Warren Zevon, Waylon Jennings, Dave Von Ronk, Doug Sahm, Alan Lomax . . . the list of peers Bob eulogized on the Never Ending Tour grew a little longer every year.

The Times They Are a-Changin' closed after 28 performances.

---

[493] In 1995, songwriter James Damiano sued for plagiarism, claiming Dylan stole his song "Steel Guitars" after he handed it over to Dylan in 1988. Though dismissed the following year, Damiano appealed his suit and has continued his legal battle to the present day.

■ ■ ■

The trilogy he began with *Time Out of Mind* echoed generational angst in much the same way *Bringing It All Back Home, Highway 61 Revisited,* and *Blonde on Blonde* refracted youth revolt during the '60s. It also launched Bob Dylan on a whole new examination of his essence. Albeit a very different Pied Piper from the one who had marched on Washington with Martin Luther King Jr., Dylan firmly reestablished himself as a Yuppie role model by the time he released *Modern Times*.

His writing process had changed. He no longer whipped out inspired masterworks at a single intoxicated sitting. He came to the studio serious, sober, and prepared. As Los Lobos's David Hidalgo described a typical recording session, Dylan brought "20 verses that he's got laid out, and he'll pick and choose and rewrite while he's going."

While not the spontaneous Bob of yore, he connected with youngsters as easily as he did with their parents and grandparents. On the open road, they were right there with him. He'd spoken to the generations once; he spoke to them again, this time as a survivor. Ironically, Dylan's constant reinvention addressed a cultural identity crisis fostered by such Bobcat superfans as Steve Jobs and Paul Allen.

"When things come at you very fast, naturally you lose touch with yourself," observed Marshall McLuhan years before the Internet began to disintegrate the recording industry. Pop music had been the first casualty, but by the Great Recession of 2008, the daily newspaper, network TV, movies, even book publishing were all under digital attack. Dylan's answer was to tune out, turn off, and wise up.

"It's peculiar and unnerving in a way to see so many young people walking around with cell phones and iPods in their ears and so wrapped up in media and video games," he said. "It robs them of their self-identity. It's a shame to see them so tuned out to real life."

He might grouse about the Web, but gave Jeff Rosen permission to exploit each new app.[494] Bob stayed Old School and followed his own advice about remaining tuned in to real life. He was rewarded accordingly.

While Dylan claimed for a time that he never saw either *No Direction Home* or *I'm Not There*,[495] both films earned multiple honors. *No Direction Home* won a George Foster Peabody Award. Todd Haynes's oddball art-house movie only took in half of its $20 million production cost at the box office, but won actress Cate Blanchett a Golden Globe and an Oscar nomination in her role as Amphetamine Bob.

The Pulitzer jury passed over *Chronicles*, but did issue a special citation praising his music. Dylan was in Russia on his Never Ending Tour when he got the news, but sent son Jesse to pick up the plaque.

David Amram, a classical composer who watched Bob evolve from Village wunderkind to international phenom over the years, heard "This is the *new* Bob Dylan!" with regularity whenever an exciting new talent hit the concert circuit.

"But, of course, Bob Dylan became the new Bob Dylan every two years himself," he said. "The thing that endears me to him is that he's still out there, searching and trying to get a deeper understanding of life, and he's still not content with what he's doing. That's what I think most good artists are like. They're always trying to improve, to advance, to go into other areas that they haven't

---

[494] His one-line description of Twitter: "Short term gain; long term loss."

[495] Haynes gave him a DVD before the film's release, but assumed he'd watch old westerns and noir detective yarns instead. Five years later, Dylan conceded, "It was all right."

worked in before, and to take the thing that they did before and do it even better."

Roseanne Cash predicted Dylan would be writing songs on his death bed, same as her famous father. "It's like Matisse creating the 'Jazz Dancers' when he was in his 80s," she said.

Dylan's first watercolor exhibition debuted in 2007, centering on his 1994 *Drawn Blank* collection. Scanning and digitally reproducing his black-and-white sketches on deckle-edged paper, Dylan created 322 paintings with gouache and watercolor washes.

"I've always drawn and painted, but up until recently nobody's taken an interest," he said. "Now I'm scrambling to keep up."

∷ ∷ ∷

During Barack Obama's final campaign swing, Bob played Minneapolis on election eve 2008, stepping out of the spotlight when the future president spoke. The senator from Illinois seemed as unlikely a character to Dylan as any he'd ever invented—the son of a white Kansan and a black Kenyan, embodying the polar opposites of Blind Willie racism.

"I think Barack has Jefferson Davis back there in his ancestry someplace," said Dylan. "And then his father, an African intellectual, Bantu, Masai, Griot-type heritage—cattle raiders, lion killers. I mean it's just so incongruous that these two people would meet and fall in love."

Ever vigilant over his political neutrality, he stopped short of endorsing Obama. He recalled instead the broad support George W. Bush once enjoyed.

"As far as blaming everything on the last president, think of it this way," said Dylan. "The same folks who had held him in such high regard came to despise him. Isn't it funny that they're the very same people who once loved him? People are fickle. Their loyalty can turn at the drop of a hat."

Beginning as far back as LBJ, Bob saw the Presidency as a no-win proposition.

"Most of those guys come into office with the best of intentions and leave as beaten men," said Bob. ". . . It's like they fly too close to the sun."

In April 2009, Dylan returned to the studio to produce *Together Through Life*. Begun as the soundtrack for a road movie,[496] his 33rd studio album was a collaboration akin to *Desire*. He wrote most of the songs with former Dead lyricist and *Silvio* coauthor Robert Hunter. "Sometimes you get out from behind the wheel and let someone else step on the gas," said Bob.

From "If You Ever Go To Houston" to "Beyond Here Lies Nothin'," his voice was so froggy that his words frequently got lost. Further, the Hunter/Dylan lyrics didn't have the same impact of the triumphant trilogy that had begun with *Time Out of Mind*. Honing a Rio Grande border sound, *Together Through Life* was all Tex-Mex in the same way *Oh Mercy* had a New Orleans sound and *Love and Theft* resonated the Old South. For a time, Dylan reinvented himself as an actual resident of the Long Star state, though there was no evidence that was true.

Despite its shortcomings, *Together Through Life* topped the *Billboard* charts the same week it was released. A month later, Bob was back in the studio recording a Christmas album. An obvious spin-off of the *Theme Time Radio Hour*, *Christmas in the Heart* contained seasonal chestnuts[497] like Judy Garland's "Have Yourself a Merry Little Christmas" and Bing Crosby's "Little Drummer Boy," and

---

[496] *My Own Love Song* (2010) starred Renée Zellweger and Forrest Whitaker.

[497] An oddball music video of "Must Be Santa" featured Dylan in Santa drag at a polka party while couples half his age danced.

went into release just before the holidays. Idiosyncratic as ever, Dylan granted his sole *Christmas in the Heart* interview to a free newspaper produced by and for the homeless. All royalties were earmarked to fight world hunger.

Why? Why not? If nothing else, he'd earned a right to his eccentricity.

:: :: ::

On a rainy afternoon in July 2009, Dylan donned a pair of boots, a hoodie, and two raincoats before trekking off from his tour bus to scout real estate. His boot heels wandered to a down-market neighborhood of the once-prosperous seaside resort of Long Branch, New Jersey.

Bob still savored a bargain. Just two years earlier, he had extended his portfolio to Scotland,[498] far beyond his holdings in Minnesota or Malibu. He paid more than $4 million for a secluded Edwardian mansion in the Cairngorm hills south of Inverness and put brother David in charge of fixing the place up. Dylan kept on rolling, antenna keen at every N.E.T. stop for the next property that caught his fancy. He had a special fondness for places where his peers had come of age.

"I was in Elvis's hometown—Tupelo," he recalled. "I was trying to feel what he would have felt back when he was growing up."

Dylan secretly visited several such homesteads.[499] During a stay in Manitoba, he found Neil Young's boyhood home and knocked at the owner's door in much the same way Bobcats had taken to showing up on the doorstep of the old Zimmerman place in Hibbing.

---

[498]   In 2004, the University of St. Andrews awarded Bob an honorary music degree.

[499]   Bob made pilgrimages to the homes of Hank Williams, Buddy Holly, Roy Orbison, Jimmie Rodgers, Rembrandt, and Anne Frank (Amsterdam), among others.

"I wanted to see his bedroom," said Dylan. "Where he looked out of the windows. Where he dreamed. Where he walked out the door every day. Wanted to see what's around his neighborhood in Winnipeg."

Similarly, he'd visited John Lennon's Liverpool home as part of a £16 tour regularly conducted by the British National Trust. This particular rainy day in Long Branch, New Jersey, he was in the neighborhood where Bruce Springsteen wrote "Born to Run." Bob hovered near the porch as the cops pulled up.

"We see a lot of people on our beat, and I wasn't sure if he came from one of our hospitals or something," Officer Kristie Buble later recalled to ABC News.

Responding to a dispatch call about a drenched derelict outside a modest house with a "for sale" sign in the front yard, the 24-year-old patrol officer and her partner Derrick Meyers approached with caution.

"What is your name, sir?" Buble asked.

"Bob Dylan."

"Okay, Bob, what are you doing here?"

He might have told her he was traveling with Willie Nelson and John Mellencamp as part of a summerlong whistle-stop tour of minor league baseball parks, but Buble remained dubious. She and Meyers had heard similar indigent tall tales. He had a show that very evening in nearby Lakewood. He'd decided to kill time by going for a stroll.

When he failed to produce identification, the cops put Dylan in the back of their squad car, called in the incident, and asked where he was staying. A big hotel next to the ocean, said Bob. Sgt. Michael Ahart was waiting when they pulled into the parking lot of the Ocean Palace Resort and Spa.

"Sarge, this guy says he's Bob Dylan," said Buble.

Ahart peered through the window at the rain soaked wraith.

"That's not Bob Dylan," he said.

The police found a wary roadie near one of three large tour buses and asked if anybody was missing.

"Who's asking?" he demanded.

Wary herself, Buble patiently explained. She asked to see Bob's passport. She and her sergeant studied the photo, then Bob. They told him to get out of the squad car.

Buble could be forgiven the mistake. Both she and her partner were born the year Bob played Live Aid. Craig Spencer, a Long Branch police spokesman with several years on both officers said, "If it was me, I'd have been demanding his autograph, not his I.D."

But times had changed. Kristie Buble had only a vague notion who Bob Dylan was. During the inevitable media onslaught that followed, she complimented Dylan for not losing his cool. He could have been an asshole. He was not. Assured that he was indeed the voice of a generation—if not her own—she told reporters that she'd given him a tip of the hat and wished him well.

"Okay," she said. "Have a nice day."

EPILOGUE

The past is never dead. It's not even
past.

—William Faulkner

There's Bob Dylan and there's Bobby Zimmerman. Mostly one equals the other. The world knows a lot about the former. Bookshelves creak. There are not one, but *two* Bob Dylan encyclopedias, each weighing in at more than three pounds. Bob Dylan is as iconic an American literary figure as Walt Whitman, Ralph Waldo Emerson, or Mark Twain. By comparison, Robert Allen Zimmerman is an orphan.

"The land created me," said Dylan. "I'm wild and lonesome. Even as I travel the cities, I'm more at home in the vacant lots."

Wikipedia delivers the basics, from Hibbing childhood and Dinkytown adolescence to Village transfiguration somewhere near the end of the Eisenhower Administration. As his vast fan base mushroomed, so did his struggle to remain himself. How much Zimmy exists inside Dylan? As much Sam Clemens as lived inside Mark Twain. On one level, the pen and birth name are synonymous. On another, the emotional gulf between man and myth is so deep and wide as to be unfathomable.

The boy from Hibbing is now as permanently interwoven into American folklore as Sam Clemens growing up barefoot and poor along the banks of the Mississippi. Yet Mark Twain's storied career has become a veritable showcase[500] compared to Dylan's fiercely closeted life. Once his Never Ending Tour resurrected him in the American imagination during the 1990s, Dylan padlocked the door and Zimmy threw away the key.

"They say, 'Dylan never talks.' What the hell is there to say?" he complained. "That's not the reason an artist is in front of people."

At the release of *Tempest* in the autumn of 2012, he cracked the door just a little. *The Tempest* was William Shakespeare's final play—a fable about an aging necromancer atoning at life's end with the assistance of a captive nymph. Dylan nixed any similarity to his own life. He pointed out that there was no "*The*" in front of *Tempest*. Any comparison to Shakespeare's swan song was mistaken. It was not as if Bob Dylan had reason to lie.

"People are going to say, 'Well, it's not very truthful," he told *Rolling Stone*'s Mikal Gilmore. "But a songwriter doesn't care about what's truthful. What he cares about is what should've happened, what could've happened. That's its own kind of truth."

That Dylan insisted on secretly meeting Gilmore to discuss *Tempest* at the rear of a Santa Monica restaurant disguised in ski cap, wig, and black leather jacket was equally irrelevant. Don't pay attention to the man behind the curtain. Listen to what he *says*; don't dwell on who he *is*.

"The old goes out and the new comes in, but there is no sharp borderline," Bob instructed Gilmore. "The old is still happening while the new enters the scene, sometimes unnoticed. The new is overlapping at the same time the old is weakening its hold. It goes on and on like that. Forever through the centuries. Sooner or later,

---

[500]   After critics excoriated an unexpurgated centennial edition of Mark Twain's *Autobiography*, Garrison Keillor warned, "Think twice about donating your papers to an institution of higher learning, Famous Writer. Someday they may be used against you."

before you know it, everything is new, and what happened to the old? It's like a magician trick, but you have to keep connecting with it."

■■ ■■ ■■

At President Barack Obama's request, Dylan connected with him at the White House on February 11, 2010. He sang "The Times They Are a-Changin'," not as anthem in commemoration of the 50th anniversary of the civil rights movement, but as requiem better suited to the second line at a jazz funeral. While others who were gathered there for the occasion roused with hope over moving up from the back of the bus, Dylan drawled as if in defeat. A half century on, congressmen, senators seldom heeded calls beyond their own. Still, Dylan continued to express cautious optimism.

"America is to me a rising tide that lifts all ships," he said before setting off on yet another leg of his Never Ending voyage. The president awarded him the American National Medal of the Arts a couple of weeks later but Bob didn't show. He was on the road again. He did 102 shows that year. Two more slid by before he returned to the White House.

Five days past his 71st birthday, Dylan appeared in the East Room to accept the Medal of Freedom. Of the 12 recipients,[501] he was the only one in shades. Before draping the nation's highest peacetime laurel over the singer's narrow shoulders, the president beamed. He recalled listening to Bob's music while he was still an undergraduate and the whole world had opened up to him.

---

[501] Madeleine Albright, Toni Morrison, John Glenn, Shimon Peres, former Supreme Court Justice John Paul Stevens, Asst. Attorney General John Doar, Center for Disease Control director William Foege, labor leader Dolores Huerta, and three posthumous honorees.

"There is not a bigger giant in the history of American music," the president intoned. "All these years later, he's still chasing that sound, still searching for a little bit of truth and I have to say, I am a really big fan."

Others were not.

"We are like night and day, he and I," Joni Mitchell declared in a 2010 interview with the *Los Angeles Times*. "Bob is not authentic at all. He's a plagiarist, and his name and voice are fake. Everything about Bob is a deception."[502]

Echoing dozens of detractors Dylan had sidestepped over the years, Mitchell fingered Bob as a product of pop music's star-maker machinery. A quarter century earlier, she'd preached the precise opposite.

"When I heard Bob Dylan sing, 'You gotta lotta nerve,' I thought, 'Hallelujah, man, the American pop song has grown up!'" she said. "It's wide open. Now you can write about anything that literature can write about.'"

Perhaps she was just much older then, but betrayal and petty jealousy had always plagued Dylan. Former acolytes like Mitchell kissed him off the way Judas kissed off Jesus.

"People have tried to stop me every inch of the way," he groused to Mikal Gilmore. "They've always had bad stuff to say about me."

He shed old friends accordingly and apologized for nothing. Synthesis was how Hank and Woody and a hundred others had written

---

[502] Mitchell later called her interviewer, Matt Diehl of the *Los Angeles Times,* "a complete asshole" with an I.Q. "somewhere between his shoe size and his knees." She maintained that her remarks were taken out of context, but even so, ". . . musically, (Bob) is not very gifted. He's borrowed his voice from old hillbillies. He's got a lot of borrowed things. He's not a great guitar player. He's invented a character to deliver his songs. Sometimes I wish that I could have that character—because you can do things with that character. It's a mask of sorts."

songs before him and it was how a hundred thousand would do so after he was gone. Call it borrowing, paraphrasing, theft, Dylan knew the practice as songwriting.

He shrugged off similar carping over his painting. When the *New York Times* exposed 18 oils on display at Manhattan's Gagosian gallery as reproductions of famous photos rather than the "visual journal" of Bob's Far East tour as advertised, Internet wags began referring to "The Asia Series" as "Bob Dylan: The Paint-By-The-Numbers Edition." Bob returned to his easel without comment.

He did not keep silent when pundits took potshots at his politics. In a 2011 column titled "Blowin' in the Idiot Wind," the *New York Times*'s Maureen Dowd scolded him for eliminating "The Times They Are a-Changin'" and "Masters of War" from his repertoire during a N.E.T. stop in China. Didn't matter that Bob had quit protesting after both anthems were written. Dissent was a young man's pastime. Besides, every Western act had to submit to "harmonizing," as the People's Republic preferred labeling its censorship policy. So his choice seemed clear: submit a playlist or don't play at all.

Any supposition that he "sang his censored set, took his pile of Communist cash and left" was absurd on its face. Dylan said as much in a reply he had Jeff Rosen post on his website. He might not have roused the rabble in Shanghai, but "we played all the songs that we intended to play."

In his final word on the subject of critics, he told *Rolling Stone*, "Fuck 'em. I'll see them all in their graves."

⁘ ⁘ ⁘

Bob signed with Simon and Schuster to do six books after *Chronicles*. One would be a tie-in with the *Theme Time Radio Hour.* He planned three others once he finished *Chronicles II* and *III*.

"I'm always working on parts of it," he said, though investing time and energy at his age could be exhausting. So why do it?

Kudos, speculated Randy Newman. Bob's contemporary called the occupational compulsion "trying for Shakespeare," and cited poets from Billy Joel and Paul Simon to Goethe and Dante as similarly afflicted. Denying that it was on one's agenda amounted to artistic hypocrisy, yet no writer worth his salt wanted less.

"You can't *try* to do art. You can't *try* to do Dante," said Newman, laughing as he added, "but you try *real* hard."

Bob tried harder than most.

"Dylan, yeah," said Newman. "Definitely. Yeah. He would never admit to it. But I believe he wanted the laurel, won the laurel, and wore the laurel."

That's why he sang his songs around the world year after year; why he showed up at the White House in shades; why he embroidered the truth; why he discouraged Dylanologists from dogging his heels—but not so much that they lost interest all together.

The New York Times' Jon Pareles defined Dylan as "sly and transformative . . . sometimes viewing his past selves with avuncular pride and amusement, sometimes staring into the abyss, sometimes tempering youthful spite with empathy."

Dylan read voraciously. B. F. Rolfzen's classroom investment back in 1957 paid off in a dazzling synthesis of Shelby Foote, Shakespeare, and Skip James; Milton, Melville, and Mick Jagger; Blake, Baudelaire, and B. B. King, et al., et cetera, ad nauseam.

On occasion he'd spin off on his passion for the Civil War. He knew the Bible, the Gnostic gospels, and the Book of Mormon and could discourse for hours on theology. He was very well read, but then he'd remember he was Bob Dylan, and sing the blues instead.

But chasing Shakespeare into the seventh decade could be a dicey game, especially for one who'd been through all of F. Scott

Fitzgerald's books. Dylan downplayed erudition and identified with ancient blues croakers. Just a vagabond, he insisted to those academics who made him required reading in freshman lit.

:: :: ::

Following his first visit to Memphis, Bob speculated that Elvis might have founded a religion.

"First of all, El-vis in Hebrew means God," he said. "El is God in Hebrew. And Elvis is just a reiteration of the tribe of Levi. And anybody who wears jeans is a Hebrew. Also, anybody who wears a baseball cap backwards, that's a yarmulke. That's heavy, eh? The world operates on principles that we know nothing of."

Bob had played footsies with the hereafter his whole life. He'd never abandoned astrology as a periscope into the future, but neither did he reject the mystic Essene who fished for souls in Galilee 2,000 years ago. He delighted in trotting out the Book of Revelation during interviews. Priests and rabbis couldn't tell whether his tongue was in or out of his cheek. Bob was redeemed, or so he said, but would not elaborate.

As the end of the Mayan calendar approached in 2012, transfiguration became his latest supernatural obsession. Not the sort of miracle that switched Saul to Paul on the road to Damascus or made Jesus glow next to Moses and Elijah on Mount Hebron, but transformative nonetheless.

"Transfiguration is what allows you to crawl out from under the chaos and fly above it," said Bob. "That's how I can still do what I do and write the songs I sing and just keep on moving."

He stopped short of self-canonization, but hovered dangerously close to hubris. His peers, he said, were Medal of Freedom winners, not just other singer-songwriters. People with a purpose, a calling . . . a *higher* calling.

People like Elvis? Graceland had become a shrine, after all. Identified by its iconic music wrought-iron gates, Presley's private residence inspired a half million pilgrimages each year. It was second only to the White House. Each August on the anniversary of his death, the faithful gathered in remembrance around the royal grave.

Before he overdosed, Elvis was to Memphis as Dylan is to Hibbing. Millions know Memphis as the home of the King. Not quite as many have trekked to northern Minnesota, but the numbers grow each year, according to the Hibbing Chamber of Commerce. Seventh Street west of Hibbing High has been renamed Bob Dylan Drive just as the stretch of Highway 51 outside Graceland is now Elvis Presley Boulevard.

The Friends of the Hibbing Public Library buy new books with proceeds from the sales of Beatty Zimmerman's recipe for banana bread and facsimiles of the Bob Dylan Drive street sign. In the library basement is a permanent Dylan exhibition detailing every nuance of his childhood. Maps of Dylan walking tours are available at stores or cafés along Howard Street. Stop in the L&B Café for a cherry pie à la mode. Visit the railroad crossing where young Bob nearly slid his Harley into eternity.

Each May, the city stages its annual Dylan Days[503] celebration to commemorate the hometown hero's birthday. Bob and Linda Hocking bought Zimmy's bar some years ago and rededicated it as Dylan Days headquarters. Bob memorabilia line the walls and ceiling. A

---

[503] Not to be outdone, Duluth renamed a 1.8 mile stretch of lakefront highway Bob Dylan Way on his 66th birthday. Marked by signs depicting Bob in front of a microphone, the road gets another commemorative manhole cover dedicated each birthday and becomes Highway 61 revisited once more during the annual Duluth Dylan Festival, which began in 2011.

huge doe-eyed portrait of Echo Helstrom stares from the neon sign on the street. The Dylan soundtrack never stops.[504]

"My dream is that he'll come back," said Hocking, "and if the Never Ending Tour ends, it ends where it began, where he did Little Richard. It would be a dream come true if he came back and played his last concert at Hibbing High School."

◼◼◼

From Johann Sebastian Bach to Louis Armstrong to B. B. King, musicians loved the ladies and seem to have sired more illegitimate children than most other mortals. William DeVogue believes Bob Dylan fit the pattern. In July 2011, he set out to prove Dylan was his dad.

"I found his management company online and faxed my story, my photo and a picture of my mother taken when she was a young woman," said DeVogue.

Tina Voyes was a folkie who lived in the Village 50 years ago. Like Paul Clayton, Bob Gibson, Mike Bloomfield, Janis Joplin, and so many others, she was also an addict. She gave Will up for adoption when he was three.

Tina spent the next four decades in and out of rehab while Will spent roughly half that time looking for his mother. When he found her in a Boston suburb, years of drug abuse had taken its toll. The story of his birth trickled out slowly. She told her son she'd been under the influence when she met Dylan. Nine months later, Will was born.

---

[504] Unfortunately, it did stop early in 2014. Because of business conditions Zimmy's was forced to close. Despite this, Bobcats remained hopeful the setback was temporary and vowed to continue with the year's Dylan Days celebrations, albeit at a different venue.

For years, rumors of Bob progeny buzzed the blogosphere. From Minneapolis to New Orleans, Dylan had allegedly loved them and left them, but quizzing him about unplanned pregnancies was taboo. Had she not confessed it in her memoir, Suze Rotolo Bartoccioli might have gone to her grave with the secret of her own abortion. When she died of lung cancer at 67 on February 25, 2011, Suze had indeed left a son, but it wasn't Bob's.

DeVogue believed that he was Bob's. When he thought he had enough evidence, he spoke with Jeff Rosen and Dylan's loyal gate-keeper did not dismiss the story out of hand. In fact, he demanded more details as soon as possible. Will's resemblance to Dylan, and the young Tina to Suze, Baez, or Sara Dylan, was just too strong. Dylan had a type in his salad days. Tina fit it perfectly.

"I told Jeff I didn't want anything," said DeVogue. "I still don't. I just wanted to know if Bob Dylan was my father."

DeVogue asked for a blood test. He received a terse reply the following day:

Dear Will,

First I want to confirm I received your email. Secondly, I want to let you know that I ran the particulars you mentioned by Mr. Dylan again. He has no recollection of any of the events or people that you describe. I know this is disappointing to you, and I'm sorry that this path on your journey has proven to be a dead end.

Sincerely,
Jeff Rosen

DeVogue persisted. He found a lab online that did DNA testing for under $200. They didn't even require blood. Will could swab the inside of his cheek. Dylan could do the same and within a week, they'd know.

But Rosen's initial zeal faded as fast as it first came on. He no longer returned phone calls, letters, or e-mail.

A year passed. During that time, DeVogue took his campaign to the Internet. He created a website, did newspaper and TV interviews, and began videotaping his and Tina's story for a documentary.

In August 2012, he heard from a Southern California woman who believed they might have something in common.

"Bob Dylan's my dad!" declared Isabella Vincenza Birdfeather.

So certain was she that her late mother, L.A. disc jockey Barbara Birdfeather, had trysted with Bob in the early '80s that Isabella began calling herself Izzy Dylan. Indeed, her physical resemblance to the young Bob, down to her cornflower eyes, was even stronger than DeVogue's.

But Isabella's reception at Rosen's office was as chilly as Will's. DeVogue hatched a plan. They couldn't get Bob's cooperation, but they could run the DNA test on themselves to see if they were siblings. They did so and the results came back doubtful: only a 9 percent chance they were brother and sister.

"I don't understand it. It means one or both of us are probably not his," said DeVogue. "But I'm not going to give up."

■■ ■■ ■■

Back in 1985, before his legacy became a concern, Dylan said, "I figure you just go ahead and live your life. And you move on to the next thing. And when it's all said and done, you let the historians figure it out."

The truth about Bob Dylan likely will not fully emerge until he passes, if then. For more than 30 years, he has successfully bought off, discredited, intimidated, or manipulated all who might divulge too much. Even his bus drivers sign a nondisclosure agreement. They adhere to it or risk never driving again.

Same with the vast array of scholars, critics, and authors who write about Bob. Access is all, but any who venture deeper than the music find themselves shut out. In 2010, with Bob's blessing, Princeton professor Sean Wilentz[505] published *Bob Dylan in America*—a weighty exercise in deep-tissue Dylanology that briefly made the *New York Times* bestseller list. In a promotional appearance on *The Colbert Report*, Wilentz acknowledged having met Dylan, but refused to talk about him. Those few to whom Bob has granted an audience similarly fear shunning—Ruth Tyrangiel, for example.

Dylan's one-time girlfriend lost her palimony case, appealed, lost again, and was hit with a court order in the late '90s to pay Dylan's lawyers $6,000 for her deposition. The case never advanced to the point where she was able to depose Bob. These days, she lives less than a quarter mile from his Malibu compound, still hopeful of reconciliation.

Though they lived within miles of each other near the beach in Santa Monica, Bob Neuwirth and Dylan hadn't spoken for years. Still performing his own truncated version of a Never Ending Tour, Neuwirth recorded a song ten years ago titled "The Call" about a late night voicemail from an old musician pal.

> Got a message last night
> Coming in loud and clear
> I tried calling right back
> No one was there.

---

[505] Wilentz is also official historian for www.bobdylan.com.

Neuwirth reminisced about raising hell during "them bad good ol' days": cutting corners, stealing scenes, courting a pair of dark-haired sisters who sounded suspiciously like Joan and Mimi Baez. They might try it again sometime "for old time's sake," he sang. But while he might sing about the past, he won't speak of it.

"I don't like to talk about it," said Neuwirth. "I'd rather talk about the future."

▪▪ ▪▪ ▪▪

As he approached his 72rd birthday, Dylan and his Never Ending juggernaut rolled on, stronger and more perplexing than ever. In March 2013, the venerable American Academy of Arts and Letters admitted Bob as an honorary member. Founded in 1898, the Academy numbers only 250 members. Normally, new faces are admitted only when one of them dies, but for Bob they made an exception.

"Bob Dylan is a multi-talented artist whose work so thoroughly crosses several disciplines that it defies categorization," said Academy executive director Virginia Dajani.

Bob didn't show for his May induction, but did send a thank-you note. He felt "extremely honored and very lucky."

"I look forward to meeting all of you some time soon," he said.

In August, *The Bootleg Series Vol. 10* materialized from the East West Touring Company archives. Subtitled *Another Self Portrait*,[506] the double album featured unreleased outtakes from the original *Self Portrait* as well as *New Morning, The Basement Tapes*, and *Nashville Skyline*. Continuing a marketing strategy that dribbled forth a

---

[506] As with the original, *Another Self Portrait* featured a self-portrait that bore scant resemblance to Dylan. Unlike the abstract smears of *Self Portrait, Another Self Portrait* looked like Graham Nash circa 1980.

few new old cuts year after year, *Vol. 10* implied many more volumes to come.

A far more audacious sales ploy followed in November with the release of *Bob Dylan: The Complete Album Collection, Vol. I.* Milking the yuppiest of Bobcats for all they were worth, *Vol. I* (could there ever be a *Vol. II?*) sold as a harmonica-shaped flash drive and contained every album Dylan has ever released as well as a couple CDs of unreleased singles. Price: $319.98.

▪ ▪ ▪

Highway 61 parallels the Mississippi River bloodline that cleaves the American heartland from Duluth where Bob Dylan was born, and runs all the way to New Orleans. Up and down that river road, the soundtrack of the American dream still resonates in juke joints and coffeehouses. There is symphony to the bleat of the long-distance trucker's horn, the chug of locomotives, and the whine of jetliners crisscrossing the continent. Bobby Zimmerman heard the yawp before he could crawl.

"Just like Shakespeare was gonna write his plays, the Wright Brothers were gonna invent an airplane, like Edison was gonna invent a telephone, I was put here to do this," he said. "I knew I was gonna do it better than anybody ever did it."

As he grew older, Highway 61 carried him farther and farther from his roots. Route 66 intersected east to west through the American West. Interstate 95 traced a throughline from Maine to the Gulf. Highway 1 hugged the Pacific coastline all the way from the Mexican border to Canada. Bob Dylan traveled all those roads and more.

He insists he never returns to his hometown, but, as with so much of what Dylan says, that isn't true.

"He's come here many times," said David Oxman,[507] a lifelong resident who knew Bob as boy and man. "He drives up from his brother's place. He sits outside his mother's house. He goes by our synagogue and Hibbing High."

Bob Dylan may have quit Hibbing, but Elston Gunn never got past Howard Street. Even when he's not there, Dylan's hometown holds on to him. Whether true or just remembered that way, Robert Zimmerman grew up amid circuses, carnivals, barnstorms, and big bands. Hibbing was where he met "Miss Europe, Quasimodo, the Bearded Lady, the half-man half-woman, the deformed and the bent, Atlas the Dwarf, the fire-eaters, the teachers and preachers, the blues singers. I remember it like it was yesterday."

For 50 years, Dylan transited the earth in search of sideshows, and an entire generation followed. On the occasion of his 70th birthday, journalist Ian MacDonald went beyond calling him the voice of his generation and dubbed him "The Dalai Lama of cool, the Moses of Acid Enlightenment . . . Dylan seems fated forever [to be] between wanting to tell us something and wanting to be left alone."

---

[507] Oxman, a Mesabi Range cable TV executive, made his remarks in 1994. He died 15 years later at the age of 86.

ACKNOWLEDGMENTS

Bob Dylan's life is my life; Bob Dylan's life is your life. Bob Dylan's life is all of our lives. He claims he's never been the voice of anybody's generation, but has to know how utterly disingenuous an assertion he's making. There's not a boomer who hasn't been touched by his anthems, ballads, and aching declarations of love. Gen Xers and Millennials have joined the chorus in recent years. The guy's our laureate. Period. End of argument.

And yet Dylan's enduring mystique totals more than the sum of his songs. His words have heft and weight and range not simply because his answers have been set down on paper, successfully rescued from blowing in the wind. Dylan never stopped asking the questions. His recent pitch for Chrysler during Super Bowl LXVIII resonated way beyond product placement or brand recognition because Bob himself resonates. His critics hopped on him like ticks on deer, but face it: What is more American than getting top dollar for selling out?

Make no mistake about the American part. Bob Dylan may have been born a Jew with Eastern European roots, but American is what he is, through and through. Always has been, forever will be. He couldn't have gotten away with the life he's led as a citizen of any other nation on earth.

Deconstructing that life was a challenge. Celebrities prize their privacy. Dylan carries the disappearing act to a whole different level. His inner circle never speaks. One pierces the Bob veil on pain of excommunication. I wouldn't want any who spoke with me punished, so I offer my heartfelt thanks by identifying them only with their initials: C. B., I. B., L. C., W. D., P. F., J. E., J. K., R. C., A. J.

W., M. Y., M. G., W. G., S. G., H. T., R. T., J. D., N. H., E. P., B. O., M. O., F. H., F. M., P. M., P. M., B. L., and J. L.

Biography always begins with those Quixotes who went before, and so it was with Bob. My enduring gratitude to his several biographers: Dave "Dylan" Engel, Bob Spitz, Toby Thompson, Howard Sounes, Ian Bell, Marc Eliot, Kevin Odegard, Michael Gray, Clinton Heylin, Paul Williams, Anthony Scaduto, Seth Rogovoy, the late Robert Shelton, and a host of others who bit off pieces of the myth, chewed them through, and digested a morsel of truth now and again, unsterilized by the Dylan publicity machine.

Similarly, I thank the journalists who have dogged Dylan's steps over the decades, unmasking him one layer at a time. My old friend and *Los Angeles Times* colleague Bob Hilburn heads a list that includes Edna Gunderson, Mikal Gilmore, Ivor Davis, David Gates, Jon Pareles, Jonathan Cott, Ron Rosenbaum, Stephen Holden, the late Al Aronowitz, John Bauldie, and Hubert Saal.

William Knoedelseder is more a brother than a friend—an older, wiser, and far more frenetic brother, but a brother nonetheless. In addition to more hair, he owns a far larger record collection and has a finely tuned appreciation of what's in it. An otherwise normal, productive American, he too succumbed early to the insanity of writing for a living. In that capacity, he has acted as sounding board, occasional editor, and consultant, never failing to add insight and insult to my prose. I remain deeply grateful for his constancy and good humor in the face of certain disaster.

Other ink-stained wretches who encouraged along the way: Jim Brown, Charles Champlin, Michael Cieply, Carol Pogash, the late, great Irv Letofsky and Jim Bellows, Ken Fields, Mark Gladstone, Bob Zeller, Rhys Thomas, Tom Szollosi, Dan Sullivan, Jill Stewart, Martin Smith, Bob Sipchen, Cathy Scott, Henry Schipper, Gus Russo, Sue Russell, Dave Robb, Bill Steigerwald, James Janega,

Danelle Morton, Susan Edmiston, Dan Moldea, Linda Marsa, Lisa Law, Larry Lynch, Dave Kinney, David Cay Johnston, Steve Long, Robert Scott, Kathryn Casey, Diane Fanning, and Kathy Cairns.

Thanks to Ira Abrams and Pam Pierce for their friendship and open-door policy. More than one chapter was written on their dining-room table. Ditto Pat & Jim Broeske, Julie Payne & Steve Luckman, and the redoubtable Dorothy "Dot" Korber. Gary Rosenberg reminded me daily of the Wonder of Days and the mantra my late father Carl McDougal drilled into me throughout his 85 years aboard this celestial mud ball: Pay Attention.

My able researcher and right-hand man Richard Ryan was an indispensable aide from start to finish. Likewise, Leonard Pickard read every word twice (thrice?), keeping syntax, voice, and grammar corralled so that gibberish came to equate English. Deborah Rybak also read behind each chapter, correcting errors, cracking wise, and offering sage storytelling advice. Alice Martell, my agent since the beginning, will remain so to the end. Christina Roth picked up editing chores where Eric Nelson had to leave off, and has handled the job like the pro that she is.

No one undertakes a book without the support of family. Mine is extensive and begins with the little red-haired girl who has been by my side for a generation. In addition to my first-line editor, Sharon Murphy McDougal is my forever Valentine. Close behind her are the legion of men and women, boys and girls whom I am proud to call my own: John & Jessica Trent, Kate & David Vokoun, Michelle Jones, Mindy & Scott Sames, Shelley Ashton, Sharon & Rick Turlington, Fitz & Sharonne Dearmore, Jen & Ray Dominguez, Andrea & Gadney Adkins, Cody & Austin Conklin, Megan Cole, Alex Cole, Ryan Dominguez, Zoe, Mia, and Wesley Vokoun, Devin, Maggie, & Callie Dearmore, Jessica MacGregor, Pat & Lynn McDougal, Neal & Jamie McDougal, Erin & Liam McDougal, Sean McDougal, Lola

McDougal, Don McDougal Jr., Ally Mills, Colleen McDougal, David & Sheila Murphy, and Mike & Amy Riley.

Thanks to the lawyers: Neville & Cindy Johnson, Josh Hardison, Lynn Bergwerk, Tom Girardi, Cary Goldstein, Amy Eskin, Pierce O'Donnell, and Marvin Rudnick.

My gratitude to old friends and new: Larry Josephson, Allan Peach, Mike Meenan, Corey Mitchell, Tim McRaven, Michael Gould, Jim Foster, Richard Lewis, Marcia Stehr, Frank Beacham, Pam Murphy, Rhonda Gardenheir, Larry Mollin, Carl Harrison, Gary Friedman, Lea Cox, Bill Katz, Tim Hays, Delilah Jones, Billi Gordon, Marla Frees, Joanne Fish, Ed Gray, Shari Cerney, Leo Hetzel, James McLendon, Norbert Litzinger, Richard & Armida Manifor, Wayne Rosso, Ed Sallee, Phyllis Graves, Bryn Friedman, Tom & Molly Webb, Beth & Rudy Vokoun, Carly, Jamie, Rebecca, Kirsten, and Jennifer Sullivan, David & Emily Sheldon, Ernie Sanchez, Ed & Molly Beckers, Jennifer Johnston, Diane & Mike Randleman, Michael Rybak, Jeff & Cindy Pierce, Virginia & Leon Stith, Judy & Ralph Sorenson, Jeff & Shareen Ross, Cheryl Rhoden, Brad Lindsay, Noah & Christina Levinson, Nathan Levinson, P. J. Letofsky, Brian Zocolla, Clara Kuperberg, Richard Kyle, Ellen Count, Jeannie Myers, Karen & Eric Koch, John & Christine Beshears, Jim Cervantes, Pat Block, Patricia McFall, Caryn, Don Lattin, Jeanne Moore, Andrew Alpern, Richard Bluett, Deborah Brower, Jim & Tish Coblentz, Dave Cogan, Susan Daniels, Lawrence Houghteling, Gary & Jaynese Davis, Mark Dowie, Anne & Ram Ben Efraim, Leslie Reynolds, Casey Abrams, David Brenner, Brenda Koch, Colin & Halle Knoedelseder.

And thanks finally to Bob, for his inscrutability, his interpretations, his humanity, and his Dylanesque fight against the fading of the light. It would be nice to have a sober conversation with Zimmy, maybe be his friend, but that possibility seems remote, fanciful, and ultimately wrong. Perhaps he has been right all along: what he has to say is said in his songs, and has little currency in any other form of human communication.

In spite of all his very human flaws, in Bob we trust.

BIBLIOGRAPHY

Books

Aaseng, Nathan. *Bob Dylan: Spellbinding Songwriter.* Minneapolis: Lerner Publications Company, 1987.

Abbott, Lynn, and Serogg, Doug. *Out of Sight: The Rise of African American Popular Music, 1889–1895.* Jackson: University Press of Mississippi, 2002.

Alper, George, ed. *Bob Dylan Through the Eyes of Joe Alper.* Joe Alper Photo Collection LLC, 2008.

Amburn, Ellis. *Dark Star: The Roy Orbison Story.* New York: Carol Publishing Group, 1990.

Aronowitz, Nona ed. *Out of the Vinyl Deeps: Ellen Willis on Rock Music.* Minneapolis: University of Minnesota Press, 2011.

Barker, Derek. *The Songs He Didn't Write: Bob Dylan Under the Influence.* Beccles, Suffolk, Eng.: William Clowes Ltd., 2008.

Bauldie, John, ed. *Wanted Man: In Search of Bob Dylan.* New York: Citadel Press, 1990.

Blake, Mark, ed. *Dylan: Visions, Portraits, and Back Pages.* London: DK Publishing Inc., 2005.

Beacham, Frank. *Whitewash: A Southern Journey through Music, Mayhem & Murder.* New York: Becham Story Studio, Inc., 2007.

Bell, Ian. *Once Upon a Time: The Lives of Bob Dylan.* London: Mainstream Publishing, 2012.

Birdfeather, Barbara. *The Birdfeather Astrological Space Book: Tales of the Universe.* Los Angeles: Nash Publishing, 1969.

Boucher, David. *Dylan & Cohen: Poets of Rock and Roll.* New York: Continuum, 2004.

Boyd, Pattie. *Wonderful Tonight.* New York: Three Rivers Press, 2007.

Bradford, A. T. *Out of the Dark Woods: Dylan, Depression and Faith.* London: Templehouse Publishing, 2011.

Brend, Mark: *American Troubadours: Groundbreaking Singer-Songwriters of the 60s.* San Francisco: Backbeat Books, 2001.

Broven, John: *Rhythm and Blues in New Orleans*. Gretna: Pelican Publishing Company, 1995.

Buell, Bebe, with Victor Bockris. *Rebel Heart: An American Rock 'n' Roll Journey*. New York: St. Martin's Press, 2001.

Burnett, T-Bone, Sam Shepard & Ken Regan. *The Rolling Thunder Logbook*. Cambridge: Da Capo Press, 2004.

Cash, Johnny. *Cash: The Autobiography*. New York: HarperCollins, 1997.

Cisco, Walter Brian: *Henry Timrod: A Biography*. Madison: Farleigh Dickinson University Press, 2004.

Cohen, John. *There Is No Eye: John Cohen Photographs*. New York: PowerHouse Books, 2001.

_____. *Young Bob: John Cohen's Early Photographs of Bob Dylan*. New York: PowerHouse Books, 2003.

Cohen, Leonard: *Beautiful Losers*. New York: Vintage Books, 1966.

Cott, Jonathan, ed. *Bob Dylan: The Essential Interviews*. New York: Wenner Books, 2006.

Crampton, Luke, & Dafydd Rees, with Wellesley Marsh. *Dylan*. Hong Kong: Taschen, 2009.

Crosby, David, and Carl Gottlieb. *Long Time Gone: The Autobiography of David Crosby*. New York: Doubleday, 1998.

_____. *Since Then: How I Survived Everything and Lived to Tell About It*. New York: G. P. Putnam's Sons, 2006.

Curtis, Jim. *Rock Eras Interpretations of Music & Society, 1954–1984*. Bowling Green: Bowling Green State University Popular Press, 1987.

Dannen, Fredric. *Hit Men: Power Brokers and Fast Money Inside the Music Business*. New York: Random House, 1990.

Dawidoff, Nicholas. *In the Country of Country: A Journey to the Roots of American Music*. New York: Pantheon Books, 1997.

Denisoff, R. Serge. *Tarnished Gold: The Record Industry Revisited*. New Brunswick: Transaction Books, 1986.

Dettmar, J. H., ed. *The Cambridge Companion to Bob Dylan*. New York: Cambridge University Press, 2009.

Doggett, Peter. *There's a Riot Going On: Revolutionaries, Rock Stars, and the Rise and Fall of the '60s*. New York: Canongate, 2007.

Dylan, Bob. *Chronicles: Volume One.* New York: Simon & Schuster, 2004.

Dylan, Bob, and Barry Feinstein. *Hollywood Foto-Rhetoric: The Lost Manuscript.* New York: Simon & Schuster, 2008.

Dylan, Bob. *Lyrics, 1962–1985.* New York: Alfred A. Knopf, Inc., 1985.

_____. *Tarantula.* New York: St. Martin's Press, 1994.

_____. *Writings and Drawings.* New York: Knopf, 1973.

Elderfield, John, and Kasper Monrad. *Bob Dylan: The Brazil Series.* New York: Prestel, 2010.

Eliot, Marc. *Death of a Rebel: A Biography of Phil Ochs.* New York: Carol Publishing Group, 1995.

_____. *Rockonomics.* New York: Citadel Press, 1993.

Ellison, Jim, ed., and Bob Dylan. *Younger Than That Now: The Collected Interviews with Bob Dylan.* New York: Thunder's Mouth Press, 2004.

Engel, Dave. *Just Like Bob Zimmerman's Blues: Dylan in Minnesota.* Rudolph, Wis.: River City Memoirs-Mesabi, 1997.

Faithfull, Marianne, with David Dalton. *Faithfull: An Autobiography.* New York: Little, Brown and Company, 1994.

Faragher, Scott. *Music City Babylon: Inside the World of Country Music.* New York: Birch Lane Press, 1992.

Feinstein, Barry, et al. *Early Dylan: Photographs and Introduction by Barry Feinstein, Daniel Kramer, and Jim Marshall.* Boston: Little, Brown and Company, 1999.

Fire, Emelia Gypsy. *Bohemian Tales: An Inspiring True Story.* Australia: Southwood Press Pty Ltd, 2003.

Flanagan, Bill. *Written in My Soul: Conversations with Rock's Great Songwriters.* New York: Contemporary Books, Inc., 1987.

Friedman, Albert B., ed. *Viking Book of Folk Ballads of the English Speaking World.* New York: Viking Press, 1956.

Friedman, Jon. *Forget About Today: Bob Dylan's Genius for (Re)Invention, Shunning the Naysayers, and Creating a Personal Revolution.* New York: Perigee, 2012.

Gill, Andy. *Classic Bob Dylan, 1962–1969: My Back Pages.* Zürich: Olms, 1998.

Gill, Andy, and Kevin Odegard. *A Simple Twist of Fate: Bob Dylan and the Making of Blood on the Tracks.* Cambridge, Mass.: Da Capo Press, 2004.

Ginsberg, Allen. *Howl and Other Poems.* San Francisco: City Lights Books. 1959.

Gitlin, Todd. *The Sixties: Years of Hope, Days of Rage.* New York: Batnam Books, 1989.

Goodman, Fred. *The Mansion on the Hill: Dylan, Young, Geffen, Springsteen and the Head-on Collision of Rock and Commerce.* New York: Vintage Books, 1998.

Goss, Nina, ed. *Montague Street: The Art of Bob Dylan.* Brooklyn, N.Y.: Charles Haeussler, 2009.

Gover, Robert. *One Hundred Dollar Misunderstanding, A Novel.* New York: Grove Press, Inc., 1961.

Graham, Bill, and Robert Greenfield. *Bill Graham Presents: My Life Inside Rock and Out.* New York: Doubleday, 1992.

Gravy, Wavy. *Something Good for a Change: Random Notes on Peace Thru Living.* New York: St. Martin's Press, 1992.

Gray, Michael. *Bob Dylan Encyclopedia.* New York: Continuum, 2008.

_____. *Song and Dance Man: The Art of Bob Dylan.* New York: E. P. Dutton & Co., 1972.

_____. *Song and Dance Man III: The Art of Bob Dylan.* New York: Continuum, 2000.

Gray, Michael, and John Bauldie. *All Across the Telegraph: A Bob Dylan Handbook.* London: Sedwick & Jackson, 1987.

Greene, Joshua M. *Here Comes The Sun: The Spiritual and Musical Journey of George Harrison.* Hoboken: John Wiley & Sons, 2006.

Greenfield, Robert. *Dark Star: An Oral Biography of Jerry Garcia.* New York: Harper, 2009.

Griffin, Sid. *Million Dollar Bash: Bob Dylan, The Band, and The Basement Tapes.* London: Jawbone Press, 2007.

_____. *Shelter from the Storm: Bob Dylan's Rolling Thunder Years.* London: Jawbone Press, 2010.

Gross, Michael. *Bob Dylan, An Illustrated History.* New York: Grosset & Dunlap, 1978.

Hadju, David. *Positively 4th Street: The Lives and Times of Joan Baez, Bob Dylan, Mimi Baez Farina, and Richard Farina.* New York: North Point Press, 2001.

Hannusch, Jeff. *I Hear You Knockin': The Sound of New Orleans Rhythm and Blues.* Villa Platte: Swallow Publications, Inc., 1985.

_____. *The Soul of New Orleans: A Legacy of Rhythm and Blues.* Ville Platte: Swallow Publications, 2001.

Hayes, Kevin J., ed. *Conversations with Jack Kerouac.* Jackson: University Press of Mississippi, 2005.

Hedin, Benjamin, ed. *Studio A: The Bob Dylan Reader.* New York: W. W. Norton & Company, 2004.

Heide, Robert, and John Gilman. *Greenwich Village: A Primo Guide to Shopping, Eating and Making Merry in True Bohemia.* New York: St. Martin's Griffin, 1995.

Heine, Steven: *Bargainin' for Salvation: Bob Dylan, a Zen Master?* New York: Continuum: 2009.

Heylin, Clinton. *Bob Dylan: Behind the Shades Revisited.* New York: HarperCollins Publishers, Inc, 2001.

Hjort, Christopher. *So You Want to Be a Rock 'n' Roll Star: The Byrds Day-By-Day, 1965–1973.* London: Jawbone Press, 2008.

Hoskyns, Barney. *Across the Great Divide: The Band and America.* Milwaukee: Hal Leonard Corporation, 2006.

Irwin, Colin. *Bob Dylan: Highway 61 Revisited.* New York: Billboard Books, 2008.

Kingsbury, Paul, ed. *The Encyclopedia of Country Music: The Ultimate Guide to the Music.* New York: Oxford University Press, 1998.

Jackson, Blair. *Garcia: An American Life.* New York: Penguin Books, 1999.

Jackson, Mary Allan. *Prophet Singer: The Voice and Vision of Woody Guthrie.* Jackson: University Press of Mississippi, 2007.

Johnson, Tracy. *Encounters with Bob Dylan: If You See Him, Say Hello.* San Francisco: Humble Press, 2000.

Knopper, Steve. *Appetite of Self Destruction: The Spectacular Crash of the Record Industry in the Digital Age.* New York: Soft Skull Press, 2010.

Koon, Bill. *Hank Williams, So Lonesome.* Jackson: University Press of Mississippi, 2001.

Kooper, Al. *Backstage Passes and Backstabbing Bastards.* New York: Backseat Books, 2008.

Law, Lisa. *Flashing on the Sixties.* Santa Rosa: Squarebooks, 2000.

Ledeen, Jenny. *Prophecy in the Christian Era.* St. Louis: Peaceberry Press of Webster Groves, 1995.

Lee, C. P. *Like a Bullet of Light: The Films of Bob Dylan.* London: Helter Skelter Publishing, 2000.

Lennon, John. *John Lennon: In His Own Write.* New York: Simon & Schuster, 1964.

Levine, Michael. *Deep Cover.* New York: Dell Publishing, 1990.

Lindsey, Hal, with C. C. Carlson. *The Late Great Planet Earth.* Grand Rapids: Zondervan, 1970.

Lott, Eric. *Love and Theft: Blackface Minstrelsy and the American Working Class.* New York: Oxford University Press, 1993.

Mackay, Kathleen. *Bob Dylan: Intimate Insights from Friends and Fellow Musicians.* New York: Omnibus Press, 2007.

MacLeish, Archibald. *Scratch.* Boston: Houghton Mifflin Company, 1971.

Marcus, Greil. *Bob Dylan by Greil Marcus: Writings, 1968–2010.* PublicAffairs, 2010.

Marcus, Greil. *Mystery Train: Images of American in Rock 'n' Roll Music.* New York: Plume, 2008.

_____. *The Old, Weird America: The World of Bob Dylan's Basement Tapes.* New York: Picador, 1997.

McDermott, John, and Edward E. Kramer. *Hendrix: Setting the Record Straight.* New York: Warner Books, Inc., 1992.

Miles, Barry, comp., and Pearce Marchbank, ed. *Bob Dylan in His Own Words.* New York: Quick Fox, 1978.

Mössinger, Ingrid, and Kerstin Drechel, eds. *Bob Dylan: The Drawn Blank Series.* New York: Prestel, 2008.

Muir, Andrew. *The Razor's Edge: Bob Dylan and the Never Ending Tour.* London: Helter Skelter Publishing, 2001.

Nadel, Ira B. *Various Positions: A Life of Leonard Cohen.* Austin: University of Austin Press, 1996.

O'Dell, Chris, with Katherine Ketchum. *Miss O'Dell: My Hard Days and Long Nights with The Beatles, The Stones, Bob Dylan, Eric Clapton, and the Women They Loved.* New York: Simon & Schuster, 2009.

Okun, Milton. *Something to Sing About!* London: The MacMillan Company, 1968.

Palmer, Robert. *Deep Blues: A Musical and Cultural History of the Mississippi Delta.* New York: Penguin Books, 1981.

Porterfield, Nolan. *Jimmie Rodgers: The Life and Times of America's Blue Yodeler.* Jackson: University Press of Mississippi, 2007.

Reid, Jan, and W. K. Stratton, eds. *Splendor in the Short Grass.* Austin: University of Texas Press, 2005.

Ricks, Christopher. *Dylan's Visions of Sin.* New York: HarperCollins Publishers, Inc., 2003.

Rogovoy, Seth. *Bob Dylan: Prophet, Mystic, Poet.* New York: Scribner, 2009.

Rotolo, Suze. *A Freewheelin' Time: A Memoir of Greenwich Village in the Sixties.* New York: Broadway Books, 2008.

Rushby, Chris. *Bob Dylan, The Illustrated Biography: Classic, Rare, and Unseen.* New York: Metro Books, 2009.

Santelli, Robert. *The Big Book of Blues: The Fully Revised and Updated Biographical Encyclopedia.* New York: Penguin, 2001.

_____. *The Bob Dylan Scrapbook, 1956–1966.* New York: Simon & Schuster, 2005.

Santoro, Gene. *Highway 61 Revisited: The Tangled Roots of American Jazz, Blues, Rock, & Country Music.* New York: Oxford University Press, 2004.

Sawyers, June Skinner. *Bob Dylan: New York.* Berkeley: Roaring Forties Press, 2011.

Scaduto, Anthony. *Bob Dylan.* London: Helter Skelter Publishing, 2001.

Scheurer, Timothy E. *Born in the U.S.A.: The Myth of America in Popular Music from Colonial Times to the Present.* Jackson: University Press of Mississippi, 1991.

Scobie, Stephen. *Alias Bob Dylan: Revisited.* Calgary: Red Deer Press, 2003.

Seeger, Pete. *American Favorite Ballads.* New York: Oak Publications, 1961.

Shaw, Arnold. *What Is the Secret Magic of Belafonte.* New York: Pyramid Books, 1960.

Sheehy, Colleen J., and Thomas Swiss, eds. *Highway 61 Revisited: Bob Dylan's Road from Minnesota to the World.* Minneapolis: University of Minnesota Press, 2009.

Shelton, Robert. *No Direction Home: The Life and Music of Bob Dylan.* New York: Ballantine Books, 1986.

Silkman, Ty. *Bob Dylan: Alias Anything You Please.* London: Reynolds & Hearn, 2008.

Sloman, Larry "Ratso." *On the Road with Bob Dylan.* New York: Three Rivers Press, 2002.

Sounes, Howard. *Down the Highway: The Life of Bob Dylan.* New York: Grove Press, 2001.

Spitz, Bob. *Dylan: A Biography.* New York: Norton, 1991.

Spitz, Robert Stephen. *The Making of Superstars: Artists and Executives of the Rock Music World.* New York: Anchor Press, 1978.

Stein, Jean. *Edie: An American Biography.* Edited by George Plimpton. New York: Alfred A. Knopf, 1982.

Thompson, Toby. *Positively Main Street: Bob Dylan's Minnesota.* Minneapolis: University of Minnesota Press, 2008.

Thomson, Elizabeth, and David Gutman, eds. *The Dylan Companion.* New York: Dell Publishing, 1990.

Torgoff, Martin. *Can't Find My Way Home: America in the Great Stoned Age, 1945–2000.* New York: Simon & Schuster Paperbacks, 2004.

Trager, Oliver. *Keys to the Rain: The Definitive Bob Dylan Encyclopedia.* New York: Billboard Books, 2004.

Turner, Steve. *The Man Called Cash.* Nashville: W Publishing Group, 2004.

Van Ronk, Dave, and Elijah Wald. *The Mayor of MacDougal Street: A Memoir.* Cambridge, Mass.: Da Capo Press, 2005.

Von Schmidt, Eric, and Jim Rooney. *Baby, Let Me Follow You Down: The Illustrated Story of the Cambridge Folk Years.* Amherst: University of Massachusetts Press, 1979.

Webb, Stephen H. *Dylan Redeemed: From Highway 61 to Saved.* New York: Continuum, 2006.

Weberman, A. J. *Dylan to English Dictionary.* New York: Yippie Museum Press, 2005.

_____. *My Life in Garbology.* New York: Stonehill Press, 1980.

_____. *RightWing Bob: What the Liberal Media Doesn't Want You to Know About Bob Dylan.* New York: The Yippie Museum Press, 2009.

Wesissman, Dick. *Which Side Are You On? An Inside History of the Folk Music Revival in America.* New York: Continuum, 2005.

Wilentz, Sean. *Bob Dylan in America.* New York: DoubleDay, 2010.

Williams, Paul. *Bob Dylan, Performing Artist: The Early Years, 1960–1973.* New York: Omnibus Press, 2004.

_____. *Bob Dylan, Performing Artist, Volume 2: The Middle Years, 1974-1986.* New York: Omnibus Press, 2004.

_____. *Bob Dylan, Performing Artist, Volume 3: Mind Out of Time, 1986 and Beyond.* New York: Omnibus Press, 2004.

_____. *Dylan—What Happened?* Glen Ellen, Calif.: Entwhistle Books, 1979.

Williams, Richard. *Dylan: A Man Called Alias.* New York: H. Holt, 1992.

Williamson, Nigel. *The Rough Guide to Bob Dylan.* London: Rough Guides Ltd., 2006.

Woliver, Robbie. *Hoot!: A Twenty-Five Year History of the Greenwich Village Music Scene.* New York: St. Martin's Press, 1994.

Yetnikoff, Walter, with David Ritz. *Howling At the Moon.* New York: Roadway Books, 2004.

Zollner, Frank, Ingred Mossinger, and Kirsten Drechel, eds. *Bob Dylan: The Drawn Blank Series.* New York: Prestel, 2007.

Zollo, Paul. *Conversations with Tom Petty.* New York: Omnibus Press, 2005.

_____. *Songwriters on Songwriting.* Cambridge, Mass.: Da Capo Press, 2003.

Film

Bob Dylan, 1975–1981: Rolling Thunder & The Gospel Years (A Totally Unauthorized Documentary). Dir. Joel Gilbert, Highway 61 Entertainment, 2006.

Bob Dylan, 1990–2006: The Never Ending Narrative. Rob Johnstone. Chrome Dreams, 2011.

Bob Dylan Revealed. Dir. Joel Gilbert. Highway 61 Entertainment, 2011.

Dont Look Back. Dir. D. A. Pennebaker. Docudrama, 1967.

Eat the Document. Dir. D. A. Pennebaker. ABC Television, 1972.

No Direction Home. Dir. Martin Scorsese. Paramount Pictures, 2005.

Pat Garrett and Billy the Kid. Dir. Sam Peckinpah. Warner Bros., 1973.

Renaldo & Clara. Dir. Bob Dylan. Circuit Films, 1978.

Tangled Up in Bob: Searching for Bob Dylan. Dir. Mary Feidt. Feido Films, 2007.

The Other Side of the Mirror: Bob Dylan at the Newport Folk Festival. Dir. Murray Lerner. Columbia, 2007.

Misc.

"artur the xxxx," comp. *Every Mind Polluting Word: Assorted Bob Dylan Utterances*. Don't Ya Tell Henry Publications.

Bob Dylan on Pacifica & KPFK. Pacifica Radio Archives.

Boy from the North Country: Bob Dylan in Minnesota. Dir. Jim Bickal. Minnesota Public Radio, 2011.

Press Releases, Misc.

"Bob Dylan Hospitalized, Cancels Tour." *Reuters*. May 29, 1997.

Corona-Pacific Productions, late '60s.

"Dylan Press Conference Introduces New Columbia Records Studio." *Columbia Records*. December 16, 1965.

"Dylan: Star-crossed Romeo." *United Press International*. February 10, 1975.

Employee Minutes, October 31, 1995.

"He Has Been Released." *Associated Press*. June 3, 1997.

Skirball Cultural Center, Los Angeles. "Experience Music Project Presents: Bob Dylan's American Journey, 1956–1966." February 8– June 8, 2008.

"Tape of Bob Dylan Press Conference Offered for Sale." *Corona-Pacific Productions*. 1966.

Newspapers/Magazines

Alterman, Lorain. "Dylan Is His Own Dilemma." *New York Times*. January 20, 1974.

Anderson, David E. "Gospel According to Bob." *Religion and Ethics News Weekly*. May 21, 2005.

Andriotakis, Pamela. "On Tour." *People*. July 16, 1984.

Aronowitz, Alfred G. "Dylan's Big Nonelectric Comeback." *Life*. February 9, 1968.

_____. "Enter the King, Bob Dylan." *Saturday Evening Post*. November 2, 1968.

Bauder, David. "Times Still A-Changin'." *Daily Breeze*. May 26, 2006.

Bennetts, Leslie. "Not Across My Daughter's Big Brass Bed." *L.A. Times*. April 21, 2004.

Brizzolara, John. "The Footsteps of Some Kind of Monster." *Reader*. 1995.

Burgess, Donald. "'Self Portrait' Not Best Dylan Effort." *Los Angeles Herald-Examiner*. August 2, 1970.

Cannon, Geoffrey. "Dylan at Wight: A New Voice and a New Style." *L.A. Times*. September 14, 1969.

Castin, Sam, and Daniel Kramer. "Folk Rock's Tambourine Man: Bob Dylan." *Look*. March 8, 1966.

Cocks, Jay. "Freak Fresco of Hell." *Time*. May 24, 1971.

Cohen, Harold. V. "He Has Re-Routed Course of Folk Music, Bob Dylan: An Original." *Pittsburg Post-Gazette*. January 31, 1966.

Cohn, Nik. "Dylan in England: Trauma or Triumph?" *New York Times*. September 9, 1969.

Crowe, Jerry. "Bob Dylan Is Hospitalized With Respiratory Infection, Cancels Tour." *L.A. Times*. May 29, 1997.

Cutright, Maura. "Bob Dylan: Singing Spokesman for Your Kids' Generation." *Pageant*. March 1965.

Emerson, Ken. "Will the Real Bob Dylan Please Stand Up?" *Boston After Dark*. April 23, 1969.

Farrell, Barry. "The Rarest Rock Show of All." *Life*. August 13, 1971.

Flanagan, Bill. "Bob Dylan Interview." *Mojo*. August, 2009.

Garvin, Allen. "What in the World! The Soaring Dropout." *Tri-City Herald*. March 6, 1966.

Gates, David. "Bob Dylan." *Newsweek*. March 13, 1989.

_____. "Positively Broadway." *Newsweek*. November 6, 2006.

_____. "The Book of Bob." *Newsweek*. October 4, 2004.

Getlin, Josh. "Defining Dylan—If That's Even Possible." *L.A. Times*. October 15, 2006.

Gilmore, Mikal. "Bob Dylan: The Rolling Stone Interview." *Rolling Stone*. September 27, 2012.

_____. "Dylan's Lost Years." *Rolling Stone*. September 12, 2013.

Gleason, Ralph J. "Perspectives: Dylan on Paper A Genius in Words & Pictures." *Rolling Stone*. June 21, 1973.

Goldberg, Steven. "Bob Dylan and the Poetry of Salvation." *Saturday Review*. May 30, 1970.

Goldstein, Richard. "Dylan: 'We Trust What He Tells Us.'" *New York Times*. October 22, 1967.

Goodman, Howard. "'Ten of Swords'—A Dylan Bootleg to Beat All Bootlegs." Knight-Ridder. March 23, 1986.

Grant, Lee. "Dylan show resonates with passion." *Union-Tribune*. February 2, 1995.

Green, Frank J. "Dylan Is Spillin' Over Into Classroom." *The San Diego Union*. April 28. 1986.

Greene, Andy. "Dylan Goes to Washington for Historical Show." *Rolling Stone*. March 4, 2010.

Greene, Gary. "Record Roundup: It Comes Out Me." *Tucson Daily Citizen*. July 24, 1965.

Harber, Joyce. "Dylan in Dixie for a Disc Date." *L.A. Times*. November 20, 1967.

Heckman, Don. "Once Gable Was King—Now It's Bob Dylan." *New York Times*. September 12, 1971.

Heissenberger, Patti. "Dylan Signs on for Batiquitos Festival." *Rancho Bernardo Journal*. 1988.

Hentoff, Nat. "Playboy Interview: Bob Dylan." *Playboy*. March 1966.

Hilburn, Robert. "Backstage With the Dylan/Band Tour." *L.A. Times*. January 8, 1974.

_____. "Bob Dylan Waxes Eloquent." *L.A. Times*. January 20, 1974.

_____. "Dylan Back with Single and Album." *L.A. Times*. November 23, 1971.

_____. "Dylan, Band Will Go on Tour." *L.A. Times*. November 3, 1973.

_____. "Dylan Biographer Still Into Subject." *L.A. Times*. May 16, 1972.

_____. "Dylan Returns to the Forum." *L.A. Times*. November 17, 1978.

_____. "Peckinpah Lures Dylan From Behind Wall of Privacy." *L.A. Times*. February 18, 1973.

_____. "'Self Portrait' Dylan's Latest." *L.A. Times*. June 26, 1970.

Hume, Martha. "The Commercialization of Bob Dylan." *Village Voice*. November 28, 1978.

Infusino, Divina. "Backstage Was Quiet for Dylan, Petty." *The San Diego Union*. June 11, 1986.

_____. "Dylan Covers All the Phases." *The San Diego Union*. 1986.

_____. "Poet Laureate of the '60's Is Coming to Town Tomorrow As Meaningful Minstrel of '80s." *The San Diego Union*. June 1986.

Jackovich, Karen G. "Take One." *People*. December 12, 1988.

Jahn, Mike. "Self-Portrait of the Artist as an Older Man." *Saturday Review*. May 11, 1968.

Johnson, Pete. "Dylan Falling in Love with Love." *L.A. Times*. April 7, 1969.

Jones, Allan. "An old scruffy man acting suspiciously . . ." *Uncut*. January 2010.

Kermod, Frank, and Stephen Spender. "Bob Dylan: The Metaphor at the End of the Funnel." *Esquire*. May 1972.

Kloman, William. "Dylan, Cohen, Hardin—Poets for Our Time." *New York Times*. April 27, 1969.

Kot, Greg. "Review of Time Out of Mind." *Rolling Stone*. October 2, 1997.

Kwitny, Jonathan. "Bob Dylan as a Poet." *Wall Street Journal*. March 29, 1972.

Lahr, John. "The Pathfinder: Sam Shepard and the Struggles of American Manhood." *The New Yorker*. February 8, 2010.

Lange, Andrew. "Bob Dylan's Secrets of Anti-Aging." *Huffington Post*. November 2, 2009.

Laurence, Robert P. "Review of Concert Shows The Real Dylan Got Away." *The San Diego Union*. November 19, 1978.

Lyman, Rick. "Dylan's Life Now Has Come Full Circle." *New York Times*. 1997.

Male, Andrew. "Dylan Director Comes Clean." *Mojo*. June 12, 2007.

Marcus, Greil. "Dylan's 'New Morning.'" *New York Times*. November 15, 1970.

Marvin, Peter. "Bob Dylan by Anthony Scaduto." *New York Times Book Review*. February 20, 1972.

Maslin, Janet. "Bob Dylan: Brave New World at Budokan." *Rolling Stone*. July 12, 1979.

McGregor, Craig. "Dylan: Reluctant Hero of the Pop Generation." *New York Times*. May 7, 1972.

Meehan, Thomas. "Public Writer No. 1?" *New York Times Magazine*. December 12, 1965.

Mendelsohn, Jill & Tingley, Judy. "Letters to the Editor." *Look*. April 4, 1966.

Mercer, Johnny. "The Times They Are A-Changin'." *Orange County Illustrated*. December 1965.

Miller, Samantha. "Tangled Up in Bob." *People*. March 16, 1998.

Milward, John. "Dylan, Petty roll into the USA." *USA Today*. June 1986.

Missett, Bill. "Dylan Tops Busy Concert Week." *The Blade-Tribune*. November 23, 1978.

Moberg, David. "The Folk and the Rock." *Newsweek*. September 20, 1965.

Morrissey, Lawrence. "Trouble in Mind." *Humble Press*. 1974.

Morse, Steve. "Changin' Along with the Times." *Boston Globe.* December 30, 1995.

Newman, Melinda. "Dylan Can't Spin These Unauthorized Looks Back." *Variety.* April 21, 2009.

Oliphant, John. "Dylan's 116th Dream." *Boston After Dark.* June 23, 1970.

Orth, Maureen. "Dylan—Rolling Again." *Newsweek.* January 14, 1974.

_____. "It's Me, Babe." *Newsweek.* November 17, 1975.

Ostroff, Robert. "Viva Durango." *Oui Magazine.* July 1973.

Pareles, Jon. "A Tribute to Bob Dylan, Both Reverent and Rowdy.*" New York Times.* November 9, 2007.

_____. "The Restless Road." *New York Times.* September 29, 1997.

Rich, Motoko. "Who's This Guy Dylan Who's Borrowing Lines From Henry Timrod?" *New York Times.* September 14, 2006.

Rockwell, John. "A Relaxed Dylan Sings in Chicago." *New York Times.* January 6, 1973.

Saal, Hubert. "The Return of Bob Dylan." *Chicago Tribune.* April 28, 1968.

_____. "Dylan Is Back." *Newsweek.* February 26, 1968.

_____. "Dylan's Country Pie." *Newsweek.* April 14, 1969.

Scaduto, Anthony. "'Won't You Listen to the Lambs, Bob Dylan?'" *New York Times Magazine.* November 28, 1971.

Schjeldahl, Peter. "Dylan, No Longer Tormented." *New York Times.* June 21, 1970.

Segel, Jules. "Well, What Have We Here?" *The Saturday Evening Post.* July 30, 1966.

Sloan, Robin Adams. "Q&A." *Los Angeles Herald-Examiner.* March 1, 1973.

Stein, Pat. "Dylan Bores Young, Reminds the Old." *Blade-Tribune.* 1988.

_____. "Dylan on Carlsbad Stage Saturday." *Blade-Tribune.* August 4, 1988.

Varga, George. "A Look Back At Dylan's Best Years." *The San Diego Union.* March 25, 1991.

Varga, George. "Bob Dylan Revisited." *The San Diego Union*. August 5, 1989.

_____. "Celebrating 30 Years, All-Star 'Bob Fest' Was Positively Dylan." *The San Diego Union*. October 19, 1992.

_____. "Dylan's 'Good' album is an enchanting work." *The San Diego Union*. November 12, 1992.

_____. "Orbison Tribute a Crying Shame." *The San Diego Union*. 1989.

_____. "Young, at Heart, Shows Mastery of Many Musical Moods." *San Diego Union-Tribune*. October 31, 2008.

Wasserman, John L. "Bob Dylan through a Lens Darkly." *Life*. August 11, 1967.

Wener, Ben. "Dylan Delivers Fine Set." *Orange County Register*. July 18, 2011.

Williams, Jack. "Anti-Hero Returns to Bring Crowd to Its Feet." *San Diego*. November 18, 1978.

Williams, Paul. "Sometimes I Wonder." *Reader*. December 1994.

Ybarra, Michael J. "Tennyson, Milton and . . . Bob Dylan?" *L.A. Times*. January 21, 1998.

Zelman, David. "Dear Bob, It's Time for a Free Concert." *New York Times*. January 13, 1974.

Chicago Daily News. "Bob Dylan." November 26, 1965.

Courier-Post. "Dylan Remains Enigma in Screen Debut." May 16, 1973.

Current Biography. "Bob Dylan." May 1965.

Hollywood Citizen-News. "Bob Dylan." November 27, 1965.

Hollywood Citizen-News. "The Soaring Dropout." March 5, 1966.

Hollywood Reporter. "Dylan Forms Label, Elektra-Asylum Set To Handle Distribution." December 10, 1973.

KRLA Beat. "Famous Songwriter Bob Dylan Mystery Man to Most Americans." July 7, 1965.

L.A. Times. "Chayefksy, Michener Sign NBC Contracts." January 18, 1974.

_____. "Dylan in Dungarees Gives Fans a Bonus." January 2, 1972.

_____. "Interview with a Reluctant Idol." September 7, 1965.

_____. "Singer Bob Dylan Wows 'Em at Isle of Wight Pop Festival." September 1, 1969.

Life. "Boom in Protest Songs with a Rock Bent: The Children of Bobby Dylan." November 5, 1965.

Los Angeles Herald-Examiner. "Dylan Forms Record Company." December 19, 1973.

_____. "Q&A." December 30, 1973.

Mojo. "Dylan at Newport: Who Booed?" October 26, 2007.

Music Rebels. "Bob Dylan: Just Like a Genius."

New York Times. "It's All Right, Ma, I'm Only D.J.-ing." April 30, 2006.

_____. August 12, 1966.

Newsweek. "Just Plain Folk, Please." September 13, 1965.

_____. "Looking for Dylan." June 14, 1971.

_____. "Strange Interlude." January 30, 1967.

_____. July 28, 1969.

_____. June 22, 1970.

_____. September 18, 1969.

Pittsburgh Post-Gazette. "Bob Dylan: An Original." January 31, 1966.

Redbook. "The Heroine of Folk Music Raps Its Hero: Joan Baez Says Bob Dylan Should Quit Playing Up to the 'Negative Feelings' of His Young Fans." December 21, 1966.

Rolling Stone. May 10, 1973.

The Star. "Some See Him As a Prophet, Others as a Moralist." May 21, 2005.

The Sun-Herald Sunday Magazine. "Children of the Golden Ghetto."

Time. "Abstract." May 31, 1971.

_____. "Rock 'n' Roll: Message Time." September 17, 1965.

_____. January 14, 1974.

Variety. "Dylan Hits Road After 8-Yr. Lapse." November 7, 1973.

Bennett, Dan. "Dylan and Petty hit arena for first stop on U.S. tour." 1986.

Edelstein, Joel. "Bob Dylan, Tom Petty Mesmerize Audience."

Kinsman, Michael. "Tangled Up in Truth."

Landey, Jennifer. "Music Bob Dylan: From 'Rue Morgue Avenue' to Street Legal."

Mood, John. "Beautiful Raucous Dirty." *Reader.*

Warth, Gary. "Solid Set from Dylan Opens Summer Pops on High Note." *BC?* February 2, 1995.

INDEX

Dennis McDougal,
writer for the *Los Angeles Times* and the *New York Times,* has won more than fifty awards for his hard-nosed coverage of the entertainment industry. He is the bestselling author of eleven books, including *The Last Mogul: Lew Wasserman, MCA, and the Hidden History of Hollywood* and *Five Easy Decades: How Jack Nicholson Became the Biggest Movie Star in Modern Times.* His book *Privileged Son: Otis Chandler and the Rise and Fall of the LA Times Dynasty* was produced as a two-hour PBS documentary.